THE USES OF SENSE

THE USES OF SENSE

Wittgenstein's Philosophy of Language

CHARLES TRAVIS

CLARENDON PRESS · OXFORD
1989

Oxford University Press, Walton Street, Oxford OX2 6DP
Oxford New York Toronto
Delhi Bombay Calcutta Madras Karachi
Petaling Jaya Singapore Hong Kong Tokyo
Nairobi Dar-es-Salaam Cape Town
Melbourne Auckland
and associated companies in
Berlin Ibadan

Oxford is a trade mark of Oxford University Press

Published in the United States
by Oxford University Press, New York

British Library Cataloguing in Publication Data
Travis, Charles
The uses of sense : Wittgenstein's
philosophy of language.
1. Language. Philosophical perspectives.
Theories of Wittgenstein, Ludwig, 1889–1951
I. Title   409'.2'4
ISBN   0–19–824942–X

Library of Congress Cataloging in Publication Data
Data available

Set by Pentacor Ltd., High Wycombe, Bucks
Printed in Great Britain
at the University Printing House, Oxford
by David Stanford
Printer to the University

To my parents,
Philip and Agnes Travis

Preface

One fine spring afternoon in 1982, I was sitting in John McDowell's living room at 17 Merton Street in Oxford, explaining to him why I had never found 'the private language argument' very convincing. A few patient and searching questions later, it suddenly occurred to me first, that perhaps there was a good argument there after all; second, that it would be an important fact if there were, since the argument points in the right direction on some central topics in philosophy where the temptation to make bad starts has proved powerful in recent times— and not only among philosophers; and third, that I should write a book about this. I believe that the first two of these hunches have proved to be correct.

Part of the importance of an argument against private language is in pointing away from a certain conception of our psychologies, and particularly of our attitudes—those usually referred to as 'propositional' and others. On the conception, we fix the facts about, say, our beliefs, intentions and expectations—and particularly their content or semantics—by ourselves, and independent of the perspectives others might have on us; as it were, simply in virtue of the way we are constituted on the inside, or (perhaps even literally) intradermally— together, if you like, with the internal history of that constitution. On some versions of this conception, the emphasis is placed on the point that if, for example, Odile believes that Montreal is east of Cincinnati, then for her to do so is for her to be in some particular intradermal state, specifiable (individuable) in other terms—neurologically, per-haps, or by a machine table, or something of the sort. As it is sometimes put, her believing what she does must consist in her standing in some specified relation to a syntactically specified object, thus one which is a fit subject for computations—as beliefs surely are—and moreover to formally specified ones. Whether Odile's belief has one semantics or another would then be derivable (modulo causal histories) from the nature of the otherwise -specified state involved. On other versions, the point of emphasis is that the content of Odile's belief (at least where true exact determination of that content is at stake) is determined by some domain of 'inner facts' which are open to observation—or anyway direct observation—only by her; as it were, by the precise course of her experience, given the way that experience 'feels from the inside'. It is a short step from this to the view that seeing, or knowing what the precise content of her belief is, demands standing in a relation to some special domain of 'inner' facts in which only Odile herself can stand. So to know, or perhaps even to be able to appreciate precisely what it is that Odile believes, one would have to do nothing less than be Odile herself. (At this point, the connection with private language is already obvious.) As McDowell has recently argued[1]—in a way that is both incisive and illuminating—these two versions are really but slightly different elaborations of the same underlying view. What the present book will argue is that that underlying conception involves an essentially false view of how propositional attitudes come by their semantics; that it is essential to what these attitudes are that their content be assigned 'from the outside' by reacting to facts that are available equally to all of us.

A second central import of the private language argument is for a certain view of the content or semantics (or, if you insist, meanings) of public words—yours and mine, say. On that view, the content of Odile's words, 'Montreal is east of Cincinnati'—where she informs Hugo of this, say—is uniquely fixed (again, if you like, modulo causal histories) by her attitudes towards them—notably, on most views, by some relevant set of her intentions and beliefs. This sort of view has been popularized by, and is rightly associated with the name of H. P. Grice. It takes more work than actually will be done in this book to show that such views contain, strictly speaking, literal falsehoods. But the argument to come certainly suggests that they reverse the direction of fit. For they at least suggest that in asking after the content of words, we are free to appeal to semantic facts about attitudes of the speaker, where these are available anyway, no matter what the solving of further problems as to the disambiguation of words might show. Whereas, it will be argued here, there are exactly the same problems to pose for the semantics of attitudes or thoughts as there are for the semantics of words; further, their solutions lie along exactly the same paths, and *via* appeals of the same sort to just the same further facts. Moreover, the Gricean view suggests that once we do fix the right facts about the speaker's attitudes, and again modulo causal stories, there can be only one semantics for the words in question which is the semantics that those attitudes require, so that there is a way of just reading off the semantics of the words from the right set of attitudes (with their semantics fixed). One of the main theses in what is to come

---

[1]   See McDowell [1986].

is that, in an important sense, that simply could not be. In that sense, the Gricean story has not identified the factors on which the semantics of words depends.

I have elaborated here on these matters of importance since, as it has turned out—unfortunately—they will receive much less attention in the main text than they merit. In fact, Gricean views have turned out not to get discussed at all. Just getting to the point of being able to discuss these questions properly has been enough of an exercise for the present. A fuller discussion of them will, I hope, be the subject of a sequel.

I have used the discussion of private language, in this book, as a focal point for a discussion of Wittgenstein's opposition to a certain picture of semantics—a picture shared by Frege, by Russell, and by Wittgenstein's earlier Tractarian self, among many others—and of the positive alternative to that picture that Wittgenstein proposes in the *Investigations*. Accordingly, I have read the argument as directed against that picture. (Note that the pictures in question are pictures of *semantics*: not of this or that sort of semantic item, but of semantic properties and what it is to have them in general.) Of course, semantics is not the only topic of the *Investigations*. Nor does the present topic exhaust the import of the private language discussion. That discussion certainly *looks* as if it is about certain topics in the philosophy of mind: pictures of sensations and the like; and more generally pictures of psychological properties. No doubt that is correct. In fact, there is a connection between the semantic themes here and those pictures of our mental lives—a connection which is at least stated in the last section of the last chapter of this book. But I think it no disgrace to admit that there is much more in the *Investigations* than is touched on here; and I certainly do admit it.

There is certainly little enough about semantics on which Frege and Russell agreed. The differences between their views are useful for locating that common property which otherwise is liable to go unnoticed. I will not say at this point what their shared picture of semantics is, nor what Wittgenstein's alternative to it is. I have stated the first point, and the core of the second, as clearly as I am now able to in chapter 1. There is no point in mere repetition. But the differences between Frege and Russell also deserve some comment. For on the face of them, they certainly suggest that any private language argument would apply to the one philosopher differently than it does to the other. In those differences, much of the further import of the argument lies. If one *must* choose, I think it is probably better to see the main target of the current argument to be Frege; though Russell is far from being spared by it.

The application of a private language argument to Russell seems obvious. For, after all, Russell insisted that language *must* be private, and that it would be 'absolutely fatal'[2] if it were not. Language must be private, on Russell's view, because at the bottom of the path of the logical analysis he then believed in, reference must be to private objects. As we will see (in chapter 2), reference to private objects is not an essential feature of private language. But it is certainly a sufficient one. (On one currently popular view of Russell, it is possible to extract this aspect of his views on reference, and delete it as an anachronistic embarrassment, while retaining a substantial and important part of those views intact. Since Russell had arguments purporting to show that names, at least, must refer to private objects, it is not obvious that this is so. What is the response to these arguments? Later, particularly in chapters 6 and 7, we will consider what sort of response to them is anyway available, and just how much of Russell's view of names then survives, and on what conditions. The result will be, *inter* alia, a somewhat different view of current doctrines of 'direct reference'.)

If private language is impossible, then there must be *something* wrong with Russell's views. It is worth noting that 1918—the year in which Russell propounded these views in a series of lectures in London[3]—is the same year in which Frege published an extended attack on the idea of private language[4]. Frege's official view, at least, is thus that our languages, at least, and more generally any language, fit either for communication or for the expression of the thoughts which concern us (for example, thoughts about mathematics) must be public. Frege's picture of semantics, whatever it may be, is surely meant to fit at least some such languages. So if one wanted to show that picture to be wrong, it would not do simply to produce a private language argument and stop. As far as the conclusion of the argument is concerned, Frege would just read that as something which had been part of his view all along.

It may well be that Frege was committed covertly to private language. There are, for one thing, his well-known views on the senses we attach to the first person pronoun, and to proper names. But these might be regarded as peripheral and unfortunate appendages on his central system. I do mean to argue in what follows that Frege's picture

---

[2] Russell [1918], p. 195: 'When one person uses a word, he does not mean by it the same thing as another person means by it. I have often heard it said that that is a misfortune. That is a mistake. It would be absolutely fatal if people meant the same thing by their words, . . . because the meaning you attach to your words must depend on the nature of the objects you are acquainted with, and . . . different people are acquainted with different objects.'

[3] Russell [1918].

[4] Frege [1918].

of semantics is ultimately incompatible with the demands of publicity. But, in terminology suggested by Michael Hallett, this is not so much because Frege thought in terms of one (or higher finite N) speaker languages, but rather because he thought, as it were, in terms of no-speaker languages. For Frege, any semantics for language or thought to have is the semantics it is, and requires what it does, in essential respects, at least, in the nature of the case, and quite independent of any reactions we might have to it. So the semantic facts of a language being what they are does not require there being any speakers of that language at all. A language may be just there to be spoken, semantically full-blown and insulated from any effects on it that speaking it might have. Which no-speaker languages there are to be spoken—that is, which semantics there are for some language or other to have—is, on the Fregean view, a fixed point. The question for a natural language such as English is: with which no-speaker language does it share a semantics? It is at that level only that the reactions of its speakers may play a role. For all that, the semantic of a language, or the senses of its expressions, is meant to be something available for all of us to grasp. The domain of senses is intrinsically a public domain. What will be argued is that semantic facts could not be simultaneously thus graspable and thus insulated from our reactions to them. The impossibility of private language then eliminates one of the alternatives that leaves.

In any event, the present strategy is not to argue that Frege was really some sort of closet private linguist. Rather, the function of private language in the present discussion is quite different. The first task in what follows is simply to describe an alternative picture to the Fregean one—one which is equally an alternative to Russell or to Tractarian Wittgenstein—and to identify in it certain central principles which are incompatible with the Fregean view. That done, private language is then introduced simply as an example of a violation of those principles. The point of the private language argument is to show that it is the violation of those principles which makes private language impossible—which yields the result, that is, that private items could not be viewed correctly as having any semantics at all. The conclusion is that the principles in question are ones that we—or rather semantics—could not live without. So they must be part of any correct picture of semantics. Since they conflict with the Fregean picture, that picture must be wrong—at least to the extent that there is conflict. Since they require the main features of the Wittgensteinian alternative, that alternative must be correct, at least with respect to those features.

I now come to the most pleasant task of a preface—that of giving credit where it is due. Pleasant as it is, I think that there is more than *politesse* involved here. For the credits reveal my own intellectual history, and hence the origins of the ideas expressed here. Seeing their origins may help to understand them better. To begin then, I was greatly inspired, and largely set in my present philosophical ways, by two of my undergraduate teachers at Berkeley, Thompson Clarke and Hans Herzberger. Clarke gave me an appreciation of Wittgenstein and of Austin, and also gave me some form of the idea which appears in this work as S-use sensitivity. Herzberger taught me a style of approaching problems which, while difficult to characterize, has been invaluable. His dispassionate way of setting out a problem is something I can at least aim for, though probably not achieve. In addition, while still an undergraduate, I was helped along present paths by Montgomery Furth at UCLA, and later, while a graduate student there, I was helped much further along them by Keith Gunderson.

From the beginning, of course, I was greatly impressed by the works of (the later) Wittgenstein and J. L. Austin. Unfortunately, I think, Austin has generally been read in quite the wrong way, so that in so far as he has been influential at all, it is quite peripheral aspects of his work which have captured the attention. That is a shame. There is nothing wrong with the idea of illocutionary forces, though not much has ever been done with it. But what matters most in Austin is his views on epistemology and on more central parts of semantics—views which are the culmination of a tradition beginning with Cook Wilson, and moving (by way of reaction) through H. A. Prichard, and largely echoed today in the writings of such philosophers as John McDowell. (So, one might say, an Oxford tradition despite itself.) More than just echoes of these views are to be found in the present work as well.

Two other cases of action at a distance must be mentioned here. These are Hilary Putnam and Noam Chomsky. Again, both of these men have been influences on me from the very earliest days. I hope that the influence of Putnam on this book will be obvious. From the early sixties on, I have always thought that Putnam was one of the very few who understood what was important about Wittgenstein, and who further developed Wittgensteinian thought in proper directions. His philosophical instincts have been—in my opinion—*nearly* infallible, and have moved his thought through the years in a natural progression so that the fundamental insights of early articles such as 'What Theories Are Not'[5] remain intact and retain full value when placed in the light of his current version of anti- (metaphysical) realism (a version with which I find myself largely in agreement). Chomsky's

---

[5] Putnam [1962a].

influence on the present work will be, I expect, less evident. I can only say that Chomsky presents a style of thinking about problems which I find not only immensely appealing but helpful. It is not so much Chomsky's views which are in play here as—I hope, at least—his way of organizing a topic.

I now come to proximate causes. As noted at the outset, I would not even have thought of writing this book, much less resolved to do so, were it not for John McDowell. His help did not end with that, but, applied regularly in small but highly concentrated doses, informed the work throughout. Next, I certainly would not have got the ideas here to anything like their present degree of clarity or development—such as that is—without the continued criticism, discussion, and some-times resistance put up by John Campbell. He has seen many drafts of this, and expended much effort on it. The result may not be what he could unreservedly endorse; but there would have been much less of one without him. I have also been helped, in ways I would not want to have missed, by the efforts, both critical and supportive, of Hilary Putnam and of Crispin Wright. Since the fall of 1986—thus, through-out the last three drafts—I have been further helped by discussions with Michael Hallett, Jim Hankinson, and James McGilvray. Through-out, I have also benefited substantially from criticism by and numerous discussions with Katherine J. Morris.

This book is dedicated to my parents, Agnes and Philip Travis, whose invaluable boundless faith in me has never been conditional on rational justification for it—or on anything else.

C. T.
Montreal
December 1987

Contents

1

Two Pictures of Semantics

In 243,[1], Wittgenstein asks the following question:

Would a language also be possible in which one could describe or express his inner experiences—his feelings, moods, etc.—for his own use?—Then can't we do that in our usual language?—But I don't mean it like that. The words of this language would have bearing on that which only the speaker could know about; on his immediate private sensations. Thus another person cannot understand this language.

Thus he explicitly introduces the problem of 'private language'. Whatever privacy is here, and whatever his arguments may be, one fixed point is that Wittgenstein holds private language to be impossible. But why is that thesis interesting? This book can be seen as a story about why it is. It is a story about a small set of principles central to Wittgenstein's thought which are argued for by the way in which private language turns out to be impossible. It is also and equally a story about a certain picture of semantics which those principles require; a picture of the sorts of semantic facts there may be, of semantic properties, the ways in which items may have them, and the effects and uses of their doing so.

Chapters 2, 4, 5 and 6 will set out the principles involved, and show what philosophic work they do. They also aim to show that the principles are correct, and that it is reasonable to accept them independent of any results of a private language discussion. But private language yields a different sort of argument in favour of them. The strategy, in broad brush strokes, is to test the principles by constructing a thought experiment in which they fail. If there are facts about the semantics of private language, then what those facts are, and what it would be to know them, cannot conform to the principles in question. The result, it will be argued, is that there can be no semantics for

---

[1]   Throughout, otherwise unidentified numbers refer to sections of Wittgenstein's *Philosophical Investigations*. The English translation sticks close to Anscombe's, since that is the familiar one. But I have deviated from hers where I thought some philosophic purpose required it, and where the German seemed as well or better served in the alternative way.

private language; that private language can express no judgements, much less ones which might be true (or false). Private language is impossible *because* it is impossible for there to be either judgement or thought which is not governed by these principles. Otherwise put, the joint assertion of semantic fact and denial of the principles for that fact yields contradiction. The desired conclusion is that the principles are correct, and, specifically, that where items do have semantics, the facts about their semantics, and the facts those items might express, are governed by those principles. Central to the principles is the denial of what will here be called the dominant picture of semantics, as that denial is contained in what will here be called the alternative picture. Also central is the account, in the next chapter, of what makes judgements about semantics correct. The desired conclusion is that the alternative picture, together with that account, apply wherever there is semantic fact. Of course, on the description thus far, it is the principles as a whole which are tested by private language; conceivably this particular part of them could have been idle in the collapse of semantic fact which takes place there. But as the story unfolds, we will see that they are not idle.

How these principles require the semantic picture to be developed here, and how they clash with its alternative, will become clear when the principles are developed. This chapter aims at no more than saying what the picture and its alternative are. The alternative has been the dominant picture at least since it was presented with great clarity, precision and elegance by Frege. 'Dominant', in fact, is an understatement. The picture is attractive enough to have been shared by nearly everyone, up to and including the present day. (Though Frege's version of a shared picture must be seen as containing proprietary elements.) The Wittgensteinian alternative to it, to be developed here, has had so far little influence. This book aims to rectify that situation by showing what is intuitive and attractive about that alternative view, and, again, to do this independent of any effect the private language discussion might have for it. But this chapter does not aim to do that. It aims merely to specify the defining characteristics of the picture, no matter how unintuitive they may, for the moment, seem. The strategy will be to explain the dominant picture first, and then to develop the present picture by considering what one must do to disagree with that one. Disagreement, we will see, is no easy matter. Which may partly explain the attraction the dominant picture continues to exert.

It bears emphasis that both pictures, being, as they are, pictures of semantic *properties*, concern whatever items may have them, and not exclusively words. They are at least as concerned with thought as with expressions of it; with concepts as with predicates. The dominant view is just as likely to inform current discussion of belief and other such attitudes, for example, as explicit discussions of language. And it is likely to inform such discussions by people who would not consider themselves Fregean. On the other side, it is important always to keep in mind that the entire Wittgensteinian view of having semantics, as it will be presented here and illustrated in the case of words, applies intact to what words express and our attitudes towards that—so, *inter alia*, to believing, meaning, intending, expecting and their objects. Further, semantic pictures have metaphysical correlates. The features the present picture finds in predicates and the concepts they may express are reflected in the properties we may have concepts of; the features it finds in bearers of truth find their reflections in the facts such items might state. By implication, at least, the dominant picture is equally one of what properties and facts are like.

Viewing the significance of private language as here viewed means construing it as a sort of transcendental argument—a story about how things must be, rather than merely about how they are—and one with a rather traditionally heavy metaphysical moral at that. It is hard to resist seeing the private language discussion as having some such force. But such argument does run counter to Wittgenstein's stated views on doing philosophy. To be impressed by how things must be, he tells us, is typically to be in the grip of a picture; whereas what we ought to ask is not how things must be, but how they are. So private language is an exceptional case. Part of the task in discussing it will be to explain why Wittgenstein is entitled to the exception.

1. SEMANTICS

It remains to be said what is meant here by semantics. The key notion is *semantic property* A semantics will be a set of semantic properties; a semantic item an item with semantic properties. It will not be important to give the notion *semantic* property sharp boundaries. It will be good enough if a semantic picture fits a large or important class of central cases. The notion *semantic* might then be broadened or narrowed a bit to capture what the picture fits. But I will now list some central cases of semantic properties, and consider some principles for expanding from these to new central cases.

Some central semantic properties are ones of saying, or of having said A (of B), and, less importantly, of meaning A, for any values of A and B which yield sense here. Some other properties are saying A to be so, and saying A to be B. Still other properties are more specific ones which entail some of these, such as those of calling A (a) B, describing or characterizing A as (a) B, or expressing the judgement that A is (a) B. A second class of central cases is epitomized by being true (false), being true of A, saying what is true, and saying what is (would be) true of (in situation) A.

Intuitively, 'true' evaluates how an item fares in virtue of others of its semantic properties—perhaps how, in virtue of them, it relates to the world. So to be true, the thought goes, an item must have other semantic properties of some appropriate sort. Whether words are true, for example, depends on what they say or said. So there must be something which is what they do (did) say if they may be either true or false. Similarly, if a promise is kept, then whether it was depends on what was said would be done, so on what was said in the words that made it, so there must be something that was said in those words; if an order was obeyed, then whether it was depends on what was said was to be done, so there must be something said in the words which gave it; and so on.

Call being true, being kept or obeyed, and the like evaluative properties. Then the general thought—intuitive, though perhaps not universally correct, is that if words or other items have evaluative properties, then they must have other non-evaluative semantic properties; in the case of words, properties of roughly the first mentioned sort. Strictly speaking, neither picture to be presented depends on this intuition being right. But it is a useful guide to further properties one could recognize, which, if recognized, would be semantic. Further, there seems at least this much right about it: if an item has an evaluative property—say, being true—then it is a sort of item which is liable to have some non-evaluative semantic properties as well; there are some such properties which it at least might have or might have had. And if it instances an indefinitely large sort— thoughts, say, or words—then there are some such properties which are had by some members of that sort, and members of the sort characteristically have some such properties. However, nothing on either side of the issue to be presented requires assuming this. If it grates on intuition, then let it be a purely optional assumption, useful only as an indication of some of what we will here recognize as semantic properties.

From the above two core samples, the class of semantic properties may be made to grow. Promises, orders and questions, for example, are neither true nor false. But orders and promises say things. An order may say that A is to do B. So orders and promises have semantic properties of a general sort on which evaluative properties may depend. That is good enough reason (by fiat if necessary) to take them to have some evaluative properties which depend on this semantics in the way that other evaluative properties such as being true depend on the same sort of semantics in other cases. *Inter alia*, orders may be obeyed. Whether a given situation counts as one of an order having been obeyed depends on what the order says just as whether a given situation makes words true depends on what they say. So we can take being obeyed (and similarly being carried out and being filled) as evaluative properties of orders. Questions do not say things. Neither do requests. But requests may be carried out. That is an evaluative property. So requests must have, as a rule, other semantic properties on which that evaluative property depends. Requests ask things. Their being carried out by given doings depends on what they ask in the same way as an order's being carried out depends on what it says. So asking A is a semantic property. But questions, too, ask things. So they may have evaluative properties in virtue of that. And so on. All this is no more than intuition. But it is just these intuitions which pick out (roughly) the subject-matter of both the pictures to come. A semantic picture need not fit all of these properties. We can revise intuitions if necessary to fit it. But the differences between present rivals will be settled in the centre of the field, and not on the periphery where such revision might be to the point.

Let us now consider semantic items. The semantic properties considered so far have their most obvious applications in the case of words. Or almost. It is true that people can say things, and also mean things, though perhaps not in a relevant sense of that treacherous word. On the other hand, people cannot be true (nor carried out) in the relevant sense. Are people semantic items? Say what you like about that. That might be one reasonable way of describing their beliefs, intentions, expectations, and so on. It is a reasonable way of seeing how Wittgensteinian principles apply to such things. But if it seems unnatural to speak in this way, then legislate it away.

There are more interesting things to say when we consider a property like being true. Words, perhaps, may have that property. But then so can (some of) what words express, or what they say, or what is said in them. Such potential bearers of this property might be called thoughts. As the name suggests, thoughts may be thought or believed as well as said or expressed. Or at least I will so use the word, since (some of) what we think and what we believe may be true. Since thoughts may be true, they must have, as a rule, other semantic properties on which their truth depends. Thoughts do not say things. What is said, for example, does not. So they must have other non-evaluative semantic properties which parallel in function those semantic properties of words. We will not yet worry about general names for those properties. But we note their existence. The important point is that the semantic pictures now at issue apply to these properties as well.

Words may have the property of having been spoken at 3 p.m., and also the property of having said that Montreal is an island. There is an intuitive difference between these properties: the second, but not the first, is a matter of how the words were to be understood. To know when a given 'Mary had a little lamb' was spoken, we need not know which understanding of it was the proper one; to know what it said, we must know this. That P is a property which, for example, words have just in case they are properly understood to have it might be thought to be part of what characterizes P as semantic. That is a vague intuition of as yet uncertain worth. In the next chapter, something specific will be made of it within an account of which situations would be ones of an item's having one semantics or another. It will then turn out to point to something characteristic of semantic fact. But it does not yet have a serious role to play.

2. THE DOMINANT PICTURE

The many accounts of semantics on the books differ in numerous respects. The idea of a common picture is the idea of a common core in all, or virtually all, of these versions. The task of this section is to display that core in its most essential features. The strategy will be indirect. I will first consider a few intuitive, and, I hope, thoroughly familiar ideas. These ideas contain a bit more than what is crucial for the picture, though, I will suggest, very little more. But they point in the right direction. Having presented them, I will then extract this core picture from them.

Though this book aims ultimately to treat all semantic items uniformly, it will help in the beginning to consider a plausible distinction between items of two sorts. Intuitively, some items, like words, or at least like English words (or German or Chinese ones, etc.), are liable to change their semantic properties. On one plausible view, there are other items which are not so liable: what was said in words, for example, or what was thought, or what is believed; in short, the items we have labelled thoughts. Words may change their semantics at least in so far as they may change what they mean over time. 'Ching' is Cantonese for *green*. But given that it comes to be used sufficiently differently by Cantonese speakers, it may come to mean *blue*. On usual views, words may change their semantics in other ways too— over time, and perhaps across other parameters as well. On the other hand, if, at a given time, Odile says, 'The walls are blue' or 'The milk is sour', then what she said in those words cannot change its semantics in any of these ways. And it is natural to conceive of it as not liable to changing semantics at all, so as having whatever semantics it does have *immutably*. It is not as if what she said—for example, that the milk is sour—might be true today and false tomorrow. As we usually conceive things, either the milk is sour or it isn't. And that fact, whichever it is, settles the status of what she said once and for all. Similarly for any of its other semantic properties. It will help to treat these two cases separately at first, and to begin with thoughts.

The semantics a thought now has is, on the plausible view, a semantics it could not *ever* lack. But that is not yet to speak of the semantics it could have had. In fact, the first intuitive thought combines naturally with a second. Suppose I say that my chair is full of feathers, and the thought I thus express is true. For all that, it might have been false, and would have been, for example, if someone had let the feathers out. The thought's being true (or false) depends on how the world is, and the world might have been different than it is in relevant respects. On the other hand, it is natural to think that while some of the semantics of the thought might have been different than it is, other parts of its semantic could not have been. The thought might have been false, given suitable co-operation from the chair, for example; but it could not have been a thought that the milk was sour, no matter what. Let us call those semantic properties that the thought could not have lacked its intrinsic semantics.

Here is the first intuitive idea to approach the core of the picture: some items, such as thoughts, have an intrinsic semantics; for such items, their intrinsic semantics fully determines their entire semantics. The intrinsic semantics of a thought fully determines the semantics it now *has*, or, since it cannot change its semantics, the semantics it has, full stop. Moreover, its intrinsic semantics fully determines the semantics the thought would have in any circumstances which might have been the actual ones. Nothing other than the thought's intrinsic semantics could be needed to determine, or could play any role in determining, all the facts as to which semantic properties that thought has in the actual situation which obtains apart from the thought's semantics—the facts of matters other than its semantic properties—no matter what that actual situation may be. So first, if a thought, W, has a semantic property Q, then W's intrinsic semantics is incompatible with lacking Q, in this sense: there cannot be an item with that intrinsic semantics about which one could state a fact in saying W to lack Q; and, in particular, one could never state a fact in saying W to lack Q. Such things might have been so, had the world been different than it is; but as it is, they cannot be so. Second, for any semantic property, Q, W's intrinsic semantics cannot be compatible both with having and with lacking Q, in this sense: there could not be both an item with W's intrinsic semantics about which one stated a fact in saying it to have Q and an item with that intrinsic semantics about which one stated a fact in saying it to lack Q; and in particular, it could not be both that one could state fact in saying W to have Q, and either that one could state fact in saying W to lack Q, or that one could ever fail to state fact in saying W to have Q. So there is no room for a further factor to decide which of these things is the case, given the world as it in fact is. If an intrinsic semantics does all this work, we will say that it is *crucial* for the semantics of the item which has it, and that that item has a *crucial* intrinsic semantics.

Consider now words. For example, English words. Here the case is complicated by the fact that, as we have already decided, English words have no intrinsic semantics. At the very least, they might do such things as change meanings. But they might, in the actual world, vary their semantics in other ways as well. Or it is plausible to think so. On one view, English words, such as 'The chair is full of feathers', might, as it were, express different thoughts at different times. So that, if the chair was full of feathers yesterday but is empty now, one might hold that those words were true yesterday but are false now (though the thought they expressed yesterday—that the chair was then full of feathers—and the different one they express today are both true at any time). In that way, words might be seen as varying their semantics over time. Words might also be seen as varying their semantics across other and more general dimensions. Their semantics might vary across speakings of them, for example—even across speakings produced at one time. As might happen with the English sentence 'I am hot', on one view of the matter. So that the semantics such words had *as spoken in such-and-such speaking* might differ from the semantics they had as spoken in another.

All of these above sorts of variation are variations that can, perhaps even might, occur in the world as it actually is: the range of semantics words would thus sometimes count as having are all semantics which are consistent with the world being that way. But the last two sorts differ from the first. Intuitively they represent what words could do consistent with their having the semantics they now do, and not merely what they could do through ceasing to have that semantics. They might even be seen as representing what the words *must* do on other occasions given the semantics they have on this one; what that present semantics requires of them elsewhere, given the changed values of the parameters across which their semantics varies. It is consistent with the present semantics of 'The chair is full of feathers', for example, that it should express a different thought tomorrow than it does today. In fact, this may even seem to be required by that present semantics. And, though it may have different semantics tomorrow than it does today, those differences are only what its present semantics requires them to be. Similarly, the present semantics of 'I am hot' requires that it now express different thoughts in different mouths. On all of those speakings it retains that present semantics, and acquires exactly that further semantics which this semantics requires. These ideas are somewhat rough. But, for present purposes, they are properly suggestive.

Intuitively, some words sometimes express thoughts. When words do so, their semantics is largely, if not entirely, that of the thought they express (*modulo* some purely formal transformations.) Notably, the words are true (if we choose so to speak) iff the thought they express is. Words, unlike thoughts, may have properties of expressing thought A, saying A, and so forth. But—trivially in the first case—which of these properties they have is determined, by formal rules, by the thought they express, or by its semantics. Where words do not express a thought—as 'I am hot' does not when not in a mouth, or as 'is full of feathers' does not, even in a mouth—they are plausibly seen as standing to *some* item with an intrinsic semantics in the same way that words which express thoughts stand to those items—the latter words to a concept, perhaps, and the former to a meaning, or propositional or thought schema, or something on these lines.

All this suggests the following idea. The semantics of a thought (or other item with an intrinsic semantics is, on the first idea, determined by its intrinsic semantics. Words cannot have an intrinsic semantics. But they could have a proper part of their semantics which does for them what the crucial semantics of a thought is supposed to do for it. (We might think of this as a semantics which, if some item did have it intrinsically, would be a crucial intrinsic semantics for that item.) We might simply call this their crucial semantics. The idea is that they do so. Now, or on any occasion for word's having a semantics—*tout court*, for example, or at a time, or on a speaking—those words have a crucial semantics which fully determines the semantics they have on that occasion in the sense, described above, in which an intrinsic semantics is meant to fully determine the semantics of an item (or items) which have it. This is the first main intuitive idea about words.

There is a second intuitive idea about words which is worth considering. It is suggested by this thought: 'the chair is full of feathers' may express different thoughts on different occasions. But something about the way it now is determines which thought it would express on any occasion where it did so—for example, at any time or on any speaking. Similarly for 'I am hot'. The idea concerns the way in which this something does the determining it does. Take 'I am hot' as a model. Those words now have a certain semantics *tout court*. The intuition is that, on a speaking, they retain essentially, though not necessarily exactly, that semantics, and may acquire more. For example, they may then express a thought which is true (false)— something which they do not do *tout court*. The semantics they retain on a speaking may not quite be all of their semantics *tout court*. One might want to say, for example, that, *tout court*, they have the property of being neither true nor false. On a speaking, they may lose that property, and gain instead the property of being true. The idea, in this case, is that the semantics they retain across occasions fully determines their semantics on any such occasion, given the other facts of that occasion.

The idea in general form is now this. Some words, now, or on some occasion, have a semantics which they may retain across a variety of occasions for their having semantics. At least if they are unambiguous—or on a reading of them if they are ambiguous—some part of this semantics, not necessarily a proper part, fully determines the semantics they would have on any such occasion, given the other facts of that occasion; it is not compatible with their having, on that occasion, any of several divergent semantics (in the previously stated sense of compatibility). Since we have already appropriated the term 'crucial', let us call this element of a semantics, for words that have it, a *critical* semantics. Like any semantics, a critical semantics is something words are liable to lose: 'I am hot' could, conceivably, change its meaning over time. The important point is what a critical semantics does for items that have it; what it determines as to what *would* be so of an item with that semantics. That words *would* say what was true if spoken in such and such way, for example, is one variety of semantic property they may have. Their critical semantics is what fixes this variety of property for them.

As conceived here, critical semantics differ from crucial ones. There could be items with a given critical semantics which differed in the semantics they had; so in the semantic facts about them. It is consistent with the world being as it is that such a variety of items should actually be producible. There could not be items with a given crucial semantics which did that. What there could not be, for a given critical semantics, is an item, on an occasion for its having semantics, whose having that critical semantics was compatible with any of various divergent sets of semantic facts about it on that occasion. So while the critical semantics of 'I am hot' is a semantics it has on a speaking, it is not its crucial semantics on a speaking. But it fixes what that crucial semantics must be, given the other facts of that speaking.

It is worth adding two notes to the above before moving forward. First, it is important to distinguish between the semantic determinacy brought about by crucial (or critical) semantics on the above thoughts, and what we might call the Fregean *tertium non datur* principle. This latter principle says that for any semantic item, W, and any semantic property, P, either W has P, or it lacks (does not have) P, *tertium non datur*. The ideas expressed above do not say that. For all that has been said so far, a given crucial semantics might fail to decide whether an item has or lacks P. The important point is that if that is so, then nothing else decides the item's status in this respect either. In that case, it is not a fact that the item has P, and we do not state a fact in saying so. But it is not a fact that the item lacks P, and we do not state a fact in saying that either. In that case, the item's having that intrinsic semantics is incompatible both with its having P, and with its lacking P, in the stated sense. With Fregean *tertium non datur*, sets of semantic properties which might be the semantics of some item would always have to be maximal sets: one could not add another semantic property to them without getting a contradictory set of properties. But we are not supposing that.

Second, so far we have spoken of intrinsic or crucial semantics as determining the full semantics of an item. And we will continue so to speak. But usually people have been interested in the determination of a particular class of semantic properties, namely, evaluative ones. And, given the prominence of truth in philosophy, the properties specifically at issue have usually been truth-involving ones—pre-eminently ones of being true, of being false, of being true (false) of (item or situation) A, and of being true (false) in (situation) A. Further, people have often conceived of a crucial semantics as not containing such truth-involving properties. The second point is non-compulsory for present purposes. As for the first, no harm is done, for present purposes, if we restrict the picture in this way. Anyone who thinks that that makes the dominant picture more likely to be right is welcome to do so.

Now for the core of the dominant picture. It seems to me that what is most important in the ideas just sketched—and what will be predominantly at issue in what follows—is not the idea that there are such things as crucial or critical semantics—that is, proper sub-parts of a semantics which do (some or all of) the jobs just sketched—but rather the idea that there are such jobs to be done at all. The crucial idea, that is, is that a semantic item has a semantics which is determinate in the way just described. Here is the idea for thoughts (or any items whose semantics is immutable). Suppose that W is a thought, and P any semantic property. Then we cannot work ourselves in to each of a pair of situations, in one of which we would state a fact in saying W to have P, and in the other of which we would state a fact in saying W to lack P. Nor into a pair of situations in one of which we would state a fact in saying W to have P, and in the other of which we would not do so. Now consider words. Let W be any words, and O any occasion for their having a semantics. If words have a semantics at a time, then O may be a time. If they have a semantics on a speaking, then O may be a speaking of them. In general, O may correspond to whatever way in which it is correct to speak of W as having a semantics. (For example, 'in this book, "privacy" means . . .') Let P be any semantic property. Then we cannot work ourselves into a pair of situations in one of which we would state a fact in saying W to have (have had) P on O (at that time, on that speaking, etc.), and in the other of which we would state a fact in saying W then to have lacked P, or at least fail to state a fact in saying W then to have P.

This, then, by current nomenclature, is the dominant picture. It is a picture of the way in which semantic items have whatever semantic properties they have. (Again, without loss to the argument, it may be restricted to truth-involving properties.) We will find that it is a picture which Wittgenstein is centrally concerned to dispute. Let us say that an item whose semantics is determinate in the above way has its semantics classically, or is a classical item, or simply is classical. Then on the dominant picture, all semantic items, or certainly all well-behaved ones, are classical. Wittgenstein's view is that no item could be classical; to think that it could be is to make a mistake as to what it is to have a semantics. The rest of this book is about what kind of mistake that is.

Given this core, the idea of items having a crucial semantics can, I think, be added at no risk. Suppose, for example, that a thought has its semantics classically. Suppose, now, that we posit a crucial intrinsic property of the thought—call it P. If we stick our necks out enough as to which property P is, then we might, perhaps, be refuted. But suppose we are willing to be open-minded as to what P is—that is, as to how it may be identified other than as the crucial intrinsic property of that thought. The only way in which we could be refuted, I think, is by finding some other semantic property, Q—preferably a truth-involving one—and showing that, if there is such a property as P, then it may be a fact that an item has P and has Q, and also may be a fact that an item has P and not a fact that it has Q. But that is just what we cannot do decisively if the candidate thought's semantics is determinate in the present sense. We cannot produce the required contrast with that thought. And we cannot introduce some other thought into the discussion without running the risk that that thought lacks P. But, rather than insist on this idea, I simply drop the idea of crucial properties from the core of the picture.

On one natural view, semantic facts supervene on others. Consider some words, and an occasion on which they have semantics. All the non-semantic facts of that occasion, or all the facts other than semantic facts about those words—everything about how that occasion is, the semantics of those words aside—leave only one way for those semantic facts to be. Or in so far as they do not—in so far as there are, if any, then various sets of semantic facts compatible with all the other facts—there are no semantic facts about the words. The work to be done here will challenge the idea, on at least one understanding of it, that other facts leave only one way for semantic facts to be. But it will equally challenge the idea that their not doing so provides any reason to think there are no semantic facts. The world will exhibit, so to speak, an extra dimension along which semantic facts may vary; an extra factor at work in fixing them. We will then see that semantic facts fail to supervene on others just in the way that any fact—in principle—fails to supervene on others. In a sense, there is nothing special about semantic facts, though they have a central role—here, at least—in establishing the general point.

On one view, there is a part of the semantics of a thought which supervenes vacuously on other facts: there is only one way for that semantics to be, full stop, since the thought's having precisely that semantics is part of what it is for it to be the thought it is. In a sense, this idea, too, will be challenged. The point is not that a thought, for example, that my chair is full of feathers, might have been anything at all. But the sort of indeterminacy we will discover in the semantics of any item at all—thoughts included—is, *inter alia*, an indeterminacy in the facts of what semantics a given thought could not have lacked without ceasing to be that thought; a variability in the properties which identify it as being the thought it is. Which will mean that the most significant parts of what has usually been taken to be intrinsic to a thought are, in an important sense, not. And it will be shown that thoughts cannot have a crucial intrinsic semantics—one which fully determines, in the present sense, what there semantics is. This will emerge as compatible with the idea that one can always view the semantics of a thought as immutable, in the sense of not being subject to change.

We now have a view of what is so of what the dominant picture applies to. But we must note a qualification which may be built into it on what it is meant to apply to. It is reasonable to take it, at least, that it is not meant to apply to inconsistent sets of semantic properties. So also, perhaps, not to items which cannot be assigned a consistent semantics. Such items might count as vacuously fitting the description of the picture provided here, since there would be no semantic property, Q, such that we could state fact in saying them to have Q. But they could not have such a thing as a crucial semantics. So they would not fit those versions of the picture which posited one. Which would mean nothing. The picture was not made for them; they might as well be ruled outside the scope of the present discussion.

Thinking along lines something like this, Frege, in at least some of his moods, and others following him, have held that the picture, or at least their versions of it, is not meant to apply to 'everyday' languages such as English or German, but rather to yet-to-be-constructed languages which would meet the requirements of 'serious and exact scientific discussion' (however they would identify that). On that sort of move, Wittgenstein has the following comment (120):

> When I talk about language (words, sentences, etc.) I must speak the language of every day. Is this language somehow too coarse and material for what we want to say? Then how is another one to be constructed?—And how strange that we should be able to do anything at all with the one we have!

The comment reveals Wittgenstein's aim. The point is *not* merely to show that the dominant picture does not apply to this or that. It is *not* to show, for example, that 'ordinary language', though in order as it is, does not fit the picture. It is rather to show that there is *no* semantic item which fits the picture, and, ultimately, that there could be none. That is certainly reason for wanting a transcendental argument, of the sort which I will claim the private language discussion to provide. (Though this does not yet explain how Wittgenstein is entitled to such an argument.) Conversely, if the dominant picture fails for some particular sort of item—English sentences, say—the defender of it still wins if he can display some other sort of item—thoughts, say—for which it does not fail. This defines the ground rules for the ensuing discussion.

3. TWO FALSE STARTS

In arguing against the classical picture, one might adopt either of two general strategies.[2] One might try to show that the picture is senseless:

---

[2] This sort of choice is often exhibited in the natural sciences. Suppose we take seriously the idea that relativistic mechanics is the truth. Now consider the Newtonian definition of kinetic energy. We might say that it makes no sense, since it appeals to notions of mass and velocity which make no sense. Or we might say that it is wrong, since, given what mass, velocity and energy must be, kinetic energy cannot be defined in that way. (See Putnam [1962b] for discussion.)

that somehow or other, in stating it, we have appealed to some
(putative) notion that is not, and could not be well defined. Or one
might accept the picture as sensible and coherent, and argue that it is
false—either of given semantic items, or, consonant with our am-
bitious Wittgensteinian aims, of any semantic item. In this book I opt
for the second more straightforward approach. But it must be said that
the phenomena to be produced could be read as demonstrating the first
thesis. Again, this chapter will not *argue* that the dominant picture is
wrong, but simply describe an alternative to it: a picture such that *if* it
is right, then the dominant one is wrong.

The main idea for an alternative picture will be a generalization of
Wittgenstein's intuition that, in some way, the present semantics of an
item leaves its 'future application'—so at least some of its evaluative
semantic properties—open; that 'the application of a word is not
everywhere bounded by rules' (84), 'the extension of the concept is *not*
closed by a frontier' (68). This section will consider two developments
of that thought which do not do the work of conflicting with the
dominant picture, and one development which might do so, though we
will not pursue it here.

The first development comes by viewing concepts, or their boundaries, as vague. If the concept is being a chair (or the words, 'is a chair'),
for example, then the point would be that there are some items which
neither determinately fit the concept (or those words), nor determinately fail to do so. It is just undecided whether they are chairs or
not. That observation, if correct, certainly counts against a Fregean
tertium non datur principle. But it does not count against the
dominant picture. For if the point is right, then nothing decides
whether the words or concepts are true of these items. So it is simply
not a fact that they have the property of being true of those items—one
could not state fact in saying them to have such a property—nor,
equally, is it a fact that the words or concept are not true of the items.
Grant all that, and the status of those words and concepts with respect
to these truth-involving properties is perfectly determinate, in the
relevant sense. So far, at least, they may be supposed to have their
semantics classically.

The first requirement for disagreeing with the picture, then, is that
there be semantic facts—on the thought being developed, such things
as facts as to a concept's 'future applications', or the future proper uses
of words. It is then required, second, that some or all of these have an
appropriate status with respect to the current semantics of the item(s)
in question. (This underlines the point that one cannot disagree with
the picture simply by being a semantic sceptic, that is, by denying that
there are semantic facts. As the present account will try to show,
Wittgenstein was no such sceptic.) The appropriate status would seem

to require that, in some sense, whether these (candidate) semantics facts are facts must not be settled by the current semantics of the item. So, in an appropriate sense, it must not follow from that semantics that they are. On the other hand, if they are facts about the item, then that they are, it would seem, must follow in some sense from the item's current status. So, it would seem, they—say, the relevant facts about future applications—are facts which, in a sense, do follow, and, in a sense, do not follow from the item's (current) understanding. As Wittgenstein points out,[3] it is easy for one or both of these senses to appear to be a queer sense. Much of the current job is to explain them so that they do not appear queer.

Let us try a second development of the thought. If the words 'is a chair' are true of an item, then they might have been false of it at least in this way: with a sufficiently different history, 'chair' might have meant *table*; the words might then have said what was false of the item. Let us engage in a little (social) science fiction. Imagine that we are at the moment of the (fictional) introduction (by the English Academy) of the word 'chair' into English. Not knowing what its future history will be, we could not then say whether it would now say something true, for example, of my armchair. That fact might suggest an idea. We think that the meaning of 'chair' is fixed somehow by its *past* use. But why should we be biased in favour of that particular time direction? Why should the semantics of 'chair' not depend on the ways it will be used in the future as well? Future uses, for example, might give us reason to revise our views on what 'chair' really said all along.[4]

Now let us apply this line of thought to the problem of semantic determinacy. Is 'is a chair' true of my armchair? If that depends on *future* uses of it, then we might just have to wait and see. Or anyway, the future could, in principle, show us wrong if we answered, 'Yes.' So it is not determined *yet*, one might say, that it has that property. But it might turn out to be determined some day that it does. That would then be a semantic fact about those words which would not be determined by their current status.

There may be much worth while in the core thought here. But again, it does not yet provide a way of disagreeing with the dominant picture. First let us distinguish two things that future use might be supposed to do. It might be supposed to determine that the words 'is a chair' *now* have the property of being true of my armchair. Or it might be supposed to determine that at some time in the future they will have that property. In the first case, we so far have every reason to say that

---

[3] E.g., in 193, 194, 195 and 197.
[4] Very sensible suggestions have been made in this direction by Crispin Wright— though not in this sort of case. See Wright [1986a], especially pp. 273–4.

they have that property classically. Not all the events have yet taken place which are required to make it so that they have the property. Still, that is what the course of the world will show. So, on the description so far, we would, in point of fact, state a fact in saying those words to have a property. And we would never fail to state a fact in saying this; nor would we ever state a fact in saying them to lack the property. Or so it seems. Consider the second case. By the same reasoning, the words will, in the future, have the property of being true of my chair classically. As for the present, well, they just do not have that property yet. So one would never state a fact in saying them now to do so. Again, we have found no instance where the words do not now, and will not in the future, have their semantics classically.

There is another possibility. Suppose that what future uses determine is neither of the things mentioned above, but rather this: that, while it is not now true to say that those words are now true of my armchair, and one would not state fact in saying so, in the future it will be true to say that those words *now* have the property of being true of my armchair, and one would *then* state fact in saying so. We await an account, of course, of how such a thing could be. But if it were so, as we will see, it would be a good candidate for disagreeing with the picture. There would be something which in the future will count as a fact. But that something would not *now* (yet) count as a fact. The fact—when it does come to count as such—would be one about what the semantics of the words *now* is, and what their now having that semantics requires. But one would not yet state truth in saying it to be a fact.

There is the matter of the semantics of the words being what it is; and there is the matter of the semantics of the words being such-and-such. What can now be said truly on the latter score does not exhaust everything involved in the former fact. As one might put it, there is a distinction to be drawn between the fact *of* the item's having its present semantics, and the fact *that* it has such-and-such semantic properties. Such is what would be so on this line of thought. But here we will not pursue it further in quite this form.

4. S-USE

Wittgenstein comments (432):

Every sign *by itself* seems dead. *What* gives it life?—In use it is alive.

Use, the suggestion is, is a factor on which the semantics of an item depends. Let us explore the idea that use may be an extra factor, in addition to the semantics an item now has, on which the semantic

facts about it may depend; so a factor which may yield any of various
sets of such facts about the item, compatibly with its now having the
semantics it does. It is not easy to see how such a thing could be. But if
it could, that would explicate the sense in which 'current semantics'
does not determine future applications. We will leave it to the next
chapter to explain the sense in which 'current semantics' does do this.
This chapter will consider the sense in which 'the future development'
is not 'already present' (cf. 197); the next will explore the sense in
which it is. The two taken together should remove the queerness
which Wittgenstein says we *may* find in the idea that, for example, in
understanding a word, we 'grasp its whole use'.

It is plausible enough that the semantics of *some* items depends on
their use. I will ultimately argue that the semantics of all semantic
items does so. But 'use' may refer to many phenomena. For the
moment we want to consider one particular kind of use. In the core
case, it is the use made of words by a speaker in a particular speaking of
them; for example, the use of the word 'banana' made by Hugo in
saying, 'The bananas are ripe.' We will call such a use a speaker use,
henceforth abbreviated to *S-use*. Presently, we will broaden the notion
somewhat. But for the meantime, let us confine attention to words.
What we want to consider, then, is the relation of an S-use of words W
to the semantics of W, and to W's semantics on that speaking.

I want to call attention to a particular phenomenon—or, since I will
not yet argue for it,[5] a possible phenomenon—which I will call *S-use
sensitivity*. By itself, S-use sensitivity is not an alternative to the
dominant picture. But it has a variety of important uses in what is to
come. Here is an example of it. Suppose that the refrigerator is devoid
of milk except for a puddle of milk at the bottom of it. Now consider
two possible speakings, by Odile, of the words, 'There's milk in the
refrigerator.' For the first, Hugo is seated at the breakfast table, reading
the paper, and from time to time looking dejectedly (but meaningfully)
at his cup of black coffee, which he is idly stirring with a spoon. Odile
volunteers, 'There's milk in the refrigerator.' For the second, Hugo has
been given the task of cleaning the refrigerator. He has just changed

---

[5] The problem is that for *any* putative example of S-use sensitivity, there are many
not obviously wrong strategies for avoiding the consequence that it really does exhibit S-
use sensitivity. Nor are these strategies beyond the ingenuity of most philosophers. They
really need to be dealt with one by one. But doing that seriously would involve such a
long digression that we would never get on with the business of this chapter, nor of this
book. (Though I will argue seriously for one instance of S-use sensitivity in chapter 4.) I
began to argue seriously for S-use sensitivity in Travis [1975]. I was initially impressed
by Austin's presentation of the phenomenon, primarily *via* his epistemological work,
but also *via* his treatment of such examples as 'France is hexagonal' in Austin [1962]. My
most serious and systematic—and I hope successful—efforts at establishing the
phenomenon are in Travis [1981] and Travis [1985].

out of his house-cleaning garb, and is settling with satisfaction into his armchair, book and beverage in hand. Odile opens the refrigerator, looks in, closes it and sternly utters the above words.

I claim that the example bears at least the following description: though there is no ambiguity in the English words 'There is milk in the refrigerator', or none relevant to the differences between the two speakings, Odile's words in the first case said what was false, while in the second case they said what was true. Both spoke of the same state of the world, or the same refrigerator in the same condition. So, in the first case, the words said what is false of a refrigerator with but a milk puddle; in the second case they said what is true of such a refrigerator. Optionally we may also say that what was said in the words in the first case differs from what was said in those words in the second. The speakings may also differ with respect to yet other semantic properties. For all that, either speaking might have occurred, with that semantics, at any one given time—10 a.m. on Sunday, say.

I will not argue here that the above description of those speakings is correct. The present point, after all, is not to prove the dominant picture wrong, but to identify something which would be at odds with it. Correspondingly, what we want to see at present is what would happen if there were phenomena like the one described, either in this case, or in similar ones. In any event, where different speakings of words may thus differ in their semantics, consistent with their all having been made at some one given time, we will say that the semantics of the words is S-use sensitive (with respect to the properties that vary across the speakings).

Since S-use sensitivity is so important for what follows, I will present one more initial illustration of it. Consider the words, 'Hugo weighs 79 kilos' and the following situation: when Hugo steps on the scale in the morning, it reads 79 kilos, and that is a stable result. However, it is now after lunch; fully dressed (in winter clothing), Hugo would register 81 kilos on the scales. Now consider two speakings of the words. For the first, Hugo must weigh 79 kilos, and no more, to qualify for some sporting event. There is a discussion as to whether he does qualify. Odile, who has seen him step on the scale, tries to settle the matter by revealing her information on the subject. She says, 'Hugo weighs 79 kilos.' For the second, Hugo is about to step on to a very delicate trestle bridge across a ravine which can take a maximum of 80 kilos without snapping. Or Hugo is placed on a balance scale to weigh out 79 kilos of gold (for some weighty purpose). The question is whether Hugo ought to step on to the bridge, or whether that really is 79 kilos of gold, and not more. Odile volunteers, 'Hugo weighs 79 kilos.' Again, the claim is that Odile spoke truth in the first case and falsehood in the second. So that the essential parts of the descriptions of the first example fit this one as well. In that case, the words 'Hugo weighs 79 kilos' also exhibit S-use sensitivity. (Similar examples could be constructed around a turkey which was said to weigh 5 kilos, and does so if you include the kilo of stuffing inside it. And so forth.) Here we may say that the English words 'weighs 79 kilos', used as meaning what they do, and as speaking of weighing 79 kilos, may make any of various distinct contributions to what is said in speaking them, with corresponding differences in the conditions for the truth of what is said. In this way at least, the words 'Hugo weighs 79 kilos' have different semantic properties on different occasions, and, as a result, used literally, may say both true things and false things of Hugo in a given condition at a given time. That is, there are things of both sorts to be said in speaking them.

Now I want to engage in a digression. Consider once again, 'I am hot.' The intuition was that something about its semantics *tout court*—in particular, something about what it means—determines what its semantics would be on any speaking of it (where spoken as meaning that). Now consider a different kind of case, as illustrated by the ambiguous English sentence, 'Mary had a little lamb.' Some speakings of that sentence speak of meat eating. Some speak of pet keeping. Both sorts are consistent with what the sentence means as such. We have the intuition, I think, that nothing about the meaning of that sentence—either *tout court*, or on a reading—determines its semantics on a speaking in the way that the semantics of 'I am hot' might initially seem to determine its semantics on a speaking. (I will ultimately argue that this initially plausible view is incorrect in that case as well.) It is not as if it were part of the meaning of 'Mary had a little lamb' that when certain other factors are present in a speaking it speaks of meat eating, and when certain ones are present it speaks of pet keeping. It is conceivable that some day someone should discover rules to that effect. But nothing about our understanding of the sentence leads us to expect this. Nothing in that thought counts against the idea of critical semantics for words, for one thing, because that idea is explicitly restricted to unambiguous words. Though 'Mary had a little lamb' provides an idea on why it perhaps should be so restricted.

The point of the digression is this. 'I am hot' and 'Mary had a little lamb' provide us with two paradigms of the variation of words' semantics across speakings of them. Intuitively, S-use sensitivity, as illustrated so far, fits the paradigm of 'Mary had a little lamb' and not that of 'I am hot.' On the present view of semantics, it does so. Nothing about the meaning of 'There's milk in the refrigerator', for example, identifies (in other terms) the conditions under which it would say what was true of a refrigerator with but a milk puddle. This thought does argue, I think, against the idea that words have a critical semantics. It certainly counts against the idea that one can account for their semantics on an occasion in terms of specifiable features or parameters of occasions in general, or indices, or something of the sort, and some function from values of these to at least some sort of crucial semantics for words on a speaking, or a thought expressed in them (a 'content' in David Kaplan's terminology[6]), where this function is fixed by the semantics of the words involved. However, rather than following out that line directly, I will let the idea of a critical semantics, like that of a crucial semantics, stand or fall for the same general reasons that the idea of having a semantics classically will stand or fall. So, for example, aside from the specific arguments that might be brought against usual thoughts about 'indices' and what these might do,[7] there will be the general point that the semantics of words on a speaking is non-classical, hence there is indeterminacy in what the values of such things as functions over indices would have to be in any given case. But this is to look ahead.

S-use sensitivity must have metaphysical correlates. We will use these correlates to broaden the notion. Suppose that, as is plausible, we take 'Hugo weighs 79 kilos' to speak of the property of weighing 79 kilos, and to say Hugo to have it. Similarly, we might take 'There's milk in the refrigerator' to speak of a property of containing milk, and to say the refrigerator to have it. For each sentence, we have considered a pair of speakings of it. If we identify what the sentence says (and says on each speaking) in this way, then we must conclude the following. Hugo counts as having the property in question for the purposes of one speaking, or for the purposes of evaluating it, and as lacking that property for the purposes of (evaluating) the other speaking. Otherwise, given the description of what was said both times, there is no accounting for the contrast in truth value. Similarly, the refrigerator counts as having the property in question for purposes of (evaluating) the one speaking, and as lacking it for purposes of (evaluating) the other. So the property of weighing 79 kilos is one Hugo sometimes counts as having (as he is at a given time, in a given condition), and sometimes counts as lacking (at that time.) Similarly for the refrigerator and the property of containing milk. The 'sometimes' here points to variation across occasions for considering whether Hugo (the refrigerator) has the property in question, or, if we like, across occasions for using words to say him (the refrigerator) to do so.

---

6 See Kaplan [1988].
7 For some of these, see Travis [1981].

When having a property, P, is liable to exhibit this kind of variation across occasions, for some range of objects, we will say that having P is S-use sensitive, and that P is an S-use sensitive property. We might also say, if we choose, that, on the same reading of 'sometimes' as above, it sometimes counts as a fact that Hugo weighs 79 kilos, and sometimes does not count as a fact, or counts as not a fact, that this is so. Equivalently, we might say that the fact that Hugo weighs 79 kilos sometimes counts as obtaining and sometimes does not. When a candidate fact exhibits this feature, we may say that it is an S-use sensitive fact.

Suppose we decided to say that there was an S-use insensitive property of weighing 79 kilos, and that this is the property spoken of in the words 'weighs 79 kilos'. (If it is not, then it is difficult to see what property those words would speak of, or what words might express exactly that property.) Given the S-use sensitivity of the predicate, we would then have to say that some speakings of it are strict and literal, so really do speak of that property, while others are not. For example, for the above pair of speakings by Odile, at most one member of the pair could exhibit a strict literal use of the words. It would then need to be decidable, in principle, which member, if either, exhibited the strict literal use, and decidable in general which speakings of the words did so. But first, the phenomenon of S-use sensitivity, if it exists, excludes this possibility. It is built into the notion that if Odile's speakings do illustrate the phenomenon, then on both of them the words bear their (strict, literal) semantics. Second, it is apparent that there could be no principled way of deciding which of at least some contrasting pairs of such speakings merited the privileged status. That is a point to be argued in arguing for S-use sensitivity. (An example of such an argument will be given in chapter 4.) But it is part of what is being supposed here in supposing S-use sensitivity (of words) to exist.

One might respond to all this by saying that 'properties' like weighing 79 kilos, containing milk, being blue, etc., are actually not good choices for properties. If they were properties, it might be allowed, they would be S-use sensitive ones. But that is enough reason, the claim would go, to suppose them not to be. We may say that the words 'weighs 79 kilos' speak of weighing 79 kilos. But strictly speaking, what they actually do is (roughly) to speak of a family of properties. A literal speaking of them, if fully intelligible and coherent, might speak of some one of these properties in particular. But the words as such speak of all the members of this family indifferently. It is worth considering why responses to the phenomena along these lines are at least highly likely to be bad ones. For the remainder of this chapter, I will then simply suppose them to be wrong.

If 'weighs 79 kilos' or 'contains milk' refers to a family of S-use insensitive properties, the question is what the members of this family might be. Suppose for the sake of argument that Odile spoke of some one of these properties in speaking truly of the refrigerator. Then we may speak of 'the property Odile (then) attributed to the refrigerator'. (Or we might prefer to speak of 'the property of the refrigerator in virtue of which what Odile said was true'.) Call this property Q. We now have the means to attribute that property to other items, and to consider whether other items, or the refrigerator in other states, have it. Will Q be an S-use sensitive property? The key point is this. In deciding that Odile spoke truly of the refrigerator, we solved one problem, or a few, about how to sort things into those containing milk and those not. But in principle there may always be more. In fact, we can easily think of countless more: suppose that what was in the refrigerator was a slice of cheese or cheesecake, or a vial of secretions of rabbit mammary glands, or a pint bottle of thoroughly coagulated (or very sour) milk, or synthetic milk with the same molecular structure as milk but which had never seen a cow; and so on. (Similarly, consider the property we decided Hugo has, even after lunch, if—but only if— his morning weighing showed—or suitable ones would show—79 kilos. Would he have that property if the earth's gravitational force were to be halved overnight? Or if, to take a Wittgensteinian example, he began occasionally to grow and shrink spectacularly and for no apparent reason?)

Most of these problems, and others, are problems for Q as well. And the point is that it is reasonable (and so, I am claiming, correct) to solve them in different ways on different occasions for doing so: their correct solutions depend on the circumstances of the solving. Does a refrigerator with a slice of cheese or cheesecake on the bottom count as having Q? Yes, perhaps, if you are an orthodox Jew (engaged in certain activities); no for many other purposes. (Note also that a vial of rabbit's milk, whatever we think about its being milk, or an ordinary full pint bottle of milk in the refrigerator would *not* have been enough to make Odile's true words true. Such things would not make the refrigerator count as having the right property for the purpose of assessing Hugo's house-cleaning. There may be milk all right, but it is not *in* the refrigerator in the right sense; what it is in, of course, is vials and bottles.) On the evidence, Q will not be an S-use insensitive property either. Nor will we make further progress towards expunging S-use sensitivity by repeating the move and speaking of some property attributed on occasion in speaking of Q.

The thought was that if 'the property of containing milk' would be S-use sensitive (if a property at all), then we may 'refine away' the S-use sensitivity by speaking of some property of containing milk *on some particular understanding of what it would be to do that*. The picture now on offer, as illustrated in the above discussion, goes against that thought. On it, we specify the property we want to speak of—the particular understanding of being/doing such-and-such—however we like. There may then be, or arise, reasons both for and against taking some item or items to have *that very property we specified*. It may then be that on some occasions for considering those reasons, they are correctly (truly) judged to show the item(s) to have that very property, while on other occasions they would be correctly judged to show the same item(s) to lack that property. No refining that we could ever do could guarantee that there could not ever be, in this way, two mutually conflicting and sometimes correct views of that very refinement and what it requires.

I do not think we have any idea how to specify a property which, in principle, no item could have S-use sensitively. In any event, that is part of the present view. First, we do not know how to specify a property such that problems *could* not arise as to whether an item had it, given all the other facts about it, and all the reason they provide for counting it as having the property, and for not doing so, where these problems did not have, *tout court*, uniquely most reasonable solutions. Second, we have no idea how to specify in advance what the solutions to all such problems are to be in specifying which property it is.[8] Properties that we could not in principle specify cannot be the ones that figure in our thoughts, words and judgements.

If a given property, like the mentioned one of containing milk, is S-use sensitive, then its S-use sensitivity is unlikely to be eliminated by restricting the range of items it applies to. The problems that may arise for refrigerators, or others like them, would arise for breasts, bottles and stomachs, or other potential containers of milk as well. Nor do we know of some other item, rather like a refrigerator, and, as it were, cohabiting with it—a shadowy object, which we sometimes fill with milk in putting milk in the refrigerator—which is not liable, in principle, to have the property of containing milk S-use sensitively. There might, perhaps, in fact be items about which there are not two things to be said as to whether they contain milk. (Though these items are less easily found than one might think at first: the case of the refrigerator with the full pint bottle also contrasts with that of the refrigerator which is wall-to-wall milk, prepared to trap the unwary

---

[8] Pioneering work in the direction of this point has been done by Hilary Putnam and by J. L. Austin. Putnam does not go quite as far as the present point; Austin, I think, does. It is especially worth mentioning Putnam [1970], a striking passage in Austin [1946, at p. 89 in the third edition], and the difficult but rewarding Austin [1952/3].

opener of it in a deluge.) But these *de facto* univocally milk-containing items, if any, are not ones which are not liable to be in a state in which they sometimes would, and sometimes would not, count as having the property in question. S-use sensitivity, the suggestion is, is an intrinsic feature of the properties—and of the facts—in terms of which we think and speak about the world. It might reasonably be said to be put there by something essential in the way we do that thinking.

S-use sensitivity, as developed so far, does not force a break with the dominant picture. Nor is that the point of it. The picture might be saved, so far, in either or both of two ways. First, we might deny that such things as English sentences—'Hugo weighs 79 kilos' or for that matter, 'Snow is white'—have such properties as being true, at least *tout court*. With Austin, we might deny that sentences were the right sorts of things to be either true or false. If we like, we can continue to say that they may have such properties *as spoken in a given speaking* of them. So far, it has not been shown that the semantics of words on a speaking—the semantics of Odile's words in one of the above cases, for example—is a semantics that such an item does not then have classically. Second, we might posit further semantic items, such as what was said in Odile's speaking of the words 'There's milk in the refrigerator' on some specific occasion, or the thought she then expressed. The item of such a sort which she thus produced on one such occasion need not be the one she produced on another. Again, we have so far produced no reason for thinking that these items would not be classical.

It is important that, to follow this line, we *must* deny that an English sentence like 'There's milk in the refrigerator' may simply have the property of being true (of or in a given situation). For if a sentence may have or lack that property, then the fact that Odile might speak it truly (but literally) of a given situation shows that that sentence must sometimes count as having the property, so that one sometimes states fact in saying it to do so, while the fact that she might sometimes speak it literally but falsely of the same situation shows the sentence sometimes to count as lacking the property of being true, so that one sometimes states fact in saying it to do that. In that case, the dominant picture would not fit it, which at least gives us some idea what it would be like for the dominant picture not to fit.

Alternatively, we could just allow that the dominant picture does not fit English sentences. That would not be the end of the picture, so certainly not a victory for Wittgenstein. For there remain the other posited entities: what was said on a speaking of a sentence, and so on. But we may now note something suspicious about this move. If a refrigerator is liable to have a property S-use sensitively, or if a property is liable to be S-use sensitive as applied to refrigerators, or to that one, we are not likely to eliminate that possibility by finding further items, enough like refrigerators that they are eligible for having the property in question, but enough unlike refrigerators that they are not eligible for having it S-use sensitively. Could the matter really be fundamentally different with semantic items and their semantic properties? That is the question I will raise in the next section. To repeat, however, the existence of S-use sensitivity is not by itself inconsistent with the dominant picture. Nor does the alternative picture consist merely in positing it. The alternative picture has not been stated yet. It is yet to come.

5. THE ALTERNATIVE PICTURE

We are now quite close to a description of how the dominant picture could be wrong. There is but one more crucial step to take. This section describes that step.

English is notorious for containing the means for its own semantic description. Some have thought that to be a bad thing. Good or bad, English contains the means for speaking of the semantic properties which interest us, and which, rightly or wrongly, we sometimes take some items to have. Any universal feature of English words, or the properties they speak of, will be features of these semantic properties as well. Further, any such feature which is an essential part of speaking English will also be a feature of any technical vocabulary by which English might be expanded. Notably, it will be a feature of any such vocabulary specifically reserved for speaking of the property spoken of in some English words on some given speaking of them—as illustrated by the account in the last section, if correct, of how the more 'refined' or precise properties we might hope to talk about in place of such mundane ones as being blue or weighing 79 kilos, would still be infected, in principle, with S-use sensitivity. So it would be a feature of any semantic property we might speak of *on occasion* in speaking English. If English has the right universal features, or even if enough of the right general features of English are essential features of its semantic vocabulary and the properties that vocabulary refers to, then it may be that the dominant picture is demonstrably wrong. Roughly speaking, if what goes for the property of weighing 79 kilos goes for semantic properties such as being true, being true of my armchair, or being true of an item just in case it is red, then, we will see, the dominant picture is wrong. Using the last section as a source of clues, let us now consider what the right universal features might be.

The first interesting feature is S-use sensitivity itself. Suppose that it is a universal and essential feature of English that its predicates and the properties they speak of are S-use sensitive. Then semantic properties, or at least those we can speak of and take items to have (call these the expressible ones) are S-use sensitive. So if P is an expressible semantic property, then P is S-use sensitive. If so, then there are some items which, as they now are or might be, sometimes count as having P and sometimes do not. Which means that we could sometimes speak truth of them in their present condition, and state a fact, in saying them to have P; and sometimes similarly speak truth of them and state a fact in saying them to lack P, or at least would fail to state a fact or speak truth in saying them to have P. There are various possible occasions for considering whether these items have P. On some of these occasions, the correct (true) judgement is that they do; on others, it is that they do not, or at least it is not that they do. For such items, the dominant picture is mistaken; these items are not classical.

The dominant picture is not to be rescued here by trying to identify the items for which P would be S-use sensitive and ruling that they are not eligible either for having or for lacking P—as one might say that English sentences are not the right sorts of things to be either true or false. By hypothesis, *P* is S-use sensitive. So there must be the possibility of items that would manifest this; if not sentences, for example, then something else.

This does not yet spell the demise of the dominant picture. If every expressible semantic property is S-use sensitive, then some semantic items have some of their semantic properties S-use sensitively, so non-classically. For all that, there could be some semantic items which have none of their semantic properties S-use sensitively, so are classical. For it is consistent with the notion of S-use sensitivity that, if P is S-use sensitive, then there should be *some* item which has P, such that we could not possibly work ourselves into each of two positions— or could not even now coherently conceive of ourselves doing so— such that in the one we would state fact in saying the item to have P, and in the other we would (could) not. And it is conceivable that the item which did this for P did the same for all of its semantic properties. So, for example, words might be non-classical semantic items while thoughts remained classical ones.

One idea broached in the last section for refrigerators and containing milk was that there could not be a refrigerator which *could* not be in a condition in which it would exhibit S-use sensitivity for containing milk, and that, if not, then it would seem that there could be no other item which did this either. It was suggested that this cast some suspicion on the idea that thoughts, or some other semantic item we might construct, might do what words could not do (if they cannot) in the way just described. Such suspicion is, I think, well placed. But we must now be careful about its source. If the situation with the refrigerators reflected some universal feature of English, or the properties it speaks of, then the grounds for the suspicion would be clear. But there may be several phenomena in play in the case of refrigerators.

The most straightforward candidate universal feature to consider is this: for any expressible property P, there can be no item which could not be in a condition to exhibit P's S-use sensitivity. If that is universal, then clearly thoughts (as a whole) cannot be classical where words are not. But it is a bit too strong to be a plausible universal, at least without considerable auxiliary argument. Further, if it does fail to be universal, it most plausibly fails for abstract entities—ones which cannot change their properties at all. (For example, could the number 3 be in a position to exhibit the S-use sensitivity in the property of being odd?) So thoughts would be reasonable candidates for exceptions to the rule here. In any case, this feature, whether it holds for semantic properties or not, points in the wrong direction. I suggest we look elsewhere.

The refrigerator with the puddle, we decided, bears the property of containing milk S-use sensitively. But that is consistent with the existence of *some* items which, in point of fact, are very well behaved vis-à-vis that property, so that there was never more than one thing to be said truly as to whether those items contained milk. What is less plausible is that there should be an item which did that, and further which was so well behaved that it exhibited no S-use sensitivity in any of its properties, or any of the properties we would expect an item to have or lack if it had the property of containing milk. Suppose, for example, that a given refrigerator is well behaved for the property of containing milk. There remain such properties as having an inside temperature of 2° Celsius (might not microclimates inside the refrigerator give us reason to say sometimes one thing and sometimes another about this?), being five years old (from exactly what moment do we start counting its age: date of purchase, on leaving the assembly line, on beginning service?), and being white, among others. The expectation would be that at least some of these are S-use sensitive in the case of this refrigerator.

The universal feature suggested by this intuition is as follows: Consider an expressible property P, and all the expressible properties which an item is eligible for having if it has P—that is, all those properties, Q, such that some item might have P and Q. Call these properties properties of the same category as P. Then if any item has P,

S-use sensitively or not, there must be some properties of the same category as P which that item has S-use sensitively (or whose S-use sensitivity it exhibits). This, I think, is a plausible universal and essential feature of English. Those who dislike this talk of categories may substitute this equally plausible one: any item which has P, S-use sensitively or not, has at least some of its properties S-use sensitively.

It follows from this principle that any thought or other semantic item has at least some of its properties S-use sensitively. But it does not follow that any of these are *semantic* properties. A thought, W for example, must either have or lack the property of having been thought (or expressed) in the Rijksmuseum in Amsterdam.[9] Perhaps it exhibits S-use sensitivity only with respect to properties like this. The sensitivity here might result from what would count on various occasions as being *in* the Rijksmuseum, for example, if the thinker was crossing the threshold at the time. That would not be interesting for present purposes. However, the issue is whether the above principle continues to hold as a universal and essential one if it is restricted to any indefinitely large class of (mutually independent) properties in the same category as P. In that case, it has the right consequence for the semantics of any semantic item, semantic properties forming the right sort of indefinitely large set. Similarly, it has the right consequences for an item's truth-involving properties, in case we choose to restrict the dominant picture to them. For there is always an indefinitely large range of possible items, like the Rijksmuseum, for a semantic item (which may be true) to be true of or not; items of which it either would or would not be true, or *tertium datur*. For each of these, there is the corresponding truth-involving property.

Whether or not this excursus into the metaphysics of English is correct, it at least shows what we want the alternative picture to be. There are two main points in it. First, all expressible semantic properties are S-use sensitive. Second, any semantic item exhibits S-use sensitivity for at least some of the expressible semantic properties it may have (or lack). Officially, that is the alternative picture. It captures the intuitive Wittgensteinian thought by letting an item's *present* semantics be the semantic properties it now, or on some given occasion, counts as having—the ones it would now be true to say it to have—and letting its 'future applications' be the semantic properties (or truth-involving ones) it similarly might count as having on other occasions. The idea is that from the facts of this occasion alone we cannot fully predict the semantic facts which will count as holding on

[9] There would have been no such property were there no Rijksmuseum, of course. But then, neither would there have been a property of being true of the Rijksmuseum. There is nothing distinctive of semantic properties in this respect.

others. Which semantic facts count, on some other occasion, as
holding of W is not fixed solely by the facts of this occasion, nor,
specifically, by what count on this occasion as the semantic facts
about W.

It has already been spelled out how this picture conflicts with the
dominant one:[10] if an item has some of its semantic properties S-use
sensitively, then it does not have its semantics classically. The
metaphysical excursus shows some of what motivates the alternative
picture. First, as far as we can see, there are no S-use insensitive
properties (though it might require more phenomenology to convince
some of this). Second, as far as we can see, there are no items which
have all their properties S-use insensitively. Semantics would have to
be a very exceptional case for there to be classical items. There is no
apparent reason why it should be. It would be better, of course, if we
had a satisfying explanation of why expressible properties *should* be S-
use sensitive. Supplying that is the main task of the rest of the book.
The main idea will be stated in the next chapter. In any case, the
position was that the holder of the dominant picture was making a
mistake as to what it was to have a semantics. We now have at least a
description of what sort of mistake this is supposed to be. It is not so
much that the dominant picture has a mistaken conception of what a
semantics is, as that it has a mistaken idea of the way in which an item
might have one, and of what the effects of its doing so might be.

There is, I think, still something in the idea that, just as there can be
no *sort* of item enough like a refrigerator to have the property of
containing milk, but enough unlike it that no member of that sort
could have that property S-use sensitively, so, for any semantic
property P, there can be no sort of semantic item some members of
which might have P, but such that no member of that sort could have P
S-use sensitively. The problem, of course, is to say what a sort is. The
right general idea, I think, is to insist that a sort have indefinitely many
distinct (potential) members, each pair of which differ in some of their
properties of the category of P. This would certainly make the idea
apply to thoughts: for any expressible semantic property of some
thought, there is or could be some thought which had it S-use
sensitively. But, while I think that is true, this is an auxiliary and
subordinate—which means optional—part of the alternative picture.
The official alternative picture is just what it has been said to be.

---

[10] Strictly speaking, we need to rule out the possibility of semantic items with no
expressible semantics. Since we could not discuss the semantics of these items—nor
would they be fit for 'serious scientific discourse'—I am assuming that there is no point
in taking them into account. The private language discussion will reinforce that
impression.

If the semantics of an item is S-use sensitive, that is to say that there are different occasions for considering its semantics and differences, from one such occasion to another, in what the facts count as being as to what its semantics is. What might such occasions be like? Let us begin with a simple case. Suppose that the English sentences 'Snow is white' and 'There's milk in the refrigerator' are either true or false (or *tertium datur*). Suppose that they bear these properties S-use sensitively. 'Snow is white', for example, might sometimes count as bearing an understanding on which it is true, but also might sometimes count as bearing one on which it is false (for example, when it occurred in the context of a denial that the greyish stuff picked up from the sidewalk, or composing the besooted snowman, was snow.) Then occasions for considering the semantics of words might just be occasions for speaking them. Let us fictionalize a bit. Odile, considering producing the second sentence, where Hugo is idly stirring his coffee, might ask herself: 'If I said that, would I be speaking true words?' Given all the facts of the case (the puddle, etc.), the correct answer on that occasion would be no. That would be the right answer to anyone who raised, on that occasion, the question whether those words had the property of being true. So, on that occasion, they count as lacking that property, and as having the property of being false. But similarly, if she posed the same question on the occasion where she was about to comment on Hugo's house-cleaning, the answer would be yes. If English words may have the property of being true, then this is one sort of variation in occasions for considering them which may lead to their exhibiting S-use sensitivity in their having of that property.

Suppose we now consider, not the English words 'There's milk in the refrigerator' but rather *Odile's* words, on an occasion, 'There's milk in the refrigerator', or those words on her speaking of them. For example, suppose that Odile, thinking of Hugo's coffee, left a note with those words on the refrigerator. We might discuss the semantics of that note—for example, whether it is true. But that note cannot be written on a variety of occasions. How can the semantics of that note, or Odile's words, or what she said, etc., be an S-use sensitive matter? Across what occasions for considering it might such S-use sensitivity arise? The answer may be: across occasions for evaluating the note, or what she said. Here is an example of how a pair of such occasions might contrast. It is meant only as an illustration, and not as a demonstration of S-use sensitivity for the items in question. *Case I*: Hugo pours his coffee, goes to the refrigerator, reads the note, opens the door, and says to himself, 'That's false.' *Case II*: Hugo does *not* pour himself a cup of coffee. He has no time for that. But on the way out he notices the note. Later, at lunch, he meets someone who persuades

him that milk is a contaminant on the order of dioxin. Remembering
the note, he says to himself, 'I guess that means we need a new
refrigerator.' Ruefully examining the refrigerator that evening, he
concludes, 'Well, the note was right.' If semantics is S-use sensitive,
then it is at least conceivable that Hugo should be right both times.
Hugo's use of Odile's words, in each of the above cases, is not an S-use
of them. We will call it a purpose use of them, abbreviated to *P-use*.
Notes, thoughts, etc. may all have P-uses. A thought, for example, is
something from which we might draw inferences. The point, then, is
that the semantics words or a thought or any other item counts as
having is liable to vary across P-uses of it.[11]

   That semantic items may vary the semantic properties they count as
having across P-uses of them may initially seem more plausible for
words than for such things as thoughts. The semantics of Odile's
words depends, plausibly, on the circumstances of their speaking:
change those circumstances enough, and the semantics the words
would then have had would differ from the semantics they in fact had
(which is not to suggest that there are equivalences between semantic
facts and others). Circumstances must show, for example, whether
'weighs 79 kilos', as she spoke it, is more reasonably construed so as to
be possibly true of what weighs 81 kilos with clothes on, or so as not to
be. Such depends on such things as the purposes for which the words
were produced. Or so I have suggested. Conceivably, the correct
assessment of these circumstances (for a given speaking) might vary

   [11]. If S-use sensitivity is pervasive, then is the concept of S-use sensitivity S-use
sensitive? One could hold it to be an exceptional case. But I would expect it not to be
one—if only because there is no point in having a concept unless there is a contrast to be
marked, so two sorts of case; and where there is a distinction to be drawn, it is no doubt
to be drawn differently on different occasions. From that perspective, the core S-use
sensitivity of S-use sensitivity would be as follows. On different occasions, distinguish-
able ranges of phenomena or states of affairs would count as what it was to be S-use
sensitive, or what this then would consist in. There would be variation in what S-use
sensitivity should be taken to be like; what is to be neglected and what not in detecting
it, or what range of cases to attend to. In the first instance, that would mean that for
some concepts, C, or properties, P, and some items, V, it would be an S-use sensitive
matter whether V fit C or had P S-use sensitively. This need not mean that there are any
concepts or properties which are S-use sensitively S-use sensitive. But on the right
conception of what it would be for them to be so, there might be. (That conception
would not be that of the dominant picture, on which it is intrinsic to their semantics
that it forbids S-use sensitivity. On the wrong conception, there can be no S-use
insensitivity, just as—as will be shown later—on the wrong conception there could be
no such thing as knowledge, or as proof—and similarly for most philosophically
sensitive concepts.) The dominant picture cannot accommodate S-use sensitive S-use
sensitivity any more than it can any other sort. The alternative picture can. If S-use
sensitivity is S-use sensitive, then its species of relativity to occasions is *not* thereby self-
refuting in the way simple *subjectivity*, or relativity to persons, is notorious. To the
extent that S-use sensitivity is S-use sensitive, the ensuing claims about it must rely, for
their content, on being made on proper occasions. The hope is that they may do so.

from one occasion to another for evaluating them: sometimes this factor counts as outweighing that one, sometimes not; with the result that it sometimes counts as so that the words are properly understood in such-and-such a way, and sometimes not. The semantics of a thought, however, would not seem similarly to depend on the circumstances of its production or expression. Circumstances might determine *which* thought Odile expressed in a given speaking, but, given that she expressed *this* thought, it is plausible that they cannot determine in the same way what the semantics of that thought is.

The situation for thoughts is not exactly the same as that for words. But there are close parallels. The main and most general point about thoughts is this. Given sets of semantic properties may count as entailing or requiring others; given sets as being consistent or inconsistent. If an item is true of whatever is red, then it is true of whatever is crimson; being true of whatever is red and being false of whatever is crimson form an inconsistent set of semantic properties. What the semantics of a given thought is always depends on the answers to some questions as to what given sets of semantic properties require or entail, or what they are consistent with. If given sets of semantic properties vary across occasions for considering them in the semantic properties they count as entailing or requiring, and if some such set is one which, on some occasion, counts as part of the semantics of a given thought, W, then what the semantics of the thought counts as being will also vary across such occasions. If it is an S-use sensitive question what a given set of semantic properties entails, then it is an S-use sensitive question what the semantics is of a thought which at least sometimes counts as having those properties. If any thought counts, on some occasion, as having some set of semantic properties with S-use sensitive entailments (or requirements), then any thought will vary the semantics it counts as having across some range of occasions for considering what the entailments of some such set is.

If there is S-use sensitivity in ordinary non-semantic properties, then it is plausible that there would be S-use sensitivity in what given semantic properties entail, and that that would be so at least because of the involvement of those semantic properties with the world. So, just as the semantics of Odile's words may depend on other facts of their production—facts of the world which are not facts as to those words' semantics—so the semantics of a thought may depend on other facts about the world, and depend on them in a way such as to make that semantics S-use sensitive. Suppose that a thought has the property of ascribing the property of being blue to an item. Then what being blue turns out to be, and the reasons the world turns out to provide for taking this item and others to be blue or not to be may show something about what the condition for the truth of this thought must be. But what they count as showing about this may be an S-use sensitive matter, and may be so in ways that make it an S-use sensitive matter whether the item in question satisfies that condition. The thought was that the item was blue; given the facts about its spectrographic properties and the somewhat unstable reactions of normal observers, such a thought would sometimes correctly be counted as true, and sometimes not (assuming that that really is what the thought was). Conversely, if it is settled that, in any case, the thought is certainly true—as may be the case on some occasions—then it may sometimes count and sometimes not as being a thought which ascribes the property of being *blue* to something. Being blue may sometimes count, and sometimes not, as the property that such a thought was about.

A casual reading of the *Investigations*, in or with its English translation, reveals a striking problem about Wittgenstein's use of the word *Satz*. Throughout, and even within one paragraph, this word is translated sometimes by 'sentence', and sometimes by 'proposition'. When we try to put the matter right by choosing between these, we quickly find that this cannot be done. The present account of Wittgenstein's picture of semantics helps illuminate why this should be so. The view it suggests is that—as far as such distinctions go—Wittgenstein uses the word in a way which is univocal and consistent throughout: neither as meaning *proposition* as opposed to *sentence*, nor vice versa. His aim was to avoid drawing technical distinctions between one sort of semantic item and another. For the problems that interested him, and his theses about those problems, are equally problems and theses about any range of semantic items we choose to discuss. They are not to be escaped by moving from one sort of semantic item to another, ceding one sort of item to the alternative view, or denying that it has appropriate semantic properties altogether, and then preserving the dominant view for some well-chosen sort of item. In particular, for Wittgenstein, it does not matter whether we decide to say that English words may be true or false, or we reserve such talk for some other item, such as what is said in them, or thoughts.

Nor can it be shown conclusively that English words cannot have such properties as being true by showing that any English words which we counted as having such a property would sometimes have to count as having it, and also sometimes as lacking it. English words could not have such a property *tout court;* but, as illustrated above, the many occasions for speaking given words may themselves provide a range across which those words vary by sometimes counting and sometimes not counting as being true. That, I think, is why Wittgenstein does not line up with Austin[12] in declaring that sentences are not the right sorts of things to be either true or false (though both agree in their general rejection of the dominant picture). If 'Snow is white' sometimes counts as true, then it must exhibit S-use sensitivity in its having of that property. But then, so, in principle, would any item that might have it.[13] '*Satz*', then, on Wittgenstein's use of it, is best read as ignoring such distinctions as those between what is produced in or with words on some speaking of them, and those words as such—much in the way that the English word 'words' cuts across such distinctions.

Well, then, if English sentences are either true or false, *which* of these is the sentence 'Snow is white'? The question points to an aspect of S-use sensitivity which is of fundamental importance for Wittgenstein. If that sentence sometimes counts as true, and sometimes as false, then the circumstances of any given occasion must show in which way it counts on that occasion. Circumstances of some occasions may simply fail to do this. Sometimes the sentence counts as saying one or another thing which now counts as true; sometimes as saying what now counts as false. On now (while reading this) considering the question what it does say, we have no more reason to count it as doing the former thing rather than as doing the latter, nor vice versa. We cannot count it as doing both. So we must count it as doing neither. But then it cannot now count either as true or as false. Which is not to say that it could never do that.

In general, where an item may sometimes count as having P and sometimes as lacking P, circumstances of an occasion must decide what, if anything, it then counts as doing, so that an item which may do both of these things may also, on some occasions, fail to count as doing either. It will so fail wherever circumstances fail to determine enough as to how things are to be counted as being P or not—to choose, that is, between the various ways of doing this, each of which would be correct on some occasion or other. Occasions on which an item fails to count either as having P or as lacking it are occasions on which it is indeterminate what it would be for the item to have that property, hence, equally, what one would be taking to be so in taking it to do so, or saying in saying it to do so. On such an occasion, no definite thought would be expressed in words which ascribed that property to the item, or at least none definite enough then to permit of determinately correct evaluation as either true or false. Hence

---

[12] In Austin [1950], especially pp. 119–121.

[13] This is the biggest point of difference between Wittgenstein and Austin. Both recognized S-use sensitivity. Austin, however, unlike Wittgenstein, insisted that English sentences were not the right sorts of things to be either true or false. Perhaps Austin's thesis can be shown. But not by phenomena which admit of interpretation as the S-use sensitive having of that property by English sentences.

Wittgenstein's continued insistence, throughout the *Investigations*, that only in appropriate circumstances do words make sense; only in a suitable home or in suitable surroundings do they express a thought with content definite enough to permit, *inter alia*, evaluation in truth-involving terms. Outside of such surroundings, they—like the present thought that the sentence 'Snow is white', is true—do not count either as saying something true or as saying something false.

Thoughts were initially conceived of as having an immutable semantics. And it may well be part of a proper conception of them that they do so. To say that is to say that any occasion for saying what their semantics is is an occasion for saying what their immutable semantics is; the semantics a thought counts, on an occasion, as having is one it then counts as being unable to change or to lose. If that is how we conceive of thoughts, then so be it. All that is consistent with there being different truths to tell, on different occasions, as to what the immutable semantics of some given thought is, and with there being some semantic properties which it sometimes counts as having immutably, and sometimes as lacking immutably. To think otherwise is, in Wittgenstein's words (104), to: 'predicate of the thing what lies in the method of representing it'.

2

The Making of Semantic Fact

Consider occasions for producing or considering or otherwise treating a semantic item, W. On which of these, or under what circumstances would W count as having some given semantics, S (as thus produced or considered or etc.) rather than some other? How might facts of an occasion contribute towards W's then counting as having one semantics rather than another? (The question may seem slightly off target for some semantic items—thoughts, say—in so far as there is, or may seem to be, only one semantics that those items could have. But, if that is so, the question is still answerable. If W could have only one semantics, then, depending on what S is, W counts as having S on all or none of the occasions for considering it. And other facts of an occasion—that is, facts other than that it is W that is then being considered—can make no contribution to determining which semantics W then counts as having.)

As the parenthesis suggests, one paramount reason for posing this question here is that an answer to it may tell us what room is left by other variations across occasions for variation in the semantics a given item may count as bearing—in other words, whether and, if so where, there is room for semantic S-use sensitivity; so just when and how the alternative picture of semantics, sketched in the last chapter, may get a grip. This chapter suggests an answer to that question which is uniform for all semantic items, and which provides room, in a uniform way, for any such item to have its semantics S-use sensitively. If the answer is correct, then all semantic items have their semantics S-use sensitively, at least in principle.

Much of what will be said here may seem platitudinous at first. I think that it is not. Nor do I think that it is apodictic. Nor do I think that it will be demonstrated in this chapter. I will set out a model of having a semantics, or, more pretentiously, what it is, and is like (for an item) to have any given semantics. The point, for the present, is to see what work the model does; to keep track of just where, in connection with what other philosophical problems (notably, epistemic ones) essential appeal will be made to its core idea. Gradually, I hope, reasons will emerge for thinking the model right—especially in chapters 4, 5 and 6. The last chapter will try to show why the model must be right. Be that as it may, it will do for the present to note how the model does much work one reasonably ought to want done.

What will be said here by way of answering the initial questions runs orthogonal, at first sight, at least, to many other proposed answers to them—for example, answers in terms of speakers' (or other's) intentions or expectations. Pursuing the matter in depth would, I think, show it to be inconsistent with most of those answers. But it is not the purpose of this book to show any such thing. What I am interested in here is the correctness and consequences of this account; not the correctness or incorrectness of any other.

One feature of the present model is that it allows us to define a natural and interesting notion of privacy as that notion might figure in the idea of private language. Roughly, language, or more generally, the semantics of an item is private just where the model fails to apply. I will try to show at the end of this chapter that that notion of privacy is of central concern to Wittgenstein, and at least a large part of what is at stake in the private language discussion. If my contention is correct that the model leaves semantics always at least in principle an S-use sensitive matter, then this shows how private language may serve as a test case for adjudicating between the dominant and the Wittgensteinian pictures of semantics. If private language is impossible, then the model must fit wherever items may count as having a semantics at all. If that is so, then there is always room for the Wittgensteinian picture to apply. In so far as the dominant picture leaves no such room, it must be mistaken.

1. A PARADIGM

One paradigm of the way an occasion fixes the semantics an item counts as having on it is provided by the way in which words may have a semantics on a speaking, where the occasion may be viewed as choosing between a variety of semantics, all compatible with the semantics the words count as having in their language, that is, with what the words mean; so as choosing between a variety of semantics, each of which the words would count as having on some occasion (speaking) or other. Where an occasion thus chooses between semantics for words W to have, I will say that the occasion *disambiguates* W, and I will refer to this phenomenon as *disambiguation*. This use of the word ought not to suggest, of course, that W are necessarily ambiguous words in their language. Nor ought it suggest that someone confronting the words on that occasion would thereby confront some problem of working out how to understand them; or that anyone would do anything other than unreflectively understanding W correctly.

The phenomenon in question is illustrated, but not exhausted, by ambiguous sentences, such as the English, 'Mary had a little lamb.' This may say something about meat eating; and it may say something about pet keeping. On some occasions it does the one thing, and on other occasions, the other. The important point to keep in mind is that on some given occasion, one or another of these things may be what it *does*: what the words said, on some given speaking, was that a certain Mary ate some meat of a certain sort. That is a fact about their semantics on that speaking. Or so intuition goes. That is what it is for an occasion to disambiguate words; for it to choose between one semantics and another which are possible ones for them to have.

But the phenomenon occurs for more than ambiguous words. Or at least it does if there is anything to the suggestions of first-order (that is, non-semantic) S-use sensitivity made in the last chapter. To remind ourselves of this, let us add one example to those of that chapter. Suppose that Hugo says to Odile, 'There are grapes in the pantry.' The pantry is bare except for a packet of raisins. Are Hugo's words true or false? The suggestion is: on some speakings, 'grapes' is true of raisins, and on others not. There may be a fact as to which it is on Hugo's speaking. But to see what the fact is, we would have to see more of the circumstances of that speaking than we have been told so far. If that is right, then here too there is at least opportunity for the occasion of Hugo's speaking to disambiguate his words—in particular, his word 'grape' in just the mentioned respect. Do these two understandings of 'grape' point to an ambiguity in that word? Perhaps. But there is no particular reason to think so.

The view so far is that where there is a variety of semantics that an item might sometimes count as having, and where it does in fact count as bearing one of these, other facts of that occasion must somehow select this semantics from the variety. In at least two respects that view need not be reductionist. First, it is no part of the view that the other facts which contribute to the selecting must be in any sense non-semantic facts. Second, it need not be part of the view that it is possible to identify or specify any given other facts of the occasion such that for the item to count as having that semantics is for those facts to hold (of an occasion). On the first point, consider again 'Mary had a little lamb'. Those words, as spoken on some occasions, count as being a remark about meat eating, which is a partial characterization of the semantics they then count as having. One range of facts which may certainly contribute to their so counting are facts as to the meaning of that English sentence 'in isolation'. Nothing in the present view demands that one be able to say how an occasion contributes to the words counting as having that semantics while overlooking those semantic facts about that English sentence. Similarly for words like 'There's milk in the refrigerator.' If the suggestions of the last chapter are correct, then part of what an occasion of speaking these words must determine about what counts as their semantics as so spoken is what the words count as requiring of the refrigerator if they are to be true.[1] For a typical speaking, at least, the problem will be one of choosing between the various things that may sometimes count as what it is for a refrigerator to contain milk; to choose, that is, what is to be taken so to count for the purposes of characterizing what was said in that speaking of those words. Again, this is (typically) part of characterizing the semantics of the words on that speaking. That an occasion must typically do just this selecting is fixed, plausibly, by what those words mean in English—specifically, by its being a fact about what they mean when they say a refrigerator to contain milk. It is given that fact that the salient work for an occasion will often be to fix what, for relevant purposes, is to count as containing milk. Again, in making that problem fit the present paradigm, we are not supposing that there must be some way, without reference to such other semantic facts, of saying which facts of a speaking make the solution to that problem for that speaking what it is.

It may also be so on an occasion that an English sentence, such as 'Mary had a little lamb', then counts as having such and such a semantics, rather than such-and-such a range of others. That phenomenon, too, is meant to fit the present paradigm. One may pose questions as to on what (sorts of) occasions the sentence so counts, or, of a given occasion, what about that one makes the sentence then so count. The present account of having a semantics is meant to describe, so be true of, such problems as well. It will, in fact, propose a general answer to any such question. But if such questions have answers, as they are now being supposed to, it need not follow either that any of those answers which isolates specific facts of some occasion manages to avoid mentioning semantic facts, or that there must be ways of isolating facts of a speaking which count as simultaneously deciding both that the sentence counts as having the semantics that it does (i.e., meaning what it does), and that the words as spoken counted as having the semantics that they then did.

This last observation introduces the second point about reductions.

---

[1] When the occasion of the speaking must fix this is on occasions for treating the words, so spoken, as having one semantics or another (and where there is a proper way of doing so in relevant respects). It is not here excluded that the occasion of the speaking might do this work differently on different such occasions for treating those spoken words.

Typically we understand speakings of 'Mary had a little lamb' as we do unreflectively, and, as a rule, correctly. As noted above, we do not typically achieve understanding through working out some problem about how the words were to be understood. Sometimes, specific disagreements arise as to the understanding of particular words. Or, without any disagreement, someone who takes himself not to know enough about the facts of some speaking, may ask how the words thus spoken were to be understood, and sometimes, perhaps, why. It is being supposed here at least to be the rule that where such questions arise and where or in so far as there are facts about what semantics the words did count as having, conclusive reasons can be given for understanding the words in that way. It does not follow that there is any account of why W counted as having semantics S which would correctly answer all such questions about W (on that occasion) which could arise. That is to say, it does not follow that it is possible to isolate facts of an occasion for W's counting as having S such that, except in the context of a particular asking of a question as to why W did so, those facts deserve the title 'What made W then count as having S'. Perhaps no facts of the occasion deserve that title *tout court*. Both these points about reduction will become clearer in a moment when we come to considering the epistemology of semantics.

The main idea so far is that a semantic item, W, counts, on an occasion, O, as having a semantics, S (or some particular semantic property P) just where all the other facts of O make it most reasonable to take W as having S, or to understand it as having, or in a way on which it does have S. (What counts as) the proper understanding of S, on O—the understanding on which it has the semantics it then counts as having—is the most reasonable one in the light of all the other facts that then obtain. That idea, as it has been applied to the examples thus far is fairly banal. It is less banal to suppose, as I now am supposing, that this disambiguation model, as set out above, applies in a substantive way to any semantic item, and all questions, for any occasion, of the semantics it then counts as bearing. There are at least two points at which banality stops. One is this. As mentioned in the last chapter, it is both natural and traditional to suppose that some semantic items—thoughts, for example—have their semantics immutably, and at least a crucial part of this intrinsically. Or at least that there are such items to be talked about if only we choose to do so. In a recent work, for example, Christopher Peacocke says the following:

On the notion of content used throughout this essay, what is required for a given content to be true is always intrinsic to that content: it is something constitutive of the content's identity.[2]

2 Peacocke [1986], p. 46.

Peacocke's notion of a content is roughly the present notion of a thought. The idea that there are, or that we can define, semantic items that can be viewed in this way—that that is a possible view of some semantic items—is not peculiarly Peacocke's. Rather, it is more or less common currency. For Peacocke's contents, or for thoughts traditionally conceived, and for at least an important part of their semantics, the present disambiguation model could apply at best vacuously. For any semantic property relevant to determining under (or on) what condition a given content would be true, the only fact about an occasion for considering that content which could play a role in determining whether the content then counted as having that property is the fact that it is that content which is then being considered. For, if, say, that content does count having that property, then one could never be considering a content without that property and be considering that content. So it would be pointless, and at best misleading, to speak of a content, and, at least, its crucial semantics, as fitting the disambiguation paradigm. The present view, in contrast, is that there cannot be semantic items which are stipulated to have their semantics in the way Peacocke describes. If contents, or thoughts, are genuine semantic items at all, then the disambiguation paradigm has a non-trivial application to them. Facts of an occasion may have a substantive role to play in determining the semantics a given content or thought then counts as having. The point will hold for any semantic property. And, in principle, any other fact of an occasion could in principle play such a substantive role. The next section will describe how it might do so.

Where the model gets such substantive applications, it ceases being banal. We may note a second point at which this will happen. A substantial part of assigning semantics to an item involves recognizing entailment relations between semantic properties. Given that an item counts as having some semantic property, P, it will also count as having all the properties the having of P entails, and as lacking all those incompatible with P. For example, simplifying a bit, if W says things to be red, or expresses the property of being red, as the words 'is red' might correctly be said to do, then given the way some item V is, W's having that property may entail that it also has the property of being true of V; lacking that property, without V's having been otherwise, might be incompatible with saying things to be red. Or, again keeping in mind that we are simplifying, if W counts as saying things to be red, and V counts as having the property of being red, then that may entail that W has the property of being true of V. Similarly, if W says a particular item to be red at a certain time, as the words 'It's red', on some speaking, may do, then that may be incompatible with W's counting as false, given the way that item is at the time, independent of its being spoken of. Conversely, the fact that W is true of V, given that it is a fact, together with the way V is, or the properties it counts as having, may entail that whatever W is saying, it cannot be that V is red. Such, anyway, are intuitive thoughts.

It is a natural idea that whether one semantic property, or having it, entails having or lacking some other is a question whose answer is independent of occasions of considering it. So suppose we were to pose conditional disambiguation problems: given that an item has (or counts as having) semantics S, on what occasions (where it so counts) would it count as thereby also having semantic property P? And how might other facts of some such occasion contribute to its counting in one way or the other in this respect? Then, on the natural idea, the model of disambiguation presented by 'Mary had a little lamb' could apply only vacuously: the only fact about an occasion that could make having semantics S then count as entailing having P would be the fact that, anyway, S does entail P. And there could not be two sorts of occasions, on one of which an item counted as having S and as thereby required to have (lack) P, and on the other of which the item counted as having S but lacking (having) P. There could not be that kind of choice to be made between two semantics for an item to have.

The application to be made of the disambiguation model in what follows centrally involves denying this natural idea. On the model, other facts of an occasion have, in principle, a substantive role to play in determining which semantic properties count, on that occasion, as entailing which others; or which ones count as those we are required to recognize an item as having given that we count it as having such-and-such others. We may note that denying this idea is fundamental to Wittgenstein's ideas on following a rule: it may be perfectly determinate which rule a given rule is, and still open for determination by occasions what following the rule in such-and-such case is to come to, or requires. If, for example, the rule is that one is to bring a red item, say, in response to a certain order, then that rule may certainly count as telling us what to do at a certain point—and in a way that decides whether the rule has been obeyed, given what has been done. But that is only against a background which is adequate for determining what counts as following the rule correctly. And it is at least conceivable that there should be different backgrounds which would determine different things in this respect. Different ways of following a rule are always conceivable. And—in present terms—other facts of an occasion have a role in fixing which of these ways counts as right (when). Wittgenstein's idea that there may be that much room for the determination of a criterion for following a rule correctly comes unnaturally to some—so much so that it has sometimes been a temptation to misrepresent and to trivialize it. Just as the present account of having semantics is meant to apply to semantic items as such, and not, for example, merely to words, for example, so Wittgenstein's remarks on rules are remarks on *rules*, and not just on formulations of them. But it will be time to say more about that issue after this account of semantic fact is in.

In any case, the idea of first order S-use sensitivity—for example, in predicates such as 'is red'—indicates one main direction in which the present model of disambiguation may find application in the area of fixing what semantic entailments may count, on an occasion, as being. What other semantics is entailed, for example, by the property of saying items (or an item) to be red? Presumably, on any occasion, some range of properties of saying what is, or would be true in such-and-such circumstances, or of items in such-and-such conditions. But exactly which of these properties are entailed by that one? In the simplest case, a start on that question would be to pose the question which of these conditions count as ones of an item's being red, or ones in which it is red. If the phenomena of ground level S-use sensitivity are as has been suggested, then the answer to that question, at least, will vary from occasion to occasion of posing it. So that facts of an occasion have a substantive role to play in determining which of various sometimes-correct answers to it then count as correct. There may be some conditions which sometimes count as ones in which an item, V, is red, and sometimes count as ones in which it is not. The phenomenon may translate to the semantic level: if there are such conditions, then there may also be ones such that the property of saying what would be true of an item in that condition sometimes counts as entailed, and sometimes as not entailed, by the property of saying something to be red. In this way, other facts of occasions may have a substantive role to play in determining which other semantics an item must count as having given that it counts as having some initial semantics. If semantic entailments thus depend on the facts of an occasion, then so too does the semantics any item has. So, too, there could not be items having an intrinsic crucial semantics in the way Peacocke supposes his contents to do; items which have their semantics in such a way that every part of that semantics with a role in determining just what the items would be true of is such that the idea of disambiguation by occasions applies to that bit of semantics at best only vacuously.

2. A REASONABLE JUDGE'S REACTIONS

The last section described the scope that the idea of disambiguation is here meant to have. But to feel the intuition in favour of the model now to be described, it will be best to keep the case of 'Mary had a little lamb' particularly in mind. The innovation here, if any, is to extend what is natural in that case to the other cases described above as well. Again, I am not at the moment concerned to prove that the model is correct, but merely to describe it. The hope is that the book as a whole will provide reasons for believing in the model's applications. The first thing that we will now suppose, then, is that there are semantic facts—that is, facts as to the semantic properties of semantic items—and that there are such facts in nearly enough, just those cases where we would intuitively take there to be such. It is, in fact, tendentious to call this a supposition. For there to be such facts is simply for it to be so that, 'Mary had a little lamb', for example, sometimes is to be taken in one way rather than another—for example, as a remark about meat eating. But surely, that is not something we *suppose* to be so; there is no question about it. Still, I allow things to be put in this way by way of concession to someone who may be inclined to be sceptical as to there being such facts, or at least to feel some sceptical tendencies. Chapter 7 will provide a more detailed examination of what it is for this 'supposition' to be correct. Meanwhile, it just is part of the model. We need note one point about it. To suppose that there are semantic facts is explicitly not to suppose that for any semantic item, W, and any semantic property, P, it is either a fact that W has P, or a fact that W does not (or, on every occasion for considering W, either counts as a fact that W does or that it does not). There may be (presumably exceptional) cases where W does not correctly or determinately classify in one way or the other with respect to having P. If Odile says that Hugo spoke falsely, for example, then if Hugo happened to say the right thing (for example, that Odile spoke truly), what Odile said may be unclassifiable with respect to the property of being true. Similarly, some speakings of 'Mary had a little lamb' may fail determinately either to be remarks about meat eating or to fail to be such remarks. Such phenomena, by themselves, provide no reason to 'retract the assumption' that there are semantic facts. They merely show that there may be some cases where there is no fact of some matter.

Fallibility

It will come as no surprise that we and our reactions—in the first instance, to particular candidate semantic items—are at the core of the present story of the making of semantic fact. By 'we', I mean you and I and most of our friends, in the first instance, and any one else with a suitable competence in the language in question (where one is) and an appropriate background in the activities in which the semantic item in question is being or is to be employed—with some prejudice, perhaps, in favour of including people in this class; that is, including anyone who performs enough the way we would expect an understander of the relevant item to perform, or who has had a relevant background which we would regard as a 'usual sort'. We may think of this core reference class as 'the community' if we like, as long as we remember that 'the community' is something pretty amorphous. Just who, for example, form 'the community of competent English speakers'? Moreover, the class of people who form 'the community' for some particular semantic item—those with appropriate backgrounds in the activities in which that item fits—is likely to cut across 'the community of English speakers', whatever that may be. Not all English speakers are fit for understanding remarks about dace and bream, for example. Nor need all those fit for taking some such remark in some appropriate way rather than some other be speakers of English. As a rule, though, our, or the community's, contribution to fixing semantic fact is not going to vary with choices between remotely plausible ways of separating off 'the community' from others.

One key point in the present model concerns the way in which we stand at the core of the story of semantic fact. Though our understanding items in one way or another is crucial for their having the semantics they do, and though it is crucial that we have such understandings of items, our role must leave room for the following thought. Whatever my reactions to any semantic item, it is conceivable that I should be understanding it incorrectly. For the item to have the understanding, hence the semantics, it does—for that to be the proper understanding of it—is not simply for it to be the case that that is how I do understand it. The point generalizes. It holds for you, me, and some specified collection of our friends. It holds, in fact, for any determinate group of people, or (potential) understanders of the item in question; anyone who might take it to have one semantics rather than another. Again, the point seems plausible enough if we think of some speaking (by another) of 'Mary had a little lamb'. I took it to be about meat eating; but that fact, by itself, leaves it conceivable that I should have understood it wrongly. The point may seem less plausible in other cases. But it is part of the present model to maintain it in full generality. For any semantic item, it is conceivable that I, or any fixed group, should mistakenly take it to have semantic property P. In particular, this is meant to hold for what I myself say.

It might be tempting to think of the above point as indicating to the normativity of semantics: to say that an item has some given semantics, S, is to say that it is *properly* understood as having, or so as to have S; that that is how it *ought* to be understood. No doubt there is an interesting normative element in semantic fact. But I think that the point here is much simpler. What it indicates is merely the objectivity of semantic fact; an objectivity built into the notion of fact itself. The same point would hold, for example, about non-semantic properties like being copper or red, or, as will later be insisted, being a chair or a game. No matter what I take to be so about an item in taking it to be copper, the fact of my doing that leaves it conceivable that it should not be copper. Similarly for any particular reaction, or judgement, of any other specific group. If there are facts as to some things, and not others, being copper, then no one is oracular about them, as one might put the point. The account to come of semantic fact may be viewed as explicating what this sort of objectivity may come to.

Doing What A Reasonable Judge Would Do

Suppose that you take some semantic item, W, to have some semantics, S, or understand it in a way on which it would have S. Again, you might think of yourself here as taking some speaking of 'Mary had a little lamb' as about meat eating. Suppose that, in doing so, you grasped or responded to all the other facts of the situation that would impress a reasonable judge one way or another in the relevant matter; all the facts to which such a judge might react in one way or another with respect to taking W to have S. Suppose, further, that there is no such fact which you reacted to other than as a reasonable judge would; you were impressed by all the other relevant facts just as a reasonable judge would be. Then, the present thought goes, you were correct in understanding W as you did, and in taking it to have S. This thought may be summed up in saying: you were correct in taking W to have the semantics you did take it to have if you thereby responded to all the other relevant facts as a reasonable judge would. To this we will add, 'only if'.

The thought just expressed may seem perfectly anodyne. For suppose that W did, indeed, count as having S. Then surely, one would think, that is what a reasonable judge of the matter would take it to do—at least if there were not some fact which such a judge had missed, and on which W's so counting depended. That, one might think, is just part of what it is to be reasonable in such matters. So, the thought would be, saying that you reacted as a reasonable judge would is just another way of saying that you got it right, and no more than that. But the equation of correct responses with those of reasonable judges might also be put to more substantive work. Suppose, for example, that it were already established that Odile and Hugo were the reasonable judges, or that their reactions, whatever they might be, would be those that a reasonable judge would have. Then, *via* the equation, it can be determined whether you were correct in taking W as you did by seeing whether your reactions in doing so matched those of Hugo and Odile, or those that those two judges would have. Such would provide a test of your correctness.

Given the idea of fallibility, of course, no matter how Odile and Hugo react, it is always conceivable that their reactions should be wrong. This is simply to say that it cannot be established that their reactions are those of a reasonable judge merely in virtue of the fact that it is Hugo and Odile who are reacting. There remains the following idea. Even though it is not a conceptual truth that Odile's, and Hugo's reactions, in virtue of being their reactions, are those a reasonable judge would have, it might still be possible to establish that, in this particular case, they will, in fact, react or perform in the reasonable way, with the reasonable judge; that they here instantiate, contingently, what a reasonable judge would do. And it might be possible to establish this independent of facts as to which reactions they actually will or would produce; so, in particular, independent of the facts as to the semantics W actually counts as having. If that is so, then, again, the possibly anodyne thought turns out to have a substantive application. More generally, whenever (if ever) it is possible to establish whose reactions, or which reactings would be those of a reasonable judge, or those in step with what a reasonable judge would do, and it is possible to establish that without appeal to facts as to what the reactions produced in those reactings would be, the thought that the correct reactions are those a reasonable judge would have can be made to do some work. Without reference to establishing things, when there are facts as to whose reactions, or which reactings, would be the reasonable ones, where these facts being what they are is suitably independent of, and does not simply derive from, those reactions being what they are, then, and to that extent, the possibly anodyne thought can be put to substantive work. The hope would be that we may be able to put actual judges, beginning with ourselves, to substantive work as instruments for detecting what the reactions of a reasonable judge would be. The remainder of this section is concerned to describe how actual judges may be made to do that work.

The central idea of this chapter is then this: *for an item to have a semantic property P is for it to be so that a reasonable (informed) judge would take it to have P.* Similarly, it counts as having P just where a reasonable judge would so react to it. The main problem to be treated here is how there may be suitably self-sufficient facts as to what a reasonable judge would do with respect to W. The main idea will be: such facts may be made by facts about reasonable judges, where, for qualifying as one of these, there is no particular reaction to W (in particular, with respect to having or lacking P) which one is required, in the nature of the case, to have.

Epistemology

The present account of semantic fact rests most crucially on a certain epistemology, the main points of which will now be set out. Frequently enough, to begin with, we do take semantic items as having one semantics or another. This need not mean that we are prepared to say, explicitly, just what semantic properties we are taking them to have. It may consist simply in the fact that there is some way in which we are understanding an item, where that is a way of understanding it on which it does or would have such-and-such semantics. Sometimes, for example, we understand 'Mary had a little lamb' in a certain way; so understood, it is a remark about meat eating, so it has the property, for example, of saying something about meat. Now, wherever we do take some item, W, as having some semantics, S, it is always conceivable that we should be wrong. Which is to say that it is conceivable that there should be further facts, and there may even be conceivable further facts which would show us wrong. So there are conceivable doubts as to what we thus take to be so; conceivable ways in which one could at least coherently doubt that it was so, that is, that W had S.

The first cornerstone of the present epistemology concerns the status of conceivable doubts. That status will be discussed and argued in much more detail in chapter 4. But it is a status on which Wittgenstein insists, and specifically in the context of discussing the status of semantic fact.[3] The general idea is a simple one. For example, I am now seated in a chair typing. It is possible for me, or more accurately, for someone in my position, to doubt whether it is really so that I am now seated in a chair. That is to say, there are doubts it would be possible for me now to have; ways in which I now could succeed in doubting whether I was now so seated—if, that is, I could bring myself now to have the right attitudes towards the right further thoughts. Which is to say that it is conceivable that there should be further facts, and there may even be conceivable further facts which would show that I am not now seated in a chair, and such that, when those facts were in, I would see that they, and my not now sitting in a chair, were

---

[3] A *locus classicus* for this insistence is 84. That passage will be discussed in more detail in chapters 4 and 6.

compatible with, as it would then emerge, all the reasons I would actually now have to take myself to be sitting in a chair. For all that, in another important sense, there may now actually be no doubt at all as to whether I am so seated. I do not doubt it; it would not be reasonable to do so.

So for all that there are conceivable doubts, in the sense just described, that fact in itself does not show that it is not now correct to judge, or take it, that I am sitting in a chair, or that I do not know that I am, or that this is, or even might be a case of, my not now sitting in a chair. Nor, as will be further suggested in a moment, does it even show that the facts which I now grasp or perceive in now taking myself, as I do, to be seated in a chair, are not enough by themselves to constitute this being a case of my (hence of someone's) being so seated. For one thing, one of the facts which I may now simply see to be so is just the fact that I am now seated in a chair. This is a situation in which I am so seated, and it may be just that about the situation which I am now in a position to—and do—recognize. The moral we will here draw may be summed up by saying: by itself, the existence of conceivable doubts for A as to F shows nothing. In particular, where there are in fact no doubts, in the way just described, it cannot show that A does not know F, or even that this might not be a case of F. For, at least if A, despite the conceivable doubts, does count as knowing F, then, of course, this could not fail to be a case of F. (At this stage of the game, this way with doubt may seem dogmatic. The reasons for thinking it the right way will be set out in detail in chapter 4. Meanwhile, this will just be the model.)

The idea so far is simply that, while conceivable doubt is a universal, there are still two kinds of cases. In one kind of case, there actually is some doubt as to F, so that it could not be, so far, that we know that F is so. In the other, there is no doubt as to F. Returning to the semantic case, where we take some W to have some S, there may be no doubt about it. That is, presumably, frequently enough the case. Where it is, we may also know, or count as knowing, that W's semantics is as we thus take it to be. Even where we do count as knowing this, there remain, of course, conceivable doubts as to its being so.

It is possible, then, for us to be in situations of knowing W's semantics to be as we take it to be, hence knowing what W's semantics is, and knowing that we know this. A situation of our knowing that W has S certainly illustrates what it is like for W, or an item, to have S; it exhibits the sort of situation that would so count. Plausibly, the factors in that situation to which we react in then taking W to have S are such that for them then to hold just is for this to be a case of W, hence of something having S; just those factors are enough to make W thus classify as it does. For if we react to those factors as we do and thereby know W to have S, then our reaction is a proper one. There is no factor which we have under- or overvalued, when it comes to having S. Given that those factors are present in that situation, one is entitled to take it that W has S. But then, of course, that is just how a reasonable judge would react to those factors. So, if there really is no doubt as to W having S, how a reasonable judge would react in and to that situation. But then, by the anodyne equation, given those factors in this situation, this just is a case of W's having S. Since semantics just is, on the present scheme, a matter of those reactions to other factors which it would be reasonable to have, for one to be truly entitled to take W to have S just is, plausibly, for W to count as having S. I will say more in a moment about just how this idea is to be built into the present account.

There is, however, another side to this coin. Since, where we react to a situation by taking W, in it, to count as having S, there always remain conceivable doubts as to this being so, it is always possible for there to be deceptive situations. Sometimes, we simply perceive or recognize the fact that W counts as having S. But sometimes we may take ourselves to be in a situation in which we do that, where we do not, for the reason that W does not then count as having S. There may be such situations which, while we are in them, give us no means of telling that we are in that sort of situation rather than in one of genuinely recognizing that W has S, or recognizing the semantics W has. It is possible for us to be fooled, and to be fooled because, from our perspective on it, the one sort of situation looks just like the other. Such would be for us to be in a deceptive situation. One might reasonably ask what distinguishes deceptive situations from non-deceptive ones. The answer, of course, cannot refer to the way the situation looks to us. I will suggest an answer to this question in a moment. But first let us take a closer look at the presently operative notion of doubt.

The present story about doubt will follow closely the present account of semantic fact itself. That this should be so is suggested by a point emphasized by Cook Wilson.[4] If we judge that W has S, then *ipso facto* we judge, or at least take it, that there is no doubt about this. If we judge that there is some doubt about it, then we may still be of the opinion that W has S, or suspect or guess that it does, or think that it probably does. But we do not truly judge that it does. To judge P is, anyway, to have no doubts about it. Here, then, is the parallel. 'We', or 'the community', on the above amorphous notion of community, are

---

[4] See Cook Wilson [1926], especially pp. 98–113.

again at the core of the story of doubt. The core fact is that we just do doubt in certain situations and not others, and then, in any situation, in certain ways and not others. Certain doubts come naturally to us— or sometimes they do. We may take this to mean: certain doubts come naturally to human beings, or to ones with backgrounds sufficiently like ours.

But now for the second point. It is always conceivable that we are not doubting something that we absolutely ought to doubt. (*On Certainty* 223: 'For mightn't I be crazy and not doubting what I absolutely ought to doubt?') That is, wherever we take there to be no doubt as to W's having S, it is always conceivable that we should be wrong about this; there are always conceivable doubts as to there really being no doubt as to W's having S. There are conceivable ways in which there could turn out to be a doubt after all. Which is just to say: our word, for any given giving of it, is never necessarily the last word. So we might ask, in what sorts of circumstances would we be failing to doubt what ought to be doubted? The beginnings of an answer again parallel the story of semantic fact: conceivable doubt, by itself, shows nothing. So, where we take there to be no doubt, the existence of conceivable doubts about that does not show that we do not know that there is no doubt, or even, necessarily, that there might be some, much less that there really is at least some little bit of doubt after all. There really is *conceivable* doubt. But conceivable doubt, as such, has no epistemic role to play. So we may be in a position of taking there to be no doubt, of correctly taking there to be no doubt, and, in fact, of knowing that there is none. Such situations, where they are identifiable as such, again illustrate what it is like for there to be no doubt. They exhibit what it is (or may be) about a situation which makes it classify in that way. Again, in addition to such situations, there may also be deceptive situations with respect to doubt, in the sense of 'deceptive' described above. We recognize two kinds of situation here. It is fair to ask what in fact distinguishes the one kind from the other. It is now time to answer that question.

We come now to a second crucial epistemological idea. Briefly put, it is this: where we take some W to have some S, and we take there to be no doubt about it, that is a case of W's having (or then counting as having) S unless there is more to the story. That is, such is a case of W's having S unless there is a further fact, or are further facts of the case which demonstrate that W does not have (or count as having) S. 'We' here need not mean specifically you and I. Any generally reasonable judge of (relevant) semantic matters will do; any member of 'the community', as that has been described above. More might be said, of course, about what it would be for other facts to demonstrate that, despite our natural reactions, W did not have S. At this point we will simply note that a demonstration that such was so would be something that fits our concept of demonstration. That concept will be described in more detail in chapter 5. But the following general description will fit: other facts demonstrate such a state of affairs when a reasonable judge would take them to demonstrate that; that is, when such a judge would react to those facts by taking such a state of affairs to obtain.

This epistemological idea, on the present account, must be squared with the idea of fallibility already discussed. W's having S cannot simply consist in our reacting, or reacting naturally, to the other facts of the case by taking W to do so. There must always be a gap between the one thing and the other if there are to be any semantic facts of the matter at all; a gap which leaves it at least conceivable that our reactions were, or would be, wide of the mark. If there is (demonstrably) no such gap, then, on the present model, that in itself counts as enough further story to demonstrate that there was really no semantic fact of the matter, so that it was not a fact that W counted as having S. But the epistemological thought provides an account of what that gap might consist in. It consists in the possibility of there being, or having been, facts which would show, or would have shown, our reactions wrong. For our reactions to be what they are and for there to be no such further facts is, on the account, for the case in question to be one of W's counting as having S.

The same core epistemological idea applies to doubt. Where we take there to be no doubts as to F, or where 'we' would take there to be none, there are no doubts about F unless there are some further facts which demonstrate that there are; that one ought to doubt, in such-and-such ways, whether F is so. So one might tell the following story about doubt: we begin with the fact that for someone in our position (or in some particular position) it would not come naturally to have doubts as to F (or, in the more general case, it would come naturally to have such-and-such doubts, but not such-and-such others). That settles the issue as to whether there are then doubts as to F, and if so, which ones, unless there are further facts which demonstrate that there is some discrepancy between the doubts that come natural to us, and the doubts that one really ought to have. That is the way in which our reactions (or human ones) stand at the core of the story of doubt. Without them, there would be no such story; they fix what the doubts really are, though they do not require that the doubts that there are be identical with those which would at first come naturally to us. (This story will be elaborated considerably in chapter 4.)

The core idea in itself may seem platitudinous. What is not

platitudinous about it on its present application is just this: for us, or some reasonable candidate understander, to react as just described, and for there to be no further facts to show that reaction wrong, is *all* that need be so for something to be a case of W's having, or counting as having, S. There need be no further account, beyond this one, of what distinguishes deceptive cases from ones in which someone really is recognizing, or perceiving, what semantics an item has; in which he is understanding it correctly. It is not yet ruled out, of course, that there may be some such further account in other terms; an account which isolates facts of situations to which a reasonable judge might react such that when, and only when, they are present, it is correct that W counts as having S, and when they are absent, the case is at best a deceptive one. But if no such account is available; if every specification of facts which would make for W's having S leaves over some conceivable deceptive situations in which those facts hold, that fact in itself is not enough to demonstrate that W does not count as having S. So that, if we would naturally take it to do so, and there is nothing else to counteract the effects on the semantic facts of our natural reactions, then W does, in fact, count as having S.

This is an appropriate point for a plausible thought about what is wrong with (some forms of) verificationism. Suppose that a verificationist sets out to give an account of the meaning of some term such as 'copper', 'cold', or 'red', or, better, of the properties of being copper, cold or red. He assembles the best tests we have for distinguishing copper from other things, or red from other colours. He then announces, for example, that to be copper just is to pass those tests, or that 'copper' is true of just what does pass those tests. Such a verificationist would be wrong for this reason: it is a fundamental part of our nature that we are always open to new reasons; always prepared to be impressed, for example, by as yet unimagined reasons for taking something to be, or not to be, copper, and to be so impressed by these that we would weigh these more heavily, in some cases at least, than the passing or failing of the specific tests the verificationist mentioned, whatever these might have been. Trivially, given our genuine openness to novel reasons, one could not say in advance exactly which reasons these new ones might be. So it is conceivable that something should not be copper despite passing all the mentioned tests, or be copper despite not passing them. It is conceivable that there should be such items or situations, even when we cannot precisely conceive of what any specific such one would be; that there might be such follows simply from the stated general fact about our nature. If the verificationist's project requires otherwise, then we can say in advance that it could not be carried out.

Still, the verificationist might have been on to something; an important part of his project may be worth saving. Suppose that some item passes the verificationist's chosen tests, for example, for being copper, and that, though we are prepared to recognize that that might not be the last word on the subject, in fact there are no further reasons suggesting anything other than what the tests show, and which would impress us as weighing more heavily than the chosen tests; there could have been things we had not anticipated, but there aren't. Then, one might say, for that to be so just is for the item in question to be copper; there is nothing else which is required for it to be so, which we have not already stated in the above description of the case. We may then have identified what it is for *this* to be a case of something's being copper, even though that is not what it would be in every conceivable case for something to be copper. This idea of that 'residue' to verificationism—verificationism without the analysis, as it were—is the idea we have now applied to the realm of semantic fact.

On this view of the matter, the verificationist has fallen short, for example, in saying what distinguishes cases of something's being copper from cases of something's not being that, not because there is some well-defined correct classification of all possible cases (of what would be copper and what would not be) which he has got wrong—as if he has failed to identify some set of features which are the real ones which mark those cases on the one side of the classification, and are absent from those on the other—but rather because our approach to the world leaves open a possibility for any system for classifying to be wrong. For all that, there may remain a residue of possible cases— perhaps even all those we might actually confront—such that he has shown what the right way of classifying them would be (or at least how to classify them correctly). That these cases classify as they do may depend on nothing more than just what he has stated. Whether such a residue would be any comfort to a verificationist depends precisely on his views of what sorts of semantic facts there are or ought to be; what a semantics is like, and what it is like for an item to have some such. The rest of this book can be seen as aiming to give reasons why this residue should be comfort indeed.

Gaps

Our original question was: what characterizes cases of W's (or an item's) having (or counting as having) semantics S; or, what makes a case classify that way rather than as one of that item's lacking that semantics? But we might now pose another question: when ought you (one) to judge that W counts as having S, or, simply, when ought one to take W (or an item) as having S? Admittedly, this is a change of question. We were first inquiring after the features which mark a case as one of a certain sort. We are now asking after the reasons one might have for taking a case to be of a certain sort—apparently more an epistemic matter. But, on the present model, the questions are linked by the epistemology just described. It may be that if you take certain facts to hold, then you ought further to take it that W has S; that is a commitment that reason and your initial commitment make for you. It may also be that facts which thus ought to lead you to judge such a thing show what it is like for W to have S: a case where they hold just is to be judged, and counted, one of W having S—*ceteris paribus*, of course—unless there are facts which provide a demonstration that it ought to be counted otherwise.

Suppose that, in a given situation, you confront a semantic item, W. You react to W, and to the facts of that situation, by taking W to have S. You have no special reason to think that there might be further facts to demonstrate otherwise, or that your reactions deviate in any way from those a reasonable judge in this situation would produce. Or so you (would) judge. Then, on the model as set out so far, you ought to judge that W has S, or that is where those facts ought to lead you. That is not to say that you could not thus be wrong about W's semantics. Just what sort of gap is there for you still to have missed the mark? On the present model, the gap divides exhaustively into two cases as follows. First, there might be some further fact in that situation which you had not recognized or reacted to, such that when you were presented with that fact, and had appreciated just what fact it was, your reactions towards W, given it, would change so that, given that those were the facts, you would no longer take W to have S. For present purposes, this is a straightforward matter. Thus we will not consider that possibility any further in what follows.

A second possibility is that there are facts you reacted to—whether some specifiable facts F, or simply the facts of that situation—to which you did not react properly, which is to say: as a reasonable judge, in that situation would react. The weight you assigned to those facts was not that which a reasonable judge would assign them. These two possibilities, as mentioned, exhaust the field. If neither is realized, then you reacted to all the facts that would impress a reasonable judge in the matter of W's semantics, and were impressed by all of them just as a reasonable judge would be—or at least you reacted to the facts of the situation as a reasonable judge would. Given that, there is no remaining possibility that your reaction was wide of the mark. On the model, a converse point holds as well. For any particular reaction to W that you produce, both of these sorts of gaps always exist in principle.

It is always conceivable that there should be further facts, then unrecognized by you, which would change your reaction. And it is always conceivable that your reaction to the facts to which you did react should turn out to be not that of a reasonable judge. Which is to say, on the present account, that there could always turn out to be further facts which would demonstrate that this was so.

The question then is: what sorts of further facts might demonstrate such a thing? The answer on the present model, ignoring possibilities for gaps of the first sort, is: facts about the reactions of further judges (to the facts to which you reacted) might show this; and, ultimately,[5] only such facts could show it. If further judges, with a claim to reasonableness in the matter at hand which is otherwise as good as yours, would react other than by taking W to have S, then you, in so taking it, reacted other than as a reasonable judge would. Which is to say, on the present model, that you thereby took the semantic facts to be other than they are. If, on the other hand, such further judges would react as you did, then your reaction was that of a reasonable judge, and you thus got the semantic facts right. (On the present view of semantics, you might *sometimes* take some W to have some S where there was no fact of the matter. That, too, might be shown by the reactions of further judges to the facts to which you reacted. It would be shown where the facts about the reactions of such judges would not justify either the claim that such judges would react by taking W to have S, or the claim that such judges would react by taking W to lack S—as might happen, for example, when there was not enough stability in their reactions. Whether failure for there to be semantic fact might come about in any other way is a topic to be treated in chapter 8.)

On one crucial point, this remark about further judges requires amplification. Suppose that you react by taking W to have S. You then find that some further group of judges, J, with an otherwise good claim to reasonableness (as far as you can see), do not share your reaction. It might be that their claim to reasonableness in this matter was, collectively at least, demonstrably or recognizably better than yours. So that a reasonable judge would conclude that they, and not you, had got these semantic facts right. And so should you conclude. Not

---

[5] 'Ultimately': under some circumstances it might be possible to demonstrate that a given reaction of yours was not reasonable by your own lights. It might, for example, be demonstrably out of character for you; or we might be able to exhibit principles of reasonableness to which you subscribe, and which that reaction demonstrably fails to meet. On the present story, if the reaction was unreasonable by your lights, then, *ceteris paribus*, it was not the reaction of a reasonable judge. But note the force of the '*ceteris paribus*' here. If the reaction was reasonable by your lights, then whether it was also reasonable depends, in the way about to be described, on facts about the reactions of further judges.

infrequently, we do adjust our semantic perceptions in just this way.[6] But there always remain conceptual gaps between J's reactions and the facts as well. J could turn out to be reacting other than as a reasonable judge would. In which case, you might still turn out to be right. J's reactions might be shown wrong by the reactions of yet further judges (something we often appeal to to adjudicate such disputes). What are wanted, in order to establish your deviation from the facts, are facts which would establish what further (otherwise reasonable) judges would do—not what such-and-such further judges would do,[7] but what such further judges in general would do, and, for any specified group of such judges, what yet further ones would do (if there are, or if not, then if there were such). Nor need there be facts as to what every such further judge would do. There need be nothing that every such judge would do; if you have gone wrong, then so might an indefinite number of other individuals. Generalizations of the required kind do not require confirmation by every instance to which they might apply.

Any given semantic facts, on the present model, depend, for being facts, on the reactions an indefinite number and an indefinite collection of judges would have to other facts, in situations in which those facts might count as obtaining or not. The other facts a given semantic fact depends on, then, can be no more and no other than what some indefinitely large range of (otherwise reasonable) judges could react to—at first approximation, facts that we and members of our community could be in a position to react to; and, in any case, facts that members of some relevant community could react to. To some, this feature of the model may smell like (semantic) anti-realism. Is it? Considering the amorphous sort of term that 'anti-realism' is, it may be that the best answer to that question is an unequivocal, 'Could be.' But let us discuss the issue briefly. We might first ask: must the other facts on which any given semantic fact depends be ones which we, or an indefinite number of reasonable judges, could know or recognize to obtain? If one thinks of the paradigm of 'Mary had a little lamb', then it would not be implausible to answer yes. Consider the question whether some speaking of those words was a remark about meat eating. It is hard to conceive of an answer to that question depending on some fact in principle beyond our ken. If the most reasonable reaction to all the facts one could confront were to take the words to be

---

[6] As I use 'nubile', it may apply to males as well as females. A colleague of mine finds the application to males deviant. Which already makes me suspect that I might not have got it right. But both of us may decide this, if we care to take the trouble, by consulting usage—that is, how others react to it.
[7] Though given judges may *show* what further reasonable judges would do; there may be no doubt that further reasonable ones would agree in their reactions with these given ones.

a remark about meat eating, then what would the point be of supposing that nevertheless it might not be?

But the present model does not require a positive answer to this question. We might, for example, entertain the following fantasy. For some item, W, and some semantics, S, there is some fact obtaining which a reasonable judge, or reasonable judges, could never know to obtain, but which is such that if reasonable judges were presented with that fact, for example, by being told that it is, or might be, a fact, they would react by taking that fact to be relevant to the question whether W has S. They might just react, for example, by judging that if that were a fact, then that would show that W really did, or did not, or could not, have S. The present account allows that sort of fact about reasonable judges to be relevant to the semantics W has. Hence it allows room for us to conceive of there being that sort of other fact which was relevant to W's semantics. The general point suggested by this fantasy is just this: that the sort of contribution any given other fact can make to the obtaining of any given semantic fact is completely determined by the grasp of that fact that a reasonable judge could have; the perspectives he could have on it, the attitudes that permitted him to take, and the reactions he might have while relating to the fact in those ways. If, for example, the most a reasonable judge could do was to imagine F to be a fact, then the effects of F on W's semantics are determined by the reactions such a judge would have while imagining this.

Any sort of linking of semantic facts to the facts we could react to could be regarded as anti-realism. It should be noted, then, that this sort of anti-realism, if that is what it is, says virtually nothing about what sorts of semantic facts there might be. The sorts of facts there might be about any item's semantics are, on the present account, just the sorts of facts which it is part of our intuitive reactions to take there to be.[8] Unless, that is, there is a demonstration, in some particular case, that our taking there to be facts of that sort is a mistake; that our reactions in particular cases do not yield up enough facts as to in which

[8] At this point, the present model reinforces, and is reinforced by, an idea expressed by John McDowell (see McDowell [1981]). McDowell's thought, in present terms, might be expressed this way. It may just be a fundamental part of our reactions, in semantic matters, that we take there to be semantic facts of a certain sort, and that we take ourselves to be capable of, and sometimes successful at, recognizing these, and seeing them to obtain when they do. Given that root fact, someone not prepared to see the world, *inter alia*, in terms of such facts and our grasping of them, might just not be in a position to qualify as a reasonable judge in relevant matters. So if we try to imagine stripping all facts of this sort away from the world, there may be no correct way of describing how other facts could ever succeed in putting them back. We begin with the views we in fact take of the world and its semantic items, holding these subject to correction where needed, on the plan just sketched here.

cases a reasonable judge would take such 'facts' to be facts. Again, chapter 7 will provide a more detailed picture of what a demonstration of this sort would look like. But the point is that the model, if anti-realist, is anyway ontologically permissive, and not restrictive. Given that there are semantic facts of some given sort, the model does say something about what it would be for that sort of fact to obtain, and how other facts may contribute to its obtaining. Other facts may do so when, and only when, we, or reasonable judges, react to them by taking them to provide reason to take those semantic facts to obtain, or simply react to them by taking there to be such reason. The facts which matter are, then, the facts to which we could react; which may, in a given case, help identify which facts they are.

Craziness

Where we understand semantic items in one way or another, the correctness of our understandings depends on the reactions of further judges whose claim to reasonableness in such matters is otherwise at least as good as our own. Which judges are these? The present model applies to the answering of this question too: claims to reasonableness are a matter for the reactions of reasonable judges to decide; we take some people to be reasonable, or in the relevant community of judges, and others not; there is a possibility for our doing so rightly or wrongly; the model explains how this is so. This is not quite to say that if someone qualifies as such a reasonable judge, *we* must be capable of recognizing him to do so. Our recognizing reasonable judges, and our ability to do so, constitutes one central sort of case. But there might be others. For example, it is conceivable that some judges should be identified as further reasonable ones by judges whom we recognize as reasonable, though we ourselves cannot recognize these first-mentioned judges as within the relevant community. And there might be other sorts of cases as well.

All this suggests a paranoid fantasy of a familiar philosophical sort. Suppose we take W to have S. Some other group of judges, J, takes W to

As McDowell recognizes, this picture extends naturally to our mental lives in general. It is fundamental to our way of viewing the world that in doing so we sometimes see, for example, cases of someone being angry; we see and sometimes feel (displays and episodes of) anger. That someone is angry may be part of what we observe and do not infer. For someone deprived of seeing these features of the world, there may be no general correct account of what count as cases of anger. The best we could hope is, by example, to sensitize him to those features. Anger belongs to a world in which it is found within the observable. Similarly for propositional attitudes or sensations. This was also J. L. Austin's view of mental life (see Austin [1946]). Chapter 4 will show why observation should work like that. Chapter 7 will provide metaphysical underpinnings for the idea of such facts being fundamental.

lack S. It just so happens that, because of what comes naturally to us, there are no facts which we could possibly be confronted to which we would react by recognizing J as the reasonable judges of W. We would always be more impressed by our own reactions, no matter what reasons there in fact were for taking J as the exhibitors of what a reasonable judge would do. Nevertheless, it is J, and not us, who are exhibiting how a reasonable judge would react. That is how a reasonable judge would react to the reasons there in fact are for taking J to be doing that. We can imagine seeing others in such a position. We can imagine its being reasonable for us to judge that they were in such a position. And if that is the reasonable thing to judge about them, then that is the position they are in. Such people would be mistaken about W's semantics, and incapable of recognizing that they were. But if we can imagine others in that position, then why not we ourselves? Is it not conceivable that semantically we, or our intuitions, have just gone crazy?

If the notion of semantic fact leaves room for such a fantasy, then two questions arise, one epistemological, and one metaphysical. The epistemological question is, how can we ever know, or with what right do we ever take it, that we are not in such a position? The metaphysical one is, what in fact distinguishes cases of our being in such a position from cases of our not being (granted that there is any conceptual space for such a position at all)? The present answer to the second question is this. There is just as much room for the fantasy as there is room for there to be demonstrations, in present matters, which we could not recognize to be such. There is just as much room for that as the present model allows. We need not maintain that the model leaves no such room. But nor need we provide any general description of just that room that it in fact does leave. On the contrary, what is needed for there to be such a refractorily deceptive situation is a specific enough story about the particular facts which would make for it. It will be in terms of that story that we will be able to see what it would be not to be in that particular circumstance.

As for the epistemological question, we can say this. If the model leaves room for such refractorily deceptive situations, that is to say that where we take W to have S, there are conceivable doubts of just this sort. But once again, to say that there are conceivable doubts is not to say that there are doubts. Often enough, where we take W to have S, there is no such doubt. We would not take there to be; and we would be performing as a reasonable judge in so reacting. Often enough, we can be in a position to know that there is no such doubt. Where any of that is so, the situation we are in fact in is one where W counts as having S, and not a deceptive one of the sort described. But any of that is often recognizably so. Which, given the conceptual space for such doubts in the first place, is all that is needed for carving out the metaphysical distinction which the second question requires. Which is just to repeat that point which the present view of epistemology was aimed at making.

The Strategy Reviewed

The aim has been to give some account of when a semantic fact would hold; and an account on which there are some. The approach has not been to show how to describe the holding of a semantic fact in other terms—not, that is, if that means, where W has some semantic feature, P, identifying other features of W which, wherever they were present, would be good enough to qualify the item with them as having P. The aim is not to supply, in such a case, features which might be detected by someone with no ability to discern the presence or absence of P itself, and which might, for such a person, supplant all reliance on those with some ability to see what has P and what does not.

Such other features of cases of having P, if they could be supplied, would provide the means of detecting cases of something's having P. But there is a more general requirement whose satisfaction will do just as well. It will do if such cases are often enough detectable, and if we can say how they are. If so, then there is such a thing as being P, something which it is to do so, and that is something items often enough may do. For any concept, C, such a general requirement might be satisfied in either of two ways. One might distinguish cases of an item's fitting C from others by appealing (primarily) to intuition as to what it is to fit C; or one might do this by appealing directly to intuitions as to what does fit C (or so counts on occasion). (If C is unfamiliar, either sort of intuition might be supplied by explanation.) Either sort of intuition, if reliable, may show often enough where there are facts as to C's application; so, too, that there are some. If either is reliable enough, then there is a way that cases do divide into ones of fitting C and others. And some things sometimes do fit C if that is how the intuitions go. Where C is a semantic concept, the present preference is for intuition of the second sort.

Semantic facts are detectable, the present thought goes, if there are reliable detectors of them, and if these detectors are often enough identifiable. But there are. We detect or discern the semantic facts often enough by relying on ourselves as detectors of them, in the first instance; or more generally, by relying on those who are recognizably reacting to the relevant semantic items (on relevant confrontations of them) as a reasonable judge would then react to them. In any given case, such judges will be those with the best independent claim to be so reacting, or those whose reaonableness in the matter is not in doubt. Often enough, there is no doubt as to who these judges are, and often enough no doubt that we are among them. Occasions of absence of doubt are no doubt required if such judges are to be recognizable. One might then ask how such cases are to be detected. But the form of answer to that has already been described: by relying on reliable detectors of them, where we are typically among these. The meta-question thus introduces no new elements.

Like most other facts that concern us, the semantic facts we take to hold are of sorts we may sometimes observe to do so. We hear someone speak of meat, for example, and do not merely infer this from other properties of the sounds that leave his mouth. If there are situations of our observing semantic fact, then each such situation goes paired with a range of possible deceptive ones—situations which would seem to us just like one of our observing W to have P, but which were not that, since they were not ones of W's having P. Wherever we take some W to have some P, such situations represent conceivable doubts about it. It is thus important to insist that conceivable doubts by themselves show nothing. Their mere existence cannot be enough to show, in a particular case, that more information is needed to settle whether W has P, or that we need to command other facts before we can be justified in so taking things. For if such doubts did automatically show this, then their existence would place W's having P beyond the bounds of what it was open to us to observe. There are, then, situations for us to be in where, though there are conceivable doubts as to W's having P, no such doubt has any force. Such situations, too, go paired with ranges of deceptive ones. But again that introduces no new element to the story. Such is a sort of rationale for the form the present account takes—for those, at least, who locate semantic facts among what we sometimes observe.

3. S-USE AND ENTAILMENT

Note how the above model of semantic fact makes room for sensitivity to occasions in the having of a semantics, hence for the S-use sensitivity of semantic properties. Different occasions for considering a given semantic item present different situations in which, and to which, a reasonable judge might react. The reasonable judge could be— and could be shown to be—an S-use sensitive device[9]: in some

---

[9] This is a bit different from saying that reasonable judges are S-use sensitive. The reasonable judges, on O, of W's semantics—that is, the particular judges who, on O, qualify as the most reasonable ones—may be S-use sensitive devices. If J is such a judge, J ·

situations, he would react by taking W to have S, and in others by taking W not to do so. If such are the reactions a reasonable judge would have, on two occasions, O and O* respectively, then W has its semantics S-use sensitively.

That the reasonable judge would be an S-use sensitive device may be shown, at least if it can be shown that evidence of the sort presented in the last chapter is what it seems to be. Consider a simple case: a ripe winesap apple, V, and the words 'That apple is red', spoken of V. There are many such speakings which a reasonable judge would now take to have the property of saying V to be red. That is a start on characterizing the semantics of those words as thus spoken. For some such speakings, the reasonable judge would take the words to be true of V. In doing so, he would assign no, or no decisive, weight to any considerations in the opposite direction which might be provided by the apple's (for the most part) very white insides. For other speakings, however, a reasonable judge would respond to just those facts about the insides by taking the words, so spoken, to be false. (I leave it to the reader to construct the details of a pair of contrasting speakings which would make a reasonable judge react in each of the above ways.) If these are the right facts about a reasonable judge, then the words 'That apple is red', now count as having had the property of being true of V on some speakings and having lacked it on others, where they also count as having had, on all of these, the property of saying V to be red.

The above illustrates how different other facts about a speaking might make a reasonable judge react differently in assigning semantics to words. And it has been explained, in the last chapter, how a speaking may be regarded simply as an occasion for considering the semantics which given words then count as having. As also previously noted, the above sort of variation in a reasonable judge's reactions does not by itself force us to recognize *semantic* S-use sensitivity. For, so far, it might be denied that the words 'That apple is red'—as opposed to what was said in them on some speaking, or those words *as so spoken*—ever count as having the property of being true of V. It is only if they sometimes so count that they must count as doing so S-use sensitively. On the other hand, the present view of semantics allows us to regard those words as liable sometimes so to count. If we do so regard them, then we do now have an illustration of semantic S-use sensitivity. For the reactions a reasonable judge would now have to the speakings just

may also pass in and out of counting as a reasonable judge, or an exhibitor of what a reasonable judge would do, as J moves from occasion to occasion. The crucial point concerns variation across occasions in the facts as to what a reasonable judge would do; not in those as to what J, a sometimes reasonable judge would do. Still, if reasonable judges are, on the whole, S-use sensitive devices, that is excellent reason for thinking that that is what the reasonable judge would be.

described exhibit what now count as the reactions a reasonable judge would have, on the occasion of each of those speakings, to the facts of it. Which is to say that a reasonable judge, confronted with the facts of some such occasions, would react by taking the words 'That apple is red', to say what is true of V, whereas, when confronted with the facts of other such occasions, would react by taking those words then to count as saying what was not true of V. Such would parallel the reasonable judge's reaction to other facts in the matter of whether V then counted as being red. That the words do so count would be a reasonable explanation of why it would then come naturally to us to understand and treat them as we then would.

The room which the present model makes for semantic S-use sensitivity, as just described, is room which is always present in principle. That is not to say that S-use sensitivity is always there to be exhibited. Consider, for example, what was said in one of the above speakings of 'That apple is red'—one, perhaps, on which (from our present perspective) what was said was clearly true. Perhaps we can find no pair of occasions, and no semantic property, P, such that on one of these a reasonable judge would react by taking that item—what was thus said—to have P, and on the other of them, such a judge would react by taking that same item to lack P. Perhaps a reasonable judge would never react by taking that item not to have P. In that case, the item would count as having P S-use insensitively. We might then say that that item has P intrinsically (or that it now counts as doing so). So the model also allows the possibility that there may be some semantic items, W, which (sometimes or always) count as having some of their semantics intrinsically. The important point is that what is required for such things to be facts is no different from what is required for semantic S-use sensitivity. For such to be, or now count as, a fact, there must be, or now count as being, the right facts as to how a reasonable judge would always react, in the face of any constellation of other facts. And such facts are always linked, in the way described in the model, to our own reactions and to those of further judges who would be recognizable as otherwise reasonable. The framework must be in place, and W must fit properly into it if it is to count as a fact that W has P intrinsically. That is a framework which always allows for the possibility of W's having P S-use sensitively, and which makes it conceivable that, and how, this could turn out to be the case.

The opposing view would be one on which at least some concepts are intrinsically S-use insensitive; on which something in their being the concept they are is a bar in principle to their ever manifesting S-use sensitivity. That thought collides with the idea that the semantics of any semantic item is irreducibly dependent on the reactions to it of those with the best (adequate) claim to be reacting as a reasonable judge would. At least there is collision for any concept that may be specified or picked out without specifying each *candidate* for fitting it. If C can be specified, on occasion, without mentioning V, there are then at least two incompatible reactions for *some* judge to have: taking V to fit C; or taking V not to. Nothing intrinsic to C, no part of what a judge would react to in reacting to it, could rule out in principle each reaction being one produced on some such occasions by the judges then best *independently* qualified to judge. So nothing intrinsic to C could rule out its manifesting S-use sensitivity. Not even the stipulation that C is to be S-use insensitive would do the job.

This room for S-use sensitivity is room not only for the S-use sensitivity of any given semantic property, but also for S-use sensitivity in the relations which count as holding between any given semantic property, or semantics and any other—notably, in what any given semantics counts as requiring. Suppose that it is given that W has some semantics S. The question is then whether, given that, it also count, as having some further semantics, S*. The answer to such a question may well depend on whether it must (or, conversely, can) so count; whether, for example, having S* is part of what having S requires. For example, suppose it is given that W says something to be red. Does that fact require that it also count as saying what is true of *this* (some sample of red, say)? On the present model, W's having S requires that it count as having S* just where its having S *counts* as requiring that. And its having S, or simply having S, counts as requiring this just where a reasonable judge would react to the facts of an occasion of considering that question by taking such to be required.

The model leaves the possibility always open that we should be able to find some pair of occasions for considering the question what having semantics S requires; such that the facts as to what a reasonable judge, on the one occasion, would find S to require are relevantly different from the facts as to what such a judge would find on the other. It provides us with a general picture of what it is for semantic fact to hold, on which it is always conceivable that this should be so. Suppose, for example, that we now regard having S as simply being something which requires having S*; requiring that, we might now take it, is just part of what it is to have S (or what S is). One thing that remains conceivable is that we should find ourselves placed in situations—though we may not yet know what these would be—in which those are no longer our reactions; in which we no longer regard S in those ways; and for which there is no demonstration that we are then reacting wrongly. There is no showing, that is, that it is our present reactions, and not those of the other occasions (or neither) which show what must always count as so.

Another conceivable development is that, though our own initial reactions do not vary across occasions, there turn out to be further judges, otherwise reasonable by any independent standard, whose reactions do so vary. The weight of their reactions, and the reasons for taking them to be exhibiting what a reasonable judge would do, may mount up until it is more reasonable to count their reactions than it is to count our own as those of a reasonable judge. Since they react as S-use sensitive devices, that is what a reasonable judge in these matters would be. In that case, we would be mistaken about the relation between having S and having S*, in a way in which we might turn out to be mistaken about any semantic fact whatever. The present idea is that there are always ways for that to happen—possible states of affairs in which it would have happened—no matter how strongly attached we may now be to our present reactions in such matters. If we were to rely on induction, then the history of philosophy might make it reasonable to conclude that it is more than just barely conceivable that there should be such outcomes, even in the most favoured cases.

The relation between having given S and having given S* might thus turn out to be S-use sensitive. It might turn out, for example, that having S sometimes counts, and sometimes does not count, as requiring having S*. Or that relation might also turn out to be S-use insensitive. The most important part of the above story concerns what is required for its counting as a fact that having S requires having S*, and, correspondingly, what would demonstrate, for any putative fact of this sort, that it was not a fact. What is required is the right facts about our reactions and those of further otherwise reasonable judges: we and/ or they must take S to require S*, and qualify as reasonable in doing so. It is always conceivable that such facts should fail to hold. Which, if they did fail, would be a demonstration that it did not after all count as a fact that S required S*. The requirement is the same whether or not the outcome, on applying that requirement, is that the relation between S and S* is an S-use sensitive one. If that is the nature of semantic fact, then no semantics an item could have, just by being what it is, and independent of our reactions to it, could have the property of ruling out, for an item that had it, that item's having its full semantics S-use sensitively. For, with that semantics, the item would do so if, for some S*, having that semantics counted, on some occasions but not on others, as requiring having S*. If there is no S* for which that is so, then that fact depends on facts about our reactions to the semantics in question, and not merely on its being the semantics it is.

That any given semantics depends on our reactions for requiring (and not requiring) what it does (so that not only our words, but our concepts also depend on our reactions for requiring what they do) is a central point in Wittgenstein's discussion of rules and the facts as to what they require. To see the connection between the present discussion and that one, we might begin with a question which Wittgenstein allows to be posed in 198: 'But how can a rule show me what I have to do at *this* point?' The question has a background. In preceding discussion, Wittgenstein has been concerned, *inter alia*, with this point. For any rule, R, and any case in which R applies, there are various candidate facts as to what, in that instance, would count as being in compliance with R. Corresponding to these candidate facts are various possible understandings of R. One might take R to require doing X (rather than Y) in this case, and understand it in a way on which it did require this. Or one might take R to require doing Y rather than X in this case, and correspondingly have a different understanding of R. And so on. It is at least conceivable that either understanding should be correct; at least both are possible understandings of R. Despite which, at least for many rules, we think that, confronted with some such range of candidate facts, we could separate out those which are facts and those which are not, or at least that there are facts as to how the separating is to go. For many R, at least, we think that there are, as a rule, facts as to what R requires in a given case. That is a point which Wittgenstein does not doubt. (As he puts it in 85, a rule 'sometimes leaves room for doubt and sometimes not. And now this is no longer a philosophical proposition, but an empirical one.') The question which he does raise (and discusses from 84 on into the private language discussion) is the question what is required for there to be facts of this sort.

Consider an example. We might lay down a rule for expanding a series of numbers by saying that the first member of the series is to be 0, and each other member of the series is to be two greater than its predecessor. (The rule is that each member of the series is to be that.) This might be a way of saying which series of numbers was in question. By the rule, for example, 98 is a member of the series, followed by 100, which, in turn, is followed by 102. Suppose, however, that Pia takes it that the next member of the series after 100 is 104. She takes it, that is, that that is what the rule requires for expanding the series in this case. Of course, she is wrong. That is—as Wittgenstein is at pains to point out—*a* possible way of understanding this rule, that is, a possible reaction to have to *this* rule. But it is an incorrect one. But what is it about the way things are that makes that so?

Such a vague question need not have a unique answer. But Wittgenstein certainly considers at least one answer that does not work, and at least one that does. One sort of answer that could not work would be in terms of (putative) further semantic properties of the rule. We specified some of the rule's semantics in saying what we did about what it required, in saying what rule it was. But there might be further semantic properties of the rule to be mentioned (other than the property that we got right and Pia got wrong). For example, we might be able to say that the rule requires that every member of the series be two greater than its predecessor, where it is a further property of this rule that that injunction is to be taken to mean such-and-such rather than such and such. One might think that if we mentioned enough such further properties, or the right ones, then it might be that the very fact that the rule had that further semantics, independent of anything else, simply entailed that the rule required doing what we took it to, and not what Pia took it to, in the case at hand. As Wittgenstein suggests in 84, we might try to lay down a rule for interpreting the rule as specified, a rule for interpreting that one, and so on. But, he insists, this would be on the wrong track entirely. The point is put succinctly in 198:

any interpretation still hangs in the air along with what it interprets, and cannot give it any support. Interpretations by themselves do not determine meaning.

If we attribute further semantics to the rule, in addition to that we specified in specifying it, then, as with the original semantics, there may be various understandings of what that entire semantics requires in this case, and so various candidate facts as to what it requires, just as there were with the original. There is not just one way someone conceivably could react to this new semantics. And that larger semantics itself cannot perform the task of choosing between these understandings. Something else is still needed to show which of these understandings is the correct one—or, more to the point, for it to be so that one of them is the correct one.

A second sort of answer—the sort suggested here—refers to facts about us and about further judges; judges who are or would be members of the relevant community in the present loose sense of that term: the community, that is, whose charge it would be to determine the facts of the sort now under consideration, or to take them to be one way or another—that is, those concerned with using that rule or evaluating other uses of it. (There being facts as to what the rule requires in particular cases, on this sort of answer, presupposes that there is some such community.) The facts about us which matter are facts about our reactions on particular occasions for taking the rule to require one thing or another; facts about how it comes naturally to us to take it to require one thing or another. (For any given facts of what our reactions are or would be, it may be conceivable that relevant judges should produce those reactions without its being a fact that the rule does require what those reactions would suggest it to. To think that such conceivabilities vitiate this sort of answer is to miss the point of the epistemology of the last section. It is that epistemology, I suggest, that moves Wittgenstein towards this sort of answer rather than towards scepticism about semantic fact.)

It is this second sort of answer, I suggest, that Wittgenstein endorses[10], at least to this extent: it is his view, as it is the present one, that without a suitable background of facts about our reactions, or what comes naturally to us, or to otherwise reasonable judges, there would genuinely be no facts as to what a rule required in any particular case. More important, there are always conceivable ways for our reactions to any given rule—or the reactions of suitable further judges—to be, or to have been, different than they are or would be. Had they been, or were they to be, then *that* rule would require different things in given cases, and different things would count as in compliance with it, from what is now so in those respects. The rule's being the rule that it is does not by itself settle all the facts of its semantics; in particular not the facts of its applications in particular cases. Such facts are settled only against a background of the reactions of a community appropriate for applying it: a suitable range of reasonable judges with occasion to take it as requiring one thing or another. The rule itself leaves room for a variety of such backgrounds.

The point of this chapter has been to extend that thought about rules to semantics, and to semantic items in general. In particular, the thought applies, for any given semantics (and any item), to the facts as to what further semantics having that semantics (or that item's having it) requires. In that way, the background provided by 'our' reactions (or those of suitable further judges) is required for the (full) semantic facts about any item to be what they are (where the background we do provide is only one of a variety which conceivably could have been). Notably, the point applies to the relations between any other semantic properties and truth-involving ones (such as being true, or what would be true of item or situation V): that is, facts as to the particular applications of any given semantic item. This dependence of semantic

---

[10] Wittgenstein sometimes refers to the required background of facts about us in terms of the existence of a custom or usage ('Gepflogenheit' (198)). I take it that, for relevant purposes, there is such a 'usage', or anyway facts about what usage would be, where—and just where—there are facts as to what the reactions of relevant judges would be. He also speaks of the semantic facts here as determined by 'what we call "obeying the rule" and "going against it" in actual cases' (201), that is, by our reactions in taking the relevant semantic facts to be one thing or another. In a similar connection (206), he refers to 'the common behavior of mankind' as 'the system of reference' for deciding such issues. All of which I take to be a way of expressing the model of semantic fact set out above.

fact on 'our' reactions, or what comes naturally to us, means that any given semantics leaves room for items which have it to have their full semantics, notably further truth-involving parts of it, S-use sensitively. They will do so in so far as we, or a reasonable judge, would perform as an S-use sensitive device in responding to them. It is then simply up to us to observe whether and where S-use sensitivity, whether ground-level or semantic, occurs.

In short, the picture of semantics which Wittgenstein is concerned to underline in his discussion of rule-following is a picture which makes room for S-use sensitivity no matter what semantic properties there may be. It leaves no room for our finding or inventing appropriately chosen semantics for items to have which in principle would block S-use sensitivity from arising for those items. So, *inter alia*, it is a picture on which there could not be concepts which, as such, were incapable of exhibiting S-use sensitivity in their applications, no matter what. This is part of Wittgenstein's commitment to the alternate picture described in the last chapter. A more direct commitment will be described in the next.

Wittgenstein's view of rules, and so of semantics in general, is a radical one—so much so that it appears difficult for some to read what he is saying except in trivializing ways. Take the point that a rule admits various understandings—particularly that there are various possible understandings of what it requires in particular cases. The point is not that all of these understandings are, or even might be, correct. Nor is it that there is really no fact of the matter as to which are correct and which not. But it is to say that any of these understandings are possible understandings of that rule. Moreover, in pointing as he does to 'different ways of following a rule', Wittgenstein makes the point that each of these understandings would have been correct if circumstances had been (as they might have been) different enough to make that understanding a proper reaction to the rule in question. The trivializing reading which may tempt one here involves distinguishing between rules and formulations of them. The temptation would be to see Wittgenstein's point as holding for formulations of rules, but not for rules. Thus, one might say: a given formulation or statement of a rule admits of various understandings—as the formulation of any of a variety of distinct rules; under suitably different circumstances, any of these understandings might have been correct. But a *rule* does not admit of various possibly correct understandings; a rule is identified as the rule it is by what it requires in each case where it applies; if R counts as requiring A, then whatever, under any circumstances whatever, failed to count as requiring A would *ipso facto* not be the same rule that R is. Such, if you like, is a convention for counting rules; it is definitional. So, the temptation goes, Wittgenstein, in speaking in this vein, could only be talking about formulations of rules.

To succumb to this temptation is clearly still to be firmly in the grip of the dominant picture of semantics. It is to think of semantic items as capable of having a determinate semantics such that the fact of having it could, by itself, settle all semantic questions that might ever arise. But it is just this grip that Wittgenstein is concerned to loosen. The presupposition above, that a rule could be specified or (to be) counted in such a way that it could not admit of various possibly correct understandings, is just the idea that Wittgenstein urges us to resist. In any event, Wittgenstein is quite clear that what he is talking about is rules. For example, he says,

A rule (*Regel*) stands there like a route marker (*Wegweiser*). Does the route marker leave no doubt open about the way I have to go? . . . And if there were, not a single route marker, but a chain of adjacent ones or of chalk marks on the ground—is there only *one* way of interpreting them? (85)

It is the rule, and not just a formulation, that (sometimes) leaves room for interpretation. As we have seen already, in the case of *Satz*, Wittgenstein resists trying to make semantic phenomena appear to go away, or to be isolated in some secondary domain, by proliferating sorts of items which might exhibit the phenomenon or not. We can now see that his idea that the phenomena are part of what it is to have semantics, and not just the afflictions of some peculiar sort of semantic item, shows itself in his use of the word, *Regel*, as well as in his use of Satz. The present account of semantic fact shows how it really could be rules that he is talking about.

The rule is: add two each time. On the present view, that is a way of specifying which rule is in question. In any event, it is not about a formulation. Now let us ask: what does that rule require? Here is one set of applications of a rule which says to do that. We are following a ceremony of giving each other baskets of fruit. The ceremony requires that whenever one receives a basket, he is to pass it on to someone else—after having increased the quantity of the fruit in the basket by two. Hugo receives a basket which contains, at the moment he takes it in his hands, 17 apples. He is to pass the basket to Odile. However, one of the apples proves to be so rotten that, before he can do anything with the basket, that apple has dissolved into an irretrievable mess. Should the basket Hugo passes to Odile contain 18 or 19 apples?

The fundamental fact here is that we lay down rules, a technique for a game, and that then when we follow the rules, things do not turn out as we had assumed. That we are therefore as it were entangled in our own rules. (125)

In other words, as things stand, there is no determinately correct answer to the question. Further surrounding circumstances, however, might resolve the issue, and then in either of two directions, depending on what they are. The point of the ceremony, or the way it is usually carried out, might make it most reasonable to attend to the apple count at the moment the basket passed into Hugo's hands. Or it might make it most reasonable to attend to the count after the basket had been relieved of its mess. (It might, of course, do neither.) In the first case, the answer would be 19; in the second, 18. That circumstances might accomplish such things is the core idea of S-use sensitivity. That they might do so in this case shows the rule in question to exhibit S-use sensitivity, as applied here, with respect to what it counts as requiring—a sort of semantic S-use sensitivity. This particular problem, presumably, could not arise for expanding numerical series. So nor could it be a source of S-use sensitivity in that case. But what rules out S-use sensitivity in the one case is, in an important sense, no different from what allows it to manifest itself in the other. It is our reactions to various surroundings for applying the rule which show that S-use sensitivity is manifest in the case of the apples; it is just the invariance of those reactions across variations in surroundings which we know how to produce, in the numerical case, that guarantees that no such S-use sensitivity there arises.

'But surely the rule, add two each time, requires writing 102, and not 104 after 100. No further facts, no matter what they were, could possibly ever show this not to be so. So nor does it depend on what the further facts are. It is a fact about that rule that could not be otherwise.' In a sense, this is right. Of course, the rule requires writing 102 and not 104 at that point. Of course, no further facts could show otherwise. After all, that is what a reasonable judge would find. A reasonable judge would not react, for example, by taking it that *perhaps* 102 is the right thing to write, but further facts might show otherwise. So there remains an equation between what the facts about the rule may correctly be said to be, and what a reasonable judge would take these facts to be. There is still a question of what kind of support each side of this equation provides for the other. One might hold that a reasonable judge would find as per above simply because, since those are the facts, any judge who found otherwise would *ipso facto* be unreasonable, at least in that matter. I have been concerned here to emphasize the opposite direction of fit. Reasonable judges of any such matter are generally recognizable as such, independent of the fact that what they found in the matter was such-and-such (for example, the facts about the rule as just stated). The present view is that they are always in principle so recognizable. The fact that a reasonable judge would have such-and-such reactions may then serve as part of the circumstances in which those facts, as stated, count as being facts. On the present model, it is a part which must be present if, indeed, they are so to count.

All of the preceding may be viewed as aimed against a view of what might be called a 'no-speaker' language.[11] Such a view is encouraged by a Fregean picture of semantic properties. On that picture, semantic properties are what they are, and do what they do (as Frege adds, 'in all essentials') quite independent of us, or of anyone else. Such properties may be thought of as providing us with ranges of 'possible languages', which are what they are quite independent of questions as to who, if anyone, ever speaks them, if so, under what circumstances, for what, and so on. For semantic properties conceived in the Fregean way provide a possible range of semantics for items to have. Each item of a given possible language L—each of its words or other expressions— may simply be associated (by definition, if you like) with some such semantics. Given that semantic properties are what they are, in all essentials, independent of any perspective we might have or take on them, each such item of L, simply in virtue of having that semantics, would have all the semantic facts about it fixed, independent of any questions of who, if anyone, ever spoke or understood it, and if so, when and how. Such a language would be, on the conception, like our languages in every respect except that it requires no speaker; it is a no-speaker language. Our languages might even be thought of as chosen from some list of no-speaker ones, and as being only quite contingently spoken at all. The present idea is that this is just what could not be. Languages, or other semantic items, have the semantics they do only as used by us or other reasonable judges, and given the reactions that come naturally to us in the circumstances of that use. Only against such a background can the facts be what they are as to what any given semantic properties do.

4. PRIVACY

It is part of the present model that any specified set of judges of W's semantics—whoever might understand W in one way or another—is fallible. It is also part of the model that this fallibility requires that for any group of judges, J, it be possible in principle for there to be further judges in a position to judge W's semantics. Which is to say that W's semantics is a matter which the judgings or understandings of W by an

---

[11] For this description of it I am indebted to Michael Hallett.

indefinitely large range of novel judges might help decide. Which is to say that any other fact on which W's semantics, or some fact about it, depends must be accessible, in principle, to an indefinitely large range of novel judges—that is, for any judges, J, with access to it, accessible to some potential judge not a member of J. Any fact relevant to fixing W's semantics must be a fact which an indefinite number of judges could grasp and properly appreciate; one which they could know, or which they could relate to in whatever other way was appropriate, such that it was the reaction of a reasonable judge to that fact when so appreciated, or so related to, that mattered to the question what W's semantics was. I will call this idea, with an amendment to be added in a moment, the *public access principle*, or PA.

The present account of semantic fact entails PA. But it will be noted that that account has been presented, but not defended. Someone might still reasonably reject the account, and do so in a way that involves denying PA. The present point is that denying PA provides a reasonable notion of privacy in terms of which to define private language. As will be indicated, it is also plausible that that notion of privacy is Wittgenstein's. That thought at least indicates how the private language discussion might be relevant to present semantic issues. If private language is impossible, then that argues that PA cannot be rejected. So a private language argument will be an argument for PA. The hope is that it will emerge, in the course of such an argument, that it is difficult to accept PA without accepting the present model. But one cannot accept that model without accepting the room that it makes for S-use sensitivity. So one cannot accept the model and hold on to the idea of special sorts of semantics which rule out S-use sensitivity in whatever items might have them. That is to restate the main theme of this book.

Before proceeding with this thought, it is time for the promised amendment to PA. Let us briefly entertain a fantasy. Suppose that Pia takes W in a certain way, as having some semantics S. Or at least that is what she claims to do. In doing so, she is reacting to some other fact, F; if F did not hold, or at least if certain other facts held instead, she would not take W to have S. This much we might count as idealization. Now for the pure fantasy. We are able to clone Pia. Perhaps, for example, we have a matter duplicator into which we can place her. In this way, we can generate an indefinite number of novel judges of W's semantics. Suppose that F is appropriately accessible to all these judges. Then, unamended, PA is satisfied. Suppose, now, that F is accessible only to these judges and to Pia. Suppose, further, that one could not be one of these judges without sharing Pia's reaction to F; you just cannot reproduce enough of Pia for properly grasping or relating to F without also thereby reproducing enough to share Pia's reaction to F. Intuitively, the possibility of such clones, and hence of an indefinite number of novel judges, ought not to be enough to make for semantic facts about W. If one shares this intuition, then a proper version of PA ought to rule out F as a fact reactions to which could be relevant to the facts as to what W's semantics (if any) in fact was. To that end, let us add an anti-cloning amendment to PA: for any semantic item, W, any semantics, S, which W might have, and any other facts on which W's having S might depend, those other facts must be such that they would be, in principle, accessible to—that is, properly related to by—both judges who would react to them (together, perhaps, with other facts) by taking W to have S, and judges who would react to them (together with the same other facts, if any) by taking W not to have S. That is, it must be possible for there to be judges who would have either sort of reaction.

PA suggests, in the case of words, that the facts on which their proper understandings and proper applications depend are not facts which might be hidden from us, or accessible to us alone while denied in principle to others. They should not be facts which we could present to ourselves but could not communicate, or at best could only hint at, and not actually state or show. That idea comes out very strongly in Wittgenstein's continued insistence, throughout the *Investigations*, on the publicity of the semantic items to which we relate. Here is a sample of his thoughts on what publicity involves:

How should we explain to someone what a game is? I imagine that we should describe *games* to him, and we might add: 'This *and similar things* are called games.' And do we know any more about it ourselves? Is it only other people whom we cannot tell exactly what a game is?—But this is not ignorance. (69)

One gives examples and intends them to be taken in a particular way.—I do not mean by this, however, that he is supposed to see in those examples that common thing which I—for some reason—was unable to express; but that he is now to *employ* those examples in a particular way. Here giving examples is not an indirect means of explaining—in default of a better. (71)

I shall explain those words to someone who, say, only speaks French by means of the corresponding French words. But if a person has not yet got the *concepts*, I shall teach him to use the words by means of *examples* and by *practice.*—And when I do this I do not communicate less to him than I know myself. (208)

'But do you really explain to the other person what you yourself understand? Don't you get him to *guess* the essential thing? You give him examples,—but he has to guess their drift, to guess your intention.'—Every explanation which I can give myself I give him too. (210)

If I give anyone an order I feel it to be quite enough to give him signs. And I should never say: this is only words, and I have to get behind the words.

Equally, when I have asked someone something and he gives me an answer (i.e., a sign) I am content—that was what I expected—and I don't raise the objection: but that's a mere answer. (503)

But if you say: 'How am I to know what he means, when I see nothing but the signs he gives?' then I say: 'How is *he* to know what he means, when he has nothing but the signs either?' (504)

Suppose I said 'a b c d' and meant: the weather is fine. For as I uttered these signs I had the experience normally had only by someone who had year-in-year-out used 'a' in the sense of 'the', 'b' in the sense of 'weather', and so on.— Does 'a b c d' now mean: the weather is fine?

What is supposed to be the criterion for my having had *that* experience? (509)

An 'inner process' stands in need of outward criteria. (580)

Wittgenstein is generally thought to introduce the notion of private language (though not by name) in 243 (quoted on page 1 of this book). What is striking about that passage is the reference to private items which are to be what are named by words of this language. The existence of such a private subject-matter might then plausibly be thought to be an essential part of what makes a private language private. Wittgenstein's descriptions of publicity, however, put the matter in another perspective. For they do suggest something like PA. And if violation of PA is to be criterial for private language, then the existence of a private subject-matter—that is, private items to be named—is not essential. That it is not is suggested by this later definition of privacy:

And sounds which no one else understands but which I '*appear to understand*' might be called a 'private language'. (269)

This definition allows us to make sense out of the following cases as examples of 'private semantics'—hence, since that is argued to be impossible, of no genuine semantics at all:

Imagine someone using a line as a rule in the following way: he holds a pair of compasses, and carries one of its points along the line that is the 'rule', while the other one draws the line that follows the rule. And while he moves along the ruling line he alters the opening of the compasses, apparently with great precision, looking at the rule the whole time as if it determined what he did. And watching him we see no kind of regularity in this opening and shutting of the compasses. We cannot learn his way of following the line from it. (237)

That is a one-person case of private language (or a private semantic item) with no apparent private items for it to refer to. Here is a similar but multi-person case:

Let us imagine that the people in that country carried on the usual human activities and in the course of them employed, apparently, an articulate language. If we watch their behaviour we find it intelligible, it seems 'logical'. But when we try to learn their language we find it impossible to do so. For there is no regular connection between what they say, the sounds they make, and their actions . . . There is not enough regularity for us to call it 'language'. (207)

Imagine that Pia uses, audibly, the word, 'gronch'. She uses it to refer to, or describe, or classify, various items which are observable by us, and no others—some ashtrays, perhaps, along with certain neckties and goldfinches. So far, there is nothing hidden about her use of 'gronch'. Suppose, though, that though we can see to what items she applies 'gronch', we cannot catch on to her use of it, or at least there is an appearance that this is so. Either we never have any idea as to how 'gronch', as she means it, is to be used; or we have ideas, but they seem always to be contradicted by what she says. So wherever we think we see what it is that makes it correct to describe or classify something as 'gronch', or what would make that word true of something, Pia tells us that that is not it. She goes on to apply the word where it would not apply on our understanding of it, or refuses to apply it where it would; and she insists that it is she and not we who are correct. We become convinced that this situation would go on for ever; we will never succeed both in grasping the semantics of 'gronch' and in satisfying Pia that we had done so.

There are now a variety of attitudes we might take. Facts might show which of these attitudes is correct, though it might also be up to us simply to choose or adopt one of these. First, we might adopt the attitude of taking Pia at her word, to this extent: we conclude that it will never be the case that we will succeed in grasping what semantics 'gronch' has; for if it has one, then what that semantics is depends on, or perhaps consists in, facts in principle beyond our ken. In that case, 'gronch, though it speaks only of the public world, is private language. Which is to say, if Wittgenstein is right about private language, that it could not be the case that it had any semantics at all. Second, we might take the attitude that Pia is mistaken. She might be mistaken as to 'gronch' having any semantics at all. Or she might be mistaken in her view that it is a semantics that we have not, or at least could not grasp; that we could not see all the facts on which correct applications of 'gronch' depend. On that attitude, 'gronch' is perfectly ordinary language. We could be in a position, not only of understanding it correctly, but, doing so, of seeing that Pia had mistakenly described something in calling it 'gronch'. When we, and Pia, would then be in the position just described would, like questions as to what the semantics of 'gronch' is, then depend on the facts available to all of us. The way in which it would do so is the way which the present model of semantic fact has just described: Pia would count as mistaken, and we as correct when that is how a reasonable judge would react to the facts accessible to us all. The contrast between the first attitude and this second one shows what it would be like for there to be private language without private subject-matter.

Both Margaret Gilbert[12] and Crispin Wright[13] have suggested distinguishing two notions of privacy. One notion might be associated with Frege (in some of his moments). On it, there is some realm of semantic properties accessible to all, from which you and I (and English) might each choose, by chance, the same semantics to attach, me to my semantic item, you to yours, and English to some English expression. Privacy arises when (and only when) we consider which other facts determine which semantics each of us, respectively, has attached. For (some of) the facts which settle this question in my case may be inaccessible to you, and vice versa. So we could never know each other to have chosen the same semantics, or never be in a position to react in an informed way to the relevant facts by taking this to be so. If there are such (to others) inaccessible facts with such a role to play in determining the semantics of someone's semantic item, then, in this sense of privacy, that item is private language. We might call this privacy in the Fregean way.

The second sort of privacy we might associate with Russell, or at least the Russell of 1918.[14] On this notion, it is the semantics itself that is private: the semantics that I attach to my words is in principle unavailable to you for attaching to yours, and vice versa. (Recall that for 1918 Russell, meaning is reference, the reference of a genuine proper name *must* be a private object, and proper names lie at the foundation of logical analysis.) Where an item has that kind of semantics, we will say that it is private in the Russellian way. It is just this sort of privacy that Frege was so concerned to argue against in 'The Thought'[15] (coincidentally published in the same year as Russell's just-cited lectures on logical atomism).

The present notion of privacy certainly captures privacy of the Fregean sort. It also captures Russellian privacy. The semantics which other facts determine a Russellian semantic item to have could not be a matter for determination by the reactions of an indefinite number of novel judges, when an item's semantics, if it is private in the Russellian way, is not one that an indefinite number of judges could grasp, or take it to have at all. If the question is whether other facts

[12] In Gilbert [1983].
[13] See, e.g., Wright [1986b].
[14] See, e.g., Russell [1918], especially such passages as pp. 195–6.
[15] Frege [1918].

show the item to have semantics S or S*, that is a question that no more than one judge could even grasp. If S and S* are semantics of the Russellian sort, no more than one judge could even take an item to have them. *A fortiori*, at most one judge could grasp how, if at all, any other facts (public or not) bear on that question.

On the other hand, it is not clear that the present view of semantics leaves room for a sensible distinction between Fregean and Russellian privacy. Suppose that W is private in the Fregean way. So we can all grasp W's semantics in this sense: that is a semantics each of us could take *some* item to have; and we may all know what it would be for an item to have that semantics. In short, that is a way in which we *could* understand some item. *But*: W's having that semantics depends on some other facts which are beyond our ken, or to which we cannot properly relate so that they might properly and correctly lead us (reasonably) to take W to have that semantics. Now suppose, as Frege would, that there is some sub-part of W's semantics, S, which determines of which situations W is true: W is true of a situation just in case that is what S requires. Is this a possible state of affairs? For some situation, V, consider the property of being true of V. What determines whether W has this property? On the one hand, the answer must be: S—it is a matter of what S requires. But what does S require (on this question)? On the present view of semantics, that is a matter of the reactions of reasonable judges to the fact of an item's having S: S requires having the property of being true of V just in case that would be part of such reactions (or what they establish to be the reaction of a reasonable judge.) So that is a public matter. On the other hand, since W is Fregean-private, W's having or lacking the property of being true of V is a matter of the proper reaction to facts to which, by hypothesis (indefinitely many), reasonable judges cannot properly relate. So that is a private matter. But this is a contradiction. (One might think: S may be public semantics, but what it requires in a particular case may be private because the facts of that case—for example, relevant facts as to what situation V is like—are private (in the sense of violating PA). Chapter 8 will argue that that is not a genuine possibility. In any case, it amounts to just another way of reducing Fregean to Russellian privacy.) The upshot is that the present view leaves no room for the idea of a publicly graspable semantics, in the Fregean way, which requires further semantics in virtue of the way the private (PA-violating) facts are. Chapter 8 will explain more fully why this should be.

The present model of semantic facts, then, leaves no conceptual space for cases falling between Fregean and Russellian privacy. Seeing it as Wittgenstein's view is one way of seeing how he could, and why he would use the private language discussion as an attack on what is *common* to Frege and Russell (and to his earlier Tractarian self). His opponent is not (just) someone who endorses private language, or thinks he does, but someone whose views (perhaps inadvertently) deprive him (and us) of just those resources that privacy also strips away.

3

The Uses of Language Games

If the ideas of S-use sensitivity and, specifically, the S-use sensitivity of semantics are Wittgenstein's, where does he introduce them? I believe that they are introduced at the very beginning of the *Investigations* in discussing the notion of a language game. The present chapter arranges features of that discussion to show how these ideas are introduced, and some consequences Wittgenstein draws from them.

1. EXAMPLES

In the first eight paragraphs of the *Investigations*, Wittgenstein introduces five examples of language games. Later, for example, in 48, he introduces other examples for various special purposes. But he defines the notion in terms of these opening examples. These, together with minor variants on them, will do for present purposes. The examples are as follows:

I. 'I send someone shopping. I give him a slip marked, "five red apples" He takes the slip to the shopkeeper, who opens the drawer marked "apples"; then he looks up the word, "red", in a table and finds a colour sample opposite it; then he says the series of cardinal number words—I assume that he knows them by heart—up to the word, 'five', and for each number he takes an apple of the same colour as the sample out of the drawer.' (1)

II. 'A is building with building stones: there are blocks, pillars, slabs and beams. B has to pass the stones, and that in the order in which A needs them. For this purpose they use a language consisting of the words, "block", "pillar", "slab", "beam". A calls them out;—B brings the stone which he has learnt to bring at such-and-such call.' (2)

III. For teaching the language of 2, Wittgenstein introduces two further games. In the first of these, 'the learner names the objects; that is, he utters the word when the teacher points to the stone.'

IV. The second of the two teaching games consists of 'this still simpler exercise: the pupil repeats the words after the teacher.' (7)

V. Wittgenstein also considers a more complicated variant of game II, as follows (8): 'Besides the four words, "block", "pillar", etc., let it contain a series of words used as the shopkeeper in (1) used the numerals (it can be a series of letters of the alphabet); further, let there be two words, which may as well be, "there" and "this" (because this roughly indicates their purpose), that are used in connection with a pointing gesture; and finally a number of colour samples. A gives an order like: "d-slab-there". At the same time he shows the assistant a colour sample, and when he says, "there", he points to a place on the building site. From the stock of slabs B takes one for each letter of the alphabet up to "d", of the same colour as the sample, and brings them to the place indicated by A.—On other occasions A gives the order, "this—here". At "this" he points to a building stone. And so on.'

In terms of these examples, Wittgenstein defines the notion language game as follows (7):

We can also think of the whole process of using words in (2) as one of those games by means of which children learn their native language. I will call these games 'language games' and will speak of a primitive language as a language game.

And the processes of naming the stones and repeating words after someone might also be called language-games. Think of much of the use of words in children's chanting games.

I shall also call the whole, consisting of language and the actions into which it is woven, the 'language-game'.

Language games can be regarded quite literally as games. We could, for example, easily write down rules for playing game II, perhaps as follows:

This games is to be played by two players in turns. It is to be begun by player 1 (the 'builder'.) The possible moves in the game are as follows:

Player 1: If it is player 1's turn, then he may move either by saying, 'block', or by saying, 'slab', or by saying, 'beam', or by saying, 'pillar'.

Player 2: If it is player 2's turn, then he may move as follows: if

player 1 has said, 'slab', then he may move by bringing 1 a
slab; if 1 has said, 'pillar', then he may move by bringing 1 a
pillar; if 1 has said, 'beam', then he may move by bringing 1
a beam; if 1 has said, 'block', then he may move by bringing
1 a block.
The above are all the permissible moves in the game.

There are various things which might be an aspect of playing some
game which the above rules do not yet make part of this one. For
example, we have not yet defined what winning would be. The game
could be specified in this respect. For example, we could say that player
1 has won if player 2 is left with no legitimate move. Perhaps player 2
cannot win, but might derive satisfaction from holding out as long as
possible. On the other hand, no such further features need be
incorporated into the game. We have not said why anyone might play a
game like the above. More important, we have not said what might
make it the case that they were. These are both important questions
about language games. But we are not yet ready to face them.

Language games, we will take it, are abstract objects specified by
their rules, so that A is the same language game as B just in case any
statement of A's rules is a statement of B's rules and vice versa.
Language games may be ours to specify or construct. (We may hope to
use some such constructions in describing language, or some episodes
of using it. That, too, is a later part of the story.) When we construct a
game, it and its rules are exactly whatever we say they are (and
whatever what we thus say entails). Once a game has been specified,
there may be a matter of fact as to whether further talk of some game is
talk of that game. Where there is thus a fact of the matter, the above
criterion settles what that fact is.

Given the intended uses of language games, we will adopt the
convention that a game counts as having been specified only when it
counts as clear what complying with its rules requires, and what
would count as following or violating them. But this clarity must be an
S-use sensitive matter. Suppose, for example, that in some episode of
playing II, player 1 says, 'slab', and, before 2 has responded, says,
'pillar'. Nothing in the rules of II, as specified, says explicitly what a
turn is to consist in. There are games in which one must do just one
thing licensed by the rules, and then wait until the opponent has
similarly made a move. There are others in which one may keep
moving until eliciting a response from the opponent. The rules do not
state that II is the one sort of game or the other. Moreover, if player 1
has moved correctly, then nothing in the rules says explicitly what 2's
response may be. May 2 bring only a slab, or only a pillar, or may he

bring a slab and a pillar? There are plausible candidate understandings of the rules on which any of these responses might be allowed, and understandings on which they would not. Nothing in the rules says which of these understandings is correct. Does our statement of II, then, count as a specification of a game? Is it clear what the rules as stated require?

One point to be made here is that different statements of the rules which were stated as II's rules may be to be understood in different ways in the above respects, depending on the circumstances in which they were made. For example, different statements in which it is said that if it is your turn, then you may say, 'slab' may be to be understood differently in such respects. For there may be different things to be understood as to what, in them, a turn is to be taken to be. Sometimes what would count as a turn is such that 1 took two of them above, and sometimes not. That one thing or another is to be taken so to count may be part of the proper understanding of some such statement. So if we know that II was stated in stating rules which say the above, and know no more about the proper understanding of that statement, then it may be an open question whether the rules as stated, or as they were properly understood to be, do or do not settle the above issues.

It is plausible, though, that nothing about the above statement of the rules of II makes its proper understanding one which settles these issues. Suppose that that is so. Still, we might take the rules as stated above to be perfectly clear, and that statement of them to be a perfectly clear statement of the rules of a game, as long as we are not concerned with episodes like those described above, and as long as we are not called upon to classify episodes like that as in accord with, or in violation of, the rules—as long, as it were, as we do not have applications of the rules like that in mind, or they are not to be taken as ones of proper concern. Whether that condition is satisfied is, of course, an S-use sensitive matter. When such a condition is satisfied for episodes which a proper understanding of the rules as stated would leave us unable to classify, we will take it that that statement does count as a clear specification of a game. That is why the clarity of concern here is an S-use sensitive notion.

Why allow clarity to be S-use sensitive in this way? The brief answer is this. We might amend the statement of the rules of II so that they explicitly say what resolves the above issues. But there is no reason to think that we could amend it, or any statement of any rules, so that similar problems would not arise for other potential episodes. For any problem, we can formulate rules so as to avoid it, perhaps, but for any formulation of rules, there will be problems we have not avoided. The reasons for thinking this have already been stated in chapter 1. So if what is demanded for clarity is that there should be no potential episodes which do not determinately classify as complying with the rules as stated or not, then there can be no such thing as clarity, and one could never say what any given game was. But if that much is not demanded, the result is an S-use sensitive notion of clarity on the lines described. Such a notion will serve our purposes as well as any notion could.

It is worth mentioning one final possibility. We specified II by stating certain rules. We then said that different statements of those rules might be to be understood in different ways. But *if* semantics is S-use sensitive, then a *given* statement of those rules may be to be understood in different ways on different occasions for considering it. On some occasion, it may be perfectly clear anyway what would count as a turn. What the rules as stated count as requiring on such an occasion may differ from what they count as requiring on an occasion on which there is nothing besides that statement of the rules to make this clear. So a given rule, as specified in a given statement of it, may count as requiring different things on different occasions. Correspondingly, on different occasions, different ways of stating rules may count as correct ways of stating what the rules of game A require. So which statements of rules count as statements of the rules of game A is liable to vary across occasions. The thought then arises that on different occasions there may be different correct answers to the question whether game B counts as being game A, for some A and B. For the moment, though, we leave this as speculation.

Note that whether the rules of a given game are being followed is quite independent of the question whether what was done in doing so was sensible, given the activity of which playing the game was a part. A builder is paving a forecourt and obviously needs a slab. So he says, 'pillar'. Stupid, no doubt. But if it is game II that was being played, then his move is correct according to the rules. One could construct other games for which compliance would coincide with good sense in this case. II is not such a game. As we will see, the possibility of such further games has much to do with the question which language games are being played in given episodes.

2. NAMING

Games I-V, aside from introducing the notion language game, are produced in aid of some philosophical point. The point, apparently, has something to do with naming. For Wittgenstein begins the *Investigations* with a passage from Augustine on language learning, on which he makes the following comment (1):

These words, it seems to me, give us a particular picture of the essence of human language. It is this: the words of a language name objects—sentences are combinations of such names.—In this picture of language we find the roots of the idea: every word has a meaning (*Bedeutung.*) This meaning is correlated with the word. It is the object for which the word stands.

Augustine does not speak of any distinction between sorts of words. . . .

Wittgenstein does not mind construing naming broadly: not only proper names name, but so do any words which may be said to mean, or speak of, what, on the most generous view, might be regarded as an item, or class of them. So, for example, 'red' may be said to name red, or the colour red, 'bicycle' bicycles, and perhaps even 'walk' walking. The points to be made about this picture hold no matter how widely or narrowly naming is construed.

The view attributed to Augustine appears to concern two relations:[1] one between words and what they name, and one between naming and meaning. The first relation, which we will call the naming relation, is one in which every expression stands to an item just in case it names that item. On the Augustinian picture, it is one which every meaningful expression is supposed to bear to something. The second relation is meant to individuate meaning: if words W name V, then any words would mean what W do iff those words name V. Meaning what it does is then the only thing W could do consistent with its naming V. Moreover, it is the only thing any expression could do consistent with its naming that. If we think of there being some domain of possible meanings for words to have, then this relation correlates items from that domain with items to be named: for every item to be named, there is the correlated meaning that words would have just in case they named exactly that. But reification here is optional. At least, on the picture, if we say truly that W names V, then we have said what could only be true of it given that it means what it does. Hence we have said what identifies and fixes that which it does mean. (As will emerge, the reified and unreified theses here are quite distinct, and the differences matter. But for the moment they can remain unattended to.)

It is tempting to suppose that Wittgenstein's attack is directed at one of the above two theses—either at the idea that every meaningful expression names something, or at the idea that the naming relation is individuative of meaning. In fact, Wittgenstein does find something wrong with each of these ideas as just stated. But the present suggestion will be that the main brunt of his attack is directed

---

[1] It does so if *Bedeutung* is construed as meaning 'meaning' in the ordinary sense in which, for example, an English word may mean this or that—as *Bedeutung* well can do in German. But *Bedeutung* can also mean, in effect, *referent*, in which case the two points to be mentioned collapse into one: a point concerning the relation between meaning and correct or proper use.

elsewhere. So we will first note that there are at least some textual indications against putting too much weight on either of the above two targets. The point about the first one has been noticed before. It is that Wittgenstein introduces his simple language games, or at least II, as illustrations of cases the Augustinian description would fit. For II is introduced in 2 by saying, 'Let us imagine a language for which the description given by Augustine is right.' To further emphasize the point, he says, in 48, discussing a certain Socratic account of 'simples' or 'logical atoms', 'Let us apply the method of 2 to this account in the *Theatetus*. Let us consider a language game for which this account is really valid.' The technique of 2, as applied in II, then, cannot be meant to show that not all words are names.

The idea that the discussion of language games has the second idea as a primary target runs up against two somewhat different problems. The first is signalled by this passage (10):

Now what do the words of this language *signify* (bezeichnen)?—What is supposed to show what they signify, if not the kind of use they have? And we have already described that. So we are asking for the expression, 'This word *signifies* this' to be made a part of the description.

Looked at in this way, 'A names/signifies B' is going to be some sort of accretion on an already satisfactory account of the use of A (and thereby of its meaning). It will state a fact which somehow supervenes on the facts already stated in that other description. If the expression needs to be *made* part of such descriptions, so given a role in them, then it is to some extent up to us to say just what sort of an accretion this is to be. Whether it is true that everything names something, for example, may well depend on how we make this part of our descriptions. But the same may hold for the relation between what a word names and what it means. Perhaps we can construct the accretion so that naming just follows along with meaning, in so far as there is anything to follow.

This suggestion of indefiniteness in theses about naming is continued in 13:

When we say, 'Every word in language signifies something.' we have so far said *nothing whatever*; unless we have explained exactly *what* distinction we wish to make.

Whether or not it is up to us to *decide* how our talk of naming will go, there is at least something which the concept of naming leaves open about how it is to go. There are a variety of distinct things which might be said to be so in saying that A names B. Where not enough has been filled in to determine what we would be saying in saying things of this form, there is not enough background to determine what we would be saying in saying that every word signifies something. In particular, not enough to determine that we must be saying something false. So the concept of naming must not be enough by itself to determine that any such thing to be said must be false. If we have said nothing whatever in saying that every word of a language signifies something, then *inter alia* we have said nothing false. But if it is that open what one says in speaking of naming, one might well think that—without appropriate background—we would similarly say nothing in saying that naming individuates meaning. So again, *inter alia*, nothing false.

The second problem is that Wittgenstein does not mean to deny the common-sense thought that we often can explain to someone what a word means by telling him what it names. Some nuancing is sometimes called for: the Dutch *berg* means, or, indifferently, names, mountains; but it is sometimes important to add that it is commonly used to refer to hills (and sometimes to heaps as well). But the need for nuancing does not change the main point: in giving such explanations, we do tell people what words mean. Wittgenstein accepts such things, for example, in 32, where he says,

Someone coming into a strange country will sometimes learn the language of the inhabitants from ostensive definitions that they give him; and he will often have to *guess* the meaning of these definitions; and will guess sometimes right and sometimes wrong.

That is, he sometimes will, and sometimes will not, guess the object of the ostension; what the word in question names.

The common-sense thought does not by itself decide in favour of the second Augustinian thesis. What is true of a word in virtue of its meaning what it does (and so how this compares with what is true of it in virtue of its naming what it does) is, on its face, a distinct question from what someone must be told in order to come to understand a word, or to know what it means. Perhaps we can explain to someone what a word means by telling him less, or other than what individuates what it means. Perhaps he must guess the rest, or our explanation only works against some background of what he knows already. (Though the idea that, in our ordinary explanations of meaning, we say anything less than *what the word means* is a singularly unWittgensteinian one.) But then it remains so far obscure what the difference could be between what specifies what a word means and what one might say in telling a non-understander of it what it means. Pending an account of what Wittgenstein takes this difference to be, it is impossible to see what Wittgenstein would be denying—or better, affirming—in denying the link between what a word names and what it means. And it is hard to see how any such account is to be extracted from the language game discussion. If, where a word does name something, there are aspects of its meaning which are left up for grabs by the facts about what it names, it remains to say what these aspects are. When we have a better grasp of Wittgenstein's view of the aspects there are to the meaning of a word, and the properties it has by, or in, meaning what it does, I think we will not be inclined to view the second Augustinian thesis as the main focus of his concern.

It is a natural thought that we might use language games as intermediate objects for studying such questions as what words mean in a language (for example, in English), or what is so of them in virtue of their meaning what they do. Our questions concern the relation between what words in a language mean and what they name. We might find simpler though related questions if we asked what words in a language game named or meant. For the facts, if there are any, in this intermediate case, must be fixed by the rules of the language game. And in enough cases, at least, we know what those rules are, because they are what we say they are. So we may be able to isolate the effect given rules would have for what a word meant, or for what it named, and hence the effect in such matters of given facts about how the word was to be used (and taken). For the present, we will put aside questions of meaning. We can then find in the language game discussion some clear and crucial theses concerning, in the first instance, the relation between facts about a language game and at least one class of facts about what a word names, namely, the fact, for some V, that it names V.

The first half of the main point has already been made in the cited part of 10. Let us say that a word, W, occurs in, or is part of a language game G just in case W is to be spoken in the making of some permissible move in G. Then the point is that if we are to speak of words as naming things in games they occur in, then the facts as to what they name must be fixed by, and so supervene, on the rules of the game. As for what W names in G, there is simply nothing else for such facts to depend on. So a grasp of the rules of G must provide what is needed for grasping or perceiving the facts as to what W names in G (assuming an adequate general grasp of the concept of naming). As one might put it, there is a route from the rules of the game to the facts as to what words which occur in it name; a grasp of the rules provides a path to those facts. For example, given the rules of II, it would be correct to say that, in it, 'slab' names slabs. Or, more precisely, for most purposes, and the most easily imagined ones, it would be correct to say this. That is a description we can recognize to fit a word which is to be used in the way 'slab' is to be used in II. It is enough to rely on our intuitions, or recognition abilities, for seeing this—provided those intuitions are robust enough. The point is just that the rules of II do determine the above fact about what 'slab' names; the present aim is not to show how to derive that fact from the rules.

For the second half of the main point, we need to ask the obvious question: how do things work in the reverse direction? What sort of a route, if any, is there from the facts about what a word names in a game to the facts about the rules that govern it in the game; the standards for its correct use, and the standards of correctness which govern it as used correctly? Later in the *Investigations*, in the midst of the private language discussion, Wittgenstein refers back to the early discussion of the Augustinian picture. He makes his view on this point clear by quoting with disapproval the following idea (264):

'Once you know what the word stands for, you understand it, you know its whole use.'

On his view, what a word stands for or names does not determine its whole use. So if you know what it names, you do not thereby know what its (proper) use is. The point, he takes it, is of some importance when it comes to seeing why private language is not possible. For the present, though, the point is that there is no route back from the facts as to what words in a game name to the standards of correctness which govern those words in the game, nor to the rules which impose these standards. So there is an asymmetry here between facts about the rules of the game, and the standards of correctness they impose, on the one hand, and the facts as to what words which occur in the game name on the other.

If there is no route back from facts about naming to facts about the standards of correctness which govern words, then that must be because any given set of facts as to what a word, or a set of words, name is compatible with any of a variety of distinct and conflicting standards of correctness—in terms of language games, with a variety of distinct and conflicting sets of rules which might govern those words, compatible with those facts as to what they name. As Wittgenstein puts this point,

What is the relation between name and thing named?—Well, what is it? Look at language game (2) [II] or at another one: there you can see the sort of thing this relation consists in. This relation may also consist, among other things, in the fact that hearing the name calls before the mind the picture of what is named; and it also consists, among other things, in the name's being written on the thing named or being pronounced when that thing is pointed at. (37)

Naming appears as a *queer* connection of a word with an object.—And you really get such a queer connection when the philosopher tries to bring out *the* relation between name and thing by staring at an object in front of him and repeating a name or even the word 'this' innumerable times. For philosophical problems arise when language *takes a holiday*. (38)

Wittgenstein describes what naming consists in by describing a family of different things, rather than any one essential thing, which might make us say of some W and some V that W named V. He denies that there is any one essential thing that would make it correct to say this. Moreover, he refrains from describing the consequences of the various things that might make us say that W names V. For example, suppose that, as Wittgenstein suggests, V has W written on it. In the right circumstances, that might make us say that W named V. But what are the consequences of W's being written on V? What does that fact have to do with how W is to be used? To see that, we have to look at the rules of the game in which W occurs. And the facts Wittgenstein cites tell us little or nothing about what those rules would be like.

To see how facts about naming underdetermine standards of correctness, we will consider two simple examples. The first begins with a further language game, which Wittgenstein describes in 15:

> VI. 'Suppose that the tools A uses in building bear certain marks. When A shows the assistant such a mark, he brings the tool that has that mark on it.' Take this to specify an elaboration of V, with V enriched by the obvious additional permissible moves for A and obligatory responses to them by B.

In 41, Wittgenstein raises a problem about this game:

In 15 we introduced proper names into language (8) [language game V]. Now suppose that the tool with the name 'N' is broken. Not knowing this, A gives B the sign 'N'. Has this sign meaning now or not?—What is B to do when he is given it?—We have not settled anything about this. One might ask: what *will* he do? Well, perhaps he will stand there at a loss, or show A the pieces. . . . But we could also imagine a convention whereby B has to shake his head in reply if A gives him the sign belonging to a tool that is broken.

This problem suggests, among other things, two additional language games we might construct:

> VII. Like VI but with the extra stipulation that if player 1 moves by naming a tool which is broken or missing (having used a name occurring in the game) then player 2 has no permissible move. In that case, 2 loses the game.
>
> VIII. Like VI except with an extra rule which states that where player 1 moves as in VII, player 2 may respond by shaking his head. In that case, player 1 loses the game.

Game VI, as it stands, does not provide any permissible move for B in the problem situation. Nor does it provide any relevant standards of correctness which govern B at that point. So it does not determine a solution to Wittgenstein's problem. Games VII and VIII each determine a solution to that problem, but the solutions are conflicting ones. Game VII, like VI, provides B with no permissible move in the problem situation. Unlike VI, though, it does provide a relevant standard of correctness which governs B. B is obligated to make a correct move; if he does not, then he loses the game. Game VIII, unlike either VI or VII, does provide B with a permissible move. Moreover, it supplies a standard of correctness governing A such that we can say that, in it, A has moved incorrectly, in the problem situation, and hence has lost the game. So if the problem situation were to arise, the rules of VI, VII, and VIII would each yield different results for it. The rules of VI would leave the state of play indeterminate; the rules of VII would dictate that A had won, so that B and not A had failed to meet the required standards of correctness; and the rules of VIII would do just the reverse, dictating that B had won, and A but not B had failed to meet the required standards. Now the crucial point is this: if W is the name of the tool, and V the tool, then it is equally correct to say that W names V as it occurs in VI, VII and VIII. That is something it does in all those games. So the fact that W names V is compatible with any of the above results, among others, depending on which game W occurs in, and what the rules are which make it correct to say that W names V.

Consider a second example. In a playing of II, player 1 calls, 'slab'. Player 2 goes to the supply dump, and finds no slabs except one with a corner missing. Or perhaps one broken in two. He brings the two halves. The rules of II fail to determine whether 2 has moved correctly in this sense: there is nothing in the rules which *says* whether a slab in two halves is to be counted as a slab. If we did regard the two halves as a slab for the purpose, then we would say that 2 was in compliance with the rules. If we regarded them as a slab no more, then we would not count 2 as in compliance. As a matter of fact, in daily life, we sometimes do and sometimes do not count a slab in two halves as a slab, and sometimes do each thing correctly, depending on our purposes in treating (or speaking of) the halves in one way or the other. As we will see later, we might also have occasion for correctly regarding 2's move as in compliance, and occasion for correctly regarding it as not, depending on the circumstances in which we consider that playing of II. In any case, we certainly can define two further games as follows:

IX. Like II, with the added stipulation that 2 shall count as having brought a slab if he has brought a slab that had been divided in two.

X. Like II, with the added stipulation that 2 will not count as having brought a slab unless he brings an intact slab (in one piece).

IX and X contrast with II in the obvious ways with respect to the above situation. In IX, 2, in that situation, is determinately in compliance with the rules of the game; his move comes up to whatever standards of correctness those rules impose. In X, 2, in that situation, is determinately in violation of the rules; his move fails the standards of correctness that that game imposes. Again the crucial point is that it is equally correct to say of any of these games that 'slab' as it occurs in them names slabs. So the fact that 'slab' names slabs in some game is compatible with any of these results, among others.

The conclusion so far is that the facts as to which items given words name (or refer to, or stand for) radically underdetermine the standards for the correct use of those words, or the standards to which use of those words would be subject in language games for which those facts hold. In the simplest case, as illustrated by II, suppose that a word, W, names an item, V. Then there is a triple of language games, in each of which W is a permissible move, and in each of which W names V, which divide over episodes as follows. There are some concrete speakings of W, in given possible circumstances, and also some specific doings in response to such speakings, such that, supposing W so spoken to refer to V, these speakings would be correct moves according to the rules of one member of the triple, incorrect moves according to the rules of another, and not determinately correct or incorrect (at least *tout court*) according to the rules of the third. Similarly for the responses to W. In the more general case, suppose that W is a string of words. Specify any set of facts you like as to what parts of W name, refer to, or stand for. Then there are triples of games in all of which W is a permissible move, such that all of the specified facts hold for each member of each triple, or, in the case where the specification allows a part of W to vary its reference from speaking to speaking—as, for example, Wittgenstein's 'this' and 'here' in V—the specified principles of variation, if any, hold for each member of each triple, and the specified referent, if any, is the referent, in each game, for each episode to be considered, and such that there are episodes over which the members of these triples differ as *per* the above. In fact, we may suppose that each member of such a triple has exactly the same vocabulary as each of the others, and that if any bit of this vocabulary names or stands for V in one member of the triple, then it does so in all.

Moreover, the examples point to an even stronger conclusion. In the simple case, if W names (or etc.) V, then for any episode which is either a speaking of W or a response to such a speaking, there is some triple of games, in each of which W is a permissible move and names V, such that that episode is a correct move in one of these games, incorrect in another, and neither determinately the one nor the other (at least *tout court*) in the third. So, in the simple case, if, under given conditions, W was spoken, or responded to by doing A, in the playing of a game in which W names V, then that fact is compatible with W's having been a correct move, or an incorrect move, or not determinately either. The parallel point holds for the more general case. That is what will be meant here by saying that facts about naming which hold in a game radically underdetermine the standards of correctness for uses in that game.

3. THE COMPLEMENT

Hilary Putnam, in *Reason, Truth and History*,[2] has proposed something like the converse of the thesis just presented. He states his thesis as, in the first instance, about the relation between truth conditions, for whatever words have them, and reference or naming, for the relevant parts of words with truth conditions. But he does not mean his thesis to turn specifically on the notion of truth. He is willing to include within his category of what underdetermines the facts of reference fulfilment conditions, obedience conditions, and whatever other rules or 'operational constraints' might link words with action or observation. To take Putnam's example, 'cat' names cats, we all suppose. But words including the word 'cat', such as 'The cat is on the mat' *could* be such as to be true, acceptable, or any other kind of correct you like, in or of exactly the situations they now are, while it was so that 'cat' referred to cherries rather than cats. *In some sense*, the hypothesis that 'cat' refers to cherries is compatible with all the facts as to the situations of which words including 'cat' are true, or in which they are correct.

As we will see, Wittgenstein has no argument against Putnam's point, and, moreover, no reason to resist it. In fact, it is a point Wittgenstein ought to welcome, given his general views on semantics. But if that is so, then there is an apparent problem. I have just argued for an asymmetry between facts about naming and facts about the rules or standards of correctness of a given language game: there is, it

[2] Putnam [1981].

was urged, a route from the former to the latter, but no route back in the opposite direction. But truth conditions, and the other things Putnam mentions, may certainly be regarded as standards of correctness. And Putnam's point, at first sight, is that there is no route from them to facts about what words name. If that point is correct, then it might seem that there is no route in either direction. Hence, no asymmetry either. To think this would be, I think, to misunderstand Putnam's point. But then that claim must now be discussed.

Putnam's point does not directly concern language games. Nor, I think, is it properly seen as directly concerning language or at least a language, such as English.[3] Rather, it is directly concerned with speech behaviour. Or, to make the point more palatable, with speech episodes. Suppose that we confront some collection of speech episodes, or speakings, and consider the problem of correctly assigning a semantics to it. We may suppose ourselves to know that the episodes are all speakings of some particular language, L. We may also suppose that we know the lexicon and syntax of L. So we can recognize what the words are in the speakings of concern, and also when those speakings are and are not speakings of full sentences, and which sentences those are. Suppose that, in addition to all this, we know one other class of fact: for any L-ish sentence, S, and any set of possible situations, we can divide these into ones S is true of and ones S is not true of. For example, we might be equipped with a Delphic oracle who does these things for us. So we can have as large a collection of facts as we like to the effect that S is (was, would be) true of this situation, and is/was not true of that one. Since it is the semantics of the words in question that we aim to discover, let us take seriously for the moment the idea that the above is all we know about the speakings in question, and about L. The question is, what does that tell us about the further semantics of those words? One sort of semantic fact is the fact, for some L-ish word, W, that W names cats, for example. Now Putnam's point can be put this way: suppose that there is an assignment of semantics to the words in question on which that fact is a fact, where this assignment is consistent with all the facts we have granted ourselves so far. Then there is another overall assignment of semantics, also consistent with all those facts, on which W names cherries. And, of course, there is an indefinite number of further assignments on which W names whatever you like.

---

[3] I do not claim that Putnam would agree that this is the right way to look at it. I believe, mostly from personal conversation, that Putnam is very sympathetic with the idea of S-use sensitivity, and particularly with semantic S-use sensitivity. Yet he often ignores that idea in his writing for example, in supposing that (effective) truth conditions might be associated with (English) sentences. The reason, I suspect, is ease of exposition. But that I cannot prove.

Words, we may recall, have no intrinsic semantics. So words having the semantic properties they do must depend on other facts about them: for any semantic property P of W, had enough other facts about W been different enough, in ways they conceivably could have been, it would not have been a fact that W had P. Change W's history enough in other respects, and you can change any particular bit of its semantics you like. Putnam points to an apparent problem with this. He selects a particular class of semantic properties, namely ones, for various V, of naming or referring to V. He then picks out a class of other facts on which the having of those properties might plausibly be thought to depend. He then shows that for any property of naming V, no set of these other facts, no matter which of them obtain, *entails*, for any W, that W has that property: we could consistently suppose both that all those other facts held of W, and that W, did not have the property of naming V. Let us generalize this thesis. Rather than confining ourselves to properties of naming V, let us let it apply to any semantic property at all, And rather than confining attention to the plausible other facts Putnam suggests (now where they *do* count as *other* facts) let the other facts, for property P, be *any* identifiable facts about W, whether or not about W's semantics—with the exception of the fact that W has P (and further excepting facts as to the reactions of a reasonable judge to all the other facts about W). The thesis is then that, for any semantic property P, there are (and could be) no identifiable other facts which would entail that W has P, in the sense of 'entail' just described. As suggested in the last chapter, this thesis is central to Wittgenstein's conception of semantics. That is why Wittgenstein *must* accept Putnam's thesis as stated so far.

As mentioned, Putnam points to an apparent *problem*. Intuitively, we all think that there are, often enough, facts about what words refer to—that, for example, it is a fact that 'cat' does not refer to cherries. But how could it be that other facts determine what these facts about reference are, when we cannot identify any other facts which *require* any given set of facts about reference to hold (where 'require' means 'entails' in the above sense)? Some have been puzzled by this. Some—though not Putnam—have been led by such puzzlement to be sceptical as to there *being* facts—or at least determinate ones—as to what words refer to. On Wittgenstein's view, there is no puzzle, and such scepticism is misplaced. The cornerstone of his view is that entailment, in the above sense, is just not the way in which other facts about them select a semantics for words. Rather, other facts have the effects they do *via* the reactions to them of a reasonable judge. Reasonable judges—and so indirectly we—are the instruments (perhaps occasion-sensitive ones) for classifying states of affairs into ones which do, and

ones which do not, count as W's having P. Putnam, I think, would
agree with this. If that is so, then problems of reference must be solved,
where they have solutions, by looking at the reactions of reasonable
judges to appropriate other facts. Given the role of such judges as
classifiers of states of affairs, there is no reason to expect such
problems generally to lack solutions.

Wittgenstein's asymmetry between facts about naming and facts
about correctness conditions (or rules of a language game) is one that is
meant to hold when the reactions of reasonable judges are in. That is
why there is an asymmetry. Putnam, too, has a point to make which
holds given those reactions as we know them to be. But given it,
Wittgenstein's asymmetry remains an asymmetry. To see this, we
must begin with some care about what Putnam's selected other facts
are. Putnam is interested in the relation between facts about reference
(facts, for various W and V, that W refers to V), and other semantic
facts—centrally, for words in which W occurs, facts that these words
are true of (or in) certain situations and untrue in others. So the interest
is in the relation between properties of referring to V and—centrally,
but not exclusively—truth-involving properties. Putnam puts this by
saying that he is interested in the relation between reference and truth
(or other correctness) conditions. But to speak of truth *conditions* in
connection with the facts Putnam mentions is at least misleading.[4] To
see how it is is to see both the value and correctness of Putnam's point
and that Wittgenstein's asymmetry remains after the point is taken
into account. The easiest way to see this will be to model the issues
raised here in the more limited and easily described domain of
language games.

Putnam's point is not directly about language games. But it can be
made to apply there. Suppose, again, that we begin with a collection of
episodes of speech and other behaviour. Again, we can recognize all the
words and sentences. We are told that these episodes are all, *inter alia*,
the playing of some game G—that is, the making of some move meant
to be a move in G. We do not know which game G is. Again, we are
equipped with a Delphic oracle. So we can amass an unlimited array of
facts to the effect that such-and-such episode was in compliance with
the rules, or a correct move, and such-and-such episode was in
violation of the rules. Suppose that the word, 'slab', is spoken from
time to time in playing G, and that moreover it is at least occasionally
a correct move, so that we know that G is a game in which 'slab' is a

---

[4] Although not necessarily incorrect. There is an ambiguity in the English
'conditions' which shows up in the difference between 'conditions under which P is true'
and 'conditions for P's being true'—the distinction between, e.g., the Dutch *omstandig-heden* and *voorwaarden*. Putnam has in mind, I think, *one* notion of *omstandigheden*.

permissible move (under some conditions or other). A possible hypothesis would be that, in G, 'slab' names slabs. Suppose that there is an overall hypothesis as to what game G, is on which that hypothesis about 'slab' is correct, where this is consistent with all the facts we have allowed ourselves access to. Then, Putnam would tell us, there is also such an overall hypothesis, consistent with all these facts, given which 'slab' names bicycles. And so on.

The point here, once again, is that the other facts to which we have allowed ourselves access *via* the oracle, etc., do not determine which game G is, in the sense that there is, *tout court*, just one game whose being played is consistent with those facts. That is to say that they do not determine what the rules of G are. But when we see that that is the point, we see that our asymmetry is so far untouched. There is no route from a certain sort of fact about correct episodes—no matter how bountiful the facts of that sort may be—to facts as to what words in G name. But then there is no route from those facts to the rules of G either. This gives us, so far, no reason to doubt that there is a route from the rules of G to the facts as to what words which occur in G name. It remains so that there is no route from the facts as to what the words name to the rules of G. The rules of G and the facts about naming in G are, of course, on a par with respect to a third class of fact: the facts we might learn through the oracle. That, I have said, is the welcome conclusion.

It was supposed initially that those of us with a good enough grasp of the concept of naming can simply recognize certain facts about naming within a language game—the fact, for example, that it would be correct (for most purposes) to say of II that in it 'slab' names slabs. What Putnam's point shows, I think, is something about what this recognitional ability depends on. Part of the reason we have for accepting the above description of II is that the rules of II speak of *slabs*. They say, for example, that when player 1 says 'slab', player 2 is to bring a slab. They mention slabs and not, for example, bicycles. We know that because we know what the rules of II are. After all, we are the ones who said what they are.

Even so, there may be special purposes for which it would remain incorrect to say that 'slab' names slabs if that is meant to rule out that 'slab' may correctly be said to name bicycles. In special circumstances, there might be reason for regarding the whole game in a special way— as taking a word which means bicycles, or which might just as well be taken to name bicycles, and imposing special conventions on it which required responding to it by bringing slabs. (As there *could* be a game which required bringing a slab when you heard the word 'bicycle', even though that word continued to mean *bicycle*). Or we might, on occasion, have one or another set of special reasons for not taking the fact that the rules mention slabs as deciding what 'slab' names. (For example, the fact that we already know 'slab' to be part of a language, used in the game, in which it means something else.) In such special circumstances, there might count as being no fact of the matter as to whether 'slab' names slabs as opposed to bicycles. There may be *something* correct to be said in saying it to name either.

Special reasons are called for, though, for any of these above conclusions to be correct. For it takes something special about the case, or our relation to it, to make such a thing a *reasonable* reaction. It is not that without them there is anything like a 'logical compulsion' (whatever that would be) to take 'slab' in the game to name slabs. But that, and not some competing option, is what we would naturally find to be a reasonable redescription of game II. That is a way of making sense of II for us. Saying that 'slab' named bicycles would not be a way for us to make sense of the game. It would simply remain a mystery how it could do that, given that its rules are as they are. That is what makes the first description and not the second correct (where it is so). It is our reactions which count. For us to have them, where indicative of what a reasonable judge would do, is for the facts about naming to be what they are—*inter alia*, what we say them to be in saying 'slab' in II to name slabs.

Returning to Putnam's original problem, we may now notice something about the notion of a truth condition. We are apt to think of a truth condition as parallel with a rule of a language game; as something which tells us when, or under what conditions, such-and-such would be true. It tells us that by speaking of, or mentioning such-and-such, and not by mentioning such-and-such else. That is certainly the way Frege thought of truth conditions. As noted earlier, we are not compelled to think of truth conditions in this way: for an English speaker, conditions may be *Umstände* as well as *Bedingungen*, where the former, but not the latter, admit Putnam's construal. If we do thus think of them as *Bedingungen*, though, then I think we are not landed with Putnam's result. The facts Putnam refers to under the heading of truth conditions—the facts the oracle might amass for us—do not determine what words refer to. But then, nor do they determine the truth conditions for words on the above understanding of a truth condition. On the other hand, if what given words require for their truth is that some cat be on some mat, and not satisfaction of some more complicated condition involving cherries, then we may find it incompatible with that that some part of those words should refer to cherries rather than cats—incompatible in the sense that it is unreasonable to describe them as doing so. And the fact that the other condition is more complicated may sometimes be part of the reason why the cat's being on the mat is exactly what those words do require for their truth.

So far, we know what the rules of a game are because we say what they are. We have not yet addressed the problem how we would know, or what would make it so of any given sequence of episodes or performances, that they were, or were correctly regardable as, a playing of some given language game, G, rather than, say, some other one, G*. Putnam's thesis calls our attention to the fact that we have not done this, and to some of the importance of that problem. But there are still other matters to attend to first before we are in a position to do that.

4. TRUTH

The facts as to what words name radically underdetermine the standards of correctness for the use of those words in games in which they may occur. We can now say more about what sort of correctness is left undetermined by what words name. Typically, an episode of the playing of some game is liable to be correct or incorrect in any of a variety of ways. Consider a playing of II. If player 1 says 'slab' when it is not his turn, then what he did is incorrect: though 'slab' is a permissible move for him in II under the right conditions, it is an inappropriate thing to say, according to the rules, under these conditions. That is one sort of incorrectness. But now we can also observe that, given the way 'slab' is to be used in II, to say 'slab' in playing II is to request, or ask for something. (There is as yet no basis here for distinguishing between requests and, for example, orders. So this should not be taken as describing 'slab' as a request *as opposed to* an order; 'request' need not always be so understood. Nor are we yet trying to discover facts or features whose presence would make an item count as a request; our intuitions are quite enough here.) If 'slab' is used as a request in II, then an episode which is a response to 'slab' in a playing of II may fulfil or carry out that request, or it may fail to. For it to fulfil the request is for it to be correct in one of the ways such an episode is liable to be. It is thus part of what is involved in that episode's being a correct move in II. The rules of II, then, specify what is to count as carrying out the request 'slab' makes in II; they define the standards of correctness to which candidates for carrying it out are subject, so what it would be to carry it out correctly. We may also view them, in doing that, as fixing what request 'slab' makes as used in II—a request which is carried out when those rules are complied with. So if such an episode is or would be a correct move in II, then we may say that it fulfils the request 'slab' makes, according to the rules of II or by the standards of II. We may also say that it fulfils the request 'slab' makes in II. If doing A is a response to a speaking of 'slab', therefore, then it fulfils the request made in that speaking if it would be a correct move in II and both the doing and the speaking were episodes of playing II.

The sorts of correctness involved in the language games considered so far do not touch on matters of truth. In 21, Wittgenstein suggests a further language game which changes that state of affairs:

Imagine a language game in which A asks and B reports the number of slabs or blocks in a pile, or the colours and shapes of the building stones that are stacked in such-and-such place.—Such a report might run: 'five slabs'.

This suggests the following language game:

XI. To II are added the following rules. First, 'How many A's?' is a permissible move for player 1 if A is 'slab' or 'pillar' or 'block' or 'beam'. Second, if player 1 makes such a move, then player 2 is to go to the dump and count A's (for player 1's value of A), return and say something of the form, 'N A's'. 2's move will be correct just in case N is English for the number n and there are n A's in the dump.

If a player says, for example, 'Five slabs' in a playing of XI, then he may be correct or incorrect in a variety of ways. One way for him to be incorrect is to speak out of turn, thus to say what it is inappropriate to say. Or he may be incorrect simply in that he speaks without first going to the dump and carrying out the prescribed operation. In that case, he has no right, in XI, to say what he does. But intuitively, what he says, in XI, in saying what he does, is something which might be either true or false. Words used the way 'Five slabs' is to be used in XI are correctly describable as saying something either true or false. So if his saying what he did is a correct move in XI, then part of what is involved in its being so is its being true. Parallel to the treatment of requests above, we may say the following. If 'Five slabs' is spoken in circumstances in which it would be a correct move in XI, then what it says in XI is true, so it is true regarded as a move in XI, or simply, it is true in XI. If such a speaking of 'Five slabs' was, or is correctly describable as, an episode of playing XI, then something true was said in it. If it is true in all the language games it counts as an episode of playing, then it is true. Thus is truth to be implicated in the story being told here. The reasons for the extra wrinkle in the last step will be spelled out when we come to the question we have not yet approached: when should we say that a speaking of W was or counts as an episode of playing language game G?

Radical underdetermination of standards of correctness by facts about naming holds, then, for such types of correctness as carrying out a request or being true. The fact that W names slabs and makes a request, for example, does not determine whether a given episode would count as carrying out the request W made in some game for which that fact holds. For any such episode—for many quite obviously—there are triples of games with a first member in which that episode counts as carrying out the request W made, a second member in which it does not, and a third member in which the matter is indeterminate, though in all three members W named slabs and requested something. Similarly for whatever else W may be said to name. And similarly for more complex cases. The same point holds for games in which W may be said to say something possibly either true or false. We can see that, for example, if we consider the problem that would arise, in a playing of XI, if some of the slabs in the dump were broken in half. We might then consider variants on XI such as:

> XII. a game like XI, but with the stipulation that if there are broken slabs in the dump, player 2 is to count all half slabs, divide by 2, and round down.

> XIII. A game like XII, but with the qualification that player 2 is to count half slabs only where there is a pair of them which was originally a whole slab.

> XIV. A game like XI, but with the stipulation that 2 is to ignore all half slabs.

> XV. A game like XI, but with the stipulation that if there are any half slabs in the dump, then 2 is simply to return and shake his head. (Thus, nothing of the form, 'N slabs' is a correct move.)

And so on. Similarly contrasting games could, of course, be constructed around an indefinite variety of other problems that may be made to arise for slabs under some circumstances or other. Games like XI–XV contrast in that each imposes a different condition for the truth, in them, of given words, such as, 'five slabs'. We thus reach the following conclusion. Fix all the facts as to what the parts of W name and the fact that W says what is either true or false. There remain a variety of distinct truth conditions to choose from, any of which might be the condition for W's truth compatible with those facts, and each of which yields substantively different results with respect to which situations W is true of. In fact, it would appear that there are such conditions which differ in their results for any such candidate situation.

5. S-USE SENSITIVITY

In 27 Wittgenstein comments:

'We name things and then we can talk about them: can refer to them in talk.'— As if there were only one thing called 'talking about a thing'.

We can now see just what Wittgenstein's objection to this way of thinking is. Suppose we have some set of words which are to be used in the following way. First, we stipulate what the grammatical combinations of these words are to be, which combinations are sentences, and which sentences say what might be either true or false. Second, for each word, and each grammatical combination, we stipulate what, if anything, it is to name or stand for (or refer to on a speaking). This stock of words is to be taken to be available for use, on any occasion, in playing any language game that might be played on that occasion provided that the stipulated facts about the words hold of them in that game. We now see that there is a great variety of language games to be played with words to be used in this way. In particular, if W is a sentence of such words which is to be evaluated as either true or false, S a situation of which W might be true or false, and O an occasion for speaking W, then there are games in which W so spoken is true of S, games in which it is false of S, and games in which it is not determinately either, in all of which the stipulated facts hold. Or at least this is true for a wide enough range of values of S. We can put this point briefly by saying: words to be used in this way would be S-use sensitive language. We might also think of it this way: facts about what words name leave them S-use sensitive language unless there are some further strictures on their use which make them otherwise.

Consider an example. Suppose that our vocabulary consists of the words, 'blue', 'green', 'sky', 'grass', 'the', and 'is'. 'Is' may be placed before 'blue' or 'green', 'the' before 'sky' or 'grass', and anything of the form '(The) A is B' is a truthbearing sentence. 'Blue' names (the colour) blue, 'green' names green, 'sky' names the sky or skies, 'grass' names grass, and 'the A' names some contextually definite A. (No problems will arise here over the interpretation of 'contextually definite'.) '(The) A is B' is to be taken to predicate being B of the referent of (the) A. We can, if we like, say that such a sentence names the state of affairs of (the) A's being B. (We have nothing here against broad uses of (names). Now what are the conditions for the truth of, for example, 'The sky is blue', or 'The grass is green', so used? What is to be made, for example, of the fact that when you look out of an aeroplane window at the bit of sky more or less near you, it looks transparent and not blue? Or the fact that the sky does not look blue, from the ground (typically) when it is about to rain? Or suppose that grass in cities is typically brown (as it is most of the year anyway in many parts of the world). Or that grass in cities is typically painted green so that it will not look brown, or painted mauve so that it will not look green? Different truth conditions consistent with all the stipulated facts decide such cases (and an indefinite variety of others) in different ways. Further, for different speakings of such words, and under different conditions of evaluating them as true or false, it would be reasonable to adopt different such conditions. So words subject to the above strictures and only to them are S-use sensitive language. Conversely, any language like the above which was not S-use sensitive would have to be subject to rules and restrictions of a much different sort than any considered so far. It is still an open question here whether there could be any such restrictions. It is a further question whether such things as English words might be subject to any such restrictions in virtue of what they mean in English (where they are spoken as meaning what they do mean). The next section will consider this last question.

6. MEANING AND NAMING

What naming fails to do for the use of a word now looks very much like what meaning fails to do. The suspicion thus arises that there is no in-principle cleft between a word's naming what it does and its meaning what it does—as if the facts as to what it names were compatible with its meaning any of various things, so that it means what it does only given some further fact which holds independently of these. If there is no such cleft, then, *inter alia*, Augustine did not go wrong by failing to observe it. This section will argue that that suspicion is at least approximately correct. Intuitively, to say that a word, such as 'blue', or the Cantonese '*lam*', names (the colour) blue, and to say that it means *blue* is, in most circumstances, to say much the same thing. Which suggests what is not quite the same point: that for a word to mean what it does and for it to name what it does are at least roughly the same thing; what is true of the word in virtue of its naming what it does, and what is true of it in virtue of its meaning what it does are (roughly) the same. What follows aims to show that both the intuition and the suggestion are correct, and moreover that they are nothing to which Wittgenstein was opposed. So that his critique of Augustine, whatever morals it draws, does not depend on supposing otherwise.

The suspicion, as it will be treated here, bears two important qualifications. First, it may be that there are some words which cannot correctly, or at least naturally, be said to name anything. If so, the suspicion is not meant to apply to them. It is explicitly restricted to cases where there is something a word may truly be said to name (on the present broad use of 'name'.) Second, for any given word W, it may be that there are specific idiosyncratic restrictions on its use, or specific details of its use which are not what would be determined by given facts as to what it names. The Cantonese '*fan*' or '*bak fan*', for example, may, for most purposes, correctly be said to name rice. But it may also need pointing out that they apply (for most purposes) only to cooked rice, and that *'bak fan'* literally means *white rice* (though it is the most common way of asking for rice.) Similarly, *'ga yun'* names the act of marrying (or equally, means *to marry*), though, for reasons etymology suggests, it is subject to the restriction that only women may correctly be said to do it. (If a man marries, then he *'cheui'* (takes) a wife.) Anyone who speaks more than one language can easily think of numerous examples of this sort. On the present suspicion, such facts represent specific exceptions to what would otherwise be so given the stated facts about naming—exceptions which are permissible, though optional if the suspicion is correct.

There are, inevitably, reasons for resisting the suspicion. The most attractive ones, I think, lie somewhere in the following rough thought: what a word names leaves its use open in a way in which what it means does not. So that we might quite well know what W names without knowing what its use is. Whereas we could not know what it means without knowing what its use is. In fact, if we did not know W's use, we could not truly be said to know what W means. To de-psychologize, what W names does not fix its use in a sense in which what W means does fix this. Words which differed substantially in their use would *ipso facto* correctly be said (at least for many purposes) to differ in what they meant;[5] whereas, the thought is, they might so differ in their use without thereby differing in what they named. If this rough thought is right, then there is indeed a gap between meaning and naming, though what the gap comes to will depend on the sense in which the thought is right. Since our aim is to exorcize this thought, and the thought that it is Wittgenstein's, the thought will require some sympathetic treatment.

In so far as the above thought touches meaning alone, it is perhaps something like what Wittgenstein had in mind in the oft-cited 43:

For a *large* class of cases of the use of the word 'meaning'—though not for all—one can explicate the word thus: the meaning of a word is its use in the language.

But note that this passage does not attempt to draw contrasts between meaning and naming. 'Use', of course, is a far from transparent term. Which is why the thought is a rough one. One thing that 'use' might

---

[5] Though, for all that, there might be something both were correctly said to mean. 'Green' and the Cantonese *ching* may both be said to mean *green*, though for all that they may also be said to differ in meaning, and certainly differ in their proper use. There are some occasions for describing some things truly as green where those things could not correctly be called ching.

mean is proper use: how the word is to be used, or is properly used in speaking its language (at least in full literal uses of it). The thought would then be that words which differed significantly in the ways they were properly used would correctly be said to differ in meaning. (We will presently encounter examples where pairs of words may be said so to differ even though there is something both may be said to name.) Conversely, one might say that for a word to mean what it does is for it to have the proper uses that it does, or to be usable correctly in the ways that it is. One might even venture to say that for a word to mean what it does is, bracketing syntax, for it to have whatever properties it does have which determine how (or when or where) it is properly used.

We have already encountered one sense in which, as Wittgenstein insists, meaning (alone) does not determine how a word is properly used: what a word means does not supply us with a set of (effective) standards of correctness such that the standards governing the word on a speaking are always and exactly some selection from these. So far, meaning and naming are on a par. That W names V is compatible with an indefinite variety of standards of correctness (and truth) for it, as exhibited by the indefinite number of language games in which it may figure as naming that. But likewise for its meaning what it does. All that, however, leaves open another possibility: the meaning of a word might fix some set of specific (and effective) set of principles for determining what standards would govern it on any given speaking, given the facts of that speaking. The phenomena may make this possibility seem attractive. A word such as 'blue', spoken in appropriate circumstances, is governed by determinate standards of correctness, which is only to say that, world willing, it is evaluable in terms such as 'true' and 'false'. Moreover, a fluent English speaker, confronted with such a speaking, normally perceives without effort what these standards are. The thought would then be that where this is so, there must be something to be understood about the English word— something known to the fluent speaker—from which it follows that these standards of correctness are what they are. On this thought, some 'part of the meaning' of 'blue' would fix (or be fixed by) some set of effective principles which, for any (evaluable) speaking of 'blue', would select from among the various sometimes correct ways of counting things as blue or not, that way which in fact enters into the truth conditions for what was said in that speaking. If, for example, the meaning of 'blue' does not tell us whether a car must have blue wheels for 'blue' to describe it truly, there might at least be some specific aspect of the meaning which fixes for which speakings this is required, and for which not. If this is so, there might also be a contrast at this point between meaning and naming. That 'blue' names blue does not seem to provide us with any specifiable principles for choosing between different ways of counting things as blue or not for the purposes of evaluating the truth of some given speaking of 'blue'. If such is decided by specific facts about what 'blue' means, then those facts must be independent of the fact that 'blue' names blue.

The idea, then, is that the meaning of 'blue' is fixed, in part, perhaps, by the fact that it names blue, but, over and above that, by some set of rules determining what it would say when, given that it names that. But to think that meaning *must* determine any such thing, beyond the way in which this is already determined by what 'blue' names, or that any such result is suggested by our unreflective understanding of speakings of 'blue', is to succumb to an illusion. For suppose there were no such special principles for determining how 'blue' was to be used (or how uses of it were to be understood). Suppose, in fact, that there were no fact either as to what 'blue' meant or as to how it was to be used which was not a fact simply by virtue of the fact that 'blue' names what it does. Imagine, for example, that 'blue' was a word which we just introduced into the language by stipulating that it named blue, and stipulating nothing else about it (or stipulating that there was nothing else about it which conflicts with what would be so simply in virtue of the fact that it names blue). Now suppose that 'blue' is used on some occasion to describe (the colour of) some item. Suppose that, on that occasion, and for the purposes of describing that item (or the purposes for which that description was given), it is determinate enough how to classify things as being blue or not—that is, which of the various sometimes correct ways of doing this is the most reasonable way of doing so under the circumstances. If the item is a car, for example, then circumstances make it clear enough whether, for the purposes of that classifying of it, it might do enough to count as being blue even though its seats and motor are decidedly not blue. That 'blue' names blue gives some reason to count the description as correct (and true) just in case the item counted as being blue on that occasion for describing it as being blue, or for the purposes of that describing. It takes no special further facts about what 'blue' means to determine whether that is so: the most reasonable way, on an occasion, of counting some item as being one colour or another is not a matter of what the word 'blue' means at all. By hypothesis, no fact about 'blue' provides any reason for imposing standards of correctness here which differ from the proper ones for counting items as being blue. Hence those are the reasonable—and the right—standards of correctness. The fact that 'blue' names blue, unless counterbalanced by other facts, connects the standards governing uses of 'blue' with those governing judgings of items as blue. Given the rich body of facts as to the right standards of this latter sort, that fact about naming can bring us quite far in fixing standards of correctness of the former sort.

So there is no reason to suppose that there are any special principles governing how standards of correctness for a use of 'blue' are to be decided. Given that there are enough facts as to how things are to be counted as blue or not on occasion, there are enough facts as to what standards are properly taken to govern 'blue' as spoken on an occasion. Given that fluent speakers of English are capable of perceiving, on occasion, what then would and would not count as being blue, it is not surprising that, given that they knew the above hypothesized facts about 'blue', they should, as a rule, be capable of perceiving how 'blue' is to be used, and how uses of it are to be treated and understood. There could, of course, be special principles for deciding such matters, and it could be part of what 'blue' means that there are. That would be so if the proper uses of 'blue' did not always correspond to what it determinately would be on the rule just stated. That the way that 'blue' is to be used is nearly enough captured by this rule, on the other hand, is enough to show that there are no such special aspects to its meaning.

The general principles involved here are these. First, if a word, W, names blue, and there is no other relevant fact about what it means, then W, as spoken on an occasion, will be true of an item just in case that item counts, on that occasion, as being blue (which is to say that such is the yield of the most reasonable way of counting things as blue for the purposes, or under the conditions of, that speaking). Second, if the truth conditions for speakings of words containing 'blue' are what they would be for a word whose meaning was exhausted by the fact that it named blue—as just described for W—then the reasonable conclusion is that its meaning provides no extra principles of the sort just envisioned. The presumption, of course, is that 'blue' does behave just as W would, since the salient fact about it is that it names blue. Its behaviour could not diverge too much from W's while that fact was preserved. That is why there is not much of a gap between meaning and naming. Of course, 'blue' *might* have its occasional idiosyncrasies, picked up somehow or other through its chequered history. But it could not have too many. Nor does clarity in what its proper uses would be require it to have any.

The thought, then, is that in favourable cases, where we say what a word names, we do state the facts about it on which its proper uses depend. Or where we fall short of that, the defect is remediable by specific qualifications of the sort considered. It is important to note how congenial that view of the matter is to Wittgenstein's view of stating meanings—a view which he emphasizes repeatedly throughout the *Investigations*. For, as no one would deny, we often can say, or at least successfully explain, what a word means by saying what it names. That is only one among many ways of saying what a word means. Neither it nor any other way of doing so is privileged, on Wittgenstein's view. Still, it is one way. Now, Wittgenstein's general view is that when we successfully explain what a word means, no matter what form the explanation may take, what we state is no less than *what the word means*, at least in this sense: the facts about the word which we state are such that for them to obtain is for the word to mean what it does; those facts determine about the word and its proper use(s) just what is determined about this by the word meaning what it does. In the last chapter, we encountered numerous passages in which this view is expressed. Part of the point of it is to deny that our ordinary explanations of meaning, when correct by ordinary standards, fail to express some fact—which, perhaps, we could not express, but a recipient of the explanation must guess—such that the effects of the facts we state are those of the word's meaning what it does only given that extra unexpressed fact, or such that the word means what it does only given that fact in addition to the ones we stated. What is not missing, in particular, is some set of special principles which decide what the consequences are to be of the facts which we did state. Rather, in saying what words mean, we say no less than we know about it, or at least enough such that to know that is to know what the words mean. The proper uses of the words are then the uses they would most reasonably have, given the stated facts about them. They are what our sense for reasonableness shows them to be; not what such-and-such special principles would decide them to be. That is Wittgenstein's general view of meaning and explanations of it. It is not a casual view, but one to which he attaches some importance, especially in the context of the private language discussion. There is no reason to take it not to apply in the special case where the way in which we explain what a word means is by saying what it names.

The illusion, then, is to think that if there are clear and easily discernible facts as to how a word is properly used on occasions, then there must be special principles determining what these are. Facts about what the word names, or whatever other facts there may happen to be about the word, may be capable of achieving the same effects without any such special rules on how this is to be done. But this speaks to only one possible interesting relation between meaning and use. For the 'use' of a word may refer not only to its proper use, but to its actual history in its language—its life, so to speak, among the speakers of that language: what it has been used and taken to communicate on various occasions by various people, for example.

This history, or the part of it a reasonable fluent speaker would be in contact with, may have a significant role in determining what the word's meaning what it does was supposed to determine: the standards properly taken to govern it on the various occasions appropriate for its use. Here is a general description of the connection. Suppose that words W are spoken on an occasion to describe an item, V. A fluent speaker of W's language, in the circumstances of that speaking, and sufficiently apprised as to what those circumstances are, will form expectations as to what V would be like if it was as said to be. On the model of the last chapter, the expectations thus formed by a reasonable fluent speaker, if suitably aware of the circumstances, fix the expectations one ought to have of the words or the item in these respects. These proper expectations, in turn, fix the standards of correctness to which that speaking of W is subject, given the reasons the world in fact provides for treating things as being that which W names or not.[6] But a reasonable fluent speaker's expectations in such respects will be influenced by the histories of the words of W, or as much of them as such a speaker would know. Again, if W is 'blue', and V is a car, then the fact that 'blue' typically is used, in speaking English, to describe cars of certain sorts, barring specific reason to use it otherwise, provides powerful reason for someone fluent in English to take V to be a car of that sort, and no more (if it is as described)—not, for example, to expect its hub-caps to be blue.

We now have three items in play: the history of a word, what it names, and what it means. Each of these items has a role in determining how the word is properly used, and how uses of it are properly taken. Comparing the first two items, we can see that there can be two words whose different histories determine different ranges of proper uses for them, even though there is one thing which both may correctly be said to name. To take a simple example, compare the Croatian, 'crno', and the English 'black'. Both may correctly be said to name black. However, what we would standardly describe in English as 'red wine' is standardly described in Croatian as 'crno'. (Conversely, tea described in English as 'black' is described in Chinese as 'hong' (red).) In many situations, describing wine as black in speaking English would arouse radically different expectations in a fluent English speaker than would be aroused in a fluent Croatian speaker by describing the wine as black in speaking Croatian. If the wine is typical red wine, then that English description of it often would lead one to

---

[6] In the case of 'blue', for example, such reasons could turn out to concern facts about lightwaves, even if relevant fluent speakers, in that situation, would have no expectations specifically about such facts. (The occasion may predate modern physics, for example.)

expect it to be much different than it is. On the present scheme of things, that translates in an obvious way into differences in what would be said, in such situations, in a Croatian description employing '*crno*', on the one hand, and an English description employing 'black' on the other.

The moral of the example, as developed so far, is this. If a word names black, there may still be more to know about it before one can know or see what the proper uses of the word would be. Its history can accomplish any of various things for it, in this regard, consistent with that fact about what it names. On the other hand, depending on the word involved, the facts as to what its history accomplishes for it in these respects might be summed up correctly in what we would say, on many occasions, at least, in saying that it is to be used, or is properly used, as a word which named black most reasonably would be. There is so far nothing in this which runs counter to our qualified suspicion. Nor are facts about the word's history anything like principles on how to determine what the proper uses of the word are given, the fact that it names what it does. Rather, they represent an additional class of fact which is an appropriate and fitting input to problems of the form, which ways of treating the word on an occasion would be the most reasonable ones, given that those facts hold of it.

It was earlier suggested that if a word names 'black', then, *ceteris paribus*, the standards of correctness governing a particular use of it are fixed by the most reasonable way of counting things as being black or not, given the facts of that speaking which might weigh for or against one or another of the various ways we have of making such classifications on occasion. To this we may now add two remarks. First, the rule applies only in cases where the word is used to describe, or speak of, things as being black. Its history may show that it would not always be properly taken to do that, even where used as meaning what it does. Second, it might also be that the history of a word, and the fact that that word is being used in classifying things as being black or not, are some of the facts which contribute, on an occasion, to making one way or another of doing this classifying the most reasonable one. That would be so, for example, if there are purposes for which what we call red wine could be described correctly as being black, and if that is what '*crno*' is typically used to do, its history making those purposes the relevant ones—or, if that is not so for '*crno*', if there are other similar examples where a parallel situation does obtain.

There remains the question of the relation between history and meaning. For example, do '*crno*' and 'black' mean the same? For many purposes, they may correctly be said to. Where it is correct to say that, we may also say that the facts about the proper use of each by which they differ from each other are fixed neither by what they mean nor by what they name, but simply by vagaries of their histories. On the other hand, if we decide that there is something which '*crno*' says of an item in virtue of what it means, that it is typically used to say just that of wine, and that, on many occasions, so used, it says what is true of the wine, while 'black' would not, that might also make it correct to say that 'black' and '*crno*' differ in meaning. But whatever reason it gives us to say that, it gives us just as much reason to say that they differ in what they name. If they may sometimes be said so to differ, that is so despite the fact that each may often truly be said to name black. Such would exhibit Wittgenstein's point is there are a variety of distinct things to be said in saying a word to name black. Some things may sometimes count as an instance of what '*crno*' names without thereby then counting as an instance of what 'black' names. Sometimes, but not always, that is a good enough reason for denying that both of them might name black.

The present claim is that Wittgenstein's critique of Augustine does not depend on positing some essential gap between what a word means and what it names, and further, that there is no such gap. So far, we have been discussing that critique solely in terms of various conceptions of the semantics of words in a language. But the Augustine Wittgenstein quotes is actually a description of language learning, and Wittgenstein has a criticism of it as such. The relevant part of Augustine is as follows:

Thus, as I heard words repeatedly used in their proper places in various sentences, I gradually learned to understand what objects they signified; and after I had trained my mouth to form these signs, I used them to express my own desires. [Cited by Wittgenstein in 1; translation by Anscombe.]

Wittgenstein's comment on this is in 32:

Someone coming into a strange country will sometimes learn the language of the inhabitants from ostensive definitions that they give him; and he will often have to *guess* the meaning of these definitions; and will guess sometimes right, sometimes wrong.

And now, I think, we can say: Augustine describes the learning of human language as if the child came into a strange country and did not understand the language of the country; that is, as if it already had a language, only not this one. Or again: as if the child could already *think*, only not yet speak. And 'think' would here mean something like 'talk to itself'.

So Wittgenstein thinks that Augustine, as Locke was later accused of doing, misrepresents the child as being, in certain crucial respects, just a small, weak and perhaps slightly stupid adult. What these crucial respects are must depend, of course, on what there is to be learned in learning language. So we might ask what Wittgenstein thinks they are.

We can detect at least two assumptions in Augustine's description: first, that the child is capable of learning what the words of its target language name, and can come to know this simply by being shown (samples of) what they name; second, that when the child has learned this (plus syntax), he is thereby made into a fluent speaker of the language. Wittgenstein may be criticizing either or both of these assumptions. If he allows the first, though, it is difficult to see what his criticism of the second might be. Suppose the child has learned that 'blue' names blue. He has thereby learned the sort of fact the adult in a strange country learns or guesses, on Wittgenstein's description of the case, and the sort of fact which, according to 32, might be enough (bracketing syntax) to make the adult a fluent speaker of this second language. What Augustine misrepresents the child as doing here is, after all, supposed to be what an adult could do. If the meaning of 'blue' determines special principles for deciding on standards of correctness for uses of 'blue' given that it names blue, then Augustine has provided no account of how the child learned or could have learned these principles. To that extent, he has failed to explain how the child could have become a fluent speaker. But equally, Wittgenstein's description of the adult, in 32, provides no account of how the adult could have learned these principles. Yet that description is meant to be in order. So far, there is no contrast between the child and the adult. Similarly, the proper use of 'blue' might depend on facts about its history in ways which are not fixed simply by the fact that it names blue. The child could not have known this history already, and Augustine provides no account of how he learned it. But those remarks apply equally to the adult and Wittgenstein's description of him. So Wittgenstein's criticism of Augustine cannot quite be located at that point either.

If there are such special principles governing 'blue', and if, as Augustine claims, the child does become a fluent speaker of the language in learning what its vocabulary names, then it is tempting to credit the child with innate knowledge of these principles, or at least with an innate mechanism, or an ethology in virtue of which the child would take just these principles to hold once he had caught on to the fact that 'blue' names blue. Augustine might then be credited with implicitly making a bold empirical hypothesis to this effect, and further, with being ahead of his time in doing so. He might also be criticized for making a bold but unfounded hypothesis to this effect. But I do not think that that is Wittgenstein's criticism of him. Wittgenstein is not generally opposed to the idea of innate mechanisms, or a human ethology, nor does he deny the importance of such things in our performances, either in learning, or in what we do, in our mature states, with what we have learned. In the next chapter, we will see a crucial case where he assigns an important role to such things. On the view of him suggested so far, his objection to positing innate mechanisms at this point places the emphasis on 'mechanism' rather than on 'innate'. It rests on his antipathy to the idea that there are any such special principles. If the meaning of 'blue' determines no such thing for it, then there is no need to explain how the child comes to know such principles. Since there are no such principles, there is nothing to explain, so no mechanism is called for to explain it. Given Wittgenstein's general view of meaning, then, this is not the point at which the child might contrast with the adult.

One thing the adult might know, or be able to recognize, is that such-and-such things would be so of a word which named blue—or that they would be so *ceteris paribus*, with possible qualifications and exceptions to be garnered from observing the relevant word in his foreign language in use. The adult might know such things, or take them to be so, because he already knows or can recognize what is so of at least one word which names blue, namely, the word or words in his native language which do that. This cannot be the explanation of how the child could know such a thing. There may be something problematic in the idea that the child could know such a thing, and the problem at this point may point to something Augustine has left out of account. But again, it is not obvious that this is so. Naming blue is a property that 'blue' might share with an indefinite number of other possible words. Why not adopt the bold hypothesis that the child has innate knowledge of what would be so, *ceteris paribus*, of any word with that property, or at least an innate something which yields this knowledge when he discovers of any one word that it names blue? We can, perhaps, see what might be problematic in such an hypothesis if we switch from discussing Augustine's second assumption to discussing his first.

On Augustine's description, the child may learn a fact such as that 'blue' names blue by being shown instances of what 'blue' names, or through instances of being shown what 'blue' names, or, more accurately, by being shown instances of 'blue' being used to name that thing. But to know that 'blue' names blue, the child must know which item it is that 'blue' names, so what blue, or being blue is. To benefit appropriately from the knowledge that 'blue' names blue, he must know when something is correctly counted as (being) blue. There is a *prima facie* difficulty as to how he could know such things. For the child can qualify as knowing what blue is only if he has the ability or the means to identify novel instances as instances (or not) of blue, or to identify, in novel cases, that which 'blue' names. Augustine provides no account of how the samples to which the child has been exposed might yield such more general capacities. This problem for the child is one which Wittgenstein's adult does not face; the adult's capacities in such respects are not in question. So this is a likely point at which Augustine has misrepresented the child as an adult.

The difficulties the above point poses for Augustine depend very much on just what problem one sees the child as facing above. Suppose we accept a classical view of semantics, and the metaphysics that goes with it. Then, bracketing vague or borderline cases, the world divides up, in an occasion-insensitive way, into items which are blue and items which are not. The child has been shown some items which are blue. His problem is to identify novel cases of blue and non-blue items—and to identify them as novel cases of what 'blue' names. Now Wittgenstein emphasizes in the *Investigations* that unless the child's ethology makes it natural for him to take certain novel items to instance what he was shown in the sample, and others not to, there is no possibility of his learning anything at all. (Like the adult, he might mistake what he was being shown in given samples; and hence, through correction, be moved from one natural way of proceeding to another.) So if this is the problem, then it is indeed natural to posit something like innate mechanisms—an ethology, for example, which makes it natural for the child sometimes to take it that it is a colour at issue, and to form certain natural judgements in novel cases as to whether some item is the same colour as that or not, and to do such things in much the ways that human beings in general do them. So, though Augustine does not explicitly mention any such mechanism, and does not do the empirical work needed to say just what such a mechanism might be like in human beings, this difficulty yields no very deep criticism of Augustine. Nor should it be thought that Wittgenstein would see some sort of deep difficulty here because of some generalized antipathy of his to appeals to ethology. He had no such antipathy.

For present purposes, however, the above is not a proper characterization of the problem the child faces. For knowledge of the fact that 'blue' names blue is here supposed to yield for the child fluency in using and understanding 'blue'—so, *inter alia*, the ability to recognize under what circumstances it would be reasonable to describe which items *via* that word, and, for a wide range of circumstances, what to expect of an item if, in them, it was so described. That yield is supposed to come *via* a rule roughly to the effect that 'blue' is properly used to describe something just where it is properly judged to be, or counts as being blue. But the point of Wittgenstein's discussion of language games is that there is an indefinite variety of such games in or for which items must be counted as blue or not, and that the way items would be so to be counted varies from one such game to another. What the child in his finished state must be capable of recognizing is how this variation would go, or, in terms of language games, which game(s) it would be most reasonable to be playing on an occasion in classifying an item or items as blue or not. The problem is not just (or even) one of recognizing which of the world's items are blue. Given the S-use sensitivity exhibited through language games, it is a problem of recognizing what, on an occasion, being blue is to come to, so which standards of correctness, from among the various sometimes-right ones, are the most reasonably taken to govern, on this occasion, classifications of items as blue or not. The difficulty for the Augustinian account, then, is to explain how the child could come by an adequate sensitivity to that sort of fact.

If the proper treatment of the word 'blue', on an occasion, depends on its history, and the effects of that history may be summed up in saying that 'blue' names blue, then it is not surprising that the proper treatment of blue, or being blue on an occasion, depends on its history among reasonable judges of what is blue and what is not. Both the world and our purposes have supplied us with reasons for and against various ways, on various occasions, of classifying things as blue or not, and the balancing of those reasons against each other has sometimes shown one or another of these ways to be correct. We do normally call the sky blue, and on many occasions it does count as being blue on the right way of judging such matters. The two facts are not unrelated. The sorts of interests we take and have taken in the sky, and the fact that we have often called it blue and been satisfied with that description, are some of the factors which will weigh in favour of counting it as blue on some novel occasions—not just counting it as what 'blue' is true of, but counting it as being blue. If our interests had typically been different—if, for example, for one reason or another we were typically concerned with how the sky looked close up (as we might be if we could fly), then some of these occasions might have been ones on which the sky would not count as blue. That questions of items being blue have been treated in certain ways by speakers of a language is one determinant of how things are properly counted as being blue in novel speakings of that language. It is this determinant that the child could not be in touch with innately.

The history of the property of being blue in our lives is, of course, not an arbitrary matter. We are bound by our ethology; we could not find just any way of treating that property reasonable or natural. Still, it is a history which depends on contingent factors. To that extent, it is a history the child could not have been in contact with innately, but must be brought into contact with in gaining fluency in the language.

In that respect, the child is not like an adult, and Augustine's description is flawed. The problem with Augustine's account of language learning, then, may be summed up as follows. There is a variety of distinct things to be said (or thought) in saying (thinking) a word to name blue. For such a thought to confer mastery of a word on a child, the child must grasp the proper understanding of that thought; he must be prepared to react appropriately to the fact it represents as so. But which understanding of the thought would be appropriate depends (often enough) on the history of the word in the language the child is learning (or its career within the community in which the child is to speak). Augustine has no account of how the child comes to be in touch with this history; nor any recognition that a sensitivity to it is called for. Faulting Augustine at this point does not require a wedge between naming and meaning.

To see Wittgenstein as locating the flaw at this point is to see him as emphasizing the importance of the activities we engage in in fixing the standards of correctness, not only for our words, but for our judgements as well. On this view, Wittgenstein's aim is not to drive some wedge between naming and meaning, but rather to emphasize that neither what a word names nor what it means is sufficient by itself to determine by what standards of correctness it is governed on a use of it. That thought fixes his view of the relation of language games to language: uses of language are (typically) describable correctly as moves in one language game or another; but which games these might be—and which rules might constitute them—is to be read off neither from the meanings of the words involved nor from the concepts they express. Missing that point and seeing a closer intended relation between language and the games to be played in it may make Wittgenstein seem an operationalist or verificationist[7]—so, for example, a behaviourist. But the ample reason we have now seen to ascribe the above idea of the relation between language games and language to Wittgenstein is reason not to read any such view into the text. The question remains just how, if not *via* rules of language, our activities may confer one or another semantics and standard of correctness on the items we produce. That is for the next section to address.

7. THE EXTERNALITY OF SEMANTICS

Suppose that someone speaks the English words W in speaking English. If we knew him thereby to be playing some language game G,

---

[7] Just this mistake is made in Chihara and Fodor [1965].

then we would know something about the standards of correctness which govern W as thus spoken. For these would at least include the standards which G imposes. So that it would be correct to describe W as correct in relevant respects (those covered by the rules of G) if W counted as a correct move in G. This section will discuss the question when words such as W are correctly described as a playing of one language game or another. The relation between language games and what words mean in their language, as discussed in section 6, exhibited an object level S-use sensitivity, for example, of English expressions: words such as 'blue' or 'is a chair' may make different contributions to what is said, and have different standards for their truth of items, on different speakings of them. But, as noted, at least neglecting the fact that English contains the means for its own semantic description, that is compatible with the view that words always bear whatever semantics they do bear S-use insensitively. The expectation is that the present examination of the relation between language games and words on a speaking will exhibit an at least in-principle S-use sensitivity in their semantics. The aim here is to say why such sensitivity would arise.

We have noted a general opposition in Wittgenstein to an ahistorical approach to language—to the idea that one might specify some space of possible languages, each with a fully determinate semantics which is its semantics quite independently of—in fact, without—its having, or having had, a life in some community of speakers of it, and then sensibly pose the problem, for a language such as English, which item in this space of possibilities English is. The present treatment of language games may appear as an exception to this rule. For language games are specified, or specifiable ahistorically, in terms of their rules. And we now want to ask which of these abstract items given words count as a playing of. There are several differences between this and usual treatments of 'possible languages'. First, we do not suppose that a language game is fully semantically determinate. If a move is a playing of II, for example, then it is governed by the standards of correctness which II's rules impose. But for all that, there may be a given doing, A, as done on some particular occasion, which sometimes does and sometimes does not count as in compliance with those rules, depending on the occasion on which that question is to be considered. Second, if words W do count as a playing of game G, that fact is not supposed to provide an exhaustive description of W's semantics. We thereby know something about W's semantics, but there may be more to know as well. For example, words might count as a move in II, but also as a move in IX, or in X. We might suppose that any semantic issue about W is settled by some fact about some language game being played in speaking W. But we do not suppose that there is some fact as to which language game is being played which settles any semantic question that might arise. Third, we are now interested in the semantics of words on a speaking, and not words in a language. So the semantics imposed on words by the fact that they are a playing of G need not follow them across all, or even any further uses of, the same words. These differences remove a number of objections to ahistoricism. But we will see just how far that brings us.

By present convention, W is a playing of G if W is, or is most reasonably taken to be, governed by the rules of G. Which means this: W counts as (or is correctly said to be) correct (in respects covered by G's rules) if it is correct according to the rules of G, and similarly counts as incorrect if it is incorrect according to those rules. For example, 'There are five slabs' might count as a move in G provided it counts as true if it counts as true in G, and as false if it counts as false in G. But if we take it not yet to be settled when W would count as true (or correct in whatever other respect), then we might reasonably ask after the conditions under which W would count as thus governed by one set of rules or another, where these might be the rules of some game, G. On that topic, Wittgenstein has the following to say (54):

Let us recall the kinds of cases where we say that a game is played according to a definite rule.

The rule may be an aid in teaching the game. The learner is told it and given practice in applying it.—Or it is an instrument of the game itself.—Or a rule is employed neither in the teaching nor in the game itself; nor is it set down in a list of rules. One learns the game by watching how others play. But we say that it is played according to such-and-such rules because an observer can read these rules off from the practice of the game. . . .

In effect, Wittgenstein points here to two kinds of case. In the first, the players of the game take themselves to be following such-and-such rules, and that is why we say, and it is correct to say, that they are doing so. In the second, we say that they are following such-and-such rules because we can see that in what they are doing—for example, in the activities in which they speak W, and what they do with W. Similarly, if W is spoken in speaking English, then users of W—the speaker and his audience, for example—may take W, as thus spoken, to be governed by given rules or standards, or, whether they do so or not, we (or an observer) may see that W is so governed from the activities in which it is embedded and the ways in which it is used (and usable) in those activities. We will begin here by considering the second sort of case.

On Wittgenstein's view, even if there are no relevant facts as to what rules people explicitly take themselves to be following, or would judge that they were following, it may still count as so, for some purposes at least, that there are certain rules by which their doings are governed. Bracketing for the moment any explicit views those people may have as to what rules govern their doings, the rules that would count as in force for those doings are the most reasonable rules for them—those, that is, that it would be most reasonable to have govern them, or the most reasonable such rules for those people to respect, given the place of those doings in the activities of which they are a part, and the purposes and interests of those people in those activities. For suppose, as Wittgenstein does, that there may be facts as to what rules are in force, in the absence of self-conscious views as to what these rules are. If, on the assumption that there are such rules, there is a fact as to which rules they would most reasonably be taken to be, then one judges correctly, on the assumption, in taking the rules to be that. But on Wittgenstein's view (see chapter 7), that there are such facts on the assumption is enough to justify the assumption, hence to make it true *simpliciter* to judge, that the facts are what they would most reasonably be taken to be on the assumption. But there are facts as to what is most reasonable on the assumption in so far as there are facts as to which rules would most reasonably govern a doing or saying, as done in carrying out given activities, and if there are no further special facts to show the rules in force for that doing to be something else. Facts of this last sort are ones we, or reasonable judges, may be supposed to be able to recognize.

Consider some simple examples of how these principles might work. Suppose that Hugo and Guy are paving a forecourt. Three more slabs are needed to finish the job. (Since Hugo is a reasonable workman, we might also suppose that three slabs are what he wants.) Hugo calls, 'Two pillars.' Grant for the sake of argument that this is at least a playing of V. So 'pillar' names pillars, etc. If Hugo is the paver and he has not moved out of turn, then, as far as the rules of V are concerned, what he said is correct. Yet there is something clearly unreasonable about his words given the facts. There is some sense in which he may be said to have misused language given that he needed, and wanted, three slabs, even though this sense has nothing to do with issues of truth, or anything close to that. The nature of this misuse can be captured, for most purposes, by supposing Hugo's doings to be governed by a rule to the effect that he is to say, 'Two pillars' only if he wants two pillars. If we like, we can introduce a language game—call it V*—which is like V except that it contains such rules. In V*, as opposed to V, Hugo's words would be an incorrect move. This means, on the present scheme of things, that, given that Hugo is to be described as playing language games, V* is among the games he is most reasonably taken to have been playing in saying, 'Two pillars.' So those words count as a playing of V*. Or at least they do so wherever he counts as having misused language in the above way.

Here is an example involving truth. Hugo and Odile are discussing their new apartment. Hugo says, 'The walls are beige.' The walls are, indeed, painted beige, though made of white plaster. Are Hugo's words true? There are various ways of counting walls as beige or not. On some of these ways, the walls do so count, and on others they do not. Correspondingly, it is sometimes true to say that the walls are beige, and sometimes true to say that they are not. So there are different things to be said, on different occasions, in saying so, where these things differ in being subject to different standards of truth. Nothing said so far decides which of these things Hugo said, nor, hence, what is required for his words to be true—or at least enough about this to determine whether they are true. But now suppose we consider the overall activities of which Hugo's words were a part. Suppose that Hugo and Odile are choosing a rug. For that purpose, it would not be reasonable to take 'beige', used in the way Hugo did, to be subject to standards on which it would not be true of those walls, or to use it so that it was subject to such standards. *Ceteris paribus*, then, it is not reasonable to take it to have been subject to such standards. So it is most reasonable to take it to have been subject to standards on which it is true of the walls. So Hugo said what is true, unless some further feature of the case shows otherwise. But here is a contrasting activity. When the building was built, two sorts of dividing walls were put in: ones made of white plaster and ones made of beige plaster. Both sorts have been painted many times; all are now painted beige. It has recently been discovered that the beige plaster sort give off a poison gas. So they are being demolished and replaced. The superintendent asks Hugo to find out what sorts of walls his are. Hugo, wanting new walls, says, 'They're beige.' But the plaster is white. By the most reasonable standards for that activity, what Hugo said would be false. So it is false—unless further yet unmentioned facts demonstrate otherwise.

All the above points may be put equally well in terms of language games. Suppose that you were engaged in the first activity above and you were going to carry it out by playing a language game involving the move, 'The walls are beige.' The most reasonable sort of game to choose to play would be one which allowed those words to be said correctly (so truly in the game) of walls which, like the above ones, were painted beige. So, if we are to suppose Hugo and Odile to have been playing a language game in Hugo's speaking above, then, unless there are further facts to show otherwise, it would be most reasonable to take them to have been playing a game of this sort. That this is most reasonable is shown by the nature of the activity in question. *Ceteris paribus*, then, Hugo and Odile may be correctly described, by our convention, as having been playing such a game. *Mutatis mutandis* for the contrasting case involving the bargain paint. On Wittgenstein's view, as expressed in 54, the above reasoning is a way of showing what language game was being played; hence also, given the uses language games have in illuminating the semantics of language, it is a way of showing what the relevant semantic properties of Hugo's words were.

In the reasoning of the above examples, no reference has been made to the fact that Hugo, Odile and Guy were speaking English, hence presumably using English words to mean what they do mean. That silence is proper in cases like the last one, since the choices to be made there, in fixing the language game(s) being played, are choices between various games all of whose rules are compatible with using the relevant words to mean what they do mean in English. But it is no part of the present view that such facts have no role to play, or that reference to them is always in some sense eliminable in fixing the language games that were played in the speaking of given words. The fact that Hugo used the English word 'beige' so as to be most reasonably taken to be speaking English (and that speaking English would be the most reasonable thing for him to be doing under the circumstances), and that that word has a certain history in the language are certainly facts which would make it more reasonable for Hugo to be playing some games rather than some others in speaking as he did, hence facts which might make it more reasonable to take him to have been doing that.

This view of what fixes what language games are being played contains a general picture of the semantics of words. On it, the semantics which words had on a speaking is an external matter: the semantics they have is the semantics an observer, looking at them from the outside, would take them to have, provided that observer was a reasonable judge, and knew all the facts he needed to as to what activity the speaking was a part of. That is, as long as he was not ignorant of some fact about that activity which, if he knew it, would change his judgement in relevant respects. So, for words to have some given semantics, S, is just for them to appear to have that semantics to a reasonable observer who was suitably informed about them. For someone to qualify as performing as a reasonable observer, he need not be either the speaker or the audience for the words. We, for example, may count as reasonable observers of Hugo's words. Hence neither are the views of the speaker and audience, nor any other part of their psychologies or histories are, enough to fix words' semantics. It is the judgements made from outside the game, given the facts of the activity involved, on which the semantics of words depends.

This view of the externality of semantics contains the mechanisms, at least, for S-use sensitivity in the semantics given words count as having. For suppose that on an occasion we ascribe semantic properties to given words—for example, we might ascribe the property of being true to Hugo's words about the wall. Whether we judge truly in doing this depends on what activity the speaker counts as engaging in, the place of his words in that activity, and what rules would most reasonably govern those words given that activity. If on different occasions there are different things it would be reasonable to judge in any of these three respects, then there will be a corresponding variation across occasions in the semantics truly ascribable to those words. Again, what counts is not merely the facts that obtained at the speaking of the words, but the reactions to those facts which a reasonable judge would have under the various conditions in which such a judge might find himself. So, for example, the activity Hugo and Guy are most reasonably seen as having engaged in might, on some occasions, be that of paving a forecourt, while on others it is some larger activity with places in it for various forms of idle amusement, time wasting, etc. The unreasonableness of saying 'Two pillars' within the narrower activity may not carry over into the larger. In which case, there may be different and conflicting things to be said on different occasions as to which language games were being played.

But this picture of semantics flows from consideration of only one sort of case of rules being in force. Wittgenstein does suggest that there is another. There is also the case where we take people to be subject to certain rules because they tell us that those are the rules they are following—or, for example, because they tell us that they are playing Scrabble, and we can look up the rules of Scrabble—they have been written down by the marketer of the game. So suppose that Hugo and Odile do have views about the semantics of Hugo's words, or take those words to have such-and-such semantic properties. Might this mean that the semantics of the words was fixed in some way other than that described already? The answer is that this kind of case is fully subsumable within the model presented already. Those facts about what Hugo and Odile take to be so are simply extra facts which may help fix what activity they are most reasonably seen as engaging in, or what is most reasonable for them given that. Nor need either Hugo's or Odile's or their joint views always prevail.

Hugo and Odile could be engaged in doing A, while having unreasonable views on the rules to adhere to in doing A, or those properly taken to govern A. The importance of catering to their views in talking to them may change *our* (or a reasonable judge's) views of the overall activity in which some words addressed to one of them were spoken—not simply doing A; but doing it in (what is to be understood to be) a special way, as it would reasonably be done given certain unreasonable constraints. (The difference between how one would tie his shoes, and how he would do it with one hand tied behind his back—no teeth in the first case, but perhaps some in the second.) But their unreasonable views *may* also be simply mistaken views about the standards governing words spoken as they spoke them. Which of these alternatives is realized is not a matter of what Hugo and Odile think. Where it is the first one, the most reasonable way of observing unreasonable constraints need not be what they think it to be.

Consider an example where Odile has unreasonable views. We have already said that, if the activity is choosing a rug, then the most reasonable use for the words 'The walls are beige', is as subject to standards on which the words would be true if the walls are painted beige (but not, for example, if they are painted white). Odile, however, would refuse to accept the words so spoken as true unless a bore sample of the walls showed them to be beige through and through. Moreover, she would not be disturbed if the paint on the surface of the sample turned out not to be beige. There may now be two possible views of Hugo's words. On the one hand, it remains so (for most purposes) that in that sort of situation, and for most purposes, it is true to say that the walls are beige. For most purposes, that is good enough reason to say that Hugo's words are true; Odile's view of them is simply wrong. But things do depend somewhat on what we take 'that situation' to be. Suppose that Odile's views are common knowledge. Then, if part of the activity involved is communicating with Odile, and if the place of Hugo's words in that activity is to do so, then Hugo's choice of words is not a reasonable one. If that is the situation, then it would only be reasonable to use those words if one wanted to communicate the fact which the bore sample would confirm. That may be enough reason, sometimes, to count Hugo's words as subject to standards of truth which are other than what they would be if those words were being spoken to a reasonable person. The important point, though, is that if that is so, it is so because of what is most reasonable from our point of view, given the precise nature of the activity that was to be carried out. It is not made so merely by the fact that Odile has the views she does.

I believe that all of these remarks carry over intact if Hugo shares Odile's bizarre views here. It remains so that if the activity is discussing rugs, then, for those purposes, the walls are truly described as beige. And that remains enough reason, for many purposes, to count what Hugo said as true (since that is how he did describe them, and it was for those purposes), counter to what both Hugo and Odile would believe about his words if they knew all the facts about the wall. On the other hand, when conversing with people with bizarre views, those views may need to be taken into account in judging how to speak and what to understand. The fact that Hugo and Odile would react strangely to certain words in certain situations may change how the activities they are engaged in are most reasonably carried out. If the attitudes of speaker and/or hearer do carry the day here, it is for that reason, and not by their mere existence. Note, incidentally, that two plausible views have been presented of the semantics of Hugo's words given the bizarre facts of this case. It is plausible that either of these views might count as correct on at least some occasions. If so, then this case can be made into a plausible example of the semantic S-use sensitivity which the present picture of semantics allows for.

The general rule, then, is that the rules and standards governing words—and hence their semantics—are always those which we (as reasonable judges) would find the most reasonable ones to govern those words given the facts of the activities in which they were produced. With that rule in mind, we might return briefly to Putnam's problem about reference. Hugo says to Guy, 'Bring six slabs.' Why should we view Hugo's 'slabs' as referring to slabs, rather than, say, bicycles? After all, as Putnam has shown, if there is a language game, G, in which 'slab' names slabs, and such that Hugo's words and Guy's response count as correct just in case they count as correct in G, then there is another language game, G*, in which 'slabs' refers to bicycles, and such that Hugo's words and Guy's response count as correct just in case they count as correct in G*. A precise answer awaits a precise description of G and G*. But the answer is likely to be along the following lines. For some purposes, perhaps, there is no reason to take Hugo and Guy to be playing G rather than G*; they might equally well be said to be playing either. For those purposes, there counts as being no fact of the matter as to whether Hugo's 'slabs' names slabs or bicycles. For most purposes, however, G strikes us as a more reasonable game to be playing than G*, since its rules strike us as more reasonable. The rules of G* are apt to seem contrived and overly complex. If that is so, and we are reasonable in being so struck—that is, if that is how a reasonable person would be struck—then it is reasonable, and hence correct to judge that Hugo and Guy are playing G and not G*. Again, it is the fact that certain descriptions of their words and activities strike us as reasonable and others do not that is crucial for determining what the semantics of their words in fact is.

The externality of semantics, on the present view, is an essential feature of having a semantics: what it is to have a given semantics is, in essence, to look that way to an observer standing outside the language game, and in a position to see the relevant facts about words and their surroundings. This suggests a quick way with the idea of private language. The rough thought would be that if W is private language, then there is no way it could look to an external observer, or at least no way in which it could appear to such an observer to have the semantics it would have if private. For an observer other than the speaker either could not see the facts on which W's semantics depended—he could not grasp the relevant activity and W's place in it—or could not grasp what the standards were by which W was in fact governed. But then there could be no such thing as W's looking to a reasonable judge as if it had that semantics. So it could not have any such semantics. Either W would have no semantics, or it would not be private language. Unfortunately, this way with private language is a bit too quick. As pointed out by Simon Blackburn,[8] a speaker of private language, if there might be such, might qualify as an external observer of his own words—for example, by making judgements about them at times other than their speaking. Such a speaker might practise auto-semantics, and this practice might show what the private semantics of his words was. The problem, of course, is that for this auto-semantics to have any significance, the private linguist must qualify as performing as a reasonable judge would. For his words may qualify as having some semantics, S, by seeming to do so to him only if there are facts about how they seem to him, and those facts establish how they would seem to a reasonable judge. The trick in arguing against private language is to show that the private linguist could not thus qualify as functioning as a reasonable judge, or as such a judge would. That trick I save for chapter 8. But it is interesting that language games, on the uses Wittgenstein has in mind for them, bring us this close to seeing what is wrong with the idea of private language.

In fact, the problems raised for privacy by the externality of semantics run deeper than they may seem to at first. For any semantics, S, which private language might have, *we* could not say truly of words W that they had S, not even by guessing wildly but right. For to say that is just to say that that is how W look from our perspective on them. But that cannot be how W look to us, no matter how reasonable we are. Might we then say truly that W have a semantics, though we know not what it might be? If not, then we could not speak truly in saying that W were private language. In

[8] See Blackburn [1984].

regarding words as private, we would lose our right to regard them as having any semantics at all. But if so, then there must be something which makes them look from the outside sufficiently like words with a semantics. This must be something which makes it both true for us say that the words have a semantics, and to true for us to say that there is nothing for us to say truly as to what that semantics is. It is at best doubtful that the notion of having a semantics allows for such possibilities.

It is fundamental to having a semantics, on Wittgenstein's view, that that semantics be what it would be taken to be as viewed from the outside, and that, as viewed from any perspective, it counts as being what it shows itself to be from that perspective. No matter what proprietary hold any given group might get on a semantic item, there is always room for slippage between the semantics they take an item to have and that which it in fact counts as having (in present terms, between the rules they take to govern the games in which the item figures and the rules of the games it in fact counts as part of). For the rules that correctly may be said to govern people's doings, so their sayings, are just the ones which count as most reasonable for those doings and responses to them. With that thought, we take the step from S-use sensitivity at the ground level of non-semantic discourse to the S-use sensitivity of semantic concepts and properties, and thus of questions of which semantics our words and thoughts have. For reasonableness, as judged from the outside, is liable to vary with the perspective on given doings, and the occasion for taking the view of them that that perspective affords. The most reasonable way of counting blocks, even when building a wall, may also depend on our purposes in assessing a given (wall-building) remark about blocks. So the conditions for the correctness of our judgements as to the truth of any given item are liable to depend not only on the circumstances of its production, but also on those of our assessment of it.

4
Doubt and Knowledge Ascription

If, as some say, Frege displaced epistemology from its Cartesian place at the centre of philosophy, to replace it with philosophy of language, then, as chapter 2 shows, Wittgenstein placed epistemology squarely at the centre of philosophy of language. On his view, epistemic facts are central in fixing the semantic facts and in blocking a sort of ontic scepticism as to there being any. This chapter will develop those aspects of epistemology which are most crucial for these tasks. Since some of the ideas come out more clearly in *On Certainty* than in the *Investigations*, here I will draw freely on the former. The ideas to be developed concentrate around two main ones: first, the S-use sensitivity of knowledge ascriptions; and second, the role, with respect to the truth conditions for such ascriptions, of our innate capacities to doubt. The chapter will divide into three main sections, each with various subsections. It begins with a historical survey of approaches to saying what knowledge is. The ones to be considered each link it in some way to doubts. The next section presents and defends a Wittgensteinian account of knowledge ascriptions. The third treats Wittgenstein's response to scepticism.

I will often speak of knowledge *ascriptions* rather than directly of knowledge. A standard reason for 'semantic ascent' is that it permits stating generalizations which could not be stated conveniently, or perhaps at all, without it. Where S-use sensitivity is at issue, the need for such ascent is even stronger. If there are various perspectives from which we might view someone's knowledge, and various things which it counts as being, as viewed from each of these, then we can only expect to falsify what knowledge is by examining what there is to be said about it as viewed from some one perspective in particular, or supposing there is a determinate perspective from which we view it when there is not. For example, S-use sensitivity exhibits one thing wrong with the idea one might otherwise get of *states* in which knowledge consists.

1. DOUBTS: 1.1. INDISCERNIBILITY

Odile looks through her window and sees a stag on the lawn. Does she *know* that there is a stag on the lawn? One might reason as follows. Suppose there were a cleverly arranged stuffed or mechanical stag, placed to lure poachers. If so, nothing now available to or detectable by Odile would allow her to tell that it was so; to distinguish that situation from one in which there is a stag on the lawn. So for all she knows or can tell, there might not be a stag on the lawn. So she does not know that there is one.

The example illustrates appeal to a principle which I will now describe. The principle is a conditional whose antecedent states a condition: A takes it that P; there is a conceivable situation, S, in which A would be taking something, Q, to be so which was not so; if A were or had been in S, A would not and could not distinguish his position (and what he does) in taking Q to be so from his actual position in taking P to be so. (If he were in S, everything would look and seem the same to him; it would not seem to A that he was taking to be so anything other than what it now seems to him he is, nor that there was anything about the world to affect the truth or falsity of this which it does not now seem to him that there is.) If there is a conceivable deceptive situation which pairs with the actual one in this way, then, as the principle has it, A does not know that P. (The deceptive situation need not be distinct from the actual one.) Call this the *indiscernibility principle*, or *IP*.

Some notes: First, IP's antecedent is meant to capture the idea that we could conceive of A turning out to be wrong 'for all else he knows'. It does not require specifying what this 'all else' is. Nor does it suppose that A's other information would stay constant across all deceptive and non-deceptive situations. (Any more than it would thus remain constant that Odile sees the stag, though that may be in fact how she knows there is one on the lawn.) Second, the right notion here is conceivability and not possibility; the epistemic thought will not reduce to a non-epistemic one.[1] What A takes to be so may be necessary—that all bachelors are married, that 57×13 is 741, etc. In that case, there are no possible situations in which it is not so, so none

---

[1]   Though possibility might be made to do more work here. There is, perhaps, no possible situation in which *what* A takes to be so—namely that 57×13 is 741—is not so (though on this point see chapter 5); but there is some possible situation (or so it would seem) in which A takes it of three numbers, K, L and M, that $K \times L$ is M, and cannot distinguish what he thereby does from what he now in fact did in taking 57×13 to be 741, but is mistaken, since $K \times L$ is not M. Such a situation would make IP apply. There is still room for the distinction. It is conceivable (for us) but, we would normally take it, not possible that A should turn out to be wrong in taking 57×13 to be 741.

such for A to be in. For all that, A might be in a position, or relate to P in such a way that we can conceive of someone being in that position and turning out to be wrong. For all of A's understanding of being a bachelor (being shown examples at night clubs, say), it could conceivably have turned out that some bachelors are married; given A's calculations, or his grasp of them, it is conceivable that he should have turned out to be mistaken, etc. A's position is compatible with there being further revelations (in fact to be made in the deceptive case) which would show this to be so, or make it the reasonable conclusion. If it is necessarily so that 57×13 is 741, that is not enough to ensure that one knows this.

Third, much of the caginess in the principle might have been avoided had we joined Descartes in a first-person stance (though that stance also obscures important features of knowledge). Descartes asks himself whether he could imagine turning out to be wrong in taking it that, say, he has hands or that 9×7 is 63. He would be wrong if he had mistaken what was required for having hands, or had done his calculations wrong. It is conceivable from his position that such should turn out to be so. Where Descartes poses the question, he takes responsibility for what it is that he takes to be so. Where, in the third person, we pose the question for A we, and not A are the ones who take this responsibility. It is *our* claim that A takes it that P. Suppose that A is right about P. It may be that we can conceive of revelations such that, were they to be made, they would show A wrong, and were A in such a deceptive situation, he would detect nothing to distinguish it from his actual one. As noted, the deceptive situation need not be a possible one if we retain the assumption that what A is wrong about is that P. Equally, A's mistaken thought, in it, need not be one that we would characterize as the thought that P. No more is required than that it be a possible situation in which A is wrong about something, such that A's position in it would seem different to him in no respect from the way his actual position seems to him where he correctly takes it that P. Thus, we may be able to recognize that, were certain things facts, they would show A's calculations wrong, though situations in which his calculations were wrong need not be what we could identify as ones in which what he calculated was that 7×9 is 63. Fourth, A's inability to distinguish S from its actual mate does not mean that he could not discover the difference through further investigation. To investigate further would be, for present purposes, to convert S to some further situation S*.

One might argue for IP as follows. If the condition is met, then A cannot tell whether he is in a deceptive situation or one in which P. So for all he knows, he might be in a situation in which what he takes to be so in taking it that P is not so. Hence, for all he knows it might be that not-P. But if for all he knows perhaps not-P, then A does not know that P. So A does not know that P. Arguments in this vein are debatable. One might contest this one, for example, by challenging the last principle in it. Later I will suggest that that is a wrong move, though, as a rejectionists, I will be obliged to say what *is* wrong with the argument. The immediate point, however, is not to challenge IP, but rather to see where it leads.

Until the middle of this century, IP or some minor variant was generally accepted. If one wanted to show, for some P, that P was not the sort of thing that could be known, or at least not from some given position, the trick would be to show that for someone in that position, or more generally in any position, the antecedent of IP was satisfied. Conversely, if one wanted to show that IP was something we could live with, the first move would be to try to exhibit an interesting class of cases of things we could know given IP—that is, cases where the antecedent was not satisfied. Our primary concern in this section is to survey the latter attempts. But first a note is in order on the former.

Those bent on the first project have exhibited great ingenuity, in a wide range of cases, in showing the antecedent to be satisfied. But one might wonder whether ingenuity is really called for. For suppose that S is a candidate deceptive situation with respect to A's knowing that P, so that at least, in S, A takes something to be so which is not so. Then S fails to realize the antecedent only if A could, if in S, distinguish it from the actual situation. A could not do this simply by the fact that S is a situation in which not-P, since, if S is plausible at all, in it A also takes it that P, or at least does what he cannot distinguish from doing that. So A must rely on something else which he now takes to be so, but would not take to be so in S (or vice versa.) Call this something else F. Since F is different from P, the question may arise how A knows that F distinguishes cases of P from cases of not-P, or, more modestly, this as a case of P from its being a case of not-P. We can surely conceive of (candidate) deceptive cases in which A is mistaken in taking F to have this role with respect to what he takes to be so. Further revelations, that is, would show that the non-obtaining of what A takes to be so is quite compatible with F. Since there are such cases, we might as well suppose S to be one. Since the point holds for any F, and there must be limits to A's means for marking distinctions, we can conclude that there must be some deceptive S. Which is to say that we know in advance of ingenuity that the antecedent is always satisfied.[2] If, as we

---

[2] For this reason, philosophers have often sought states or positions such that there is no such thing as taking oneself to be in them, but not being. It is difficult to see how there could be such states, or how, if there were, they might serve as a basis for knowledge of how the world is, even in necessary respects. But waiving that, it is

would normally expect, F is something logically distinct from P, then of course there are possible cases in which F but not P. So F cannot hold A proof against being in a deceptive case. But even if F is not logically distinct from P, that fact could help A only if A stands in the right epistemic relation to it. If IP is the measure of the right relation, then it is just that which seems hopeless. So, it would seem, ingenuity can only give the false impression that there is an open question where there is not. IP poses a challenge one could not withstand.

Let us say that a *doubt as to P* is a way of turning out to be wrong in taking it that P; a situation such that if it now obtains, then in taking it that P, we would be taking to be so what is not. (The situation may be one in which not-P, but it may also be counter to fact in what we are doing, in it, in taking it that P.) If A takes it that P, then a *doubt for A as to P* is a situation in which what A thus does is similarly mistaken. If a doubt for A as to P is a deceptive situation, let us call it *live* (for A). If it is non-deceptive—that is, if A is in a position to distinguish it from the actual one, let us call it *discharged* for A.

The suggestion, then, is that, for any A and P, there is always a live doubt for A as to P. This bodes ill for the project of living with IP. Still, the project is worth exploring. There are two basic strategies for it. One is to carve out an interesting domain of objects of knowledge to which we can relate so as to be immune to IP. The second is to proliferate senses of 'know', postulating a strong sense for which IP holds, and, to assuage our linguistic intuitions, a weak or man-in-the-street sense for which it does not.[3] Following Descartes, one might employ both strategies at once. Here, though, we begin with the first.

---

difficult to see how they help at all. Suppose A is in such a state and takes himself to be. Is it not conceivable that he should be in some other state, on some occasion, which he mistakenly took to have this property, and further to be a state which it was not? And is it not further conceivable, even if not possible, that A's current position should be revealed to be just this? In which case, if IP is allowed, this sort of infallibility would not guarantee knowledge. It is instructive to compare Cook Wilson [1926] on this point. The problem as he sees it is how error is possible. This is a problem for him because, on his view (and in his terms), if you judge that P, you cannot be mistaken. What you can do, however, is mistakenly take yourself to *judge* that P, and be mistaken about P, where what you really do is something-else that P.

[3] Philosophers who accept the IP have a notoriously difficult time refraining from speaking 'with the vulgar'. In a letter to Princess Elizabeth of 28 June 1643, Descartes says, 'I can truly say that the chief rule I have always observed in my studies, and the one I think has been most serviceable to me in acquiring some measure of knowledge, has been never to spend more than a few hours a day in thoughts that demand imagination, or more than a few hours a year in thoughts that demand pure intellect; I have given all the rest of my time to the relaxation of my senses and the repose of my mind.' In terms of present interests, this is to say that Descartes can only get himself into the right situation for taking the IP seriously for a few hours a year. What looks here like a plea for more leisurely working conditions for philosophers ought, on philosophical grounds, to be taken quite seriously. Wittgenstein's account of knowledge will show just how unfacetious Descartes is here being, or at least ought to be.

1.2. TRANSPARENCE

Descartes begins his third Meditation with a misdiagnosis, encouraged by his first-person treatment of what we can know, of what he had done in the second in establishing his own existence. On his view, he was able to see so 'clearly and distinctly' what he asserted in holding that he existed that, as he could also see, he could not be wrong about this. He could not doubt it because, in our technical sense, there simply was no (live) doubt for him about it. What he saw 'clearly and distinctly', on one view, was what thought he expressed in holding that he existed, and what that thought required for its truth, or, on an alternative view, simply the fact that he existed. In either case, his having *that* sort of view of the item in question—what was asserted— guaranteed that the IP could not be applied to that item, for the reason that there were no live doubts for him as to its being so.

Descartes' argument for this analysis is fairly typical of one who accepts IP. He reasons that if his view of the item, P, in question above did not provide the guarantee just mentioned, then he would not know that he exists. Given that he has just established that he does know this, that remark is taken as a *reductio*. It is easy to see what is wrong with this diagnosis. Suppose that the item in question is that A exists, and the question whether A knows this. If the worry about A's knowing this is whether IP applies, then clearly there is no worry. For IP applies only if there is a doubt for A as to that item. But such a doubt would be a possible situation with A in it in which that item is not so. Since the item happens to be that A exists, there clearly is no such situation. A's view of the matter, whether it be clear or muddled, is beside the point.

Descartes' misanalysis, however, suggested to him, as to many of his successors, how a search for knowledge (strictly speaking) might proceed. Descartes took the thought that he existed (and the one that he was a conscious being) to *exemplify* a wider class of things that might be known. The task for an account of knowledge would be to fill in, or adequately characterize, the other members of that class: items that we can at least view in such a way that there can be no premiss to make the IP apply to them and us. That view of knowledge (in the strict sense) is the subject of this section.

One of the best developers of this Cartesian view, and one of the last before Wittgenstein and Austin pointed epistemology in a new direction, was H. A. Prichard. To begin, Prichard accepts IP without question. As he puts it, 'no state in which we may be mistaken can possibly be one of knowledge.'[4] To underscore the point, and

---

[4] Prichard [1950], p. 83.

emphasize that nothing turns here on peculiarities of the modal 'may', he says later that if Descartes' 'state of mind' regarding a certain claim about triangles was one of knowledge, 'then, of course we know that in it he could not have been liable to deception; and therefore for ourselves we have cut off the doubt at its source.'[5] Here the point is quite explicit. If A and P provide us with a case of knowledge, then they provide us with a case where IP does not apply, since there is no live doubt for A as to P. It is also clear that Prichard thinks there is an interesting class of such cases.

Prichard is probably best known for his opposition to the view that knowledge is a sort of hybrid state. As he puts it, knowledge and belief are two utterly distinct sorts of things, as are knowledge and being sure, or being convinced, or 'being under the impression that'.[6] In particular, knowledge is not some particular subspecies of belief, or any of these other things—belief, say, with some other quality added on, such as being justified and true. In fact, on his view, what we know we do not believe, and vice versa. One major difference: what we believe is either true or false; what we know is neither. In effect, what we know, as opposed to what we believe, are facts.[7] Rightly or wrongly, Prichard accuses Descartes of ignoring the distinction in kind here. The idea of such a distinction he properly credits to Cook Wilson[8]. This part of that epistemological lineage was retained by Austin, as evidenced, for example, in his remark that knowing is not something higher up in the same scale as being certain, since there is nothing higher on that scale, and his view that to say one knows is to take an entirely new sort of step. Wittgenstein, too, agrees with Prichard on this score, as evidenced by his view that 'know' is a very special word, with highly restricted uses.

In his further development of the above distinction, however, Prichard parts company with Austin and Wittgenstein. On his view, knowledge is a state of mind—as are belief, and the other things from which he wants to distinguish it. The differences come in which states of mind these are. In the case of knowledge and belief, the difference is

---

[5] Ibid., p. 90.

[6] Prichard does equate knowing and being certain, but appears to use 'being certain' in a special sense, more akin to 'it is certain that' than the ordinary 'I am certain': being certain, for Prichard, is not having a feeling, or being convinced.

[7] A point argued for more recently in Vendler [1972], ch. 5.

[8] Cook Wilson [1926] makes much the same points as Prichard, though in somewhat different guise, especially in the section, 'Opinion, Conviction, Belief and Cognate States' (pp. 98–113.) As for belief being a different state from knowledge, see especially pp. 99–100. As for knowledge being an infallible state, see especially pp. 104–108. As already noted, Cook Wilson puts the point in terms of judgement, which is supposed to be infallible because it requires, in effect, what we here call semantic transparence. But note the *caveat* mentioned above: one may *think* he is judging something and not be *judging* anything at all.

unmistakable. So that, by reflecting on any one of our own mental states—if so much is even necessary—we can see and know whether it is a state of knowing something, or (merely) a state of believing something. Which is to say that, if we know something, we do or can know that we know it, and can do so merely by examining our own states of mind. Here a minor fracas with Descartes may cover up a wider area of agreement. Prichard insists that we do not recognize a state of mind as a state of knowledge by first recognizing that it has some other property—pointedly, that of being 'clear and distinct'—and then realizing that having that property is the mark of a state of knowledge. In fact, Prichard believes that there are and can be no such marks. He also thinks that Descartes held otherwise. Be that as it may, those states which Prichard wants to call states of knowledge are plausibly just those which Descartes would describe as ones in which we have a 'clear and distinct perception' of the object of that knowledge. Whether we recognize them as such by other features, or whether they are just unmistakable, as they must be on Prichard's view, their similarity becomes apparent when we consider what could make any mental state have the properties Prichard and Descartes take these respective states to have.

If A knows that P, then, *inter alia*, P, as neither Prichard nor Descartes would deny. Stronger yet, if A knows that P, then on their views, since they accept IP, there must be no live doubt for A as to P. In knowing that he knows that P, as A does or can on Prichard's and on Descartes' views, A must know that this is the case. Prichard insists, plausibly enough, that A's mental states could not bear marks viewable by A from which it could be deduced that these consequences hold. But then, how could reflection on his mental state allow A just to see that all this is so? It might help here to divide up what, on Prichard's view, A can see on reflection where A knows that P. First, A can see that he π's that P, where π is some attitude or other that he can take towards P. Second, he sees that he knows this. The first point is meant to withstand change of emphasis: A sees that what he π's is that P. Add the second point, and what A sees is, not only that he *knows* that, as opposed, for example, to believing it, but also that what it is that he knows is *that*. Suppose, for example, that P is the thought/fact that K is M—to take Prichard's example, that a three-sided figure is three-angled. Then by, or perhaps in, seeing clearly just what thought that is, A can see just what is required for being K—that is, what is thought of in that aspect of the relevant thinking—and similarly in being M, and hence, in Prichard's terms (modulo variables) 'that a certain characteristic of a K requires or necessitates that a K is M".[9]

_____

[9] Prichard, [1950], p. 102.

On Prichard's view, our attitudes towards P are transparent to us, *inter alia* in their semantics. By examining our mental states, we can see what it is towards which we are taking an attitude. In fact, we can see all there is to see about this. One thing we can see in particular is how the item in question confronts experience: if we think of it as a thought, then what possible (extra-mental) states of affairs would count for or against its truth; if we think of it as a fact, then which such states of affairs would be ones of its obtaining. Since that the item is the one it is is a feature of the mental state in question—a feature which A can 'directly observe' if the state is his—it is, at least in favourable cases, a feature about which we could not be wrong. Further, what A can see in some cases is that the item he π's does not confront experience at all; that no further states of affairs, other than what holds in the obtaining of the mental state itself, could possibly make this item untrue or not so. These are the cases in which A has knowledge that P and may know that he does so.

Given the above doctrine, it is clear how, and in just what cases, a Cartesian argument may be blocked. If it is really the case that there is no possible situation in which P would not be so, or none which A might fail to distinguish from the one he is actually in, and if A can see this to be so merely by observing or reflecting on his mental state, then there is no doubt for A, or at least no live one as to P, hence nothing for IP to apply to—contrary to what one would have expected, A's existence aside. It is also clear that the class of values of P which might have this status is limited, even if, as Prichard and Descartes thought, it includes more than just the thought that A exists. If this is what knowledge requires, then, as Prichard says, 'we are forced to allow that we are certain of very much less than we should have said other-wise.'[10] (Recall that Prichard equates knowledge and certainty in his sense.) In particular, according to Prichard, we do not know any 'inductive generalization' such as that sugar is sweet, nor anything we might give as testimony in a law court, such as that we were at home on the night of the 13th, or that that desk is mahogany. What we can know are mathematical and logical truths, at least if simple enough, miscellaneous conceptual truths, such as that bachelors are un-married, and perhaps more exciting ones as well, which ones depending on your philosophical views (Prichard gives as an example that only bodies move), and *perhaps* certain 'directly observable' features of one's own mental life, such as what one intends to do next, provided there are such features about which one just could not be wrong. If this expansion on what, 'I exist' was meant to exemplify seems still so limited that an account which restricts our knowledge to

---

[10] *Ibid.*, p. 97.

it could not be correct, then one might seek new ways to expand it, compatible with our present view of IP—that is, further ways for there to be, or cases in which there are, no live doubts for A as to P. This brings us to our next chapter in the history of the subject.

Thirty-five years ago, Norman Malcolm[11] proposed an ingenious idea for extending the realm of what was immune to IP. Malcolm, it seems, agreed with Prichard and Descartes in their particular interpretation of the maxim that if you know, then you cannot be wrong. Which is to say that he appeared to accept the IP. However, he proposed that the class of items exemplified by Descartes' 'I exist'— those items P such that, in favourable circumstances there may be no live doubt for A as to P—might be extended to include *some* of what by usual lights are empirical claims. For example, it might include some things expressible by someone in saying, 'There is a fountain-pen on the desk', or some things taken to be so in taking there to be one.

Suppose that A, in good health and lighting, is looking at his desk. There is a fountain-pen. Whether there is one or not is not, as it were, independent of the course the world takes, or more pointedly, has taken. That there is a pen on the desk is not a conceptual truth. Still, Malcolm holds, if A π's a thought that there is a pen on the desk, what thought this is, and what state it is part of may be transparent to A in the Prichardian way. Notably, it may be transparent to A how his thought answers to experience. It may also be, transparently, that the thought does not answer to experience in any way other than that in which it has already answered in A's πing the thought in the way he does—in a way one might do so staring at a pen on a desk. This last feature is not, of course, a property of every thought that there is a pen on the desk. But Malcolm's view entails that there are a variety of thoughts to the effect that there is a pen on the desk (desk and time fixed), each with a different truth condition, and that some of these do have the property. For Malcolm does hold that one may know, in a sense of 'know' for which IP holds, that there is a pen on the desk.

If A takes there to be a pen on his desk, then the truth of what he holds depends on how the world is. On the other hand, his thinking what he does in the way he does already involves the world having taken a certain course. The thought does not just pop into his mind. He sees the pen on his desk. It is not wavy or fuzzy or otherwise

---

[11] See Malcolm [1952/63]. Malcolm distinguishes two senses of 'know': a 'strong' sense, and a 'weak' or 'ordinary' sense. We will discuss his 'ordinary' sense in 2.5. Here it is only his strong sense that is at issue. Moreover, the reprinted (1963) version of his article contains a new conclusion. The idea discussed here is only that put forward in the original Mind (1952) version. I have not yet been able to find a way of making the new conclusion consistent with the rest of the text. Anyway, the original suggestion is certainly interesting.

ephemeral-looking. The lighting is good. As visual experiences go, A's here is first class. A feels fine, is not crazy, etc. For A to experience all this is already for the world to have taken a particular course, and perhaps to have answered, at least a little, to the thought in question. The usual view is that, for all that, A might be wrong. It might not be a pen, but an FM radio in pen's clothing, or a weird Martian crystal, pen-like at the moment, but on the verge of evaporation, or a spectacular hallucination, etc. At least some of these ways for A to be wrong are enough to make IP apply. If someone had planted a novelty FM radio on A's desk, then, though such is certainly detectable, and not merely in principle, A in his current position, having the experiences he does, would not detect the difference. On Malcolm's view, this might be correct, depending on just what thought A had. But it *might* also be wrong. It is possible for A's thought, in taking there to be a pen on his desk, to be such that it requires nothing more of the world than what is already the case by A's having the experiences he does in or while thinking it.

Thus, the course the thought requires of the world, and the course the world takes in that thought's thinking might exactly coincide. So, for example, if the 'pen' does later evaporate, such need not count against what *A* took to be so in taking there to be a pen on the desk. Or if it suddenly begins to play *Kindertotenlieder*, then it is no longer what A took it then to be, or is a pen in the relevant sense, but a music-playing one. Similarly, if A suddenly has experiences as if coming out of a grade A hallucination, then those experiences are delusive, or its being an hallucination is not incompatible with there being a pen on the desk in the relevant sense. If everyone else would treat the situation as one in which A had hallucinated, this merely shows that nothing is required from others by way of support for this particular view of A's, and so on.

If some thoughts to be had in taking there to be a pen on the desk are immune to IP, not every such thought is. Thinking a thought to which Malcolm's doctrine, above, applies requires the right circumstances. First, while, or in, thinking it one must be having experiences such that the world's taking that course (one in which the thinker has those) is all that is required for truth by some thought that there is a pen on the desk. For some thought to have the right properties, two semantic properties must be compatible: first, the property of being made true by the thinker's having had such-and-such experiences (the ones A has in or while thinking it), and second, the property of being a thought that there is a pen on the desk. On Malcolm's view, such properties may be compatible. But, of course, A could not have a thought of the required kind while on the bus (and not hallucinating). His experiences would not be right for making any thought of the right sort true. Second, one must somehow arrange for one's thought to have the right semantics: that is, one on which it is guaranteed to be made true by the fact that one is now having such-and-such experiences, and never to require anything further than that. Not every thought to the effect that there is a pen on the desk has this property. On Malcolm's view, some do. One might give one's thought the desired properties, perhaps, by thinking it under the right circumstances, or, on Malcolm's view, perhaps by having the right intentions towards it. In any case, Malcolm is thoroughly Prichardian on one point. For given A and P, it is transparent to A whether the above two conditions are met. With at most a bit of reflection on A's part, this is a matter about which he could not be mistaken. If they are met and A sees that they are, then he may be said to know P in the strongest possible sense: there is no possible situation for A to be in in which P is not so and A could not detect the difference; what is required for P to be so comes to no more than all the differences that P in fact does detect. Malcolm's innovation was to extend that idea to some thoughts about the ordinary empirical world.

Placing Malcolm at this pre-Wittgensteinian stage of the story is perhaps the greatest anachronism in the present account. Yet it is clear why he belongs here. This is not to deny that Malcolm was influenced by Wittgenstein. Wittgenstein does point out, not infrequently, that not everything that looks like an 'empirical proposition' is one or that there is no clear distinction between such propositions and others. Some empirical-like propositions form a framework, or fixed points, around which investigation of the truth of other propositions may be carried out. For such fixed points, we have no clear ideas on what would count for or against their truth, nor how investigating such might be carried out. Nor is this ignorance. It may be that no such investigation could be carried out—at least one which would show what the answer was. As a distinct thesis, Wittgenstein also held that sometimes there are propositions about which there simply is no doubt, or which it makes no sense to doubt; doubting them, in present terms, is just not part of the language games in which they are moves. Malcolm may have taken such things to mean that there are propositions, at least as empirical as the above-described thought that there is a pen on the desk, such that there are no possible circumstances in which they will have been shown to be false. On the present view, that is a misinterpretation. We will return to the topic of 'fixed-point' propositions in chapter 5. By then it should be possible to say why this is so.

1.3. TROUBLES WITH TRANSPARENCE

Descartes, Prichard and Malcolm agree on the following point. For an interesting class of items, we can see precisely and unmistakably both what they require for them to hold or be true, and that this requirement is satisfied, when it is. For such items, under such conditions, IP does not apply. These are the items which we may know in the strictest sense of the term. There may be other things which we may truly be said to know in some other weaker 'plain man's' sense of 'know', which, perhaps, makes much of what we ordinarily say *via* the verb 'know', true. There are two reasons for finding this general view of knowledge unsatisfactory. The first is that the analysis does not save enough of the phenomena. The second is that it is unlikely at best that there is any interesting class of items of the sort envisaged above, specifically ones which, under favourable circumstances, might be immune to IP. What Descartes' 'I exist' appears to exemplify, in short, is roughly itself.

Leaving aside Malcolm's innovation, the first point should be obvious. The items which may be transparent to us in the envisaged way are roughly conceptual truths, including, perhaps, most of mathematics. On some views, we may add to this some items about 'directly introspectible' mental states, if there be such things. Now, to put the point crudely, we would ordinarily suppose that, under favourable conditions, we might truly be said to know such things as that there is money in our pockets, or that this is where we take the bus to work. On the most generous view of conceptual truth, these are not samples of them. Nor are they immune to the IP. So, on the suggested analysis, a very large and important class of things we would take ourselves to know we do not. But an analysis of knowledge which has us being that wrong about what the notion applies to could not be right. It is as if someone claimed that no one has ever worn shoes except for some obscure band of Buddhist monks. The suspicion would be immense that such a person had mistaken what wearing shoes was. In the present case, the parallel conviction might be fortified by considering the immense disutility of a notion of knowledge which was thus restricted, compared to that of a notion with roughly the applications we took our notion of knowledge to have. Of course, we all know that sometimes we are wrong, even in cherished beliefs about the applications or even the coherence of some of our concepts. We were shown to be wrong about such things as simultaneity. And there is always the more hackneyed case of witches. But the rule is that it takes a startling discovery, or—in the case of witches—at least a massive change in world view to demonstrate such things. Whereas in the present case, there has been, in the most important sense, no discovery at all. Cartesian arguments simply present us with the fact that we are not infallible. Whatever we say or think (or nearly), there are conceivable ways for us to turn out to be wrong. But who ever doubted that? And if no one ever did, then why think that the concept of knowledge requires otherwise for it to apply? To accept this as a result would be to violate canons of sound linguistic inquiry. In plainer words, it would be unreasonable.

A cloud of dust is thrown up around the above point by the idea that most of what we say in using 'know' is really about 'knowledge' in some weaker sense. This gives an appearance of saving phenomena at least in the sense that it appears to make the bulk of what we ordinarily thus say true, or true as far as philosophy is concerned, at least. But it is merely a diversion. Suppose we ask: 'knowledge' in some weaker sense than *what*? We could, of course, introduce a notion to which IP applies by stipulation. And we might remark that this notion was 'stronger' in some sense than the ordinary notion of knowledge. But the problem with which Descartes began was to check certain of his views about *knowledge*. Even stating his problem at all involves appealing to a notion which we are all meant to share. Which one? Knowledge, of course. Descartes' problem was that he was afraid that he might have some wrong views about *that*. Claims about 'moral certainty' and the like then come to this: most of the time when we use the word, 'know', we do not use it to mean or refer to knowing. Most of the time, then, we use it to express something other than what it properly does express in English; we *say* 'know', but we are really talking about something else. First, what possible reason could there be to think this was true (as a thesis about English usage, for example), and second, what is to show on which occasions we really use 'know' to mean *know*? What argument could there be that the above view of knowledge has got this right? For the moment I will leave this at a series of questions. But we will rejoin the argument at this point in section 2, when it comes to defending a Wittgensteinian account.

Let us now graft Malcolm's innovation back on to Prichard's views. How does this help? On Malcolm's view, there are *some* thoughts about the empirical world which we can know to be true. But clearly these are not the thoughts we ordinarily express, nor do they correspond to the things we ordinarily take ourselves to know. If A is about to tell B that there is a party Friday night, then C may stop him by telling him that B already knows that. There may be a thought for B to have about parties which could not be shown wrong no matter what subsequently happens. But a thought of that sort is not what A or C have in mind. In fact, it might be observed that having Malcolmian thoughts, if possible, must require considerable skill. Most of the time in taking it that P, we do recognize things which, if they were so, would show us wrong. Malcolm's innovation, then, does not bring the transparence account appreciably closer to getting knowledge to have the applications we would have supposed it to have. This particular Cartesian line on knowledge, then, leaves us knowing too little either for knowledge to be a useful notion, or for this to be what our notion of knowledge might plausibly be taken to come to.

The first objection is in itself enough to make us look elsewhere for a correct account of knowing. Unless there is some as yet unimagined and successful technique for carving out some much wider area of objects of knowledge which are immune to IP, it is IP that will have to go. The second objection not only strengthens the first by increasing the implausibility involved, but is also of interest in its own right, not in the least because it connects present issues with Wittgenstein's views on semantics. The point of it is that there is no interesting immune area to be carved out by present Cartesian techniques. We might approach the point by recalling our initial impression that there could not possibly be anything which withstood the challenge of IP (with the noted exception that A exists, and perhaps that he thinks something or other). The thought was that, for any A and P, for A to be in a position to distinguish his actual situation from all those in which not-P, in the way required by the IP, he would have to have information which was new and different, in the sense that he might properly take himself to have it without having settled whether P. But information which satisfies that requirement is compatible, for all A knows, with at least some situations in which not-P. In which case, IP must apply to A and P, given that A has that information, no matter what it is. Finding the particular situations which allow IP to apply is a mere matter of detail. If Descartes, Prichard and Malcolm are correct, then there is an interesting class of P's for which this impression is wrong: for them, A could be in a position such that no situation could be constructed which would allow IP to apply. The question is, just what have they done positively to dispel the impression? What grounds have they offered for taking it to be wrong in the favoured cases?

Prichard's account on this score is perhaps the clearest. To take a simple case, suppose that what A takes to be so is, as we should put it, that bachelors are unmarried. By reflecting on his thought here (or, in Prichard's terms, his state of mind), he can come to see (or he already just does see) that in it, he is thinking about (the property of) being a bachelor, and taking something to be so of it (and, of course, of bachelors), and similarly of the property of being unmarried. There is nothing that could conceivably make him mistaken about that. By reflecting on what properties these are, he can see that being a bachelor is a property something can only have by also having the property of being unmarried. Again, he could not conceivably be wrong about that. The reason, it seems, is that a property which lacked that feature would simply not be that of being a bachelor, hence, not the one he is thinking of, and he could not be wrong about which property he was thinking of, nor about what is required for being that property. What is supposed here, clearly, is the transparence of thoughts, or mental states and their objects, to the people who have them. If A has the thought that P, or takes P to be so, then, it is supposed, A does or can know which thought this is, and hence, at least in the respects mentioned, what its semantics is, and can do so in a way such that there is no possibility of his being wrong about this.

Suppose the claim is that A knows that bachelors are unmarried. The backing for it, on the above story, might be put like this. A takes something to be so (if 'takes to be so' seems not neutral enough, then A π's something). A sees that what he thus takes to be so is that bachelors are unmarried. He further sees that the properties he has in mind in doing so—those he thus takes something to be so of—are such that the first mentioned requires the second for having it. 'Sees', in this use, remains a success verb. But, for purposes of IP, that is not to the point. If one wanted to construct a situation for IP to apply to here, the natural proposal would be: could there not be a situation for A to be in such that being in it would seem, to A, exactly like the situation just described, one which he has no means of distinguishing from that, in which all or some of the above is not so; either what he thus takes to be so is not that bachelors are unmarried, or the properties he has in mind are not such that the first requires the second for having it, or both? Could there not be, for example, unbeknownst to A, some test, T, for being a bachelor—that is, for having the very property he thus has in mind—which, in fact, is absolutely decisive for having that property, and such that passing that test does not require having the second property above? If such a situation is conceivable, then IP applies, and A does not know what he thus takes to be so. If the above is the backing for the claim that he knows that bachelors are unmarried, then he does not know this. On the present Cartesian view, such is not conceivable; there could be no such situation. The heart of the second objection is that this claim is wrong.

The semantics of a thought, or any given propositional attitude, would be transparent to its entertainer, A, if the item's having the semantics it does rather than some other simply consisted in A's being in some introspectible mental state; one such that one could not mistake its semantics (or if it is an attitude, what the attitude is towards) since nothing would count as doing that. Taking the right things to be so of the item, or having the right intentions towards it, for example, might do the job if they are introspectible in this sense; if one could not in principle mistake or confuse what one thus intended or took to be so, or fail to perceive anything relevant about this. Similar remarks apply to words and their speakers. On Wittgenstein's view, an item's semantics is not made what it is by any such states, in part because there are no mental states, and certainly not attitudes towards a semantics, which are unproblematic in that way: whose possessors command an authority over them which precludes in principle their going wrong as to what the semantics of *those* states is, for each question that might arise about that semantics. (One can, for one thing, always generate the unanticipated.) In part, also, the point is a matter of what we want semantic descriptions to do; what they are used for.

In any case, the view is that the semantics of an item is an external matter. The semantics of A's thought or words is what it is most reasonably taken to be given the overall activity into which it fits. What it is most reasonably taken to be is what reasonable judges would take it to be where, bracketing S-use sensitivity, these are whatever reasonable judges might be in a position to take the item to have some semantics rather than some other. Since this whole book is an argument for that view, I offer no special argument here, but take it as established.

Given the view, it is clear why there can be no transparence of the sort Prichard and Malcolm want. Malcolm's thought about the pen, for example, could turn out to be wrong because he turned out to be wrong about the way it stood up to experience. This might happen because a reasonable judge would take Malcolm's thought to be about a pen on a desk, and hence, given the other circumstances of its thinking, to be one which would be shown wrong by such-and-such future experience, either which Malcolm had not thought of, or whose significance he had misassessed. So Malcolm does not know in the supposed strong sense in which knowledge stands up to IP. Ditto for Prichard, and for anyone and any thought, whatever that person may *take* that thought to require for its truth.

Here we may note a particular case of the externality view, emphasized by Hilary Putnam over many years and in many places.[12]

---

[12] *The locus classicus* remains Putnam [1962b]. See also Putnam [1962c] for a good general statement of the position. But, of course, these are but a small sample of what Putnam has had to say on the subject.

Where A π's that P, it is always possible that one day a new test, T, might be discovered such that a reasonable judge would find it only rational to take T as a test for P's obtaining, and a weightier one than any way in which P has yet confronted experience, no matter what ways those are, and no matter which thought A took P to be. T would then have that status. In this way, at least, A could always turn out to be wrong. For this reason among others, violating our most cherished semantic intuitions is not decisive proof of having changed the subject.

More generally, reflecting on one's present state cannot *guarantee* in the way IP requires that others, judging from the outside, would find the thought one entertains to require such-and-such for its truth; nor that what one takes to be so requires such-and-such for being so. Hence such reflection cannot be infallible as to what is required for this. It cannot preclude the possibility of semantic blindness. In whatever sense it might be correct to say of someone facing a snorting and pawing pig in broad daylight that for all he knows there may be no pig, it is equally correct to say of someone face to face with what he means by being a bachelor that for all he knows he might be taking to be so what is not so in taking to be so what he thereby does. If mechanical pigs are a way of going wrong about something, then, intuitively, so is semantic blindness (or, as the case may be, lack of semantic prescience).

Does this mean that for any thought, P, that we might entertain, there are conceivable circumstances under which P would not be so? At least this: for any P, there are conceivable circumstances under which in taking it that P, we would have taken to be so what is not. For there are always conceivable circumstances in which the thought we have entertained in taking it that P would have a different semantics than it in fact does. If we allow possibilities to range wide enough, then, on the present view of semantics, there are no items which are necessarily true. Necessary truths require a treatment of necessity which limits the possible situations it must confront—say, to ones where an item retains (the essentials of) the semantics it in fact has (not that we have an S-use insensitive notion of that). Such suggests a way with knowledge of mathematics, or other items we might regard as necessary, as well as with such things as counterfactual conditionals over such domains. It also suggests that a variant IP, in terms of deceptive situations in which not-P, would have just the same applications as the present cagier version.

The point of the second objection is that if IP is valid, then what we know, leaving aside Descartes' 'I exist', and perhaps, 'I think', is precisely nothing. But whether IP leaves us knowing nothing, or merely little, it is clearly much too little for IP to be consistent with a correct account of knowledge. (If such seems merely a dogmatic rejection of scepticism, there is a non-dogmatic rejection on the agenda for section 3.) This closes the present subject. Henceforth, I will assume, at least as a working hypothesis, that IP is false. It remains to find an account of how it could be. The search begins in the next section.

1.4. A PIONEERING REJECTION

With his pioneering rejection of IP, Moore pointed epistemology down an importantly new path. His account of the matter, while incomplete in major respects, and not quite right as far as it went, was, on the other hand, not so very wrong either. But if we want a clear view of the rejection, we should separate it from another issue. It is said that Moore offered a 'proof (or several) of an external world'. He does have a paper of that title (henceforth PEW),[13] and in it he does say that that is what he has done. The question whether he has succeeded in this has been the focus of much attention. But the topic of such a proof is separable from Moore's views on what we know, as presented, for example, in 'A Defence of Common Sense'[14] (hereafter DCS), where no such proof is on offer. Though it takes both articles, at least, to show what the views are, the sole interest here is in Moore's views on knowledge. The topic of proofs of an external world must wait.

As for what we know, Moore offers, in effect, a sort of paradigm case argument. He begins by listing a large number of things he knows, such as that he has hands (or a body), that he was born at some time in the past, and that he has never been very far away from the surface of the earth. He uses this to define, for most (he says, 'very many') of us, a similar class of things that each of us knows. For example, each of (most of) us knows that he was born at some time in the past. Is Moore just being dogmatic about this? In DCS, he says that it is his *opinion* that he knows the things listed. But Moore's view appears to be this: he is more certain of these things, and moreover, of knowing them, than he would be of any philosophical argument, such as one involving IP, claiming to show otherwise. If there were a choice between taking it that he is mistaken about knowing such things, or taking it that there is a mistake somewhere in a philosophical argument, reason would always dictate that he choose the latter.

Moore's view here shares a feature of many paradigm case arguments. It is always conceivable that there is something on Moore's list

---

[13] Moore [1939].
[14] Moore [1925].

of clear examples such that he is wrong about the facts of the case. Such would be so, for example, if everyone but Moore in fact knew about the prevalence of flying saucers, experiments done on earthlings deep in space, amnesia-inducing drugs administered on return to earth, etc. Moore is supposing that no such thing is, in fact, the case. If he is wrong in this, then he has chosen the wrong example; it should be replaced with another. But what Moore is doing is using examples to illustrate a sort of case he takes to exist. His examples may be effective in doing this even if he is wrong about the facts of some particular one. What they point to is the reasonable conclusion that no philosophical argument could successfully show that we *were* that wrong all along about the sorts of cases to which our concept of knowledge might apply.

In holding as he does that there is plenty that we know, Moore shows that he rejects IP. For Moore does not suppose that there is no conceivable situation in which, for example, it would turn out that he did not have hands after all, and to which IP would apply. Indeed, in PEW, he is quite explicit on that point. For the main thrust of that article concerns the notion of proof and its relation to knowledge. About this he says that, even though he knows he has two hands, he has no proof of this, or at least in normal circumstances he does not. In defence of this, he says that a proof of such a thing would have to rule out, *inter alia*, Descartes' dreaming hypothesis, and that he is in no position to *say* how that is to be done. On the other hand, Moore does not claim that he can just claim to know whatever he likes, or whatever he likes from some pre-established list of things we all certainly do know, regardless of the ways he might be wrong about it. If there were reason to think that surgeons had deceived him into thinking that his prosthetic devices were hands, then he would not be able to claim that he knew he had hands.

What Moore is suggesting, then, in effect, is, for given P, a partition of doubts as to P into two classes, which we might as well call *real* and *mere*. For real doubts as to P, Moore had better be in a position to show that they do not hold in his case, on pain of not knowing that P. Mere doubts lack this force. These are the ones Moore need not be able to prove do not hold. His point is that, in general, the partition is interesting. The class of mere doubts is far from empty; the class of real ones is small, or perhaps null, and at least roughly specifiable, or, at any rate, real doubts are recognizable as such. Of course, how the partitioning is to be done may depend on the circumstances Moore is in. It is as he is standing in the lecture hall, for example, that he is entitled to say he knows he has hands. Perhaps there are some other circumstances in which he would not be entitled to say this.

Some critics of Moore claim that there is some sceptical, or perhaps philosophical, question as to what we know, or whether we know that P, which Moore has not answered, and which cannot be answered by means such as the above. Less interestingly, some suggest that there is a philosophical sense of 'know' in which Moore has not shown, and the above does not show, for any P, that we know that P. Such suggestions will be more profitably examined later in the story. Leaving them aside for now, there is another problem with Moore's position. This comes out when, in a particular case, we ask how the needed partitioning is to be done. Suppose that I now claim to know that there are three chairs in my office, or that Moore wrote PEW. Ordinary intuition, read as Moore reads it, tells us that these are the sorts of things one might know, and that, in my present position, I do know them. There is, for example, no obvious problem about ascertaining how many chairs there are. There are, of course, doubts for me, in our proprietary sense, as to whether these things are so. There are stories on which, without realizing it, I have suddenly lost my ability to carry out counting procedures, say, to recognize when I have counted something twice, as there are stories on which Moore secretly collaborated with some other Cambridge philosopher to the point where it is incorrect to say that *Moore* wrote PEW. These do sound rather far-fetched. So it is quite intuitive to view them as representing mere doubts.

Now consider situations like the following. Some psychologists with a grant have decided to study the incidence of loss of counting abilities. Perhaps—in fact, for all I know—there is some rare medical condition in which this happens. Similarly, a historian of philosophy has decided to research how often there have been unreported collaborations of the kind just imagined. In the second case, PEW might be one of the works under study. Suppose that the historian's assistant reports to him that PEW is one case, at any rate, where there was no such collaboration. Asked how this has been established, he says that I say so, and I know. Clearly, this does not establish the point. What the assistant says is not only incorrect, but bizarre. Part of the trouble is that it is incorrect for him to say that I know this, unless I know quite a bit more than I do. In particular, I would have to know something which shows that there was no such collaboration. It could not be said here that there is any such thing in particular that I do know. So we have produced circumstances in which we are seriously interested in whether I know that Moore wrote PEW, where I can be shown not to know by showing that I have no proof as to lack of the envisaged collaboration. This seems to indicate that the doubt in question is, when we think seriously about it, a real doubt for me as to Moore's having written PEW. It is clear how to apply the same technique in the case of the three chairs. It is also clear that if this technique does show what it seems to, then Moore will be mistaken: the partition between real and mere doubts will not be interesting in the respects listed above, and will not succeed in preserving much or any of what, on Moore's view, we would intuitively take ourselves to know.

Is the above technique a good one? We supposed ourselves to begin with an intuition that the doubt about collaboration was a mere one for me as to Moore's writing PEW. We then constructed a situation reflection on which would seem to give us the opposite intuition. But why should this new intuition count more heavily than the intuition with which we began? There are two points to make here. First, suppose that it does not. The facts would then be this. When you view my present situation in a certain way, the collaboration story represents, intuitively, a mere doubt for me. When you view it in another way, the story represents, intuitively, a real doubt for me. Either way of viewing my situation is a way in which we sometimes would view it, correctly so, according to intuition. If this sort of situation is the rule—as it would seem to be, on the present assumption—then doubts are not classifiable as real or mere at all. It is like trying to decide whether the sentence 'It's raining', expresses, in English, a true thought or a false one. There is no way of classifying it as doing the one thing or the other at all.

Second, it would seem that it could be argued that the second intuition ought to count more heavily than the first. If we do not allow the collaboration doubt to count as real, then the assistant simply is not wrong when he says that I know that Moore wrote PEW. But that is an intolerable situation. Of course the assistant is mistaken when he says this. Whereas, if we say that our initial intuitions were wrong, there are ways of explaining this away. Ordinarily, when nothing is at stake, we speak loosely. We implicate, perhaps, the right things, whereas strictly speaking what we say is false. Or we are speaking of knowledge in another sense of the term—Descartes' 'moral certainty', perhaps. The reason for thinking that I could not have been speaking strictly, literally, and truly when I said that I knew that Moore wrote PEW is just this. If I was, it would seem, nothing could make this so other than the fact that I do know this. But if such is a fact, then the assistant also speaks truly. Which he does not. Whether this line of thought is irresistible, it has attractions, at least for many. Part of the view to be developed is that it is exactly the attractiveness of this thought that makes scepticism seem hard to refute.

The upshot is that either doubts are not classifiable as real and mere at all, or if they are, the partitioning does not turn out to be interesting in the ways Moore demands of it. It is too early to say that Moore has no response to the points just sketched. But it will be better to attack that question after we have considered another way in which IP might be rejected.

2. THE WITTGENSTEINIAN ACCOUNT: 2.1. AN OBJECTION TO MOORE

On Certainty (henceforth OC) is, at least nominally, Wittgenstein's reaction to Moore. The attitude is critical, though sympathetic to a degree. One main criticism is that Moore misuses the word 'know', in sitting in his study, or standing in the lecture hall to enumerate what he knows. He ignores the fact that 'know' is a special word, requiring special circumstances for its proper use. 'We just do not see how very specialized the use of "I know" is.' (OC 11). The point is made at the start in OC 6:

Now, can one enumerate what one knows (like Moore)? Straight off like that, I believe not.—For otherwise the expression, 'I know', gets misused. And through this misuse a queer and extremely important mental state seems to be revealed.

There is something bizarre, for example, in Moore holding up his hands and saying, without further ado, 'I know there are hands here.' Similarly, suppose that a guest enters my living-room. I gesture at what is obviously an armchair and say, 'I know that's an armchair.' Both speakings are, in some sense, a misuse of 'know', hence, incorrect. But there is room for many theories as to what sort of 'misuse' this might be. Wittgenstein expresses worries as to his view on that point, as in OC 423:

Then why don't I simply say with Moore, '*I know* that I am in England'? Saying this is meaningful *in particular circumstances*, which I can imagine. But when I utter the sentence outside these circumstances, as an example to show that I can know truths of this kind with certainty, then it at once strikes me as suspect.—Ought it to?

Despite the worries, it is clear what Wittgenstein's position is. Without appropriate surroundings, the words 'A know(s) that F' express no definite thought—that is, none with a truth condition definite enough that one might reasonably hope for there to be a fact as to whether the thought was (or the words were) true or false. Here a Fregean image may help. Frege held that certain words failed to express a 'complete' thought, or truth-bearer as such, but did so on a speaking only if the content of that thought was filled in by the context of utterance. Frege's example was, 'The tree is covered with green leaves', which might express one thought spoken in the winter, and another spoken in the summer.[15] What context filled in here, on his view, was the time at which the tree was to be so bedecked. Wittgenstein would have disagreed with Frege that there was either an absolute or an S-use insensitive distinction between 'complete' and 'incomplete' thoughts. Bracketing that, Wittgenstein's position is that for a knowledge ascription to say what might be true (or false) some features of its proper understanding must be filled in by its context of utterance (i.e., facts about its speaking). The present story is an account of what those features are.

Where a speaking is called on to fulfil the role Frege points to, some speaking might fail to live up to its responsibility. So Frege's sample sentence would fail to express either truth or falsehood if it were spoken in a context which did not determine at what time the tree was to be covered. Such would be likely to happen, for example, if the sentence were printed between theorems in a textbook on set theory. Similar things might happen for knowledge ascriptions, on the present view, if spoken outside of natural enough circumstances. But that feature of the account ought not distract us from a more important one. Context is called on to perform the above role for words W precisely and only where there is a variety of distinct things to be said (to be so), thus a variety of distinct truth conditions for what is said in W spoken as meaning what W do mean in their language. Context must do this for the contributions of words to what is said in wholes of which they may be parts only when, in addition, the variety remains when the semantics of the remainders of such wholes is fixed. So Wittgenstein's view is that there is a variety of distinct things to be said in saying A to know F, for fixed A and F, and where it is knowledge that is being spoken of. It remains to make out what the variety is, that this is Wittgenstein's view, and that it is correct.

Wittgenstein illustrates the role circumstance ought to play here, and so the sort of misuse involved, by drawing a number of comparisons in the *Investigations* and in OC. In 117, for example, the comparison is with, 'This is here'. In 501, it is with 'It's raining'. In 514 and OC 348, the comparison is with 'I am here'. And in 514 and 515 there is a crucial comparison of all of these cases with, in effect, 'The rose is red'. In 117, the example illustrates the following point:

You say to me: 'You understand this expression, don't you? Well then—I am using it in the sense you are familiar with.'—As if the sense were an

---

[15] See Frege [1918], p. 27.

atmosphere accompanying the word, which it carried with it into every kind of application.

The implication is that, in crucial respects, this is not so. To a philosopher, in Wittgenstein's time as now, the point is apt to seem trivial, for roughly the same reasons that 'I am here' itself seems rather trivial. On conventional wisdom, we cannot know what thought was expressed in a speaking of 'I am here' unless we at least know who the speaker was, and when the speaking was. If the speaker is A and the speaking at T, then, abstracting from any peculiar 'modes of reference' associated with the word 'I', the thought will be that A was at the place of the speaking at T. Since it is A's speaking, this means that A was at the place at which A spoke at T. So, without knowing what thought a particular speaking of these words expressed, we can say that, whatever it was, it was certainly a true thought. We might put this by saying that 'I am here.' is true whenever it is spoken (though, of course, we never know exactly what it says unless we know the right facts about the speaking).

Such is a conventional description of how facts of a use can be required for determining what thought was expressed in given words so used. But so far from illustrating Wittgenstein's point in 117, it actually illustrates the problem he is attacking there. For, as he makes clear in 116 and 514, for example, the problem is largely one about *philosophical* practice; about philosophers considering words outside of the circumstances in which they are naturally at home, and then seeming to see all sorts of things about the words, or the concepts involved, which are just not so. For example, a philosopher considering the words 'I am here', outside of any situation in which it might be natural for someone to say that, *thinks* that he sees what the semantics of those words is. From that vantage point, the words may seem to say what is trivial, given the semantics that the philosopher seems to see them to have. Their semantics may then seem to be just what it was supposed to be by the conventional account just sketched. But then we must check whether what they say really is trivial, and whether it really is what it is made out to be by the conventional account, by checking what they would express where naturally used. The presumption would be that what they would then say is not trivial, for otherwise why use the words at all? It is certainly Wittgenstein's view that the conventional approach is wrong about what the words say, as he makes clear in OC 348:

Just as the words 'I am here' have a meaning only in certain contexts, and not when I say them to someone who is sitting in front of me and sees me clearly,—and not because they are superfluous, but because their meaning is not *determined* by the situation, yet stands in need of such determination.

If context must do more than is done when I am in front of you and you see me clearly, then the tradition on what those words do say must be wrong. In any case, the correctness of the isolated philosopher's perceptions as to the semantics of the words involved will depend on his being right as to the ways in which such thoughts as would thus naturally be expressed would be trivial, or more generally, as to which thoughts those would be.

The apt comparison, then, would be more along the following lines. When would 'I am here' be used naturally? Suppose I am arriving at the station, and you are to pick me up. When I arrive, I call you at home and say, 'I am here.' That is one wholly natural use. Is it trivial? Intuitively not. It was certainly highly informative to you; if it were not, you would have already been at the station. But is it made true merely by the fact that I was at the phone I was at while I was calling, whatever phone that might be? Consider the following. You own a priceless Picasso, which I much admire. Therefore, I take an earlier train than planned. I wait an appropriate time, and then take a taxi to within two blocks of your home. From a phone booth around the corner, I call you, and say the simple words, 'I am here'. You say, 'I'll be right there', and head for the station as pre-arranged. I wait ten minutes, then break into your house, take the Picasso, and disappear into the night. The ruse here depended on my giving you false information. How did I do that? The present suggestion is that I did it by speaking falsely in my words, 'I am here'. If I did that, then I must have done so by not being at the indicated place at the indicated time. But if I did *that*, it must have been by doing something other than being other than at the place at which I was speaking at the time at which I was speaking. So, it will be part of what was said, or of the semantics of my words, 'I am here', that there is something to be understood as to what the indicated place (and time) are to be taken to be, such that, *ceteris paribus*, at least, what I said will be false if I was not there then. In this case, for example, what I said will be false, *ceteris paribus*, if I was not at the station at the time of the call.

If the above is the right view of my words, 'I am here', then it points to two far-reaching conclusions. First, what the semantics of my words was—in particular, what was to be understood about the indicated place and time—is not something that could have been deduced from 'the meanings of the terms' alone, and hence from the 'sense the words carry into every application', not even given facts of my speaking which such meanings might have directed one to take account of (in some specified way.) So it is not to be seen by a philosophical analysis of those words in isolation from their natural use. Second, the range of different things to be said in those words, and of the differences that may exist between one such thing and another, is much wider than the analysis by the isolated philosopher would have indicated. One indication of this fact is that there will be an indefinite number of distinct things that a given speaker, in a given place at a fixed time could, say in those words, depending on an indefinite variety of other facts about his circumstances. If all this is so, then the price of speaking outside of natural enough circumstances is clear. The facts of such a speaking will not choose between the various semantics those words might have on some speaking; they will not dictate that the words be understood in one such way rather than another. Where such failure is radical enough, the words thus spoken will not bear enough semantics to say either what is true or what is false.

The above illustrates how the philosopher might go wrong by considering, or using, words out of context. It also shows an important part of Wittgenstein's position on knowledge, and on Moore. Moore disagreed with the sceptic on what knowledge consisted in. But he shared with the sceptic the more crucial assumption that there was just one thing it consisted in, so that it might be a sensible project to survey some vast range of possible objects of knowledge, to fix us as we are at a given time, and to catalogue these as the ones we do then know and the ones we do not. Whereas Wittgenstein's point, put non-linguistically, is that different things would count as knowing that F on different occasions for judging whether A, in a given condition, counts as knowing this. Nor are these things any stable function of antecedently specifiable other factors found in such occasions.

Since Wittgenstein's time, considerations have been adduced against reading the 'I am here' case in the way suggested above. Similar considerations would count against any account of knowledge ascriptions which would have Moore going wrong in the way just described. It may be bizarre for Odile now to say, 'I know I am wearing shoes.' But it would be equally bizarre for her to point at her feet and say, 'I am wearing shoes.' In neither case, on a currently fashionable view, does the bizarreness touch on issues of truth. Despite it, it is urged, Odile is wearing shoes, and similarly knows this or does not. In both cases, on this view, what is said is deducible, modulo a few specifiable points, from what our words mean in English, and is what is either true or false. Such views must be considered in due course. Present procedure, though, is to begin by seeing what there is to be said in favour of the Wittgensteinian view just described. Which means that, provisionally but unabashedly, I will engage in what is sometimes disparagingly referred to as ordinary language philosophy. Only after having done so will I consider whether it is right to engage in that. At least we *will* eventually consider that question. It will also advance the discussion greatly if we can separate two issues. Let us temporarily forget what role facts of a speaking have in determining what was said in ascribing knowledge to someone, and begin with the prior question what there is to be said, of given A and F, in saying that A knows that F. Our interest is in the variety. If that is great and rich enough, we may draw whatever consequences do follow from that as to the role of circumstance.

2.2. ORDINARY LANGUAGE

This section takes a brief look at how—and when—we actually do speak of knowledge. If that grates too much, then skip on to the topic of how the data matter. Here is one simple thing one might know: where the milk is, or that it is in the refrigerator. Here is one case. Hugo, engrossed in the paper, says, 'I need some milk for my coffee.' Odile replies, 'You know where the milk is.' Suddenly defensive, Hugo replies: 'Well, I don't really *know* that, do I? Perhaps the cat broke into the refrigerator, or there was just now a very stealthy milk thief, or it evaporated or suddenly congealed.' The reply is not only absurd, but fails to count against what Odile said. In these circumstances, it does not even tend to show that Hugo does not know where the milk is, or that it is in the refrigerator. Or such is a natural reaction.

A contrasting case. Hugo and Odile are just leaving for a weekend in the country. As they are stepping into the car, Odile asks, 'Are you sure everything is put away?' Hugo replies, 'Yes.' She then asks, 'Where's the milk?' He answers, 'In the refrigerator.' She asks, 'Are you *sure* it is?' 'I know it,' replies Hugo 'after all, that's where the milk is kept.' Again this is absurd. Knowing where the milk is kept is not good enough here for knowing where the milk is now. So the trip is delayed. Here is one view of the contrast: there is a doubt as to the milk's being in the refrigerator—namely that it was not put back—which does not tend to count against the truth of Odile's remark in the first case, but does count against the truth of what Hugo said here. Between the two cases, Hugo's relation to the refrigerator has, of course, changed. Such would not seem to make for relevant changes in his other information about it. But to remove all doubt on that score, let us turn to a second case.

Pia, perhaps eyeing a trip to Paris herself, says, 'Odile was in Paris last week.' Luc asks how she knows. Pia replies, 'Hugo told me, and he knows—he heard it from Odile himself (or: he put her on the train himself.)' So, it seems, Hugo certainly ought to know. A variant. Odile did not tell Hugo she was going to Paris, nor did he put her on the train.

On her return, he might say to her, accusingly, 'I *know* you've been in Paris; I saw the ticket stubs.' Or, 'If you had been in Geraardsbergen with your mother, she would have made you call me.' A contrasting case. Rumours have been flying. Odile, it is said, was seen with strange company in a strange night spot in Reims. Could she have changed trains in Aulnoye? Pia tries to stop the rumours: 'I know she was in Paris. I heard it from Hugo, and he certainly knows—he put Odile on the train himself.' Made in these circumstances, such a remark is absurd. It does not tend to show Hugo to know where Odile is, nor does he here count as doing so. To see the contrast with the first case even more clearly, suppose that, in the absence of rumors, Hugo was asked, during that week, where Odile was, and said, 'I don't know.' It then emerges that he put her on the train for Paris himself. It would be no defence of his remark here (by ordinary lights) to protest that after all it was possible for her to change trains in Aulnoye. So again, a doubt which counts against one claim that Hugo knows that F (the change of trains doubt) does not intuitively count against another. If there is change in Hugo's other information across these cases, it must be one in the information he counts as having as he in fact is at a given time.

Let us take it that we can now construct pairs of cases on the above model *ad lib*. We may now note two further phenomena, one of which has been exploited[16] to argue against a Wittgensteinian (or Austinian) account, the other of which appears to argue for it. The first concerns natural, the second unnatural uses of 'know'. On the natural side: Someone tells us that a chair is a Wassily. If we ask whether he is sure, he might reply that he knows it is, and he ought to know—he knows something about, or has had some experience with furniture. If his position (his qualifications) is good enough, then, intuitively, his claim here to know is correct. Similarly, the waiter tells me, 'Those are real flowers on the table.' I reply, 'I know.' If I am sensitive to the widespread practice of using artificial flowers and have looked closely, then ordinarily, my claim would count as correct. Again, Luc needs to buy hosiery. He considers going to McTeagle's. But there is a problem: 'I know they sell shoes, laces and polish. But do they sell socks?' He seems to recall that they do, but is he sure? Or: we know (suppose) who paid what to whom when. But the problem is what Reagan knew and when he knew it. What is emphasized in the anti-Wittgensteinian tradition is that such uses of 'know' are quite correct even though for none is there any specific doubt as to the point in question 'in the air' or 'in the offing'—no particular reason, for example, to think that McTeagle's might not sell shoes. So, it is thought, there is no well-defined set of doubts relevant to the truth of those claims.

[16] E.g., by Barry Stroud [1984]. Stroud's target is Austin.

The second phenomenon concerns unnatural uses of 'know'. For example, Luc is staring the pig in the eye, and we say, 'Luc knows there's a pig in the sty' or, 'Luc knows that's a pig'. Or Pia is looking at the shoes in McTeagle's *étalage* and we say, 'Pia knows that those are shoes.' Normally such remarks would be puzzling. That is a superficial remark. It points towards a deeper one, which may also help with the first phenomenon. In appropriate circumstances, perfectly natural things may be said of Luc and Pia (as they now are) in saying them to know these things. The remark about Luc would be natural, for example, if there was suspicion that he was a city slicker who had never seen a pig and would not know one on sight. It would also be natural if the suspicion was that this was a Quisneycorp 'farmworld', and that a mechanical clockwork pig (the point of the remark being that Luc is not taken in by such things, or has checked). Of course, a doubt we would count as relevant in the first case (perhaps that's the way a sheep looks, for example) we would not so count in the second, and vice versa. But this is to say that even where, for given A and F, it is sometimes bizarre (and not just plain false) to speak of knowledge, we can still construct contrasting pairs of cases as per the first two examples. Moreover, we appear to be able to build such a pair around anything we can count as a possible doubt as to F.

We can now see a similar point to be made for the first phenomenon. Suppose I was right in saying I knew the flowers were real. Now suppose that the headwaiter repeats to an assistant the rumour he heard that a firm which makes a new hyper-realistic fake flower has been surreptitiously seeding the best restaurants with them as a publicity stunt. Could that be going on here? It would, quite likely, be bizarre for the assistant to assure the headwaiter that it was not, on the strength of my word that the flowers were real and the assurance that I knew. For those purposes, I cannot be said to know. Similarly, Luc may have spoken correctly, above, in listing what he does and does not know about McTeagle's. But now suppose that we read an article on how McTeagle's has been reorganizing and eliminating less profitable lines. It would be no proof that shoes, anyway, had been unaffected to claim that Luc knows that McTeagle's sells shoes. Nor would he now count as knowing this. So for this range of cases too we can construct contrasting pairs. No matter what else we say about cases where 'no doubts are in the offing', we shall see that that fact is enough to establish the Wittgensteinian account.

2.3. READING THE DATA

The data just cited admit of various interpretations. Progress requires beginning with one. Here is the one I will defend. It begins with the principle that, for given A, at a given time, informed as he is at that time, and a given object of knowledge, P, there is a variety of distinct things to be said of A in saying that A knows that P (for example, in using the word, 'know', to mean what it does mean). Second, these things differ from each other in ways such that a possible doubt as to P which, if live for A, counts against the truth of one such claim may fail so to count against the truth of others. Different ranges of possible doubts are relevant to different claims that A (in a given state) knows that F. A third principle is, in effect, the converse of the second. For any possible doubt for A as to P, so presumably any coherent set of them, there is something to be said in saying A to know P which is shown false by that doubt, or any doubt in that set being a live one for A.

A note on how the data are taken to show this. The first two principles are shown by the existence of contrasting pairs, as in the case of Hugo knowing that the milk is in the refrigerator. The third principle is indicated by our means for constructing natural situations for saying such *prima facie* bizarre things as, 'I know that those are shoes'. It is important, of course, that the contrasting situations of ascribing knowledge be such that whatever (relevant) possible doubt is live for A in the one is live for A in the other. We are supposing that this is so of Hugo and the milk, even though, in fact, in one situation he is sitting in front of his coffee, and in the other he has just stepped out of the door. That difference does not make a difference for the relevant doubts as to the milk being in the refrigerator. If anyone doubts that point, though, the same point comes out even more certainly in the cases of Odile in Paris, and those involving mechanical pigs, etc.

Things to be said, then, in saying A to know P differ in which doubts as to P would count against their truth. The presumption is that for any single such thing there are doubts which would, or might, so count, and doubts which would not. The rule at least is that neither class of doubt is empty. Exceptions to the rule are conceivable. But the evidence is that, at least in the latter case, there are none. For the data indicate that where we take it that there is such-and-such doubt as to P, we also take it that there is something which would settle that doubt, and thereby count as settling whether P. We might elevate this to a fourth principle of the account: for anything to be said in saying A to know P, there is a non-empty class of doubts as to P which would not show this thing to be false, even if live for A, thus which do not enter into its truth condition. I will say something later about why this would be true. But I take it to be a less central part of the present account than the first three principles.

The proposal, then, is that where there is a determinate answer to the question whether A knows that F, possible doubts as to F divide into real and mere, where the class of mere ones is non-empty, and that this distinction enters into the truth conditions for what is said in saying A to know F. Restricting attention to cases where A takes it that F^{17}, I thus propose the following generalization on truth conditions for knowledge claims: 'A knows that F', where it ascribes knowledge of F to A, is true iff no doubts which count as real with respect to that knowledge ascription are live doubts for A. Note that this condition makes no mention of a requirement that it be so that F. This virtue of the account will be discussed and exploited in due course. I have also said nothing about what determines which doubts are to be treated as real for a given knowledge claim. There will be more about that later.

So, on this reading, Moore was nearly right. He was correct in observing a real/mere doubt distinction, but failed to see that that distinction must be drawn differently, in questions of knowledge, for different discussions of the same A and F, thus differently for different things to be said of Moore as he was as he lectured, in saying him to know that he had hands, or was in England. So it is also that Wittgenstein supports Moore's drawing of the distinction:

> But that is not to say that we are in doubt because it is possible for us to *imagine* a doubt. I can easily imagine someone always doubting before he opened his front door whether an abyss did not yawn behind it, and making sure about it before he went through the door (and he might on some occasion prove to be right)—but that does not make me doubt in the same case. (84)

and yet remains so critical of Moore's use of 'know'.

We have identified real doubts as one feature which distinguishes one knowledge claim from others—for fixed A and F, the only one mentioned above in their truth conditions. But are there not perhaps others? A claim that Luc knows it is a pig in the sty is true if Luc has discharged all relevantly real doubts about it. But for a given real doubt, D, when does Luc count as having done that? If the doubt is whether it is a mechanical pig, then sometimes this has been settled if Luc has kicked it, and it grunted rather than clanked. But sometimes not; some mechanical pigs might be very clever fakes. Is this not a matter that might vary from one ascription to another?

It bears emphasis, first, that I am not claiming to discover any unique 'real logical form' of knowledge ascriptions. On Wittgenstein's view, there is no such thing. That said, we may note that the question

---

[17] The point of the restriction is to avoid taking sides on the tricky question whether knowing that F *always* entails taking it that F (a question perhaps relevant to such issues as the possibility of innate knowledge). But for present purposes, A's taking it that F may be taken provisionally as part of the truth condition for the truth of any claim that A knows that F.

contains the seeds of its own answer. Where it is a real doubt that the pig might be mechanical, it may or may not also be a real doubt that the pig is cleverly made so as not to clank when kicked. If it is, then Luc cannot discharge the real doubts there are simply by kicking the 'pig'. If not, then he may be able to discharge the real doubts in this way, depending on things like our normal standards for settling such doubts, but not, in this respect, on the knowledge ascription in question. So, I will suppose, distinctions of this further sort may be handled in terms of further real doubts, and the notion of real doubt is enough for present purposes.

There remains the question what determines which doubts count as real for a given claim that A knows that F. Since, on the account, different such claims are properly understood to say different things (distinguished by their truth conditions), and one such understanding is to be distinguished from another by what one would take to be the real doubts on it, it is a reasonable view that part of the story here is that it is part of what there is to be understood about a knowledge claim that certain (sorts of) doubts are to be taken as real and certain sorts not. So one thing that may make a doubt real (or not) is that it is to be understood to be so. As per chapter 2, how words are to be understood is fixed by how competent judges of that would react to them. So the beginning of the story here is that, to speak roughly, we, if normally sensitive to the facts of the speaking (of 'A knows that F.') would react by treating certain doubts as real for it and certain as not.

Such begins the story but is not its end. For I also take it that the world is a further factor which may show that a doubt is real even where we would not initially react by taking it to be so. Luc tells Hugo, 'There are stags in these parts. Odile told me, and she knows—she's actually seen them.' We would all dismiss the possibility of mechanical stags as irrelevant to this claim. But suppose that, unknown to us, Quisneycorp actually has been sowing the landscape with mechanical stags. Then perhaps that is what Odile saw. So she did not know after all. Shown the facts of Quisneycorp endeavours, we have been taught that this possibility is a real doubt after all. What the world shows in such respects is shown, we suppose, by the reactions of reasonable judges to the facts which show it. So a doubt, D, is not real for a knowledge ascription, K, only if (a) we would not naturally take it to be and (b) there are no facts of the world which we would react to by altering this initial reaction.

It is impossible to overemphasize the importance of this 'world-involving' aspect of real and mere doubts. For the present, note how we have relied on it in formulating truth conditions for claims that A knows that F. In failing to mention, in those conditions, the requirement that it be so that F we have relied on the following thought: if there are facts to make this a case of F's not obtaining, then for any claim that A knows that F (or equivalently, any occasion for judging whether A knows that F), there are some facts which show some doubt to be real for that claim or on that occasion which A has not discharged. If there is not a stag on the lawn, and Odile takes it that there is, then Odile could not have done everything that ought to be done to settle whether there is.[18] Our initial reliance on this thought hints at lines of exploitation to be followed in chapter 5.

Having discussed the variety in ascriptions of knowledge there are to be made, we now come to a second issue which, though less important for present purposes, is more difficult to get right. For all that, it is worth a try. Moore thought that he could catalogue the things he knew, or many of them, any time he liked—for example, while standing at the front of a lecture hall. Wittgenstein thinks, as does Austin, that this is a mistake. Given the above account of variety, what is mistaken about Moore's view, and in exactly what does this cataloguing mistake consist? We can begin with a highly general remark. Consider the ascription of knowledge that F to A. Suppose that there are two distinct semantics, each of which some such ascription would have. These semantics may differ from each other, for example, in that, for given D, on the one semantics, D would count as a real doubt (for A) as to F, while on the other it would not. Then for a particular such ascription—Luc's, say—to count as having the one semantics rather than the other, there must be facts of its making which make this so—on the present view, facts which make it more reasonable to take it to bear the one rather than the other. It is conceivable for there to be none such. If there are not, then where the choice is one that must be made for the ascription to count, for some purpose, as understandable, the ascription will not so count. There will then count as being no definite thought that it expresses. If the purpose in question is one of, or involves, evaluating the ascription as true or false, then it will not be properly evaluated as being either. In which case, it will be correct to say that nothing either true or false was said in it. Such describes a risk that Moore runs in trying to catalogue what he knows. If he says that he knows that he has hands, and if there are no facts of his so speaking in the lecture hall which show which of the things to be said in saying so Moore did say, where the choices thus not made span both what is true and what is false, then what he said will be unevaluable as to truth; so he will neither have said something true, nor have said something false.

[18] Similarly, where there is a stag on the lawn, seeing it may be enough to know this. But where there is no stag, you do not see it.

It would be remarkable if this theoretical risk were never realized. For the normal case, where there are semantic choices, it is possible to construct cases where nothing makes them, and where the result is ununderstandability. Luc says, 'Hugo . . .', but nothing about his doing so shows whether his words spoke of Hugo A. or Hugo B. One might refer to 'the one he meant'. But it could be that nothing shows which one he meant. Suppose he never noticed there were two?

We are still left with the parallel oddities of 'Those are shoes', said pointing at the shoes in the *étalage* or at one's feet, and 'I/you/she know(s) those are shoes', said in the same circumstances. Since the first oddity appears not to touch issues of truth, should we not say the same about the second? There are two points to make about this. First, when you say, 'Those are shoes', you give your word for it in whatever way people normally do in asserting things to be so. But you do not explicitly say that you are giving your word. In traditional terms, it is not part of the truth conditions for what you said that you said it. A vicious regress follows from saying otherwise. Where you give your word, others are entitled to take your word for it (more or less guardedly), or not. They are also entitled to give your word for it. If someone else were to say that the things were shoes, he could back his claim by saying that, after all, you said so. Plausibly, it is just here that the oddity lies in the above case. Since there was, so far, no doubt as to the things being shoes, we do not know what to make of your giving your word that they are. What sort of assurance is this supposed to give? How could the things possibly fail to be shoes? Could they be sensitive listening devices? or the things in the *étalage* flowerpots? If we ought to have such doubts, then what is your word worth anyway? Since it is indeterminate which doubts are thus relevant to judging the value of your word, it is also indeterminate what your word is worth. None of these remarks touch on the truth value of what you actually said. If we now shift to your saying, 'I know those are shoes', then there is a sharp contrast to be drawn. For, while all of the above remarks apply equally here, it is now plausibly the case that you do say that you give and have due assurances for it.[19] Now the indeterminacy of what these assurances should be, hence whether you are in a position to give them, does yield indeterminacy for the truth of what you said.

Second, we must look more closely at the intuition that in saying, 'Those are shoes', you said what, at any event, is true. There are certainly various distinct things to be said of things in the predicate 'are shoes'. For example, some such things are true of some house slippers of which others are not. If your use of the words is odd enough, then it is not determined which of these things you did say in your

[19] And if you say that A knows that F, you do say that A has due assurances for it.

remark. But to challenge the view that what you said is either true or false, a further step must be taken. We must show that some of these things to be said are true of what you spoke of, while others are not. It would be rash to assert that there is nothing to be said in those words that is not true of the things on your feet. But it is certainly difficult to imagine any such thing. If we take it that there is no semantics your words plausibly could have had on which they would be false, and that the semantics of any words reasonably like yours would be such as to make them true if anything, then it may be correct for us to assign your words at least that much semantics—that is, the property of being true—without being able to assign them any more detailed semantics than is involved in saying that you used 'shoes' to mean *shoes* and to describe the objects on your feet. Again there is an apparent contrast with the case where you say, 'I know these are shoes.' Here, if the first three principles are right, we can easily imagine things to be said in your words which would be false, as well as things which would be true. With knowledge ascriptions we are, in this respect, always is a situation more like the one we would have been in with respect to your 'These are shoes', if the things on your feet had been slippers. It is then unclear with what right we would take some of these things to be too remote from what might have been said in your words to have any effect on evaluations as to their truth. The unclarity mounts if we ask precisely which such things might thus count as too remote.

For all the above, there are fall-back positions one might conceivably take. Suppose that Luc and Hugo, trying to catalogue what Odile knows as she stares into the *étalage*, say that, at any rate, she knows that those things are shoes. (It is not hard to imagine this actually happening as a kind of joke.) We might then take the attitude that any doubt, on that occasion, as to whether the things were shoes would be too far-fetched or ridiculous. We might also take the further attitude that, given that, whatever precisely Luc and Hugo said, or however indeterminate its semantics may be, it surely could not have been something with a semantics such as to make it false. Finally, we might take that as good reason to regard it as being true, whatever it might be. There might conceivably be occasions on which such are reasonable attitudes to take towards Luc and Hugo's words. Which is to say that they might sometimes be correctly regarded as having said something true. Such depends on the situations in which the words are viewed, not on that in which they were spoken. If this is so, it would provide a sense in which, within narrow enough limits, the cataloguing mistake might sometimes not count as being a mistake. But it would still be a mistake to try to build very much philosophy out of this. In particular, even if it is correct, it ought not to obscure the much more important points contained in the three or four principles which describe the variety of distinct things to be said in ascribing knowledge of P to A. These points stand independent of whether they leave room for fall-back positions like the one just described.

Let us now sum up the core of the present account. For a given fact, F, which might or might not be known (by someone) and a given subject, A, who might or might not know something, there are various distinct things to be said in saying A to know F. None of these things has—outside of some particular context—the property of representing the 'real' facts as to (A's) knowledge (of F), as opposed to the others, which would then (really) do something else. Each of these things differs from all the others in the conditions (or what is required) for its truth. These conditions differ from each other in terms of the drawing, for each of them, of a distinction, within the realm of conceivable doubts as to F, between 'real' and 'mere' doubts. The real/mere doubt distinction (for given F and A) is thus an S-use sensitive one. Real doubts, but not mere ones, have the property that, if live for A, they may show the knowledge ascription in question to be false. So, in general, if some of the items in question are true, then the rule will be that there are others which are false. Conversely, the falsity of some cannot show the falsity of all. Finally, where A is said to know F, circumstances of that saying must decide which of these items, if any, was (were) produced.

Whatever the demerits of the present account, let us immediately note two of its merits. First, since, typically, on it the range of real doubts for a given claim that A knows F will be highly restricted, many knowledge claims have truth conditions which allow them to be true, and some knowledge claims will be. In that sense, it is a consequence of the account that there are some things we can know. But, given the implied S-use sensitivity of knowledge, this is better put by saying that there are some things we can truly be said to know.

Second, the account offers a solution to Moore's problem. On our account of him, Moore wanted to draw a distinction between real and mere doubts, but he wanted to do this S-use insensitively. (If Moore was the relevant subject or knower, then the distinction was sensitive to occasions *he, qua* knower, might be on; but it was not sensitive to occasions for ascribing knowledge to him as he was on some given occasion.) The problem was that for every conceivable doubt as to F— unsurprisingly—we can conceive of, and construct occasions on which we would take that doubt seriously, which is to say occasions on which it would be natural to treat it as real for purposes of deciding whether Moore, on his occasion, knew F. If a doubt must be ruled real or mere *tout court*, then this seems compelling reason for ruling a doubt as real. But, by this reasoning, the category of mere doubt will always be empty.

The solution on offer is this. Any conceivable doubt might properly be treated as real on *some* occasion for ascribing knowledge of F to A. But that does not show that, when we fix an occasion for judging whether A knows that F, that doubt would count as real on *that* occasion. We allow the intuition that threatened Moore's S-use insensitive way of drawing the distinction—the intuition that for each doubt, there are occasions for treating it as real. But we allow it as an intuition about some occasions; not one about what is so of *each* occasion for ascribing that knowledge to A. Nor do we allow an inference from what is correct about each such intuition to any conclusion about what is so on all such occasions. There are conceivable occasions on which there is a doubt as to whether Odile changed trains in Aulnoye. That does not show that this is or even might be such an occasion. Correspondingly, there are some ascriptions to someone of knowledge that Odile is in Paris which this doubt might show false. But if, on some occasion, we are ascribing such knowledge to Hugo, this last fact does not show that the ascription we thus make is among these.

2.4. ARGUMENT[20]

Criticism of the sort of view just outlined tends to focus on the question whether, outside of appropriate circumstances, one fails to express a definite thought in saying A to know that F—whether the oddity involved in so speaking touches on questions of truth. As the above discussion makes clear, this is not the main point. What is at issue is not the correct description of such exceptional cases, but rather the role of circumstance in determining what is expressed, particularly in natural cases, in knowledge ascriptions. Odd uses of 'know' are interesting primarily in so far as they point to what that role might be. Which is to say that criticism of the present view had better begin with the first principle. Grant the first three or four principles, and further questions about the relation between oddity and truth can be allowed to remain moot.

The first principle states that there are a variety of distinct things to be said in ascribing knowledge of F to A. Fix F and A, and the remaining principles indicate how to construct a goodly sample of these. What

---

[20] The following summarizes argument presented in a more general context in Travis [1985].

such a sample would look like is illustrated by the data of section 2.1. The opposing view would be that if we fix A and F, then, speaking of A as A is at a given time, there is just one thing to be said in saying A to know F, where, typically, at least, this will either be something true, or something false. On such a view, most or all of the candidate things to be said in so speaking, as proposed by the present account, are not really *said* in so speaking, though they may be suggested or otherwise conveyed. There is a clear three fold task for any such opponent. First, he must specify what the one thing is that is said in thus saying A to know F, and specify under what conditions that thing would be true or false. In particular, it must be clear enough what doubts for A as to F would, if live, show that thing to be false, or at least how such is to be determined. Second, he must show that his truth condition does not yield relevant S-use sensitivity: that, while knowledge ascriptions generally do count as satisfying it or not, it is not so that, with A and F fixed, some ascriptions may count as satisfying it where others do not. Third, he must show that his unique candidate, as opposed to any of the other candidates proposed by the present account, earns the title of what is really said in such a knowledge ascription, consistent with our notion of what it is to know that F. As a subsidiary matter, he may try to explain the appearance that other things are sometimes said in such ascriptions, for example, through a theory of suggestion. But as long as he performs the first three tasks, we will not hold him accountable for doing that.

The data, on their face, make the opponent's task look hopeless. If there must be just one thing which would count as Hugo knowing that Odile is in Paris, then none of our many candidates recommends itself for that role more forcefully and convincingly than any other. Forced to say *tout court* which doubts must not be live for Hugo and which doubts may be, we can identify no unique way of doing this. The possibility of a change of trains at Aulnoye does not distinguish itself from, say, the possibility that it is all rumour and Odile never left home, as being never relevant to the question whether Hugo knows Odile to be in Paris. Yet nor does it distinguish itself, by any principled argument, from yet further doubts, as being relevant to that question on every occasion for its posing. Fix all of the facts of the world, or all those which might show a doubt to be relevant or not, and the point remains: we just have various ways of speaking of knowing such things, none more privileged, by our lights, than the others. Fix the relevant facts about Hugo—he put Odile on the train last night, and is now at his desk working on the ledgers—and the point remains: he might be discussed in any of various ways, varying, for example, with our purposes in doing so. We can identify no one way of drawing the needed distinctions here as the one our concept of knowledge requires. So also we can identify no one state of affairs, as opposed to the other plausible candidates, as the one uniquely qualified for fitting our concept of knowledge.

Given the intuitions we have, the opponent's task is to explain away most of these as false. That they should be is implausible, certainly by the usual standards of linguistic argument. The usual tactic, applied in this case, would be to select from the variety one criterion as 'the real criterion for knowledge', and then to offer a theory of why, if that is the real truth condition, we would react or draw the inferences we do in each of the vast assortment of cases where that condition does not appear to square with our intuitions. Suppose that the opponent gets this far. It still remains to be demonstrated that his initial choice of criterion was not arbitrary, but in fact is required by what the concept of knowledge is. Here the usual tactic is not to offer independent arguments that this is so. (Indeed, if there were such arguments, then the whole project of explaining most of our intuitions as false would be uncalled for.) Rather, the tactic is to claim that the criterion of choice allows smoother explanations of our false intuitions where we have them—smoother, that is, than any rival. That is, it permits the neatest account of why we would have the false intuitions where we do, on the assumption that they are false. I know of no example of such a case ever having been made out even with remote plausibility. But discussing that point would take us too far afield. The question remains why an account on which most of our intuitions are false is preferable to one, like the present one, on which, on the whole, we do say what we appear to be saying. Where is that demonstration that, after all, most of our intuitions are false? And if there is none, why should we believe such a thing?

Some criteria for knowledge do, of course, distinguish themselves somehow. There is the sceptic's criterion on which any doubt is real. And there is the reverse proposal on which no doubt ever is. The trouble with the sceptic's proposal, I have argued, is that on it we would never know anything, or not much. Not only does this jar intuition, but it also makes knowledge a useless concept. What reason would we ever have to take an interest in it? Which, since it does interest us and we do discuss it, indicates that the sceptic's proposal is wrong. The converse proposal has similar flaws. On it, we know everything we take to be so which is so. But again, this removes any point in having a concept of knowledge. Which is strong reason to think it wrong for our concept. What these points show is that it is not enough for a given candidate criterion for knowledge to be distinguished. It must also be motivated. It must be demonstrable that that criterion reflects uniquely what knowledge really is.

The above argument is open to a misunderstanding. The Wittgensteinian position is that there is an indefinite variety of distinct things to be said in saying A to know that P. The opposing position is that there is only one such (truth-bearing) thought—call it AKP—and that the other things which, on occasion, appear thus to be said, can be explained away as mere suggestion, and, in each case, a suggestion that plausibly would be made given that AKP was said. The misunderstanding is to think that, as things now stand, the issue is a stand-off: the phenomena—the great variety of ways in which we treat various knowledge ascriptions, and take them properly to be treated—can be explained either in the Wittgensteinian or in the opposing way. This misses the arbitrariness of the opponents' view. In any sense in which there is a stand-off here, it is equally so regardless of which of an indefinite number of candidates an opponent proposes for the role of AKP. Until he has convincing independent arguments to show one such candidate to be correct for that role, there is really no stand-off at all.

A comparison may make the point clearer. The word 'red', may, to all appearances, be used to say both true and false things of a suitable apple. Sometimes, for example, the inside, matters and sometimes not. Suppose that, counter to appearances, there is really only one thing to be said of the apple, strictly speaking, in this word. Then it must be possible to specify which possible state of the apple would make this thing true (unless it is something necessarily false of apples). Presumably this will be a state we might sometimes take ourselves to be speaking of in using 'red' of the apple, as reflected in our ways of evaluating what was thus said. Where we were so speaking, we would, strictly and literally, be using 'red' to speak of being red, and be speaking of what we took ourselves to be speaking of. By contrast, on other occasions where we used 'red' to describe the apple, and took what we said as something to be evaluated differently, we would not really be using 'red' to speak of being red, or would not be speaking of what we took ourselves to be. The question now is, which thing that conceivably might be expressed in the word 'red' is suitable for the role just described? If none is, then any theory of the form just sketched is wrong. For 'red' there is obviously no such privileged candidate. Nothing about what 'red' means, for example, determines whether there are conditions on the insides of an apple for the apple to count as red. So in this case, things are pretty much what they seem to be: the rule is that, in using 'red', we are saying what we take ourselves to be saying.

The same general point applies in the case of knowledge ascriptions. If knowledge is what we sometimes, but not at other times, talk about, for example, in using 'know', then there must be something which shows which occasions those privileged times are. Otherwise, the rule must be that, in making knowledge ascriptions, we are saying (to be so) just what we seem to be saying. In which case, the Wittgensteinian account is correct. If, on the other hand, it is claimed that we never really speak of knowledge, then the question is what possible reason there could be for taking knowledge to be something of which that would be so.

2.5. CONVENTION

Assuming that the linguistic argument of the last section comes out in our favour, the truth conditions for knowledge ascriptions are as portrayed here, at least in broad outline. Minimally, there is a variety of things to be said in saying A to know F; these differ in their truth conditions; and these truth conditions differ in such a way that what is a real doubt for some such ascriptions might not be for others. If, in addition,[21] as intuition tells us, principle three is at least nearly enough right that the set of mere doubts for some knowledge claims is non-empty, then IP is mistaken. It does not capture correctly any feature of our concept of knowledge. That, one might say, is what we call knowledge. Or better, what we speak of in speaking of it.

But is this the end of the matter? Does it really establish that IP is incorrect? One might seem to glimpse a residual issue. To bring it out, let us consider another appeal to linguistic fact for settling epistemic issues—one made by Malcolm in discussing his weak or ordinary sense of 'know'. Malcolm proposes a pair of examples:

(4) You say, 'I know that it won't be dry', and give a stronger reason, for example, 'I saw a lot of water flowing in the gorge when I passed it this morning.' If we went and found water, there would be no hesitation at all in saying that you knew. . . .

(5) Everything happens as in (4), except that upon going to the gorge we find it to be dry. We should not say that you knew.[22]

He analyses these examples as follows:

. . . in case (4) where *you did* know, your grounds were identical [to those in (5)]. They could be at fault in (5) only if they were at fault in (4), and they were not at fault in (4). Cases (4) and (5) differ only in one respect—namely, that in one case you did subsequently find water and in the other you did not.[23]

---

[21] This does not follow simply from differences in proper understandings because of the world-involvingness of real doubt. That is the crux of the present matter.
[22] Malcolm [1952/63], pp. 178–9 (1952 version)
[23] Ibid.

Malcolm draws two conclusion. First,

> As philosophers we may be surprised to observe that it *can* be that the knowledge that P is true should differ from the belief that P is true *only* in the respect that in one case P is true and in the other false. But that is the fact.[24]

Second,

> Now it certainly *could* have turned out that the gorge was quite dry when you went there, even though you saw lots of water flowing through it only a few hours before. . . . What [this] shows is that *although you knew you could have been mistaken.*[25]

So Malcolm rejects the principle that if you might be wrong, then you do not know, or that it cannot be correct to say that you do know if you might be wrong.

If this last principle is mistaken, then IP certainly falls with it. But, no matter how good Malcolm's linguistic data, one is apt at least to feel queasy about the result. John McDowell expresses the qualm nicely while attacking the idea that knowledge that F might consist in 'experiencing the satisfaction of criteria for F':

> It is tempting to ask: when the ground for attributing knowledge is experience of the satisfaction of 'criteria', what *would* constitute possessing the knowledge? Someone who admits the question might be inclined to try this reply: the knowledge is constituted by experiencing the satisfaction of 'criteria'—given that things are indeed as the person is said to know that they are. But does that specify something that we can intelligibly count as knowledge? Consider a pair of cases, in both of which someone competent in the use of some claim experiences the satisfaction of (undefeated) 'criteria' for it, but in only one of which the claim is true. According to the suggestion . . . the subject in the latter case knows that things are as the claim would represent them as being; the subject in the former case does not. . . . However, the story is that the scope of experience is the same in each case: the fact itself is outside the reach of experience. And experience is the only mode of cognition . . . operative. So why should we not conclude that the cognitive achievements of the two subjects match? How can a difference in respect of something conceived as cognitively inaccessible to both subjects, so far as the relevant mode of cognition goes, make it the case that one of them knows how things are in the inaccessible region while the other does not. . . ?[26]

One must be careful not to read this as a defence of IP. On McDowell's view, one may know that F because he 'experiences the fact' that F Odile may know there is a stag because she sees one, for example, even

---

[24] Ibid. p. 180.
[25] Ibid.
[26] McDowell [1982].

though taking oneself to experience a fact is not always as good as doing it; there may be deceptive cases.

We can add substance to McDowell's qualm by observing what we typically, though not always, do with knowledge claims. Knowledge is related to action, and so to policy. If A knows that F, then A has proper assurances. So if we take A to know that F, then our policy for action should be what it would be given that F. But a defender of IP now has the means to phrase his worry. Assuming that ordinary language analysis is right as to when A counts as fitting the concept expressed by 'knows that F', and S is a situation in which A does so count, why (and with what right) should we conclude that S is a situation in which one ought to act according to the above policy? *Ought* we in fact so act when, as the sceptic will urge, for all of A's assurances, it might be that not-F?

The qualm points to a general worry about ordinary language analysis. Given analysis may show us to respect or violate some principle, P, in what we are prepared to recognize as to the situations in which words W fit. So the most secure linguistic thesis, given the data on which the analysis is based, may be that W respect P (or do not). But our words and concepts are almost never one-dimensional. There are many things we take to be so of them and their proper use. And these things not untypically come into conflict. In which case, there conceivably could be overwhelming reason for rejecting a principle for W which even our most sure-footed intuitions seem to show correct. Such could be a discovery. In Malcolm's case, for example, suppose that he is right that we are prepared to count some situations both as ones of A's knowing that F and as ones in which A might be wrong. Despite that, could the connection between knowledge and action not give us compelling reason to hold that it was wrong for us to do so? How could it be correct to act without reservation on the premise that F if it might be that not-F?

Let us begin with more specific qualms. The present account, unlike Malcolm's, respects the principle, 'If you might be wrong, you don't know.' Rejecting that link is not the present way of rejecting IP. So we may preserve the thought that where it is true to say that A knows that F, it is not true to say that A might be wrong. If there is then anything definite to be said in so speaking, then it is true to deny that A might be wrong.

To respect the link is, of course, to recognize S-use sensitivities in 'might'. This may seem merely to spread conventionalism: '*this* is what we call knowledge, and *this* is what we call a case in which A might be wrong.' But there is no denial here of a link between 'might' and action. Where it is not so that A might be wrong about F, one's policy should be what it would be on unreserved acceptance of F. The thought cuts two ways. If there are facts which show this unqualified acceptance of F to be bad policy, that fact may be put by saying that it might be that not-F. If it might be that not-F, but A takes it that F, A might be wrong about this. If A might be wrong, then A does not know that F. So he cannot have discharged all real doubts for him about this. To show acceptance of F to be imprudent is thus to show that there is a real live doubt for A about it. But there are facts to show all this if there are facts to make this a case of not-F. This is to repeat the point that the world may show there to be real doubts where we would not initially have thought that. If such powers are granted the world, then it is not a mere matter of convention, or 'what we call what', whether a given state of affairs counts as A's knowing that F. Nor do links between knowledge and policy yet provide a way for current linguistic analysis, or its rejection of IP, to prove wrong.

What of 'cognitive achievement'? The achievement required for knowledge, on the present account, may be viewed as negative, or perhaps better, as global. It is not as if, where knowledge that F is at stake, there is some set of doubts, $D_1, \ldots D_n$, such that for A to have discharged them is *ipso facto* for A to know that F. There is no other information such that having it is as such good enough for knowing that F (provided that F). Rather, the requirement is that there be no real doubt which A has not discharged, so that if A has discharged $D_1, \ldots D_n$, that is good enough only provided that those include all the real doubts. If that is the achievement, then it is not one that could have been reached both by someone who counts as knowing that F and by someone in a deceptive situation. Contrast Hugo and Odile's being in Paris with a case of someone, Luc, who is in a situation (which seems to him) just like Hugo's except that in that case, Odile is in fact in Reims. As things are, Hugo counts on some occasions as having discharged all real doubts. Luc can never so count. So their achievements are not the same. Otherwise put, there is a fact Luc has failed to see: that there is a doubt that ought to have been settled before it was taken that Odile was in Paris. In Hugo's case, there need be no such failure.

On the account McDowell rejects, as on Malcolm's, what distinguishes Hugo's case from Luc's may be *solely* what neither experiences (or perceives, sees or is aware of), namely, whatever it is that in fact makes the one case a case of Odile being in Paris and the other not. It is precisely and only that in virtue of which Hugo might, but Luc cannot, count as knowing that she is there. Thus McDowell's worry as to how what is 'cognitively inaccessible' can distinguish knowledge from ignorance. But if that is a worry, might it not apply to the present account as well, even though that account posits a different distinction between the cases? For what is the status of the fact (where it is one) that Hugo, but not Luc, has achieved what was required?

Part of an answer here is provided by a view McDowell finds congenial: Hugo, but not Luc, experiences a case of Odile's being in Paris, so perceives the fact that she is there. What Hugo does is one thing it might be to experience such a fact.[27] Malcolm's view hints at more to say on the same lines. On that view, Hugo might correctly take himself to know that Odile is in Paris while also judging correctly that he might be wrong about this. We have rejected that idea. Where Hugo counts as knowing Odile to be in Paris, there is no question as to her being there; so it would be incorrect to judge that she might not be. There is, correspondingly, a fact that counts as holding of Hugo's situation: the fact of the incorrectness in it of the judgement that Odile might not be in Paris. But then, why should not Hugo, in taking Odile to be in Paris in the way he does, without doubts about it, count as perceiving that fact? Luc, of course, can perceive no such fact in his situation, since there it is not a fact. This is an example of a fact accessible to Hugo but not to Luc, even though Luc may mistakenly take himself to see such a fact.

As Austin pointed out, what one sees may be a lemon even though one could conceivably take oneself to be doing that where the object in question was a bar of soap. In that case, seeing a lemon just is your cognitive achievement. Similarly, you might see your position to be one in which there are no real doubts, even though someone might, on some other occasion, mistakenly take himself to be doing that. So too for experiencing or perceiving the fact that Odile is in Paris. Which prompts two general remarks. First, of course it is always conceivable that there should be some real doubt for us as to F while we mistakenly take there to be none. For all that, we may sometimes know that there are no real doubts about F. Second, as a special case, our ordinary language analysis could conceivably turn out to be wrong on the plan outlined. Which does not in itself bar us from knowing that it is not wrong. Finally, given all the above, one of the facts we *can* see is that IP is mistaken.

---

[27] McDowell's targets characterize themselves as 'anti-realists'. But I think McDowell has the more interesting form of anti-realism. A cornerstone of his view is that there is no antecedently fixed and fully determinate 'something' that 'the fact that F' would come to. Similarly for 'the thought that P's correspondence with reality'. What it is for F to hold may be shown by the ways we could be in contact with that fact in experience. (This may invite comparison with Wittgenstein's view that what a theorem says is shown by what the proof is that proves it.)

3.SCEPTICISM: 3.1. THE SCEPTIC'S PROBLEM

A sceptic, for present purposes, is anyone who holds that what he, or one, does or can know is roughly what it in fact would be if IP were valid: very little or nothing.[28] This description makes it clear what the sceptic would like to be so. First, he would like there to be something to say in saying A to know F, or not to, such that every doubt for A as to F, if live, shows the first thing to be false and the second true. So the sceptic's favorite doubts—dreaming, demons or whatever—would count, just by being doubts, for the truth of what he would like to say in saying us not (or never) to know such-and-such. The desideratum here touches what it is that is said and not just its truth. It would not do, for example, for the sceptic to say what is true in saying Hugo not to know Odile to be in Paris if what he said would have been false had Hugo had her followed by an operative who had phoned from Aulnoye to report that she stayed on the train.

Second, the sceptic would like to work himself into a situation in which, in speaking of knowledge, he would say what he would like to say; thus, one where what one would say in speaking of A's knowing that F would have the semantics that he wants his knowledge ascriptions and denials to have. The general rule is: what one would say on an occasion in saying A to know F is true just in case A counts, on that occasion, as knowing that F. So the sceptic would like to find or construct an occasion on which A so counts only if there is no live doubt for A as to F.

Third, he would like the situation he works himself into to be one with quite general powers of the above kind: it should be a situation such that for any F, what would be said in ascribing knowledge of F to A would fit the above bill. Preferably, the same should hold for any A. The sceptic does not aim to be sceptical merely as to Hugo's knowing that there is milk in the refrigerator, but as to Hugo's, or anyone's knowing anything within some very large class of (possible) facts. What he wants, then, is a situation in which what is said in speaking of knowledge for a broad range of A's and F's has the truth conditions to make sceptical arguments relevant, and further the truth values which make the right generalizations true. If there is no situation with general properties such as these, then a sceptic might try to settle for there being, for each A and P, some situation as per point two.

---

[28] Someone like Prichard, who holds IP valid, but nevertheless thinks that there is an interesting class of things one might know, need not be considered a sceptic for present purposes.

Fourth, the sceptic would like it to be the case, and should be able to show that what is said in the situations described under two and three shows what knowledge really is, or ought to be taken to be, and what we really can know, or ought to take ourselves to be able to know, whereas other things said in ascribing or denying knowledge or using 'know' literally in other situations, if any, do not. The sceptic's use of 'know' is to be taken to be the proper one, at least for serious philosophical purposes.

Since it is so clear what the sceptic would like to say, for example, in saying Hugo not to know that Odile is in Paris, or that he is wearing shoes, why should there be any difficulty about there being such a thing to say, or even about the sceptic's ability to say it? Why can he not work himself into a position for saying it simply by explaining, as we just have done, what it is he means to say? The answer is a special case of a general point. Where we have multiple intentions regarding our words, the intentions may always conflict. You meant to be talking about penguins, since that was the topic of discussion, and you meant to be talking about a certain kind of bird, which you had seen in zoos. Too bad for you: the bird you had in mind is a puffin, not a penguin. So either you are not speaking of penguins, or your words do not have the truth conditions you would like them to. Similarly, the sceptic means to speak of A's knowing that P, and thereby to say something with respect to which possible doubts have the status just described. The problem is whether the sceptic can do both things at once. Is there anything to be said in speaking of knowledge for which doubts do have the status the sceptic would like them to?

To make the problem vivid, suppose that the sceptic introduces the verb, 'shmizx'. He is then free to stipulate that you can only shmizx P if there is no conceivable live doubt for you as to P. He may then conclude, correctly, that there is little or nothing we can shmizx. The conclusion is perfectly banal. On the face of it, we have now explained why we do not speak (much) of shmizxing. Matters get interesting only if there is an interesting connection between shmizxing and knowing things. That there is is what is presupposed in the view that the sceptic can say what he wants. But that there is requires arguing.

The interesting relation between shmizxing and knowing need not be that shmizxing is what we speak of, in the right situations, in speaking of knowledge. It may also be that shmizxing is what we ought to be speaking of, for some interesting range of purposes, such as doing philosophy. This points to another way in which the sceptic's position runs the risk of being banal. Suppose that there are special situations in which what we would say in speaking of knowledge is what the sceptic would like to be said in knowledge ascriptions, or at least his. Why should this not be regarded as a mere curiosity? We might say: 'You know—if you do some special intellectual exercises—perhaps sitting in front of the fire and screwing up your attention in the right way— you can put yourself in a strange situation in which practically everything you might say in ascribing knowledge to yourself (or to others) will be false. So what?' It is not obvious that one should draw the conclusion from this that really, seriously speaking, we do not know anything (or much). The sceptic must do something to show that, in fact, his special situations are the ones one ought to be in if one wants the correct answers to the serious questions about what we really know. This tendentious view of the matter would certainly require argument of a pretty impressive sort. So the fourth desider-atum, the point about importance, is a highly likely point at which to begin to chip away at scepticism. Rather than doing that in what follows, however, I will aim to show good reason why the sceptic cannot get so far as succeeding in saying what he wants to at all, or at least why there is no reason to expect that he can.

3.2. DOUBTS AND GAMES

To show that the sceptic cannot say what he wants, we must illuminate enough of the way in which what is said in a knowledge ascription depends on the circumstances of its saying. This requires a different sort of analysis from that given so far. To give it, I will make two main moves. First, as noted, to speak of knowing F is the rarer and more arcane activity; the more common and familiar ones being simply to assert, deny, doubt or wonder whether F. So I will make a link between the former and the latter—given our present purposes, between occasions for speaking of knowledge and occasions for the more mundane activities.

The idea for the connection is roughly this. To count as knowing F on an occasion where one might do so is to count as having the right assurances of F; the assurances required on that occasion for A's position to count as knowledge. Which assurances these must be varies from occasion to occasion of speaking of knowledge, and may or may not be determinate on any given one. The thought is that for this to be (sufficiently) determinate is for it to be (sufficiently) determinate on which range of occasions A's assurances ought to be good enough for the mundane activities of asserting, accepting or judging that F. Sufficiency here is enough determinacy to permit assessment as to truth.

More needs to be said about what is meant by being good enough for these mundane activities. Consider an example. Hugo says to Odile, 'There's cheese and biscuits on the sideboard (if you care for some).' Odile could conceivably respond with a doubt about this—for example, 'Perhaps Luc was around and ate it all.' By our ordinary lights, such a doubt may have any of various effects. We may perceive it as showing that Hugo ought not (just) assume that, or simply say that, or that Odile and Hugo ought not to accept that there are cheese and biscuits on the sideboard without checking further, or more generally, that it is doubtful whether there is, or at least there is some doubt as to there being cheese and biscuits on the sideboard. But we may also perceive it as showing nothing, as being out of place or beside the point. That would be to perceive it as not counting against the judgement that Hugo is in a position to say whether there are cheese and biscuits on the sideboard, to give his word or to vouch for it, or the view that Odile, if she perceives his position correctly, ought to accept his word for it. Suppose that Hugo's position is such that were he to assert F, no doubt would be perceived correctly as having the first sort of effect. Then he has the right assurances of F. As with occasions for ascribing knowledge, occasions for speaking of F's being so may or may not make determinate which doubts would have which status, hence the status of Hugo's position. Again, the status of Hugo's position, as that of any particular doubt, is an S-use sensitive matter.

The second move, following Wittgenstein's suggestion, will be to portray questions of A's assurances for the more mundane activities in terms of language games of a particular sort, namely ones which specify expressions of (certain) doubts as possible moves at some stages in them. Let us call such games *d-games*. Let us begin with a simple game with no provision for doubt. Call this the *breadbox game*. This is to be played by an eater, A, and his assistant, B. When A comes down to breakfast, B is to say either 'There's bread in the breadbox' or 'There's no bread in the breadbox'. In the first case, A may respond with either 'I'll have toast' or 'I'll have cereal'. In the second, A is restricted to the second move.

A may feel that B sometimes says there is no bread when there is, or note that B sometimes says there is where A never ends up with toast. These feelings are accommodated in the breadbox* game. This expands on the breadbox game as follows. After B's initial move, A may say, 'Are you sure?' This expands A's set of possible moves. To avoid stalemates, we define a countermove for B: B is to look in the breadbox and to say, 'There's bread' just in case he sees bread, and 'There's no bread' iff he sees none. But suppose A over-uses his new option and B finds it boring. That feeling, too, may be accommodated in the breadbox** game. This gives B an extra countermove. If B has already looked in the breadbox (within a reasonable time before A's descent to the kitchen), then B may simply respond with, 'Yes.' (In this game, A is barred the move, 'Are you sure?', if A has already seen B look in the breadbox.)

The breadbox** game has the possibility for A to express doubt, but not for him to express just any doubt. So far, there is no good reason why it should contain that possibility. Suppose now A feels, not only that B sometimes says 'There's bread' when there is none, but also that he sometimes says this when it is cake and not bread that is in the breadbox. (A detests toasted cake.) This feeling is provided for in the breadbox d-game. This again adds to A's possible moves. Not only may he say 'Are you sure?', but also he may say, instead of that, either 'Are you sure it isn't used up?' or 'Are you sure it isn't cake?' In the first case, B is to look, as before. In the second, he must not only look, but break off a piece and judge whether the texture is that of bread or that of cake. He must then respond either 'It's bread' or 'It's cake.', according to his judgement. As in the breadbox** game, there is the added provision here that if B has already performed the relevant test, he may simply reply, 'Yes.' Games which, like this one, allow for the expressions of doubts are d-games.

Chapter 3 introduced a notion of truth in a game G, and linked that with the notion of truth. Let us now introduce a notion of knowledge-in-G, and try to link that with knowledge. Just as truth-in-G does not require G to be a game in which one can speak of truth, so knowledge-in-G does not require G to be a game in which one can speak of knowledge. Both concern evaluations 'from outside'. Suppose that G is a game in which F is a move that A might be in a position (in the game) to make. Suppose that A is now in a position such that for any doubt D which is a possible countermove to F in G, A has already performed all the checks which that move might require of him. That is, he has done everything that might be required of him by way of response to such a move except for reaffirming G. Then let us say that *A knows F in G*. If G is a d-game which meets the first condition, call it *relevant* (to A's knowing F).

The link between truth-in-G and truth is roughly this: if A says W, and in doing so is reasonably (correctly) regarded as playing game G, then A said something true if W is true in G. The link between knowledge-in-G and knowledge cannot be so straightforward. It may be, for example, that on a given occasion A's position is such that he counts as knowing F in all the relevant d-games he would reasonably (and correctly) be regarded as then playing. A's position may also be such that, for some range of possible occasions, O, he would similarly count as knowing F in all the d-games he might be viewed as playing on O. But A's present occasion for speaking of F need not be what makes *us* say that A knows or does not. Hugo is bent over his ledgers. An assurance from him as he is so engaged that Odile is in Paris may be as bizarre as any expression of doubt to him about this. But we may still have occasion for speaking of his knowing this. On some such, he would count as doing so, and on others, not. So, similarly, the above possible fact about a range of occasions shows us what to say about Hugo's knowing that Odile is in Paris only given that that range is the right one for showing this on our occasion for judging Hugo's knowledge.

We may now connect the first move with the second. Plausibly, we may put the fact that Hugo has the assurances of F which he ought to have on an occasion for the mundane activity of saying that F just in case Hugo counts as knowing F in all the relevant d-games he might correctly be viewed as then playing. This is to suppose that a doubt might then show Hugo's word not to be good enough, as per above, only if Hugo's overall activities make it reasonable for him to be playing (so be viewed as playing) a relevant d-game in which that doubt is a move. What makes it reasonable to play a game in which that is a doubt is just what makes it reasonable to perceive that doubt as possibly showing that Hugo is not in a position to vouch for F. So, on occasion O, A counts as knowing that F just in case A counts as knowing that F in all the relevant d-games he would reasonably be regarded as playing on all occasions for which A's assurances ought to be good enough if A is to count on O as knowing that F. If, on O, one took A to know that F, it would be reasonable, given that, to expect A's word as to F to be good enough on just those occasions.

Within this framework we can restate what the sceptic wants. Let us call a d-game, G, a d*-game if, for any F that is a move in G, any possible doubt, D, as to F is a move in G in response to F. Then, where the sceptic speaks of A's knowing that F, he wants his talk to refer to occasions for playing d-games (in the way just described) such that some of these are ones on which A would count as playing a d*-game containing F as a move. Otherwise put, the sceptic wants his occasion of speaking of knowledge to be such that what counts on it as required for knowledge is proper assurances of F, *inter alia*, on some occasions on which one would count as playing relevant d*-games. Such occasions would be among those on which a knower of F would then be expected to have proper assurances.

It is worth marking a possible confusion here which may also provide powerful impetus in the direction of scepticism. For the sceptic to say what he wants, and for it to be true, his situation must be one of which the above is determinately the case. This is to be distinguished from the case in which his position is what it is anyway heavily suspected of being: one in which there are no determinate facts as to for which occasions for speaking of F A's assurances should be good enough, nor hence which d-games count as relevant to the question whether A knows F. Suppose (to revert to old terminology) there is no determinate fact as to whether doubt D counts as real when it comes to A's counting as knowing F. One might perceive this as meaning that D might be relevant to A's knowing that F. But if it might be, one might reason, then A cannot be positively counted as knowing that F unless A has discharged D. So D is as good as a real doubt. If the sceptic's position yields enough such indeterminacies, and these indeterminacies are treated in this way, then the sceptic's result follows.

The mistake is in the first move after the supposition. To suppose that D might be real is to presuppose that there is some fact of the matter about this. But what made it look as if D might be real was precisely the fact that there is no such fact of the matter. So if the sceptic is in the position he is suspected of being in, the right conclusion should be, not that he might be right, but rather that he has not said anything with sufficiently definite truth condition at all. So there is simply no question of his being right; there is not yet anything for him to be right about.

Are the sceptic's desiderata realizable? Recall a general fact about language games: the games one would count as playing in saying F are those which are made most reasonable by the overall activities of which saying F is a part. So, to count as playing a game in which F is a move, something about one's activities must make it reasonable to say F under some given conditions, or in some sorts of circumstances, and sometimes reasonable to respond to this move by acting on F, in such-and-such particular ways. It may be reasonable, for example, to say that the rug is beige when one has examined its backing and seen it to be beige. In the right circumstances—say, where the beige ones are always Uizgurs—it may be reasonable to react to this by identifying the rug as a genuine Uizgur, and by buying it. Such may fit in most sensibly with our overall activities as rug merchants. If so, then I have just described the circumstances in which saying these things is a proper move in the language games we rug merchants would then be playing. Moreover, as the example indicates, the way in which our activities make the move of saying F reasonable is indispensable in determining what the truth conditions for so speaking are to be. Different games with F impose different standards for F's correctness. For it to be a determinate fact that some of these games rather than others are being played, there must be determinate circumstances under which F would count as correct.

We have not yet spoken of d-games in particular. But doing so suggests a further point. A given d-game may define a doubt, D, as to F. But, as the example again suggests, whether D is a doubt as to F depends on the standards of correctness for F. It is sometimes a doubt as to the rug's being beige that a celery-coloured pile may *look* beige when held against the bright green background against which it is on view. But this is not even a possible doubt in the rug merchant game just described. So a d-game, to be coherent, must be, as it were, grafted on to a doubt-free game in which there are realizable standards of correctness for the move of saying F.

All these requirements conflict with the rules of a d*-game. To put the point briefly, in a d*-game there is always doubt as to F. So also no particular doubt about F can ever count as settled. For if the doubt D requires check C in the game, then there is always the more refined doubt: perhaps D even though C was positive (as we saw in examining IP). It may, for example, be a non-clanking mechanical pig. So A could never be in a position in which he knew F in the d*-game. So it could never be reasonable to take F's word for it, nor, hence, to act on it. So circumstances for playing a d*-game would be incapable of defining which games with F counted as being played. Hence it could never be reasonable to play a d*-game. Nothing could make it reasonable both to play a game (some particular one as opposed to others) in which F was a move, and also make it reasonable to play a game in which every doubt as to F was allowed.

Since it could never be reasonable for A to be playing a d*-game, it could never be reasonable to regard A as playing one. But could not A and B be unreasonable? Suppose they agree to play a d*-game involving F, and act accordingly: wherever A says F and B expresses a doubt about it, both A and B do take this as reflecting on A's ability to vouch for it. Of course A and B may say they are doing all this. But on the present view, what they say does not by itself settle which games they are playing. In the present case, I have argued that they must be mistaken. Either there is nothing definite A is saying to be so in saying 'F', or, more probably, their policies towards doubts are what we would have to count as unreasonable, hence incorrect.

We now have a short account of why the sceptic's desiderata are unattainable. The sceptic's occasion cannot be one on which knowledge claims refer to occasions for playing d*-games because there are no occasions for doing this. The sceptic may now ask why his claims must refer to occasions in the way described, and why he cannot simply make his talk of knowledge refer directly to whatever d-games he chooses. Again there is a short answer. In our mundane activities of asserting and accepting F, we do, on occasion, recognize certain doubts as having the status of relevance for A's entitlement to assert or accept F, in the way explained, and other doubts as lacking this status. Similarly, when it comes to an occasion of discussing A's knowledge, we recognize some situations as being such that the inadequacy of A's word or position in them counts against A's knowing F, and other situations as lacking this status. Our natural policies in both respects are revisable. But they require revision just where there are facts to show us that this is so. The sceptic, in pointing to mere possibilities for error, has pointed to nothing which even tends to make us react in this way.

The above facts are important, since what counts as knowledge, and hence what the sceptic says in discussing it, is what it is determined to be by our reactions as reasonable judges to the facts on which such matters depend. It remains clear what the sceptic would like to say. But desire is not enough. What one says in speaking, on an occasion, of A's knowledge (or ignorance) that F is determined by what, if anything, does count on that occasion as knowing that F. What so counts is what our reactions show to count. As adumbrated in section 2.5, the sceptic may still have residual worries as to whether or why he must respect our natural policies in these respects. The next section will consider whether such worries might be genuine.

3.3. ETHOLOGY

Wittgenstein says (OC 475),

I want to regard man here as an animal; as a primitive being to which one grants instinct but not ratiocination. As a creature in a primitive state. Any logic good enough for a primitive means of communication needs no apology from us. Language did not emerge from some kind of ratiocination.

Along the same lines (OC 317),

This doubt isn't one of the doubts in our game. (But not as if we *chose* this game!)

That we doubt as we do is, so to speak, a part of our ethology. To borrow an image,[29] it is as if we were innately endowed with a doubting device; a mechanism whose output was that we, on some

---

[29] An image which has come to prove sometimes dangerous in recent times. But we are under no compulsion to read more of a mechanistic view of ourselves into it than suits our purposes.

occasions, accord particular statuses to particular doubts (having them or not being one way of doing so).

Wittgenstein has a number of things to say about our doubting device. Here we will concentrate on two sets of remarks. The first are typified by,

Just as in writing we learn a particular basic form of letters and then vary it later, so we learn first the stability of things as the norm, which is then subject to alterations. (OC 473)

The child learns by believing the adult. Doubt comes *after* belief. (OC 160)

One might or might not stress Wittgenstein's references to learning. In either case, his remarks in this vein suggest a number of points about—to continue the metaphor—the 'input–output' relations of the doubting device, and the relations of inputs to its 'internal states'. The first point concerns a necessary condition for there to be any output of the device at all. (For there to be an output is not merely for us to doubt or not. If there is no output then we do not doubt. It is for doubts to be assigned definite statuses, on occasions, as proper or not.) For the device to have an output for given F and some occasions for judging whether F, etc., it must have certain sorts of situations which it recognizes as ones in which no doubt as to F would be proper (i.e., to the point, as explained above). We may think of these situations, so typed, as part of its input—the givens it is provided to work with. Or we may think of them in terms of facts about its internal states: for these situations, it is prepared to output a classification of doubts which has the null class as the proper ones. To back off from the metaphor here, grasping when it would be correct to doubt whether F, or when such-and-such doubts would be proper, requires a 'prior' grasp of when there would be no doubt as to F. To de-psychologize further, facts as to which doubts as to F are proper on an occasion require for their obtaining and are determined by facts about a wide enough range of occasions on which there is no doubt.

As should be clear enough by now, the above point does not mean that it is possible for us to be in 'paradigmatic' situations for F in which we could not turn out to be wrong in taking it that F. First, although we can sometimes recognize a situation as one in which no doubts are proper, we may also sometimes mistake our situation for one of this type when it is not that sort of situation at all. We take this situation to be of a certain sort, such that in that sort of situation, doubts about mechanical pigs are misplaced. But it is not that sort of situation. It is rather one one might find oneself in in the midst of Quisneycorp's 'farmworld'. Second, experience may teach us that a sort of situation is one in which one ought to have doubts about F after all. For the device to operate, there must be some situations which it assigns doubt-free status. But that does not mean that there are some situations which must have this status. In the metaphor, the internal states of the device are modifiable.

Third, the first point has a consequence for the sceptic's project. The sceptic wants us, on his occasion, to regard all doubts one ever might have as to F as proper. As we have seen, this would mean being prepared, from the sceptic's perspective, to assign no situation we might be in doubt-free status with respect to F. No matter what our position, there are always some conceivable doubts to have about F. (That is, there is no standing up to IP.) But if Wittgenstein is right about the ethology of our doubting, to go along with the sceptic in this would be to put ourselves in a position in which our doubting device could not function at all. There would simply be no outputs. This is the ethological correlate of the point that, as the sceptic does it, there is nothing he would be saying to be so at all in saying or denying A to know that F.

As mentioned, experience may teach us that or when certain doubts are proper. The second set of remarks concerns the way in which experience might do this:

But isn't it experience that teaches us to judge like *this*, that is to say, that it is correct to judge like this? But how does experience *teach* us, then? *We* may derive it from experience, but experience does not direct us to derive anything from experience. If it is the *ground* of our judging like this, and not just the cause, still we do not have a ground for seeing this in turn as ground. (OC 130)

No, experience is not the ground for our game of judging. Nor is its outstanding success. (OC 131)

This game proves its worth. That may be the cause of its being played, but it is not the ground. (OC 474)

The main point is simple. Given facts or argument could show that a doubt was proper or not, or that a given policy of doubting was (in)correct *only* via the fact that that is how those facts or arguments affect us. Beyond that, there is no further possibility for any facts to demonstrate that our policies, or the structurings we assign to doubts, on occasions were in fact incorrect. There is no further question of the correctness or propriety of doubts; nothing further for facts to show in this regard beyond what our reactions to them show them to show. Our ethology fixes our reactions, so the statuses we will accord doubts for any given input of experience. And it is our reactions, as reasonable judges, which show what the facts of such matters are.

Relating doubts to our doubting, and that to our ethology, shows, if successful, that the fact that we recognize certain states of affairs and not others as fitting our concept of knowledge reflects, not mere surface facts of our language, but rather 'deep' facts about our natures. How might this depth help against the sceptic? We may assume that if our ethology is decisive, then the sceptic is out of business (or else we would all be sceptics). So consider the ultimate sceptical fantasy. Nature has miswired us. We do not have certain doubts where we really ought to. Our ethology condemns us to bad policy.

On the Wittgensteinian view, this fantasy is incoherent. From an ethological perspective, this is why it is. Doubts, in the mundane activities of asserting, accepting, etc., are related to policies for action. When I accept F, my further policies are what they would be given F. To say that we ought to have doubt D as to F would then be to say, or say what entails, that doing so yields better further policies. Better further policies are ones that are more worth having. Which is to say that a demonstration that D ought to be treated as proper could only be given in terms of what was worth while or pointful, or what mattered. It could only be a fact that one ought to have D if it were a fact that there is some point or worth in doing so. But what is worth while or pointful for us, and what matters, is defined by our ethology. There is no point in saying that something is worth while for us which we are constitutionally incapable of recognizing as such. And it is in terms of what is worth while for us that proofs of the propriety of doubts must be given.

In section 2.5, we considered the possibility that linguistic intuition might lead us astray by getting us to recognize something as A's knowing that F where there are, in fact, good reasons not to act as unqualified acceptance of F would dictate. There is no possibility for ethology to mislead us in this way. For there could be good reasons not to act on this policy only if there were something to show us the worth of doing so, given what matters to us. If there were something to do this, then it would ipso facto show us the corresponding facts as to the doubts we ought to treat as proper.

In the far-off kingdom of Wu, there is a race of intelligent beings who speak of themselves sometimes as shmizxing the things they take to be so. Their concept of shmizxing is much like our concept of knowledge except that, in a few selected cases, there are doubts we would treat as real in questions of knowledge which nothing could persuade these beings to treat as real in questions of shmizxing. So there are a few cases which count as cases of shmizxing but not knowledge. For the rest, the consequences of shmizxing for them are the same as the consequences of knowing for us. So when a doubt would not show one of them not to shmizx F, they build their policies on F just as we do when no doubt could show one of us not to know F.

By our lights, their policies are thus sometimes imprudent. But we cannot convince them of this. For no fact we could point out to them could show them that it was worth while to alter their policies (hence their policies of policy formation). They could, of course, see that they were sometimes wrong in taking it that F. So are we. But they could not see that their errors were of a sort to give any point to judging differently than they do, either in judging that F, or in judging that they or others shmizx it.

We *might* pity these beings. We certainly might criticize their policies, which, we might say, we would find worth while changing if we were them. We could certainly say correctly that these creatures sometimes take things to be so when they do not know them. But it would be incorrect to say that they take these things to be so when they do not shmizx them (where they are incapable of seeing that fact themselves).

The sceptic wants to speak of us. He has no outside position from which to do that, using concepts other than ours as we do in speaking of the inhabitants of Wu. (Or, if he did create one, and began to speak of shmizxing, we would not and could not care about what he said.) But our concept of shmizxing is knowledge, the very one the sceptic is using to discuss us. So the sceptic is incorrect.

5

The Limits of Doubt

This chapter will explore the S-use sensitivities of demonstration or proof—facts to the effect that (on an occasion) it has been proved that F, or that saying and/or doing such-and-such. or what was thus said done or stated proves or did then prove F. The concept in question might be described as partly epistemic. For, first, it will turn out that if B ever has the property of proving F, then that is not a property it can be said to have or lack occasion-insensitively; there will always be at least conceivable occasions on which it would not prove F. And second, what is required for B to prove F cannot be characterized independent of our perspectives on the world, or, more exactly, those provided by the occasion on which B is to count as proof or not, and, specifically, independent of what one with those perspectives may and may not correctly take to be so.

This much may already make it seem as if what will be at issue is—to use a recently coined epithet—a mere liberal arts concept of proof (or, perhaps, a mere notion of 'proving F to A'; a suggestion specifically to be rejected in what follows), where that mere 'soft' notion is meant to contrast with some other 'hard' notion. On the envisioned hard notion, a proof of F might be identified as such by purely 'internal' characteristics—the fact that its steps prior to its conclusion are true, perhaps, together with the fact that all of its non-initial steps are linked to earlier ones by inferential rules drawn from some fixed stock of 'truth, (or proof-) preserving' ones. Part of the message of what follows is that no appropriate and motivated such harder notion is available. This is not to deny the possibility of formal theories of proof. (There is no sense in ruling impossible what in fact exists.) It does say something about their applications, and about their content. Exactly what it thus says may be read off the account of proof to be represented here.

The discussion to come is meant to forge a link between the previous chapter and the succeeding one. Like the preceding chapter, this one will be centrally concerned with doubts; but in a different way. The last chapter assumed a field of possible doubts (for A to have) as to F, or ways in which one could conceivably doubt F, and went on to argue two things: first, that for purposes of ascribing knowledge of F to A, this large field must be divided up into (generally proper) sub-parts—the real doubts and the mere ones; and second, that for such partitioning to be possible at all, it must be done in an S-use sensitive way. This chapter will direct attention at the wider field of possible doubts with which the last one began. It will argue that on at least one key conception of possible doubt—one which captures a field to be divided up by the real/mere doubt distinction—what possible doubts there are as to F is itself an S-use sensitive matter. It is just this S-use sensitive notion of possible doubt that is crucial for the concept of proving F.

The notion of possible doubt at issue is captured if we think of a possible doubt as to F as a way (or a statement of one) for F (or what we think in thinking it) not to be so; a way in which it would be possible for F not to be so; so, a way the world might possibly be on which F would not be so. Let us exclude from the range of ways for F not to be so the bare supposition that not-F. This is the notion we henceforth adopt. *Prima facie*, there are, on it, two ways for D to fail to be a possible doubt as to F. First, D may fail to be a possible way for things to be at all. Second, D may fail to be a way for F not to be so. We will suppose that for D to be such a way, it must be (sufficiently) determinate *how* F would fail to be so on D. An example of the second sort of failure: let F be that there are chairs in my office, and D that I am wearing boots. Possibly I am. But how does this make for a case of not-F? Is it to be imagined that my booted footsteps make chairs dissolve? Except in special circumstances, this does not count as constituting a case—nor a way—of F not being so.

It will be argued in what follows that if D ever counts as a possible doubt as to F, then it is an S-use sensitive matter whether it is; further that, for each of the above two sorts of failure, it is an S-use sensitive matter which doubts succumb to them. Given that, there is, of course, a yet wider notion of doubt available. We may call D a *conceivable doubt* as to F if there is any occasion on which D is a possible doubt as to F. It is far from clear that this picks out any definite limited and interesting class of cases. If so, then this wider notion may still be importantly S-use sensitive. But in any case it is the more limited notion of possible doubt that will prove to matter in matters of proof.

If D may be either a possible doubt as to F or not one, then it *might* also be indeterminate which D is. Let F be that Odile has been working in her present job at least a year, and D that the earth was created last month (with memory traces, etc.). D presumably does not cast doubt on Odile's right to unemployment insurance, so in that context it is not a possible doubt as to F either. In other contexts it may be. But on yet other occasions it may simply be indeterminate how it is to be treated. For there to be any such thing as proving F, much less a proof of it, it will be argued, it must be determinate enough how candidates classify with respect to being possible doubts as to F or not. Much of the interest in what follows will be in what is required for that condition to be met. One thing, it will be argued, is that there be items other than F which neither require nor admit of proof. Meeting that requirement is one thing that requires that proof be an S-use sensitive notion.

Let us now briefly look to the future. The next chapter will be concerned with family resemblance. One of the most striking facets of that doctrine is what might be called the 'no common thread' thesis. The thesis might be put like this. Suppose that the family resemblance doctrine applies to a concept C. Now survey all cases of items to which C does or would apply. There is no common thread running through all these cases. On a strong version of this thesis, this means that there are no other features present in all the items to which C applies in these cases. On a weaker version, this means that there are no such features which distinguish all such cases from every case of an item to which C would not apply. On the weak thesis, there are no sufficient conditions for C to apply; on the strong one there are neither sufficient nor necessary conditions.

Wittgenstein urges us to verify the no common thread thesis 'by looking and not by thinking'. We are supposed just to see that there is nothing else in common to each thing we are prepared to call a chair or a game or whatever. But suppose we do see that. Why should we not reason as follows. Take any V which we might be inclined to call a chair. Any set of other facts about V (and hence all of them) are compatible with something's (and so with V's) not being a chair. So it cannot be a fact that V is a chair. (Nor, given broad enough scope for the no common thread thesis, could it be a fact that V is a non-chair.) The concept of a chair is thus (as looking teaches us) ill defined. So, within broad limits, there can never be a fact of the matter as to whether V is a chair. So, within these limits, chair-talk is not genuine fact-stating discourse.

Wittgenstein's strategy of looking rather than thinking is effective precisely because for most of us the above conclusions were never an option. (Some philosophers *have* argued in the above vein for selected domains—for example, semantic discourse. Unless their principle of selection is reasoned and powerfully motivated, they will thereby have effected a reduction of ontology to aesthetics.) But it is worth considering under what conditions Wittgenstein's recommended path would be the correct one, and under what conditions, if any, the above alternative would be correct. For one thing, looking may inform us that the family resemblance doctrine fits all, or nearly all our concepts. In that case, we will need to have Wittgenstein's path available. For another, there may be special circumstances in which what makes Wittgenstein's way correct is not available to us, so that we then must reason in the alternative way. Or there may be philosophical theories which inadvertently deprive us of our right to follow Wittgenstein's path. If so, it will be important to recognize such circumstances or theories when they present themselves. It is a mistake in philosophy to argue that since we normally do not accept such-and-such standards or principles, that these cannot be correct as applied in an *abnormal* case. An account of proof is a way of examining what kind of support Wittgenstein's way with 'no common thread' phenomena, or the view that there need be no common thread, requires, and hence seeing when that support would, and when it would not be available.

Prima facie, the doubts as to F—or at least the expressions of them— which are available to us is an S-use sensitive matter, if only in innocuous ways. Suppose that Hugo and Odile go out to buy a piano, having first measured the corner into which it is to fit. Having seen some pianos and their price tags, Odile *might* express the doubt, 'Perhaps the corner has shrunk since we left.' But suppose they had stayed home. Then Odile could not have expressed a sensible doubt in saying *that*. The availability of that expression of doubt depends on her perspective on the world—in this particular case, at least as fixed by her spatio-temporal position; but here and elsewhere perhaps in other ways as well.

This dependence on occasion may seem innocuous. For one might have roughly this thought. The doubt Odile expressed in the piano store depicted the world as being a certain way: one in which the corner was smaller at that time (call it t) than at the earlier time of measurement. Had she stayed at home, she could still have expressed the thought of the world being in that way, though she would have needed other words to do so. So the possible ways the world might be such that the piano would not fit the corner remain the same as viewed from her (hypothetical) perspective at home at t as they were as viewed from her perspective in the store at t. It is that that renders such variation as there is innocuous.

Part of what is to be argued here runs against this thought. It sees the above as an instance of a phenomenon which is not in general innocuous in this sense. What varies across occasions on the present account is not merely what words one must use to specify a given way for the world to be, but which are the ways it possibly could be (in relevant respects). What make for the variation are differences in the perspectives on the world which different occasions afford. But these differences are not specifiable in terms of such variable as spatio-temporal position. With that flagging of the goal, it is time to begin the argument.

1. MOORE AGAIN

Though Wittgenstein is sometimes hard on Moore, Moore in fact took radical steps away from the tradition, and part way, though not the whole way, towards the Wittgensteinian view—of proof as well as of knowledge. In each case, it is helpful first to set out Moore's break with the tradition, and then to build Wittgenstein's view on to that. This section, then, will look at Moore's view of proof.

The last chapter suggested that Moore's main contribution in the case of knowledge was to recognize a real/mere doubt distinction. What Moore missed, it was suggested, was the S-use sensitive nature of that distinction. His missing this may have resulted from his reliance, in example, on the first-person—a case which encourages conflation of the position of the ascriber of knowledge with that of the subject of it. So while he did recognize that what he might truly be said to know may vary with his epistemic position as a knower, he did not see that it may also vary with the position of an ascriber of knowledge to him. In the case of proof, the temptation to that particular conflation is largely absent. So Moore did recognize that the notion of proving F, so of being a proof of F, is an S-use sensitive one. That is his main break with the tradition he discusses.

But Moore also thought that the S-use sensitivity of proof could be isolated at a given level—that of a proof's premisses. Moore concentrated on the idea of the admissibility of given premisses in a proof; the question whether a 'proof' which contained such-and-such premisses might actually count as proving F, or whether its appealing to those premisses barred it from that status. That, Moore thought, was an S-use sensitive question. It might be that one could appeal to G in proving F on one occasion, but not on another. Moore's explanation for this is that G themselves may require proof on some occasions, but not on others. On the other hand, consider the question whether given premisses, G, if granted, would prove F, or whether there is a proof of F from G—roughly, whether G yield a *valid* proof of F. That question Moore treated as S-use insensitive.

Wittgenstein's most important break with Moore, it will be argued, occurs at just this point. Wittgenstein does not think that the S-use sensitivity of proof can be isolated at the level of premisses. Further, he does not think that there can be a relevant S-use insensitive notion of validity—one such that if premisses are admissible and there is a valid proof of F from them, in that sense of validity, then that 'proof' *proves* F. It remains to say why Wittgenstein thought this, and what its significance is. But for the moment let us look at Moore.

Moore's view of proof is contained in his article, 'Proof of an External World', henceforth PEW.[1] PEW is often wrongly represented as a study of the concept of knowledge. In fact, the article contains only one significant mention of knowledge, and that is by way of citing a fact that is supposed to be indisputable, and not by way of establishing anything about knowledge. True, Moore does here offer what he calls 'proofs' of an 'external world'. If these succeed, they may certainly show something about solipsism—a radical form, perhaps, of what we will later call 'ontic scepticism', that is, scepticism as to there being this or that. It may be that that contributes indirectly to the solution of some problem concerning epistemic scepticism of the sort discussed in the last chapter—that is, scepticism as to our being able to know this or that. So Moore may have contributed indirectly to the study of knowledge. But knowledge is not the topic of discussion in PEW. Rather, that article focuses on the concept of proof.

Moore says that he is responding in PEW to a claim by Kant that there is, or was before Kant, a certain scandal in philosophy. The alleged scandal was that, Kant's efforts excepted, no philosopher had ever proved (strictly, rigorously, or whatever) that there was 'an external world'. Moore's response is that, whether or not any philosopher ever thought it worth while actually to provide such a proof, there is certainly no trick in doing so. Which Moore attempts to illustrate by providing a few proofs of his own. So that in so far as there ever was any scandal, it was of a rather low-grade sort.

Here is one of Moore's proofs. It consists of two premisses and a conclusion. The premisses are what he expressed, or might have, on a certain occasion, in holding up first one, and then the other of his hands, and saying, first, 'This is a hand' and, then, 'This is another.' The conclusion is what he would have expressed on that occasion in saying, 'There are at least two hands.' There is no mention here of an external world. So, strictly speaking, this is not a proof, or anyway an explicit one, that there is an external world. In the discussion leading up to this illustration, however, Moore goes to great pains to analyse two notions: that of an external world, and that of external objects (or objects without the mind). The conclusions Moore reaches are, first,

[1] Moore [1939].

that hands are external objects, and second, that if there are external objects, then there is an external world. Let us grant Moore this much. Then, adding the first conclusion to the above proof, we may derive the conclusion that there are at least two external objects. Adding the second to that, we may then derive that there is an external world. The result would be a proof consisting of six lines and a conclusion. Let us call the proof Moore actually offers 'Moore's proof', and the longer proof just mentioned 'Moore's extended proof'. Incidentally, note that 'proof' is normally a success word: if B is a proof with conclusion F, then B proves F; if B has been produced, then F has been proved, etc. Where it is important to cancel that presupposition, I will enclose 'proof' in scare-quotes. Here, for example, we might better speak of Moore's 'proof'.

What is this illustration meant to do? Moore did not expect Kant to accept it as a proof of the external world. He did not think that Kant's reaction would have been, 'Oh yeah—I forgot about that one.' Rather, he expected that Kant would not have accepted Moore's proof. What he thinks and argues is that Kant should have accepted this result because, as Moore puts it, this proof is a proof in the strictest sense of the term; the fact is that it just does fit our concept of proof, and not just some *soi-disant* or 'as good as' notion of proof either. Moore's arguments for this, *via* some entirely general principles about proof, form the most important part of PEW.

Kant would not accept Moore's proofs, Moore thinks, because Kant would think that Moore's premises (the first two steps) themselves required proof. Prove them to Kant's satisfaction and then add Moore's proof, and—though the result might seem strange or unperspicuous—Kant would be forced to accept it as flawless *qua* proof. It is here that Moore makes his only mention of knowledge. He concedes, first, that if he did need to prove these premises on that occasion, he could not. In fact, he would not know how to begin. But second, he maintains that he does not need to prove them. He certainly knows them, so they do not require proof. Without any proof, they are admissible as parts of proofs of other things. So, Moore holds, in demanding that they be proved, Kant would be mistaken.

Moore recognizes that there might be other occasions on which his premises or ones just like them—what he would then express in saying 'This is a hand.', for example—would require proof, and would be admissible in (strict) proofs only on condition that such proof was supplied. He also thinks that on such an occasion he would have at least a reasonable chance of being able to supply such proof. For example, his premises might require proof if we were among clever surgeons who had often managed to fool people about such things as their having hands, or if Moore had just swallowed some drug, or might have done. In such a case, there would be a reasonable chance that Moore could settle whether the clever surgeons had been at work on him, or etc.—though it is also possible that, contingently, he could not. In any event, if Moore were in such a situation, then the proof of an external world which he in fact offered in the illustration would not then count as proving that there was an external world. It would at least require supplementation. But none of this shows, on his view, that his proof, when offered, did not prove its conclusion.

So Kant is mistaken, on Moore's view, as to what is required for proving F (strictly, or whatever). The mistake may be put this way. Kant would note, correctly, that there are conceivable doubts as to the thought Moore expressed in 'Here is a hand'. He would further note, also correctly, that because of this there are some occasions on which that thought would require proof, and, without it, not be admissible in a (strict) proof of something else. From this he concludes, incorrectly, that (strictly speaking, perhaps) that thought always requires proof, at least in this sense: it is never admissible as an unproved part of what (strictly speaking) proves something else—notably, that there is an external world. That Kantian conclusion about Moore's premiss depends on this further (incorrect) thought: if there is any occasion on which B would not count as proving F, then B never counts (strictly speaking) as proving F.

Kant and Moore disagree, then, both on what is required for proving (or being a proof of) F and on what is required for being admissible as an unproved premiss in what proves F. On the first score, Kant but not Moore holds that for B ever to count as a proof of F, it must always do so. For Moore, proving F is an S-use sensitive matter. Second, Kant, but not Moore, thinks that for G ever to be admissible as a premiss in what proves F (or, perhaps, anything) it must always be so; and further, that it can always be so only if it never requires proof. Moore thinks that requiring proof, and hence being admissible as a premiss, are S-use sensitive matters, where what does not require proof *is* so admissible. Moore also thinks that Kant's second mistake fully accounts for the first; Kant is wrong in the first matter exactly to the extent that his second error makes him so.

There are two possible views of what Moore does in arguing against the Kantian position. On one of these, Moore is what, on the tradition, an ordinary language philosopher is supposed to be. His point is that it is a feature of our ordinary concept of proof, and what we are prepared to recognize about it, that we at least sometimes count things as proof when they satisfy the Moorean, but not the Kantian requirement. That is what we mean by (call) proof. It is clear why this would not be a very effective way of arguing against Kant. Kant might well allow the ordinary language data, but then go on to point out that there are more stringent standards of proof available, so a stricter notion of proof that is havable for the asking, and then further argue that it is this stricter notion that ought to concern philosophers. (After all, if not philosophers, then who?)

But there is another more charitable view of what Moore is claiming. On it, what Moore is claiming is that you cannot have a notion of proof like the one Kant is supposing, or at least not one with any possible applications. (And a notion of proof with no applications is not one that ought to interest philosophers or anyone else—at least as a standard to try to come up to.) The point would be that if it is required that a proof, to prove F, must count as doing so on every occasion for offering it, then nothing could ever count as proving anything. No 'proof' could possibly count as doing what a proof reasonably ought to do on every such occasion. So any useful notion of proof—any notion with possible application—must be an S-use sensitive one.

Moore claims that, as things stood when he offered his proof, he could not have proved what he said in saying 'This is a hand'. Nor did that require proof. But circumstances could have been such that it did. If they were, then there is a reasonable chance that Moore could have proved this. None of these remarks is to be taken as merely autobiographical—a comment on Moore's personal abilities, ingenuity or etc. There is an apparent puzzle about these claims. Consider some circumstances in which Moore could have proved the point in question—for example, ones in which there are clever surgeons lurking about. And consider some proof that Moore then might have offered. Why could he not just produce that proof on the actual occasion of his saying 'This is a hand'? The answer, as Moore sees it, is that perhaps he could then have produced that proof, or at least he could then have said all the same things as were said in giving it. But then, since he could not have proven, on that occasion, what he said in saying 'This is a hand', we must conclude that that 'proof' would not then have counted as proving that premiss. This is a way of seeing how Moore's view requires that proof be an S-use sensitive notion.

2. WITTGENSTEIN'S CRITIQUE

The current majority view is that Moore's 'proof' does not prove what Kant wanted proved; whatever Kant wanted done, it is not so easy. Wittgenstein subscribes to that view. The question is, why is this so?

Several views are possible. Barry Stroud has suggested[2] that the trouble is that there is some special philosophical question, of concern to Kant, which Moore has failed to answer. It is not quite clear what Stroud means by this. He does insist that every step in Moore's 'proof' is valid. So if the 'proof' fails for philosophical purposes, that must be either because its premises are not admissible for those purposes, or because its conclusion is not what was to be proved—not, that is, the thought that would be a direct answer to Stroud's philosophical question. The point on which Stroud is not quite clear is which of these he thinks is so. He does think that Moore's premises are true, and, for the most part, ones we (or Moore at the time) could be said to know to be true. And he gives some impression of tilting in favour of the second diagnosis. In any case, either diagnosis commits Stroud to recognizing some kind of S-use sensitivity—either in what is said in saying 'There is an external world' or in the admissibility of premises.

Crispin Wright has presented several diagnoses of Moore.[3] A quite natural one, though not the one Wright ultimately accepts, could be put in present terms as follows. Moore admits that it is an S-use sensitive question whether his premises require proof. If requiring proof is an S-use sensitive matter, then the same, presumably, could be said for his conclusion. If Moore is addressing Kant's problem, then he must suppose himself to be offering his 'proof' on some occasion on which that conclusion requires proof. But now Moore is just assuming, as it were, a sort of co-ordination between his premises and his conclusion in the way they vary across occasions with respect to requiring proof. In particular, he is supposing that there are some occasions, his own among them, on which the conclusion requires proof but his premises do not. That is why those premises may be admissible in a proof of that conclusion. But one might plausibly argue that this is precisely what is not so. If we are going to have doubts, or raise questions about the existence of an external world, why not doubts about Moore's premises as well? In which case, on such occasions, we would not be able to appeal to them in a proof of an external world.

Wittgenstein's diagnosis differs substantially from either of the above. On Wittgenstein's view, Moore's 'proof' does not count as proving his conclusion because—on the occasion of his offering it— nothing *could* count as proving that; there is nothing that proving F, for Moore's value of F, might consist in.[4] The thought Moore wanted

---

[2] In Stroud [1984], ch. 3.

[3] See Wright [1985].

[4] Wright, too, would say this on his final account of the matter. But—as I understand it—Wright's reason is that Moore's intended conclusion is actually a rule or regulative principle, and not a question of fact. That, I will suggest, is not Wittgenstein's direction.

to prove did not then *admit of* proof. (Nor, in this particular case, would it on any ordinary occasion.) Let us further investigate Wittgenstein's notion of admitting of proof.

It is natural to think of 'the thought that there is an external world' as a definite thought with definite content.[5] Similarly for the thought that Moore has two hands, or the one he expressed in saying himself to. Now, if F is a definite thought, then it is natural to think that it has a certain range of properties: there are some conceivable situations which are (or would be) ones of F's being so; and there are others which are ones of F's not being so. It is further natural to think in terms of some great range of 'all the (relevant) conceivable situations there are', and to think of F as partitioning these into the two classifications just mentioned—perhaps with some residue of unclassifiable cases. Finally, it is also natural to think of the way in which F does this classifying as intrinsic to being the thought F is; thus, different ways of classifying *ipso facto* make for different thoughts. So the classification F imposes on the—or any—range of conceivable situations must be occasion-invariant.

Now for proof. Here it is natural to think that—on a given occasion, at least—there is some definite requirement for proving F, so that a candidate 'proof' succeeds or fails in proving F in virtue of satisfying or failing to satisfy that requirement. It is also natural to think of such a requirement in terms of the above thought on thoughts. A requirement on a proof of F is that it leave no doubt as to F; hence that it furnish what rules out any conceivable situation which would be one of F not obtaining (or perhaps any which would not be one of F obtaining), at least in this sense: given what the proof provides, it is not possible for the occasion of giving that proof to be one on which that situation obtains. We need not yet concern ourselves further with what is involved in a proof *ruling out* a situation (though it will turn out, on the account to come, that S-use sensitivity arises for the application of this notion as well). The important point so far is this: given the occasion-invariance of (definite) thoughts, the range of situations which must be ruled out in proving F remains constant across occasions. In that sense at least, the requirement for proving F must, on this conception, be occasion-invariant.

Wittgenstein rejects this view. First, he takes it that, though F may be as definite as thoughts ever get, the possible, and even the conceivable, ways for F not to obtain, and hence which would be the situations of F's not being so, is a question whose answer varies

---

[5] Or, for some, to think of it as definite nonsense. Which, in terms of the theory to emerge, would be to fasten on a different range of cases. That variation will not affect the general point being made here.

substantively across occasions of posing it. As we have seen, this is anyway part of the Wittgensteinian picture of semantics. Considerations about proof provide some of the most powerful motivations for it to be there. So, second, if we retain the idea that a proof must rule out all possible (or conceivable) ways for F not to be so—as we certainly can on Wittgenstein's view—then the requirement for proving F will vary substantively, and in just the respect just described, across occasions for proving F.

Let us say that F admits of proof on an occasion O if on O there is a (sufficiently) determinate requirement for proving F, and it is at least conceivable that there should be a proof which then would count as satisfying it. F does not admit of proof on O if on O there is no such determinate requirement; if whatever requirement there was (if any) was not one that any conceivable 'proof' might satisfy, or simply did not permit classification into cases of what satisfied it and what failed to. On this notion, something might admit of proof and not be provable. We might know what it would be like to prove F, but not be able to, for example, because we cannot find the right premises. As, for example, where we cannot prove that Fred embezzled the money, but are sure that we could if only we could examine a certain Swiss bank account. Or where we cannot prove that God exists, but—on some views—could do so if only the stars would one night rearrange themselves into the message, 'Believe!'

On Wittgenstein's view, then, admitting of proof is an S-use sensitive notion. But it would be more perspicuous to put the point by saying: only in appropriate circumstances will F admit of proof. Not all circumstances are appropriate for proving F. In fact, it would be correct to say that appropriate ones are exception rather than rule. Moore's circumstances were not appropriate. So he attempted to prove what did not then admit of proof. The wording here is meant to be suggestive. The suggestion will be followed up in the next section.

In *Metaphysics*, Gamma Aristotle says,

for it is lack of training not to recognize of which things demonstration ought to be sought, and of which not. For in general it is impossible that there should be demonstration of everything, since it would go on to infinity so that not even so would it be demonstration.[6]

Kant might accept the maxim. If so, then he views the question what admits of demonstration as an S-use insensitive one. One might disagree with Kant on there being a philosophical scandal simply by locating the existence of an external world S-use insensitively within

---

[6] *Metaphysics*, Gamma, ch. 4 (1006a)—trans. Christopher Kirwan.

the range of things for which Aristotle's advice not to seek demonstration is correct. Neither Moore nor Wittgenstein takes that path.
Moore takes Aristotle's dictum to point to the fact that we need to
start somewhere: we need premises, and, since there must be a start,
ones which do not require proof. He then points out that what is thus
available for us to start with is an S-use sensitive matter. Nor, on
Moore's view, is that much S-use sensitivity eliminable for some truly
strict notion of proof. For Wittgenstein, the key point is that not
admitting of proof is a by-product of the ways in which requirements
for proving F vary across occasions for doing so; and inherits S-use
sensitivity from that. Kant demanded proof of what did not *then* admit
it; so proof which neither Moore nor anyone else could possibly have
supplied. But it is the underlying variation in requirements for proof
that shows the most important way in which Moore's conception of
proof, as well as Kant's, goes wrong.

    What varies, more specifically, is what a proof must accomplish—
what possibilities it must rule out—where such variation leaves no
aspect of a proof immune in principle from variability across occasions
in its fitness for the task then required of it. That a 'proof' of F may
satisfy the requirements for proving F imposed by some occasions,
while failing those imposed by others, is not a phenomenon isolatable
at the level of premises and their admissibility. It may also be a matter
of the validity or truth-preservingness of any inferential step. Or it may
be a global feature of the proof: there is a condition which the proof as a
whole fails to satisfy; the fault cannot be located solely in any one
aspect of it—say, the premises or the inferential moves. So, on
Wittgenstein's view, Moore's 'proof' could not have counted as valid—
counter to what Moore and Stroud hold, and surprising as this may
seem. Later we will see how that could be.

    Wittgenstein agrees with Moore that Kant's conception of proof is
mistaken, and is so in missing the S-use sensitivity of proving F. But,
though Moore locates S-use sensitivity in requiring proof, he misses or
misplaces the variation in requirements for proving F, and hence
misses the consequences for admitting of proof which the S-use
sensitivities in proof entail. Those are the counts on which Wittgenstein faults Moore.

    Note one point on which Kant, Moore and Wittgenstein agree. None
of them—and certainly not Kant—takes the requirement for proving F
(in any relevant sense) to be satisfied merely by providing *true*
premises and connecting them by specified 'valid' inferential rules to
the conclusion. Kant would not doubt that Moore's premises are *true*.
Nor would he question the truth-preservingness of the inferential rules
to which Moore appeals—either in the shorter, or in the extended,

proof. Clearly, those virtues of Moore's 'proofs' would not be enough, for Kant, to make Moore's 'proofs' *proofs*.

3. PROOF CONDITIONS

For some things to admit of proof, some other things must not. Such is the force of Aristotle's dictum if his injunction not to look for proof of certain things is to be read as saying that they do not admit of it. But why should anything not admit of proof? Wittgenstein suggests, first, that, for any F, F's not admitting of proof is an S-use sensitive phenomenon, and second, that, given the first point, not admitting of proof is a by-product of the S-use sensitivity of proof. Here is the idea in brief. What may be true or false may have a condition for its truth, or truth condition. If it is S-use sensitive, then its truth condition will vary substantively across occasions. The point of a 'proof' of F (as opposed to its premises) is not to be true or false, but to prove F. While it thus will have no truth condition, it may have a proof condition. If proof is S-use sensitive, then that condition will vary substantively across occasions for proving F. A given B may satisfy some of the conditions within this range of variation and not others. Now, we know from the case of truth that where (truth) conditions for an item, W, vary across occasions, facts about a given occasion must select adequately from the range of conditions W might sometimes have. The facts of some occasions may fail to do the required selecting. In which case, W, on that occasion, will not be assessable as to truth at all. As Wittgenstein insists, if the sentence 'I am here' is printed in the middle of some arbitrary paragraph of this book, it will express no definite thought, and have no condition for its truth. Similarly for proof. If proof conditions for a candidate proof, B, of F, vary across occasions, then the facts of a given occasion must select adequately from the range of proof conditions which that variation provides. Some occasions may not be up to that task. If that is true of an occasion for any value of B, thus, *vis-à-vis* the condition for proving F, then on that occasion F does not admit of proof.

The phenomenon to concentrate on first, then, is the variation across occasions in proof conditions (for fixed F, or fixed F and B). The first task is to assemble facts which show such variation to exist. If it does, then by the above idea, occasional not admitting of proof will follow directly from that. As usual with studies of S-use sensitivities, there will always be alternate ways of reading any set of relevant data. But we will worry about that only after some reasonably convincing data are in. One point, though: if the truth conditions for W vary substantively across occasions, that is compatible with there being some uniform way of saying (for example, now) what W's truth condition is on any occasion. For example, it *might* be that the sentence 'This is red', on speaking S, is true just in case the referent of that 'this' then counted as being red. It is just that when we try to apply that uniform formulation, we will find variation across occasions in what counts as satisfying that condition; we can identify states of affairs which, on one occasion, but not on another, would count as ones of that condition being satisfied. (For example, the sentence is said of apple A, and A is a normal ripe winesap.) Similarly for proof. If proof conditions vary substantively across occasions, that is compatible with there being some uniform way of saying what the condition for proving F is.

The data to be developed in this section and the next aim at showing two things: first, that proof conditions are liable to be S-use sensitive, and that they are in the general case; and second, that there is no interesting class of proofs which satisfy the conditions for proving their conclusions S-use insensitively—that is, invariantly across occasions for proving those conclusions. To say that there is no interesting class is to say that there is no such class which would support a reasonable S-use insensitive notion of proof. Such a notion, if available, might then be held to be a stricter notion than the one discussed here, so that only what proves F in that sense would be a proof in the strictest sense of the term, and only a liberal arts notion of proof would be infected by S-use sensitivity. Following Wittgenstein, I will try to show the unavailability of such a notion by arguing the strong thesis that *no* proof counts as proving F S-use insensitively. Obviously, less might do. For the moment, though, it is the first point that is at stake. Here are some relevant data:

> *Case I*. Luc doubts that McTeagle's sells shoes. Hugo wants to prove it to him. So Hugo goes to the closet and pulls out some old shoeboxes with the McTeagle's name and logo, or some shoes with 'McTeagle's Quality Footwear' embossed on the insole. That settles the issue. If the argument needs putting into words, it might go like this: 'Here are some McTeagle's shoeboxes/shoes. So (you can see that) McTeagle's does sell shoes.'

> *Case II*. Hugo does not believe that they would actually give Odile an office with *chairs* in it. Odile decides to prove it to him. So she takes him to the office and shows him the chairs. Again, if verbalization is called for, it might go something like this: 'See. There's a chair. And there's another. So there *are* chairs in the office.' (Note the formal parallel with Moore's 'proof'.)

Case III. You want to borrow twenty dollars from me, which, fortunately, is more than I carry in cash. I tell you I do not have it, but you do not believe me. So I prove it to you. I take out my wallet and show you that it is empty. 'See,' I say, 'it's empty. So I don't have twenty dollars.' Conversely, if I had wanted to prove to you that I *did* have twenty dollars, then I might take out my wallet, remove a twenty-dollar note, and show it to you. 'See. This is a twenty dollar note. So I have twenty dollars.'

Comment. Provisionally, we have been thinking of proofs as more or less verbalized or verbalizable items. But should we? In the above three cases, words are hardly called for. You see that my wallet is empty; Hugo sees the chairs. And so on. Words can hardly make things *more* certain. And the suspicion is that if it is words we are really relying on, then they might make things less so. Those McTeagle's shoeboxes show that McTeagle's sells shoes, all right. But is it really the fact that they are McTeagle's shoeboxes that shows that? Or the fact that they have the McTeagle's name on them? Exactly how should this state of affairs be verbalized? What is the critical fact here? If you are moved by that sort of thought, then you might want to liberalize our requirement on being a line in a proof to include such things as the shoeboxes, or so-and-so's seeing them, or the state of affairs of their being like that (demonstrating), or etc. But the basic phenomena of S-use sensitivity, with which we are now concerned, will not be affected whether you include items of such sorts as proofs or you limit proofs to what is accomplished by words or thoughts.

Case IV. Moore offers to accompany Pol, who wants to sing the *Winterreise*. 'Can you play it?' Pol asks. Moore assures Pol that he can and proves it: 'I've played the piano all my life, and in the last few years have made a special study of Schubert *Lieder*. In fact, I played the *Winterreise* in recital just last week.' That is surely enough to settle that Moore can handle the part.

Case V. Odile has bought a new blind for the window. But Hugo, saw in hand, claims that it is too wide to fit. 'Oh go on.', Odile protests. So Hugo takes out his steel tape-measure and measures. Holding it next to the blind lying in the hall he demonstrates 'See—it measures 42 inches.' Then taking it over to the window frame, he again measures 'See—it measures 40 inches.' If the window measured 40 inches, and the blind measured inches 42, so the thought goes, then the blind is wider than the window.

Case VI. As we walk into the lecture room, we hear someone say, 'What a good joke. Look. That lectern is made of ice.' But the person must be looking from a bad angle. The lectern is nothing of the sort, as we then proceed to demonstrate: 'Just feel it. It doesn't feel cold. It isn't dripping. And, for good measure, if you run your hand across it you will get a hand full of splinters. So it is not made of ice; it's just a normal wood lectern.'

Case VII. Hoisting her glass, Odile says, 'To Belgium—157 years old today.' 'Go on' says Hugo 'It's much older than that.' So they consult a history text. There it is written, 'Belgium seceded from the Netherlands in 1830 and imported a king from the house of Saxe-Coburg.' Odile's case is made. Hugo buys the next round.

As mentioned already, the examples may seem slightly off the subject—for example, examples of mere informal proof, in some informal sense of 'informal'. But that is not yet our immediate problem. The more pressing concern is that the data was supposed to consist of contrasting pairs. For the point is that what sometimes counts as satisfying the condition for proving F at other times does not. So let us consider what the other member of the pair might be in each case (flagging contrasting items with an 'a'.)

Case Ia. Hugo is renowned for his collection of 'special edition' boxes—such as the hatbox with the legend 'Ronald Reagan's Strategic Haberdashery Initiative', the shoebox with 'General Rommel's Walkovers' written on it, and the other shoebox with the legend 'Tiny Tim's Macrobiotic Naturalizers'. Now we come to the McTeagle's boxes. We can see what it says on them. And the humour of it is not immediately evident. (In contrast to the others?) But just because Hugo has boxes like that—that hardly proves that McTeagle's sells shoes?

Similarly, if one were to suppose that McTeagle's used to sell shoes but might recently have stopped, or that the venerable McTeagle may have found a deal on shoeboxes that he couldn't refuse, so that for the next ten years McTeagle's will pack everything in shoeboxes, then, on those suppositions, Hugo's 'proof', or those boxes being in his closet, or the fact of their being there, would prove nothing. So if it could be that any of these things were so, then Hugo's 'proof' could not count as (a) proof.

Similarly if it could be that Luc or Hugo were hallucinating, or that it was all somehow done with mirrors, or that Luc had forgotten what a shoebox looked like, so that those things were not, then Hugo would not have succeeded in proving his point. One reason: it would then not be enough for it to be a fact that there are shoeboxes in the closet; Hugo is entitled to cite that fact only if he can *show* that it is so.

Case IIa. Hugo is standing in Odile's office, or, perhaps, sitting in a chair. He is presumably sane, sighted and in good lighting. Moreover, he is a presumed master of the concept *chair*. Odile suddenly announces that there are chairs in the office, and she is going to prove it. She then produces, as nearly as she can, the proof of case II. That is, she gestures at a chair and says 'There's a chair' and so on. We would not think that she had, after all, produced a proof that there were chairs in her office, though we might not know quite what else to think of her mysterious performance. This need not be *raw* intuition. If someone seriously wants to prove to us that there are chairs about when we are evidently sitting in one, then it would be reasonable to wonder what else might be going on other than (and instead of) there being chairs about. We may legitimately feel that we have no good answer to that question. We may now rehearse a special form of the argument of case Ia. If we were to suppose that there might be some way or other—we know not, and cannot imagine what—of *this* being a situation in which there are no chairs in the vicinity, then on that supposition, Odile's 'proof' would not be accepted as proving that, after all, there are. So if this could be a chairless situation, then Odile's 'proof' would not prove that it was not that. But Odile's raising the question of proof here makes it reasonable to suppose that this could be such a not-yet-imagined situation. So her offering it under these circumstances brings it about that her 'proof' does not count as a proof.

Case IIIa. This case could be developed either along the lines of Ia or of IIa. For the first, suppose that I am in the habit of walking about in tails and a tall black silk hat, that things are constantly disappearing into and appearing out of my sleeves (or wherever) and that I am well known for always having an empty wallet when the bill arrives, even when I have just been seen making a large withdrawal from the bank. You ask for a loan of twenty dollars, and I produce (as nearly as possible) just the demonstration of case II. This would not be accepted as proving that I do not have twenty dollars. Similarly, we may construct cases by appealing to hallucinations and all the other items in the usual bag of tricks.

Now along the lines of IIa. I take out my wallet and show you the twenty-dollar note lying there. I let you touch it, hold it up to the light, etc. Then I put it back in my wallet. Then I announce, 'Now I am going to prove that I have twenty dollars in my wallet.' I produce the same demonstration as before. What could that demonstration be other than mysterious? Certainly not a proof. For what would we now want shown for proving that? Just *how* is my demonstration supposed to prove that I have twenty dollars?

Case IVa. Suppose that Moore's hands might just have fallen off. Or that he had, or might have unscrewable, 'hands' which he might absentmindedly have left at home that day. Or that he might just have acquired unscrewable 'hands'—tricky surgeons again—which felt just like hands, but when you try to play the piano with them . . . . Or that Moore's piano playing competence might suddenly have vanished. On these suppositions, Moore's 'proof' would still leave the question entirely open whether he could play the *Winterreise*. So it would not be a proof of that. In some cases, something else might be. If the problem were simply that Moore might have been given the unscrewable, but pianistically hopeless 'hands', that could be settled—perhaps—by Moore's trying to screw his hands (counter-clockwise, of course) and thereby proving that they do not come off—*if* the problem were confined to that particular possibility. But, of course, if one were to suppose that Moore might have unscrewable 'hands', there might be no clear point at which we could properly take it that the problems had stopped.

Such is a story about what various suppositions might do. I leave it to the reader to construct circumstances in which such suppositions would properly be made—in which it would count as so that one or another of these things perhaps could be the case. (Perhaps: many amateur pianists have recently been the unwitting victims of cunning surgeons; could Moore be one of these?) I am convinced that there are such circumstances. But the story of them will have to be a good one. They are not circumstances which we find ourselves in every day. I, at least, have never found myself in any such.

Case Va. Suppose that it were so that tape-measures, even metal ones, sometimes grow or shrink—as it were, for no apparent reason—or that Hugo's might have done so. Or suppose that an object, such as a blind, might change length merely in virtue of change of position. Or suppose that—to anticipate a later theme—an inch might not really be a unit of measure, as you are now conceiving of such things, so that the window's measuring 40 of them while the blind measures 42 of them does not really entail that the blind is wider than the window. On such suppositions, Hugo's 'demonstration' would not demonstrate that the blind was wider than the window.

Suppose that blinds can vary length merely by varying their spatial position. If that were so, then we might (though need not) be left with no way of settling what the length of something (or at least a blind) was. If that were so, then nothing could be a proof of Hugo's claim—it would never be determinately so of anything that it had met the requirements for settling that issue. We might be left in such a position; but we need not. We would then be left with no effective conception of what it would be for the blind to be such-and-such a length.[7]

We would lack not only an understanding of how the notion *proof of Hugo's claim* is to apply, but also a grip on what the conclusion of such a proof is to be. If we did make this supposition about change of length through change of place, we would then notice that there were a variety of distinct things to be said in saying the blind to be wider than the window. Some of these things might turn out to be proved by Hugo's demonstration, and anyway would not be disproved by moving the blind over to the window, holding it up and showing it to fit. Whereas others of them would be disproved in that way, and correspondingly proved if the match showed the blind not to fit the frame.

If the fact were that blinds may change length with position and we knew that, we might say any of various things in saying the blind to be wider than the window— *inter alia*, that to whose truth it matters what the blind would do when held against the window; and that for which only the way the blind is in its position in the hall matters. Physicists might tell us how to settle either of these claims. But that may leave them unable to tell us which sort of claim Hugo made. It might be that nothing else settles this either, so that it is a fact about what he said that it was determinately neither the one thing nor the other. As things in fact are, Hugo expressed a thought with definite content—in so far as we ever do so. In the counter factual circumstances just envisioned, his thought would turn out to lack definite content. So apparently having definite content is an occasion-sensitive matter. (Let us postpone the

[7] Putnam tells us that Reichenbach often expressed ideas along these lines. The whole issue is discussed in a very illuminating way in Putnam [1975].

issue whether being a definite thought varies with it.) This point, too, is crucial for what follows.

Case VIa. The next two cases add little to what has been observed already. The wonders of chemistry might, perhaps, some day include a way of making ice act, for a limited time, at least, just like wood. It might sometimes be possible to suppose that chemistry may have done that already. It is also conceivable that some day a school of neoThaleans will spring up. These people might admit different forms of water, including ice and steam, but claim that everything is made of one of these three things. My 'proof' is not likely to count as a refutation of neoThaleanism. Nor is it yet clear, until the neoThaleans arrive, what would be. It is not obvious, in fact, that it would be possible to argue with them at all, or that if it proved not to be, that would be a mere psychological matter.

Case VIIa. Odile's 'proof' would not work if it were to be supposed that history books, or anyway hers, lie. But that might simply be chalked up to the admissibility of premisses. At least if what the book says is right, then Odile's conclusion follows. Matters, however, need not be quite that simple. There is, after all, a sense in which Belgium is much older than 157 years—a sense with great appeal for the average Belgian. As they would put it (rough translation), it was already a nation, though not a country.[8] That is why the attempt at secession was so successful. So Hugo might harbour a suspicion that he did not really lose after all. This is a perhaps more mundane re-creation of some of the issues of case Va.

4. SEMANTIC DOUBT

If proof is S-use sensitive, then that sensitivity is contained in the data presented already, and in more just like it. But, as noted, there are a number of ways in which the above intuitions may create the impression of having somehow changed the subject. One way is this. If we accept the data of the a-cases, then that data may be read as showing that the 'proofs' in the cases with which these a-cases pair

---

[8] That is not quite the way the average Belgian would put it. Two nations, perhaps, but not one. Moreover, the average Belgian would deny vehemently that there are any average Belgians, except perhaps, as they put it, King Boudewijn and Eddie Merckx. As this suggests, there were many reasons why the revolution succeeded.

never really were proofs. For the a-cases, or most of them, exhibit possibilities of some sort for the conclusions of those 'proofs' not to be so, though all the rest of what the proof said was so. For example, it would have been possible for Hugo to have had special McTeagle's shoeboxes made—say, because he found that amusing. But then, one might think, even in the first case of the pair, the 'proof' did not really rule out all possibility of its not being so that McTeagle's sells shoes, or of whatever its conclusion might have been. So on no occasion would this 'proof' really prove it. Or at least not strictly speaking. At most, it might settle all the doubts we happened to have on that occasion, or all those we need have had. But then, it is just that that represents the change of subject.

A second impression of changing the subject may come from the reverse direction. Consider Odile's 'proof', in IIa, that there were chairs in her office. One might feel that our intuition that that was not a proof came not from the pointing out of some specific way in which it fell short of being a proof—some specific other possibility that it left open—but rather from the fact that it would be odd to offer that sort of a proof, or in fact any proof in those circumstances. Either the trouble is that it would not have been enough to convince Hugo if he were not already convinced, or it is that it is pointless, as it were, to preach to the converted. But in either case, that intuition is one on another subject. So that, be that as it may, it remains so that Odile's 'proof' really did prove (or demonstrate) the point in question. Or so it might seem.

A minimal requirement for proof to be an S-use insensitive notion is that each pair of cases in data of the above sort must divide up on at least one of the above two lines. Either the a-case, which appeared not to count as a proof, must really have been a proof on that occasion, though not naturally then treated as such, for some peripheral reason, or the first case, which appeared to count as a proof, must not really have been a proof, though convincing enough, perhaps, for the purposes at hand; it must not have settled the point in question in the way that a proof or demonstration would have done. In any event, each pair of cases must consist either of two cases of proving the conclusion in question or of two cases of not proving it. Conversely, building a case for the S-use sensitivity of proof requires, minimally, dispelling impressions of the above two kinds.

The main line to be taken here with the first sort of impression is that if the reasoning behind it were accepted as a general principle about proof, then nothing, or much too little, could ever count as proof of anything. There would at least be broad areas of human knowledge—in fact, virtually all of it—which concerned facts which, in the nature of the case, could never be proved; a paradoxical and hence unacceptable conclusion. The point would be that for any 'proof' we could always produce or concoct some situation in which it would not count as a proof, and then for the reason that it then counted as leaving open possibilities for its conclusion not to be so despite all else it said. If it is generally correct to move from such a fact to the conclusion that that 'proof', on some other occasion, did not count as proof, then there is nearly enough no such thing as proof. But if that move is not generally correct, then the ground is cut away from under the first sort of impression—at least often enough to sustain the S-use sensitivity of proof which the data seems *prima facie* to show.

This point could be put, a bit more tendentiously, by saying that the S-use sensitivity of proof is pervasive: (virtually) any 'proof' counts as a proof only given that certain suppositions, which would sometimes be proper ones, and on which that 'proof' would be no proof, cannot then properly be made, or used to show that that 'proof' does not then fit the concept of proof. The further data to be developed in this section are primarily aimed at showing that conclusion. The aim, that is, is to show how any 'proof' can be made to do less than proving its conclusion by constructing appropriate circumstances for giving it. A secondary effect of this data, if effective, will be to do something to counteract the second of the above impressions. For it will show that the reason why Odile's a-'proof' that there are chairs in her office would not then be treated as a proof is not merely that it is pointless, but that there actually are ways for its conclusion to be wrong, even given its premises, and that it cannot count as having ruled out all such ways there then were. It is not expected that the data will establish this unequivocally. It might still be reasonable to suppose that there might be principled ways of dismissing enough of it to leave an interesting class of proofs which are so S-use insensitively, and which would then represent proof in the strictest sense. But a final assessment of the data will not be attempted until the section after next.

It bears emphasis that the present task is still restricted to data collection. The immediate task is to enlarge our collection of apparently S-use sensitive proofs. One might proceed in an *ad hoc* way. But Wittgenstein has suggested a sort of general procedure for exhibiting the (intuitive, and at least apparent) S-use sensitivity of any proof. The plan is to exhibit, for any proof, B, of F, doubts which sometimes, though not always, would be taken intuitively to show B not to prove F, and a general method for constructing these. I will call the method 'the path of semantic doubt'—though the term 'semantic' is not quite proper for all the doubts in the class, and where it does fit can be expected to do so only S-use sensitively. Exhibiting the procedure will not automatically settle that the concept of proof is S-use sensitive. But it ought at least convince that data of the sort presented so far can be produced for whatever class of proof one likes. Wittgenstein describes the method in passages like the following:

If I wanted to doubt whether this was my hand, how could I avoid doubting whether the word 'hand' has any meaning? (OC 369)

If I make an experiment I do not doubt the existence of the apparatus before my eyes. I have plenty of doubts, but not *that*. If I do a calculation I believe, without any doubts, that the figures on the paper are not switching of their own accord. (OC 337)

If I ask someone, 'What colour do you see at the moment?', in order, that is, to learn what colour is there at the moment, I cannot at the same time question whether the person I ask understands English, whether he wants to take me in, whether my own memory is not leaving me in the lurch as to the names of colours, and so on. (OC 345)

'I don't know if this is a hand.' But do you know what the word 'hand' means? And don't say, 'I know what it means now for me.' And isn't it an empirical fact—that *this* word is used like *this*? (OC 306)

'Do you know or do you only believe that your name is L.W.?' Is that a meaningful question?

Do you know or do you only believe that what you are writing down now are English words? Do you only believe that 'believe' has this meaning? *What* meaning? (OC 486)

'I know that this is a hand.'—And what is a hand?—'Well, *this*, for example.' (OC 268)

The suggestion here is this. Let B be your favourite example of a proof (of F)—occasion-insensitively, if you think there are such proofs. Then there are suppositions which, if proper to make, would destroy your proof. These suppositions depict ways for things to be such that if things really might be that way, then B could not have removed all possibilities for F not to be so—either because B would state what might not be so, or because it then might be that for all B states, F is not so, or both, or because neither of these would be determinately not so. The suppositions in question are coherent. In fact, it is sometimes possible to show, by entirely ordinary means, that what they suppose is not so (or that it *is*.) So if B is to prove F S-use insensitively, then there must be a reasonable and well motivated way of isolating these suppositions and declaring them never relevant to the question whether B proves F. The trouble is that we can construct circumstances where, intuitively, they are relevant to that.

Not all the suppositions Wittgenstein produces in this connection are straightforwardly semantic. But we can *always* find suppositions of the right sort if we permit ourselves to entertain semantic doubts. If B appeals to premisses P, and derives F from them, then we can always formulate, in one way or another, doubts as to whether the semantic rules in fact governing P really do permit that derivation. Part of the long-range task is then to show that such semantic doubts cannot be excluded as irrelevant across all occasions for proving F. In the short run, though, the aim is to show that there are some occasions on which they intuitively would be taken to count against B's proving F, thereby exhibiting more facts for an opponent to explain away.

To illustrate, let B be: 'Pol is a bachelor; so Pol is unmarried.' A supposition might then be: couldn't the concept of a bachelor be such as not to require what fits it to be unmarried? Compare: a student, Roy, knows that Pia is an invigilator; he reads it on her badge. But what is an invigilator? Any inference from that premiss which its semantics might license on occasion is one that Roy might doubt. He would have to be shown why it followed. Similarly, couldn't someone accept that Pol was a bachelor, and have just the doubt just mentioned as to B? In unusual enough circumstances (some sort of brainwashing, perhaps), we ourselves might be made to have such doubts. On such an occasion, we would only count it as proved that Pol was unmarried if the relevant facts about the concept bachelor were demonstrated (something B does not do.) And we would be reasonable in recognizing this condition on proof—or so it would seem. (So far, those relevant facts might be demonstrated—an exercise in boring everyday linguistics, perhaps.)

For the reasons just mentioned, B might not be everyone's favourite candidate for S-use insensitive proof. An expansion of it might seem to approach closer to that ideal. Consider B*: 'Pol is a bachelor; if anyone is a bachelor, then he is unmarried; so Pol is unmarried.' Such, one might think, counts as proof S-use insensitively. Or if not, then only because it would sometimes be correct to doubt one of the two premisses. So at least any S-use sensitivity here could be isolated, as Moore thought it could, at the level of the premisses and their admissibility in proof.

But wait. Could it really not be that both those premisses were true and the conclusion still false? Reflect on the semantics of (that occurrence of) 'if–then'. Does that semantics really require that if A is so, and 'If A then B' is so, then B is so? Consider the following example. A man asks me, 'How do you get to McGill?' I reply, 'If you turn left and go straight, then you will get there.' He turns left, takes ten steps, has a heart attack and dies. Was my statement false? Arguably not. Now, couldn't the if–then statement in B* have just the semantics that this example suggests—a semantics which in special circumstances (which, perhaps, now might obtain) would allow that conditional to be true while Pol was a bachelor but not unmarried? (And couldn't it be settled—that is, proved—whether that is so by ordinary techniques for investigating language?) So again, there is a doubt to be had, so presumably occasions for having it, and for settling it in proving that Pol is unmarried. The important point here is not that the semantics of 'if–then' *does* allow for such possibilities (though I confess to believing that it does), but rather that this is a reasonable linguistic hypothesis; reasonable enough so that someone (even a sophisticated philosopher) might accept both premises of B*, accept them as admissible in a proof, and still have coherent and sensible doubts as to whether B*'s conclusion followed—doubts good enough, intuitively, reasonably to block B* then from proving F.

Before drawing conclusions from this, I will mention one conclusion I will not draw. Philosophers such as Leibniz, Lewis Carroll and Saul Kripke have suggested that anything less than unquestioned acceptance of and reliance on inferential rules such as *modus ponens* deprives us of the right to accept (or reject) any argument at all. I think that these philosophers are mistaken. But none of the above need be seen as expressing a doubt about *modus ponens*. Grant the correctness of that rule. There remains the question whether the move in B* from premises to conclusion is an instance of it. It is if, but only if, the second premiss, and the particular occurrence in it of 'if–then', have a certain semantics. It cannot be necessarily so that all occurrences of the English 'if–then' do have that semantics. But it is just that that was being doubted in the illustration.

Now for the right conclusion. Any proof contains inferential moves which are correct and truth-preserving only if certain facts hold (among which may be the fact that the moves instance certain rules). Any proof may be expanded by adding to it statements of some of these facts. At first sight, the expansion may look like a nearer approximation to the ideal of what is S-use insensitively proof, or at least, on the Moorean model, S-use insensitively valid. But if B is the original and B* the expansion, let us, from the vantage point of B*, look back at B. The extra premises in B* are themselves subject to doubt (on some occasions). On some occasion, as a consequence of that, B* would not count as proving its conclusion; those premises would require proof first. But where such doubts enter into the conditions for proving that conclusion, they destroy not only B* as a proof of that, but, by the same token, B. (The shorter proof cannot generally withstand such doubt while the expansion does not.) Nor could B's inferential moves then count as preserving truth or proof across all suppositions it would then be correct to make for the purposes of assessing proof. But these points about inferential moves and expandability hold for *any* proof; they hold for B* relative to its expansions just as much as for B relative to its. Therefore no proof can count as proving its conclusion, or even as valid, S-use insensitively.

We are now in a position to re-examine Moore's proof. Both Moore and Stroud found no question as to its validity. But, by the present argument, it can be valid at best only S-use sensitively. To see how it might, on occasion, fail to count as valid, consider Odile's parallel proof of chairs in her office. The proof was: 'There is a chair; and there is another; so there are at least two chairs in the office.' Consider this supposition: perhaps chairs are not, as it were, material objects, but rather what we might call ephemera—something akin to little flashes of light, such as those one sees when there are ice crystals in the air. Think of this as a sort of 'material mode' version of a semantic doubt. Now, it would be clearly incorrect to reason: 'There is one flash of light; and there is another; so there are at least two flashes of light in the office.' Similarly, if chairs were ephemera, then it would be incorrect (invalid) to reason about them as Odile did. And if it is to be supposed that chairs really *might* be ephemera, then proving, from Odile's premises, that there are at least two chairs in the office requires, *inter alia*, proving that in fact they are not ephemera. Under those conditions, Odile's 'proof' would not prove her conclusion, not because the premises were in doubt, but because it relied on incorrect inferential moves. But, the claim is, we can construct occasions for having such doubts. On such occasions, Odile's proof would not count as valid. Similarly for Moore. Wittgenstein's point, of course, is not that Moore is on an occasion like that. Rather, given the S-use sensitivity of validity, the point is that Moore's occasion selects no determinate requirement for validity on it. So it cannot be so that Moore's proof then counted as valid.

There can be a class of proof which prove their conclusions S-use insensitively only if there is an interesting class of semantic doubts which can be isolated and ruled universally irrelevant to the subject of (valid) proof. Two thoughts might suggest that there is such a class. First, one might think that Wittgensteinian semantic doubts are fit only for people who do not know what the semantics of relevant items actually is. Whereas, the thought goes, there is a certain minimum set of semantic facts one must know in order to count as genuinely entertaining given thoughts (so premises) at all. Second, one might think that what really matters for the question whether B proves F (in the strict or potentially S-use insensitive sense of the term) is what is so *given* the semantics of all of B's constituents, so what follows from (Pol's) being a bachelor, given the concept that being a bachelor in fact is—it matters, for example, whether everything, in all possible situations, which satisfies the actual requirements for fitting that concept is unmarried.

But as soon as these thoughts are stated, they show why they are unpromising. As for the first, it just does not seem true that (S-use insensitively) there are any specifiable semantic facts which Roy *must* grasp to count as thinking that Pia is an invigilator. The point appears to generalize across all thoughts. Making something intelligible out of the second hopeful thought requires drawing an S-use insensitive line between facts which are 'intrinsic to the semantics of concept A', and facts which are up for negotiation or proof, or which depend in some way on how the world is (and how we react to it). If anything in philosophy is clear by now, it is that the prospects for that project are exceedingly dim.

5. WAYS THINGS COULD BE

As always, there are many readings of the data. Since there must be a start, I sketch here an account which takes the data at roughly face value. Suppose that B purports to prove F, and O is an occasion on which F admits of proof. Then there is on O a reasonably determinate range of doubts which are relevant to assessing whether B then counts as proving F. Each of these doubts is, of course, a possible way for things then (on O) to be, and, we will suppose, a way on which F would not be so. Each is, further, a doubt which B must settle or resolve: what B provides must settle that things, on O, are not as that doubt has them being. B might fail to settle some such doubt either because that doubt is, *inter alia*, a doubt as to something B states or provides (so that if it is correct to suppose that things might be as that doubt has them being, then that part of B itself requires proof); or because the doubt is a possible way for things to be on which F would not be so despite the obtaining of all that B states or provides (so that B leaves open the possibility of F then failing to be so in that way). If B thus fails to resolve any doubt in this range, then it does not count on O as proving F. Otherwise, it does so count.

To this account I add the thesis of S-use sensitivity: the range of doubts thus relevant to B's proving F varies from occasion to occasion. In this way, different occasions impose different proof conditions on B. Each condition refers to some given range of relevant doubts. Given that, the rule is that any such range is a *proper* subset of the conceivable doubts as to F, in the sense already given here to that last term. It may then be that B satisfies some of these proof conditions but not others, hence counts on some occasions, but not on others, as proving F.

A warning before proceeding further. It is impossible to discuss proof without using modal notions. The topic of modalities, and (for example, English) modal expressions, is a vexed one. Several thousand years of discussion have produced numerous candidate distinctions. It is not possible to discuss those proposals or to address that topic directly here. But it may be tempting to reread what is said here in terms of some such distinctions—in particular, some candidate distinction between 'epistemic' and 'metaphysical' modalities. In so far as there is content in such a distinction, the coming talk of possibility cannot be purely 'epistemic'; it is as 'metaphysical' as such talk gets, though, perhaps, not purely so. (The point of this chapter is to link epistemology to metaphysics.) But the most important point is this: a proper account of modalities will simply have to fit the facts to be stated. No more should be read into the coming text than what it actually says.

The next question, then, is: which doubts as to F are relevant on O to B's proving F? There is an obvious answer. Let D be, on O, a possible way for F then not to be so, where that possibility is not removed (so, D resolved) by B, but a doubt which is not relevant, on O, to assessing B. By the second clause, B might prove F despite D. By the first, for all the reason B provides for taking it that F, it remains possible, on O, that F is not then so. But that is absurd. If such is possible, then B does not prove F. Hence, the relevant doubts, on O, are all of the ways it is then possible for F (then) not to be so. This obvious answer, I suggest, is correct.

Reflection may make it seem as if the obvious answer could not be correct. For if it were, it may seem, there would always be far too many relevant doubts for anything ever to succeed as a proof. Suppose Hugo and Odile to be sitting in her office, and let F be that there are then chairs in the office. Surely, the thought is, it is a possible doubt as to that that Hugo and Odile are both hallucinating. But as Moore urged, and Wittgenstein agreed, if we are always going to entertain such doubts, then we had better give up on ever proving anything.

This thought rests on two confusions. First, for most F, there are in general many ways for things to be which, on some occasion or other, are possible ways for F then not to be so. And there are many ways for facts just like F not to be so. There are, for example, many ways for there to be no chairs in the office, and many ways for there to be none at a particular time—for example, the time at which Hugo and Odile sat there. But the issue on O, in considering what would prove F, is how it is possible for things then to be: whether that could be an occasion or situation which was one of F not then obtaining, and if so, just how it could be that. What is possible for some situations or occasions may not be possible for others. So the great variety of ways for *some* situation to be one of F's not obtaining need not all be possible ways for *this* situation (or for O) to be one of F's not obtaining. The great variety which the thought appeals to does not automatically show anything about what a given situation, O, could be, hence anything running counter to the obvious answer as to which doubts are relevant.

Second, for any given occasion—for example, the one of Hugo and Odile chatting in her office—there are many occasions for considering it, and what would have proved F on it. No doubt there is S-use sensitivity across those occasions with respect to the question what it was possible for that occasion to be. Such may again be misread as providing a very large variety of possible ways for that occasion to be *tout court*. Whereas what needs attending to, in this case, is what counts as so about occasion O on any one given occasion for considering O.

Pol, sitting on a terrasse in Paris, sees Yvon walk by, and calls to him to join him. 'Guess what' Pol says: 'Odile is in Paris.' 'I don't believe it' replies Yvon. 'Yes, really,' says Pol: 'She's been with me all morning.' Just then Odile returns to the table from inside and sits down. 'See,' says Pol, gesturing, 'here she is.' That, one would think, is proof. Now consider this way for things to be: Odile changed trains at Aulnoye and went to Reims instead. Surely Odile *could have* done that. So, further, that is a possible way for *some* situation to be. But the situation in which Pol and Yvon find themselves just could not be like that: that is not then a possible way for their circumstances to be.

Meanwhile, in Tervuren, Hugo is feeling pangs of jealousy. Is Odile *really* in Paris as she is supposed to be? Or did she perhaps change trains in Aulnoye and go to an assignation in Reims? Far-fetched doubts, perhaps. Then again, perhaps not. Hugo's circumstances may be ones that could possibly be that way; that may be a possible way for things to be on his occasion for considering them. That shows nothing about how it is possible for things to be from Pol's and Yvon's perspective on them. Hugo's situation (or occasion) is just not the same one as theirs—though both are occasions for considering—doubting, in the one case, seeing in the other—the same fact, namely that Odile is then in Paris. Here we see a non-innocuous version of the thesis formulated in innocuous form in the introduction: the doubts it is possible (coherently) to have as to F, and not just the possible expressions of them, vary with (our) perspectives on the facts, and not just with our spatio-temporal positions. For as our situations vary, so too there is variation in what those situations possibly could be, and with the way things could be, so the doubts that there *are* as to how things are.

Consider this way for things to be: Odile, like other important executives, has a double; it is the double and not Odile who is in Paris. Is this a possible way for Pol's and Yvon's situation to be? I have been supposing so far that it is not. And we can easily imagine circumstances being such that it is not. (Imagination is hardly called for: try having this doubt next time you are face to face with your spouse or other close friend.) But it may also be important that there are different occasions for us to talk of Pol and Yvon. We can construct some, perhaps, on which it would be true to say that this is a possible way for their circumstances to be; and there are others on which it would not be true to say this. Such would illustrate the second point about S-use sensitivity. Given the two points, the obvious answer to the original question may stand.

Whether D is a possible way for things to be, and hence whether it is a possible doubt as to F, varies across occasions for considering that, and perhaps varies further across occasions for considering any given such occasion. What, then, determines of any given occasion what the possible ways are for it to be? The Wittgensteinian answer is: the reactions of a reasonable judge to that occasion—as shown, among other things, by the facts of *our* accepting certain 'proofs' as proofs, and rejecting others, under the circumstances and in the ways in which we do so. As usual, a qualification is called for. What matters, in the end, is the reaction of a reasonable judge to all other facts which might make him regard the occasion (relevantly) in one way or another. So there are here two determinants of the possibilities for a situation: first, there are facts as to how reasonable judges would react initially from given perspectives, or with given information; second, there are facts as to how the other facts which actually obtain would change the reactions of reasonable judges when such judges confronted them— where and when there are any further facts which would do this.

Which is to say that what a situation could be, and so which doubts are possible ones in it, are world-involving matters. A reasonable judge in Pol's and Yvon's position, perhaps, would not react by taking that to be a situation in which they might be looking across the table at Odile's double. But suppose that Odile is an important executive and that it is, in fact, a hitherto-concealed fact that important executives always have doubles who frequently travel for them. That fact, if it is one, may be enough to change the reaction of a reasonable judge.

Pol and Yvon, then, correctly take their situation to be one which could not be such that Odile changed trains at Aulnoye and went to Reims instead of Paris. But it is possible to be mistaken in such matters—not only because one reacts unreasonably, but also because one is mis- or uninformed; because the world sometimes contains surprises. In matters of possibility, as with other objects of knowledge, it is in the nature of the case that it is possible for there to be deceptive cases. But it is importantly intrinsic to being a deceptive case that such is a case in which we are misinformed—hence, in which there *is* some more information, known or unknown, which *shows* it to be deceptive. That is what distinguishes any deceptive case from any non-deceptive one; hence it is built into the notion of being deceptive that in the absence of any such further story about the case, our initial (reasonable) reactions in distinguishing what is possible for (and in) a situation from what is not are *correct*. (If the question is whether being a deceptive case is a possible way for *this* situation to be, that is a question to be settled in the same way and by the same rules as those just described for questions of this general type—that is, questions as to what situations could be.)

This world-involvingness of doubts, and this role for reasonable judges, on the present account, are both things which distinguish the notion of proof now under discussion from the more subjective notion of proving F to A. Yvon, for example, may be wrong as to what the doubts are as to Odile's being in Paris—and even unshakably so. Sitting across from her on the terrasse, he (seriously) entertains fantasies as to how it might all have been done with mirrors, etc. proving to *him* that Odile was in Paris would involve proving that no such trickery was afoot; her mere presence there would not suffice. Yet, in the situation Yvon and Pol are in, her presence at the table with them then *does* suffice to prove it. Conversely, Yvon may sniff the air (in Odile's absence) and say: 'That's Odile's perfume; so she's in Paris.' Odile shares the scent in question with several million other women. So the fact Yvon appealed to does not prove she is in Paris (though he is in fact right that she is). But there may, and need be no convincing him of that.

A proof of F, on O, then, must resolve all possible doubts, on O, as to F's then being so. But what is it for a 'proof', B, to resolve a doubt, D? We might say this: B resolves D iff it states (or provides) something, G, itself not in doubt (or else proved by a sub-part of B) such that G is incompatible with things then being the way D has them being. But, it may be objected, this only exchanges one terminology for another; it gives us no effective means of picking out cases in which some value of B resolved some value of D. I think it is correct that this explanation just exchanges one terminology for another. I further think that, in the sense in which this is so, it would be equally so for any other form such an explanation might take.

What effectively decides, in particular cases, whether some B resolved some D is just the reactions of reasonable judges to that B and that D on that occasion for B's doing so. (In effect, this is just a special form of the account of what doubts are possible anyway.) There is no penetrating beneath these reactions to an *effective* and general account of how a reasonable judge would work in these respects. So, for example, Serge says of Odile, 'She might have changed trains in Aulnoye,' and Yvon replies, 'Impossible. I saw her on the terrasse just moments ago.' Neglect the fact that Yvon's reply *might* itself be doubted. Is what Yvon said, if accepted, incompatible with Serge's doubt? Or might it be so even though Odile never got to Paris? (Might it be, for example, that one can, as Yvon then may have done, see people where they are not—a serious extension of an idea facetiously suggested by television? Might further technology make us talk in such ways?) There is nothing other than, or more fundamental than, the reactions of reasonable judges for deciding this. That answer is required, of course, by the general picture of semantics at work in this book. But, I suggest, it is also required by the phenomena of proof and doubt as we have now seen them to be.

This view of the matter may jar. For there is another picture which may at least seem to afford us a glimpse of a more fundamental account of what it is for G to be incompatible with D. On this picture, G is incompatible with D just in case there is no possible situation (or state of affairs or world) in which G holds and things are D's way. (In a parallel part of the picture, an inferential rule, R, is truth-preserving iff wherever F is derivable by it from G, there is no possible situation in which G and not F.) The problem, of course, is: how is it determined what the possible situations are? What determines that there is no possible situation in which G and things are D's way? What determines that we have not just described such a situation in saying just that? Possible situations are not open to investigation or observation the way coins in my pocket might be. There is a possible situation in which such-and-such is so just in case we (or reasonable and informed judges) take it that there is; just in case they recognize that as possible; just in case such is part of our (or their) reactions. If we thus determine what the possible situations are, then the present view of proof suggests that we may very well perform as S-use sensitive devices in doing so. Which would make for S-use sensitivity in what is compatible with what, as it makes for such sensitivity in what situations could be (and correlative sensitivity in which rules are truth preserving and in what is required for them to be so, that is, over which range of cases they must be).

6. RIGOR AND LIBERAL ARTS

The core thesis so far is that proof is an S-use sensitive notion; that the requirements for B proving F, for fixed F (and B) vary across occasions; and that the variation cannot be reduced to merely a matter of the acceptability of B's premises. This section sketches a defence of that thesis. The defence will parallel closely the defence in chapter 4 of the account of knowledge presented there. To some extent, it will involve anticipating the moves of an opponent. It is always possible that some opponent will be more ingenious than I am in finding moves to make. For that reason at least, this may not be the last word on the subject.

The ultimate defence of the core thesis is the data, as illustrated in sections 3 and 4. But data admit of various readings. In certain respects, it is clear what an opponent's reading of the data must be, hence what task he must perform. Suppose the data to be organized on the lines of section 3, as an indefinitely large (that is, always expandable) collection of contrasting pairs: ordered pairs of occasion, each pair involving a given B and F,[9] where on one member of the pair B proves F (or so it appears), and on the other member B does not prove F (or appears not to). Then the opponent must be prepared to sort out these contrasting pairs as follows: for each pair, he must be prepared to hold either that on both of its occasion, B really does prove F (at least in some sense of 'prove'—perhaps some favoured 'strict' sense); or on both of its occasion B really does not prove F (again, perhaps in some favoured sense of proof). The opponent is allowed some exceptional unclassifiable 'borderline' pairs. Ultimately, he owes us an account of proof which shows how or why these pairs do classify as he does it. In any event, in just these respects, he must take the true facts to be other than they appear to be.

At first, this requirement *might* seem easy to satisfy. An opponent could just sort through the data, classifying each pair *ad hoc*. There are two reasons why this will not do. First, you cannot classify an ever-expandable collection *ad hoc*. The opponent must show suitably well

---

[9] Suppose B contains a demonstration such as, 'There's Odile'. One might hold that this very demonstration could not occur on any *two* possible occasions (though there is no need to hold this). But then one indistinguishable from it could. Which is good enough for present purposes.

how to deal with novel cases. Second, it must be so, and recognizably
so, that the notion on which cases classify in the opponent's way is,
indeed, a notion of *proof*. (Recall the discussion of 'shmizx' in the last
chapter.) I will take this to require that, on the opponent's notion of it,
there be such a thing as proof; that there are cases in which some B
proves some F. As Moore would have said, a notion for which that was
not so would not be recognizable by us as a notion of proof.

Further, I will take it that some of the values of F for which this is so
must be 'empirical' facts—such as that there are chairs in Odile's
office, or that Montreal is north of Toronto. This may seem arbitrary.
But there are at least two special reasons for it here. First, our aim in
looking at proof is to investigate questions of the form 'What other
facts must hold if it is a case of F being so?', or 'What other facts require
F to be so?', or 'Under what circumstances is it a case of F being so?', or
'Under what circumstances would such and such facts make it a case
of F being so?'—primarily for 'empirical' values of F. A notion of proof
that had no application within that domain would also have no *present*
interest. Second, suppose someone did hold that empirical facts were,
in the nature of the case, never susceptible to proof. Then the pressure
towards ontic scepticism would simply collapse. No other specifiable
facts are, strictly speaking, incompatible with 'bachelor' meaning
something other than *bachelor*—for example, 'bachelor-stage'. But
then, on this conception of proof, why should there be other facts
which did that? Moreover, I think that any notion of 'proof' which
excluded in principle proof of empirical fact would not be recognizable
as a notion of proof. But that point is less important for the present.

Before moving to the main business, there is a wrinkle on the above
which I want to discuss in some detail. As with knowledge, it is open
to the opponent, in performing the task just described, to proliferate
senses of 'prove'. One plan for doing this is, I think, important in
fuelling the idea that when it comes to proof in the strictest sense,
there is an S-use insensitive notion available. The plan's relation to the
Moorean conception of proof will be obvious. Suppose Pol says, '$P_1, \ldots$
P_n; so F', for given values of those dummy letters. Depending on the
values, it *might* be correct to respond to him like this: 'The points that
you stated *would* prove F; F does follow from that (so that, in one
sense, what you stated *does* prove F.) But what you said doesn't *prove*
F, since perhaps $P_1, \ldots P_n$ isn't so (so that, in another sense, what you
said does not prove F).' The response illustrates two possible sense of
'prove' or 'proof'. Call the first, 'proof$_1$', and the second, 'proof$_2$'. What
Pol said (his premises) proves$_1$ F; but what he said does not prove$_2$ F.

Splitting of senses here is optional. We may distinguish different
things which were said, respectively, to prove and not to prove F: Pol

said *to be so* what, if so, proves F; but what he said—the thoughts he expressed—does not prove F, since those thoughts do not then have the right status. We might rest content with that. But we will also allow that this splitting of senses, while not obligatory, is available.

Proof$_2$ is obviously an S-use sensitive notion. Pol's premises might have the right status on some occasions but not others. But what of proof$_1$? Here is a thought: if we sufficiently restrict the inferential rules—and hence, we hope, the inferential moves—which could possibly make for proof$_1$, and dub the result 'strict proof$_1$', then the result might be an S-use insensitive notion—one on which B proves F either always or never. We need only find (enough) rules which are *always* proof$_1$-preserving. And it may seem that we might do that. For is that not just what formal theories of proof—or, for example, formal logical calculi—successfully study?

This idea does not quite speak directly to the present issue, or at least offers no novel opportunities to the opponent. Here, briefly, is why. Suppose that Odile wants to prove that Hugo will buy the next round. She reasons as follows: Consider a system with the axiom 'Hugo has twenty dollars in his pocket' and the rule: 'From "Hugo has twenty dollars in his pocket" derive "Hugo will buy the next round"'. In that system, it is a theorem that Hugo will buy the next round. Obviously Odile has not proved anything. Her system lacks the right status. Here is a way of saying what status is required. The indicated 'proof within her system' would prove that Hugo will buy the next round on, but only on, occasions such that it then satisfies the proof condition for that thought which that occasion imposes. The system represents the standards for correct proof (in relevant matters) on just those occasions on which those standards are, in fact, what the system represents them as being. The fact that there is such a system contributes nothing to settling when this would be so. If we ever had reason to think that proof conditions were S-use sensitive, we now have exactly that much reason to think that it will be an S-use sensitive matter when a proof-within-her-system counts as proof, and when that system has the indicated status.

Now consider a formal system such as a propositional calculus. In an obvious sense this is worse off than Odile's system. For it does not permit the construction of 'proofs' at all. What it does permit is the derivation of certain strings of (relevantly[10]) uninterpreted symbols from others. For example, from the symbol 'P' and the symbol 'Q', we

---

[10] *Some* symbols, such as &, may be 'interpreted' by the formal theory in the sense that they are, say, associated with some particular truth-function. But that does not tell us what, if any, components of thoughts they may be taken to represent—e.g. where, if ever, they may be taken as representing occurrences of 'and' in lines of some 'proof'.

can derive, perhaps, the string, 'P & Q'. But what thought does 'P & Q' express? Obviously none. A formal calculus has applications only when combined with some 'translation scheme'—a specification of what, for example, which bits of English—we may substitute for its letters and other symbols.

In one sense, the rules of a formal calculus are beyond criticism. They are simply rules for changing certain strings of symbols into others. Let us henceforth hold the rules as such immune from criticism in every sense. Still, if the question is which 'proofs' the calculus selects as proofs, then the same problems arise as with Odile's system. Take a particular proof schema generated by the calculus, and a particular way of filling it in, substituting for its letters to obtain a 'proof', B, of some particular thought, F. Then at least two problems arise. First, for any occasion for offering this result as proof of F, the question may be posed whether what is thus offered—the recommended sequence of thoughts, or what is indistinguishable from them—really is an instance of that schema. Does B (or what is on offer as B) then really have the semantics it must have in order to instance that schema? The sorts of problems involved here were discussed in section 4 in connection with proofs that Pol is unmarried. No matter how unexceptionable the calculus, nothing about it in itself could guarantee that the answers to this sort of question are not, in the general case, S-use sensitive.

Second, suppose that, on O, B does instance some schema which the calculus predicts is correct, and which in fact in those circumstances could only possibly lead from truth to truth. And suppose B's premises are then unexceptionable. Given even the Kantian conception of proof, or anything it could be presently relevant to recognize as proof, this is not enough to guarantee that B proves its conclusion. Suppose Pia offers a 'proof' and includes as a premiss Fermat's last theorem. Suppose that Fermat's last theorem happens to be true. That last fact is not enough by anyone's lights to make Pia's 'proof' proof. Pia's 'proof' could be proof only on an occasion which affords the right perspective on the fact Fermat's last theorem states. Similarly, if B instances what is in fact a truth-preserving form of inference—just the fact which its relation to the calculus is meant to ensure—that makes B *proof* of F only on occasions which afford the right perspective on that fact. If, on any occasion, there is no or too little reason to take this to be so, then the bare fact of B's bearing relation R to calculus C, where C happens to be a good one, cannot by itself convert B into proof.

The issues here may be put in another perspective by borrowing the framework of chapter 3. Wittgenstein compares logical calculi to language games. Both are abstract 'objects of comparison' specified by their rules, and fixed by our construction of them:

in philosophy we often *compare* the use of words with games and calculi which have fixed rules, but cannot say that someone who is using language *must* be playing such a game. (81)

Part of the point is that if we view a calculus as bound to some particular 'translation' or substitution scheme linking it with language, then we may think of a calculus as a language game or part of one. Then all the general points about language games, as made in chapter 3, apply. People using the relevant words may count as playing that game on some occasions but not on others. What shows whether they do so count is the activities in which they use these words, and the most reasonable moves to make with those words as part of those activities. So a given realization of a proof schema, which would be proof by the rules of that calculus game, counts as proof in just those circumstances in which it is most reasonable so to treat it—where the move it would make from premisses to conclusion leaves that conclusion not open to further reasonable doubt. In such circumstances, and only there, will that calculus game count as among those being played. Now the question is whether the way in which circumstances make such things so is such as to make it an S-use sensitive matter whether that game is being played. That question is not settled or even advanced by the bare presence of that game among the variety there are to be played.

Now for the main business. The opponent must find a sufficiently large range of contrasting pairs such that, contrary to (first) appearance, really both members of the pair are cases of B proving F, and, in fact, such that the B involved proves its conclusion S-use insensitively. (Or at least such that any S-use sensitivity exhibited by B is attributable to the varying acceptability of one or another premiss in it.) But Wittgenstein has shown, *via* the technique of semantic doubt, how it is possible to have doubts as to the correctness of any proof—where these are doubts given which the proof would not be correct. If B consists of a sequence of thoughts, $P_1, \ldots P_n$ (perhaps structured into sub-proofs), and has a conclusion, F, then it is possible to construct doubts as to whether the semantics of one or another line in the sequence really does license the inference drawn from it. The opponent, then, must (at least) isolate a sufficient number of these Wittgensteinian semantic doubts and show them to be S-use insensitively irrelevant to the assessment of whether B has proved F, at least in the favoured sense of 'prove'. How might the opponent do that?

A hopeful thought for the opponent appeals to the fact that Wittgensteinian extreme doubts are, in the general case, *semantic* doubts. Which means that, in many cases, they involve supposing things to be in ways in which certain items would have a semantics other than that which they in fact do have—otherwise put, ways other than those the actual semantics of those items permits. Whereas, the thought would go, what matters for issues of proof is what is so given the semantic facts as they are. If the question is whether B proves F on O, then that is settled by seeing whether the actual semantics of B's constituents leaves any possible way for O to be an occasion of F's not being so—or perhaps even more generally, whether that semantics leaves any way for F not to be so *tout court*. Suppositions on which the *semantic* facts would be other than they are—the thought goes—are simply not relevant to answering those questions. If this consideration rules out enough Wittgensteinian semantic doubts, then the opponent may hope to be able to carry out his task of identifying enough contrasting pairs for each of which the B involved never really falls short of proof. (If this is to work, of course, then which facts are *semantic* facts must be sufficiently often an S-use insensitive matter, as must be just which ways for things to be given semantic facts rule out.)

In unusual circumstances, we may come to suspect—even reasonably—that we are going crazy and losing our semantic competence. We may then doubt whether the concept of a bachelor is really such that fitting it absolutely *requires* being unmarried. Investigation may even be able to settle this for us. Or, in the right circumstances, we might wonder intelligibly—and perhaps even reasonably—whether some day something might turn up—some unusual situation which would make reasonable and semantically competent judges change their minds as to whether *all* bachelors really *must* be unmarried. But, the thought goes, the semantics of the concept really does require that. As long as it does, there is no possible way for a situation to be one in which some bachelor is unmarried. On the hopeful thought, it is that fact that matters in determining which doubts count for assessing a 'proof' that Pol is unmarried. (At least for the favoured sense of proof.)

There are two troubles with this hopeful thought. First, the thought indicates how, *on an occasion*, a doubt, D, may be ruled out of consideration—if the semantics B's constituents then count as having then leaves no possible way for that occasion to be as D would have it being; if it is (or then counts as) incompatible with those semantic facts that D's way for things to be should be a possible way for that occasion to be. (As where D has Pol being a not-unmarried bachelor, and the concept requires bachelors to be unmarried.) But for the opponent to be able to classify contrasting pairs (for given B), as he must, enough semantic doubts like D must be thus ruled out invariantly across all occasions. That would be possible only if enough elements in the semantics of B's constituents is semantics those items would count as having on any possible occasion. On the present picture of semantics, the semantics of any item is an S-use sensitive matter. If that is right, then the doubts ruled out by the consideration the hopeful thought adduces will vary from occasion to occasion for offering B as proof. On that picture, there is little reason to hope that enough semantic facts will be so S-use insensitively to make a success of the project the opponent must carry out here. (This, of course, appeals to other parts of the Wittgensteinian picture to support the picture of proof. But enough actual attempts to sort out cases— candidate proofs and occasions for giving them—on the lines the hopeful thought suggests would be likely to generate more support for those other parts of the picture.)

The second related trouble with the hopeful thought may be put this way. Take a sample semantic doubt, D, which the hopeful thought would rule S-use insensitively irrelevant to proof. For example, D might be (in material mode) that perhaps some bachelors are not unmarried. Now, if there is, or could be, an occasion O such that D is a possible way for O to be (or on which D counts as a possible way for things then to be), then D cannot be ruled irrelevant to assessing proof *S-use insensitively*. To see whether there is such an O, we might ask when things would be D's way. *One* answer to that question is this: things would be that way if facts or circumstances obtained to which reasonable judges would react by taking the concept bachelor to permit its application to some items who were not unmarried.

We may now note two ways in which it is at least conceivable that there should be such facts or circumstances—though this does not mean that we need now be able to see exactly what they would be like. (If we could see that, our view of reasonable judges might be expected already to be different.) First, we already know that reasonable judges are devices who are prepared to change their reactions in the face of sufficiently strange or unexpected circumstances—a point on which Wittgenstein continually insists, and one certainly corroborated by the course of twentieth century science. So we can at least conceive of a situation turning up which was so unexpected that reasonable judges reacted to it by recognizing the possibility of D. Again, this need not involve conceiving of the details of that situation. Second, we can also conceive of discovering that we are crazy; that we—you and I, say— have had a really grade-A semantic hallucination (or delusion): we thought that Pol was a bachelor, and were then overcome (inexplic- ably, in retrospect) with an irresistible intuition that bachelors must be unmarried—whereas no reasonable judge would *ever* think that, and when the drug wears off (say) we will be amazed that we ever could have thought such a thing. (Again, we need not *now* be able to see in any detail what we then *would* think about bachelors.)

One question remains. If such things are conceivable, are there any occasions on which those are possible ways for things to be? An affirmative answer is, I think, built into the notion of conceivability. To construct such occasions, one would need to make the perspective they offered on the world one which failed to reveal whether these conceived-of situations obtained, or might obtain. (Such need not involve subtracting from our knowledge; it may involve adding to it.) Suppose, for example, that we have just had a very long run of cases in which we have seen our most cherished intuitions perish (truth has proved stranger than science fiction). Or that all the signs are that—as far as our cognitive faculties go—we really should not have had that second piece of wild mushroom quiche. In such circumstances, providing or defending a proof by citing the semantic facts—in so far as they then even would be facts—would be as useful as it now is to provide or defend proof by citing Fermat's last theorem (if that happens to be true). It is not useful because there are certain possible ways for our situation then to be. It could, for example, be one of those situations which contains another one of those intense surprises known for making cherished bits of semantic faith bite the dust. A 'notion of proof' which overlooked such possible ways for *some* situations to be, like one which permitted free appeal to Fermat's last theorem, would not be recognizable as such.

It is sometimes appealing to think of a (definite) thought's identity as fixing, and perhaps fixed, by what else it entails and/or is entailed by. Or equally, by a particular sorting out of ways for the world to be into ways which (*ipso facto*) would be ones of that thought being so, and ways which would not. Or something much along these lines. There is nothing wrong with any of these images as such. But if we think of a thought's identity as fixed in any of these ways, and by a particular realization of that way, invariantly across all occasions for considering it (thinking, doubting, investigating or proving it, among other things), then that is a way of thinking about thoughts which is challenged by the present view of proof. It is intrinsic to that view that one and the same thought may have different entailments, and hence different ranges and sorts of situation which would be ones of its being so or not, on different occasions for using it. That idea is fundamental to the ontological picture now aimed at. *Inter alia*, it is the key to our right to Wittgenstein's path in recognizing family resemblance, rather than the alternate path of ontic scepticism.

7. HINGES

Proof, on Wittgenstein's view, is an exceptional activity. In fact, only in appropriate circumstances does any given F admit of it. This last point can now be seen as simply a by-product of the more central thesis that proving F is an S-use sensitive matter, and that the conditions for doing so vary substantively across occasions for it. Appropriate circumstances for proving F are ones which select adequately from the range of sometimes correct conditions for proving F, so that in them there is a determinate enough condition which some candidate proof might determinately either meet or fail to. Inappropriate circumstances are ones which do not do such selecting. No 'proof' of F could possibly satisfy all the conditions in the range. Where the conditions it must satisfy are not sufficiently limited by the circumstances, then no 'proof' could then conceivably succeed as a proof. The preceding discussion has linked this fact to the issue of doubt. There are always conceivable doubts as to F. There could not be a proof which removed all of these. Yet any of these is referred to by the proof condition for F on some occasion. That is why no proof could satisfy all proof conditions for F, and sufficient delimitation by circumstance is called for. This is, in fact, a somewhat oversimplified picture of what appropriate circumstances do. But it makes clear the sort of question at issue.

To the above general view Wittgenstein adds a specific idea as to what appropriate circumstances would be like. An occasion on which F admits of proof is one on which there are other things which do not. Since admitting of proof is S-use sensitive, that much is hardly surprising. But further, on any given such occasion, O, there are things which must not admit of proof if F is then to admit of proof at all, and moreover if F is to admit of proof in the ways, or by the sorts of proofs it does. On other occasions, some of these items might admit of proof while F still admitted of it—though not in the ways or by the proofs it does on O. But any of these items could admit of proof on O only under conditions which would then destroy any proof of F. Specifically, these are items which cannot be doubted—so about which there is and can be no possible doubt—on O, if F is to admit of proof. The supposition that there was some doubt about any of them would then destroy any proof of F, since it would remove any (correct) way of sufficiently restricting the doubts as to F which would then count as possible. Since any determinate proof condition for these items would require resolving *some* non-empty set of doubts, and those must then be the possible doubts, there can be no determinate proof condition for these items. Hence they do not admit of proof.

Items which support proofs of F, on O, in this way Wittgenstein calls 'hinges'. The notion is introduced as follows:

Here *once more* there is needed a step like the one taken in relativity theory. (OC 305)

. . . we are interested in the fact that about certain empirical propositions no doubt can exist if making judgements is to be possible at all. (OC 308)

The term 'hinge' is then introduced in the following passages:

That is to say, the *questions* that we raise and our *doubts* depend on the fact that some propositions are exempt from doubt, are as it were like hinges on which those turn. (OC 341)

That is to say, it belongs to the logic of our scientific investigations that certain things are *in deed* not doubted. (OC 342)

But it isn't that the situation is like this: We just *can't* investigate everything, and for that reason we are forced to rest content with assumption. If I want the door to turn, the hinges must stay put. (OC 343)

The idea is stated again, slightly amplified, in these passages:

I want to say: propositions of the form of empirical propositions, and not only propositions of logic, form the foundation of all operating with thoughts (with language) . . . (OC 401)

In this remark the expression 'propositions of the form of empirical propositions' is itself thoroughly bad; the statements in question are statements about material objects. And they do not serve as foundations in the same way as hypotheses which, if they turn out to be false, are replaced by others. (OC 402)

What hinges support is meant to be something much wider than proof: all doubting (and the content of any particular doubt), all judgement, and in fact all operation with thought or language. But I think we can see the kind of support hinges provide by focusing on the case of proof. Extensions to other cases would be obvious. So far, it might seem that what hinges support in this case is, not admitting of proof, but merely requiring it or not, and, in the latter case, provability—that is, the actual availability of proofs which do satisfy the proof condition of the occasion. That is not really a separate option. For if lack of hinges left it indeterminate what required proof and what did not, by the same token it would leave it indeterminate what the proof conditions for the relevant items were, which would leave them not admitting of proof. In any event, it is clear that Wittgenstein did not have any such more limited intention—as he makes clear in passages such as these:

Only in certain cases is it possible to make an investigation 'is that really a hand?' (or 'my hand'). For 'I doubt whether that is really my (or a) hand' makes no sense without some more precise determination. One cannot tell from these words alone whether any doubt at all is meant—nor what kind of doubt. (OC 372)

What would it be like to doubt now whether I have two hands? Why can't I imagine it at all? What would I believe if I didn't believe that? So far I have no system at all within which this doubt might exist. (OC 247)

If I say 'an hour ago this table didn't exist' I probably mean that it was only made later on.

If I say 'this mountain didn't exist then', I presumably mean that it was only formed later on—perhaps by a volcano.

If I say 'this mountain didn't exist half an hour ago', that is such a strange statement that it is not clear what I mean. Whether for example I mean something untrue but scientific. Perhaps you think that the statement that the mountain didn't exist then is quite clear, however one conceives the context. But suppose someone said, 'This mountain didn't exist a minute ago, but an exactly similar one did instead.' Only the accustomed context allows what is meant to come through clearly. (OC 237)

If someone doubted whether the earth had existed a hundred years ago, I should not understand, for *this* reason: I would not know what such a person would still allow to be counted as evidence and what not. (OC 231)

All testing, all confirmation and disconfirmation of a hypothesis takes place already within a system. And this system is not a more or less arbitrary and doubtful point of departure for all our arguments: no, it belongs to the essence of what we call an argument. The system is not so much the point of departure, as the element in which arguments have their life. (OC 105)

Hinges do not support proofs of F by occurring as parts of them, or by constituting something from which F could be derived. Typically, they do not occur as parts of such proofs. (Typically they could not do so without losing their hinge status.[11]) Rather, for every part of a proof, hinges support its having the effects it then does. For any inferential step in the proof, hinges are needed for it to be a fact that all possible doubts as to the conclusion of that step have been removed—and, for any particular doubt, that it has been removed. (So hinges support the facts that that particular step was then proof- and truth-preserving; without them no such thing could be a fact.) For any premiss in a proof, hinges similarly support the fact of its admissibility; of its not then requiring proof. Note that it has already been said here that such facts—what the possible doubts are; when any given one has been resolved; and when there are none—are questions of the reactions, on that occasion, of reasonable judges. So the point may also be put this way. Hinges are items which a reasonable judge, on that occasion, would not doubt, question or investigate. That part of the reaction of a reasonable judge is essential to the part which consists of taking some

---

[11] In the same way that one typically cannot say, 'I am wearing shoes', where that is plainly so, or, 'I know that's a chair', gesturing to someone to sit down, without thereby *raising* doubts about it.

doubts and not others to be possible, taking B to resolve doubt A and so on. Without the hinge reactions, a reasonable judge would be deprived of these others; he could not make sense of any particular way of reacting in these other matters.

Consider how hinges might support resolving doubt. Odile says that Napoleon won at Austerlitz in 1805. Hugo might doubt this. He might, for example, suspect that that battle took place in 1806. The issue might be resolved, to his and Odile's satisfaction, by a judicious consulting of history texts. Imagine an occasion on which this is a correct way of judging. Now suppose one were to doubt that the earth is over 100 years old. (The doubt is: perhaps it isn't.) If that is a possible way for things to be, then the evidence of history texts can no longer count as settling Hugo's doubt. Nor, if one were then to entertain such doubts, would it be clear (or determined) what would settle whether the historical record was correct.

Wittgenstein also notes that hinges are needed to make it determinate what is being doubted in any given doubt—say, Hugo's doubt that perhaps the battle was in 1806. The general idea here should now be clear. There are many distinct doubts one might have in doubting that. What might resolve one such would not even address others. Nor would anything resolve all. Hence if the doubt is to be resolvable, even in principle, then circumstances must select adequately from among the variety of doubts it might be. If the doubt is in principle unresolvable, so that nothing could show things to be that way or not, then it does not partition states of affairs into ones of its being so and ones of its not being. But then it is not a thought with definite content.

In Hugo's case. for example, what are the conceivable ways for the battle to have been in 1806 rather than 1805? One is for it to have been fought then and so recorded—Odile misremembers or something. That is what was at issue in the above example. Another would be for it to have been fought then and the historical record falsified. But there are others. Through a fluke in the calendar, it was really 1806, though, since no one had noticed this, everyone was still writing 1805. The earth just then passed through a warp in space-time, and suddenly entered 1806, though it still seemed like 1805. Through an anomaly, the earth entered 1806 for just that one day and then went back to 1805. Or just an area around Austerlitz did that. Or the earth was really created in 1806, complete with false traces and records back-dating some of its history—that which actually occurred during the first half hour. And so on. Clearly most of these conceivabilities represent quite distinct thoughts (where they represent any at all). The point is then that without proper hinges, such as the thought that the earth is older than that, Hugo's doubt would not determinately be one of these rather than any one of the others—with which it would cease to be any definite thought, so doubt at all.

The same general points apply to the need for hinges in supporting judgement. As things stand, Odile counts as having expressed a definite thought in saying that Napoleon won at Austerlitz in 1805. But suppose we were to doubt whether the earth was over 100 years old. In circumstances in which this was to be doubted, we *might* well be able to detect a variety of distinct thoughts to be expressed in saying that. For example, perhaps a thought which was not falsified by that doubt being so, but merely depended on how the falsified historical record was, even if it was created *ex nihilo*, and another thought which would be thus falsified. Nothing in Odile's circumstances would make her thought clearly one of these rather than another. Hence, given the doubting of what are in fact then hinges, she would then have expressed no definite thought.

It is now apparent that hinges themselves, when hinges, lack precisely those sorts of support that they lend to Odile's thought. Consider the thought that the earth is over 100 years old. Suppose that were then to be doubted. Suppose that one tried to prove it by (roughly) repeating the proof Odile gave Hugo—that is, by consulting history texts and showing that they cite events over 100 years old. Clearly that could be at best no more than a parody of a proof. Things would be no better if one cited the geologic evidence, or textbook accounts of it. And so on. So far, on this occasion, there is no determination of what would resolve any such doubt, nor hence of what sort of proof condition might attach to the thought that the earth is more than 100 years old. For similar reasons, if that thought were then to be doubted, there would be not enough else then not in doubt—enough else that a reasonable judge would then not doubt even though he doubted that—to provide a fix on just which thought a thought that the earth was (or was not) more than 100 years old would then be. Or there would not be enough else of the right sort to serve as hinges. In appropriate circumstances, a reasonable judge might doubt such a thought about the earth without doubting other things, where there were enough of the right sort of other things such a judge then would not doubt to serve as hinges for that doubt, and for the thought it would then involve. Odile's and Hugo's circumstances are not among these.

Crispin Wright has suggested[12] that hinges are not genuinely fact-stating, so not true (nor false). In support of this, he cites the 'normative' nature of hinges, and the fact that we are not prepared to count anything as showing them wrong (unsurprisingly, since they do

---

[12] In Wright [1985].

not admit of proof). These features correspond closely to what has just been described above in saying how hinges support proof and other things. I am not sure exactly how Wright would argue from these features of hinges to their not being fact stating. But there is a natural idea that tends in his direction. It has, I think, two parts. The first is that, as described in the last section, it is natural to think of a definite thought, or one with definite content, as defined or individuated by what it entails and what entails it, or by the way it partitions states of affairs into ones of its obtaining and others. The second is that it is natural to think that if a thought is true, then it must be so in virtue of something else; namely, in virtue of satisfying—perhaps in tandem with the world—some particular condition for truth which is *its* truth condition. Which condition that is should be determined, if at all, by what, on the first part of this idea, fixes that thought's content, the condition being that the actual state of affairs be one which classifies, on the thought-fixing (and identifying) scheme, on the right side of the partition, or that that state of affairs contain facts which on the given thought-fixing relations, entail the thought.

Now consider some ripe candidates for (S-use sensitive) hinge status, such as: rigid rods do not change length (merely) with position; the earth is more than 100 years old; or (with Moore) there is an external world. The most striking feature of these sometime-hinges, as explored above, is that they afford no definite conception of what it would be for them to be so or not to be; it is not determined just which situations would be ones of their obtaining and which ones not. So they impose no partitioning of the sort just envisioned. So, it seems, there can be no definite requirement for their truth, hence none such that they might be true in virtue of satisfying it. So, if one accepts the above idea, they cannot be true. Of course, that does not mean that they are false. They must then be some sort of rules or regulative principles which guide our thinking about what might be true or false.

Wittgenstein, however, does not think of thoughts in that way. Nor should they be so conceived on the present view of semantics. For it is central to that view that a thought may change in the semantics it counts as having from one occasion of considering it to another. In the present context, the same thought may serve as a hinge on one occasion and admit of proof on another. On the latter it clearly must be true. There is no reason for it to lose that property in moving from the latter to the former. Suppose that that the earth is over 100 years old now serves as a hinge (for something). If it is either true or false, then it must be true. But if it is true, then that cannot be in virtue of satisfying some requirement which is its truth condition. What, then, makes it true? The answer, I suggest, is that nothing else *makes* it true; that it is true is just one of the fixed points of its semantics.

Suppose we think of a thought as individuated on any occasion by the semantics it then counts as having (reasonable enough, since thoughts entered the discussion in the first place under the pressures of distinguishing one semantics from another). Then since, on the previous idea about definite content, hinges lack it, we might ask just what thought the present 'thought' that the earth is over 100 years old is. What semantics does it now count as having? An answer would cite what is now fixed about that semantics: first of all, *that*—that it is the thought that the earth is over 100 years old; and second, I suggest, that it is *true*. There are few other semantic properties that it now counts as having. Its semantics is indeterminate in many other respects. Then again, what we have seen by now is that *any* thought has indeterminate semantics when it comes to choosing between many conceivable alternatives. In that respect, hinges are, at worst, a bit more extreme.

The semantics just mentioned, if this hinge does count as having it, allows the hinge to be, in an important sense, a determinate thought. Much about its semantics still remains to be fixed—by the circumstances of some other occasion. But the semantics it does now count as having is to be understood as a guide to how any such further fixing is to go: in the way that that semantics (most reasonably) requires. What this shows is that there is a variety of ways in which some semantic properties may depend on others. In the 'normal' case, perhaps, truth-involving properties may be most reasonably regarded as following from other ones—for example, properties of saying this or that. But in the case of hinges, it is just the other way round.

8. AGREEMENT WITH REALITY

Not everything so need be provable; but everything provable is so. So, though proof is an exceptional enterprise, it may show something of what is required for things to be so. The main morals of the present account are intimately linked with the notions of a hinge, and of not admitting of proof. Wittgenstein indicates them in passages like the following:

Well, if everything speaks for an hypothesis and nothing against it—is it then certainly true? One may designate it as such.—But does it certainly agree with reality, with the facts?—With this question you are already going around in a circle. (OC 191)

Really 'the proposition is either true or false' only means that it must be possible to decide for or against it. But this does not say what the ground for such a decision is like. (OC 200)

[Everything that we regard as evidence indicates that the earth already existed long before my birth. The contrary hypothesis has *nothing* to confirm it at all.

If everything speaks *for* an hypothesis and nothing against it, is it objectively *certain*? One can *call* it that. But does it *necessarily* agree with the world of facts? At the very best it shows us what 'agreement' means. We find it difficult to imagine it to be false, but also difficult to make use of it.]

What does this agreement consist in, if not in the fact that what is evidence in these language games speaks for our proposition? (*Tractatus Logico-Philosophicus*) (OC 203—the bracketed part was crossed out in the MS)

Giving grounds, however, justifying the evidence, comes to an end;—but the end is not certain propositions' striking us as true, i.e., it is not a kind of seeing on our part; it is our acting which lies at the bottom of the language game. (OC 204)

What prevents me from supposing that this table either vanishes or alters its shape and colour when no one is observing it, and then when someone is looking at it again changes back to its old condition?—'But who is going to suppose such a thing!'—one would feel like saying. (OC 214)

Here we see that the idea of 'agreement with reality' does not have any clear application. (OC 215)

Consider, first, a hinge on an occasion—say, that the earth is over 100 years old. It is natural to feel that everything speaks for this and nothing against it. As Wittgenstein urges, it is correct to think this too. (That is what a reasonable judge would think.) But *how* does everything speak for it? As discussed in the last section, there is no particular *way* in which anything else could count as supporting it. So other things could not prove it, nor even make it 'highly probable'. For it is undetermined what is required for supporting it in any given way; as it is undetermined whether being supported in that way is being *supported*. Where it is a hinge, the occasion as yet supplies no fix on what possibilities any 'support' must rule out.

Is it then so (and does it count as so on that occasion) that the earth is over 100 years old? Of course. That is one feature of the thought which is fixed and which, it is to be taken, any other features must be moulded to fit. Thus would a reasonable judge regard it. Which in one sense *does* fix what it would be, and be like for a situation to be one of that thought being so. It would be like *this*, for example (since it is fixed that this is such a situation). This illustrates *one* thing that agreeing with reality may be like.

A parallel: suppose we are classifying some large set of items into the chairs and the non-chairs. On an occasion, some items may classify as chairs for such and such reasons. But some items will so classify simply because there is no reasonable doubt that that is what they are. Not that no reasons could *ever* be given, on some occasion or other, for classifying those items in that way. But on any occasion, it is important that there be items which are thus indubitably chairs (or not) and that that is the best and most fundamental reason for then so classifying them. Without such facts, it could not be a fact that one candidate dichotomization rather than any of a variety of rivals was correct. There being facts as to how items classify (as chairs or not) depends on there being cases for which it is a fact that there is no doubt that such-and-such is a chair. That a reasonable judge would not doubt that certain things were chairs is part of what fixes the content of that concept. (An ostensive aspect, if you like.)

The parallel problem is dichotomizing situations into ones where the above hinge holds and ones where it does not. Like the chair in which Hugo is now seated, there is no doubt as to how the present situation classifies. It is indubitably one of that hinge being so. So is anything it is possible for this situation to be. As for the rest, that must take care of itself somehow or other, where and when problems about it arise. But there being facts as to the correct ways of dealing with such further problems depends on there being situations, like the present one, for which there is no doubt as to how they classify. The point remains that this situation *does* classify, on the correct scheme for doing so, as one of that hinge being so. So the hinge does agree with reality. And it has just been said what its doing so consists in.

Consider now a thought which is not a hinge—say, that there are now (at least) two chairs in Odile's office. There may be a variety of occasions for proving that. Each of these may differ from the others in what it is possible for it to be, hence in the possible doubts, on it, as to that thought; and perhaps in the hinges which then support such proof. Where two occasions differ in these ways, each will provide a different then-correct dichotomization of situations into those which would be ones of that thought's being so, and those which would not be that; or at least there will be different ranges of cases in each category. What sometimes counts as a possible way for the thought to be so (or not) may at other times not. Correspondingly, different things on different occasions would *prove* that the thought was so; would leave no possible way, that is, for that to classify as an occasion of the thought's not being so. Even though we may suppose the thought to be so, hence to agree with reality, S-use insensitively, such are ways in which there may be variation across occasions in what its agreement with reality would consist in.

To generalize, the way in which any thought partitions situations into ones of its being so and ones of its not, and certainly the content of these categories, is never fixed solely by what thought that thought is, but depends on what hinges support it and what possibilities its being so contrasts with. These are factors liable to vary from one occasion to another of considering, investigating, proving or judging that thought. Thus the notion of agreeing with reality is an S-use sensitive one, at least in what it requires for it to apply correctly.

Let us now consider once again the no-common-thread thesis. Consider a concept C—call it the concept of being P—two items, V and V*, which are candidates for being P, and the thoughts, respectively, that V is P and that V* is P. For simplicity, restrict attention to the strong version of the thesis. What we want to see is how this could be true—that is, how, if looking points in that direction, we may be entitled to follow Wittgenstein's recommended path of accepting the thesis, rather than the alternative path of ontic scepticism. It would be sufficient for this purpose if we could show how it could be, for any other feature, Q, of V, that both of the above thoughts were true, even though V* lacked Q.

The present account of proof allows us to show this. The key point is that the fact that V and V* are different items existing under different conditions—as might be, for example, with two chairs in different cultures or settings—may itself make for significant differences between occasions for proving the thought that V is P and those for proving the thought that V* is P. Suppose there is some occasion for proving the first thought on which it is a possible doubt that V might not be Q, and any 'proof' which did not resolve that doubt would not prove the thought that V is P. This is to say that significant among the ways for things then to be are ways on which V would not be Q, and further—perhaps thereby—not P. Now shift to an occasion, O*, for proving that V* is P. Need there be parallel doubts? Since, by hypothesis, V* is not Q, O* must be an occasion on which that is a possible way for things to be. But, as the present account of proof allows, O* *may* be an occasion on which there are no possible ways for things to be which would be ones of V*'s lacking Q and further, or thereby, lacking P. For example, it may be an occasion on which there are no possible ways for things to be at all such that V* lacks P. Or it may be one on which there counts as being a *proof* that V* is P—where that proof would work independent of considerations of having or lacking Q. It might then be more reasonable to accept that proof as proof than to remain attached to the idea that V*, to be P, *must*, no matter what else, be Q. Perhaps V* then distinguishes itself from items which are not P in other ways, or it counts as most reasonable to suppose so. By way of general moral, the ways there are on O* for V* to fail to be P can only be seen by looking; thinking without the facts of that occasion is simply not enough.

The ways in which a single thought classifies situations into those of its obtaining and those of its not vary with occasions for its doing so. If that is so, then the same must hold for thought-types, and hence for the ways in which a concept classifies items into those which fit it and those which do not. What we have now seen is that this may also make for differences in the principles governing such classification when it comes to classifying V and when it comes to classifying V*. The present account of proof is, *inter alia*, an account of how that could be. Nothing, perhaps, could be *just* like V in *every* other respect and fail to be F. Conversely, if U is an item which is not F, then nothing could be otherwise just like U but F. There must then be relevant differences between U and V*. But if U lacks Q, that does not mean that V* must differ from U in having Q—even if lacking Q is somehow salient in identifying U as a case of non-F. Similarly for any specified set of features by which V* could differ from U; there may always be more differences, and more ways of drawing distinctions than that. One reason lack of Q may matter for U but not for V* is this: U's lacking Q may on occasion, leave possible ways for things to be on which U would not be F; whereas there may be no equivalent way for things to be with respect to V*.

A convinced ontic sceptic need not be converted by, nor even believe anything in the preceding account. Then again, most of us are not in his position. Most of us nowadays are thoroughly Butlerean: we do not believe in the possibility of (classical) semantic decompositionality at the lexical level. In that sense, we take it, *everything* is what it is and not another thing. Wittgenstein's way with proof shows how we may be entitled to take things in that way. One might of course think to find one's entitlement elsewhere. More will be said about the possibilities for doing so when we come, in chapter 8, to discussing private language. If Wittgenstein's way does not yet seem attractive, it may then come to be.

6

Through the Wilderness

The aim of this chapter is to explain the idea of family resemblance as Wittgenstein expounds it, notably in 65–92. We will approach the idea first through its application, in 79, to proper names and their semantics. There are two reasons for this approach. The first is that some of the most initially striking manifestations of family resemblance in other cases—say, predicates, or general concepts such as being a chair, or a game or a number—are absent or at least not obviously present in the case of proper names. Seeing what family resemblance means in that case allows us to direct some attention away from these more seductive features of the idea, and perhaps thereby towards a more basic underlying phenomenon. What will emerge is that there is an underlying mechanism in family resemblance which is essentially the same as that which generates S-use sensitivity. In fact, it is the mechanism of semantic S-use sensitivity, as described in chapter 2, but applied here so as to generate other phenomena as well.

The second reason for beginning with proper names is that the topic is interesting in its own right. In recent years, there has been lively debate over the semantics of proper names. Though Wittgenstein's name has been mentioned, his view of the matter is one which has not been. It is worth considering how the debate might have gone had his actual position been in the field.

Until the last section, I will concentrate on what Wittgenstein actually says about names, without worrying very much about whether or how his view captures all of the features which family resemblance was meant to exhibit. In fact, we will not seriously address the question of what those features are until the last section. On the other hand, I will worry quite a bit about whether doctrines thought to be found in 79 are actually consistent with what he says about family resemblance as applied in other cases.

1. DESCRIPTIVISM AND CLUSTERS

Saul Kripke, in *Naming and Necessity*, attributes to Wittgenstein a view of names which he calls a cluster concept theory. In discussing problems with another theory linking descriptions to names, for example, he says,

The most common way out of this difficulty is to say, 'really it is not a weakness in ordinary language that we can't substitute a *particular* description for the name; that's all right. What we really associate with the name is a *family* of descriptions.' A good example of this is . . . in *Philosophical Investigations*, where the idea of family resemblance is introduced, and with great power.[1]

Kripke further characterizes cluster concept theories as follows:

According to this view . . . the referent of a name is determined not by a single description but by some cluster or family. Whatever in some sense satisfies enough or most of the family is the referent of the name.[2]

'The gist of all this', Kripke later remarks, 'is that we know a *priori* that, if the Biblical story is substantially false, then Moses did not exist.'[3]

Is Wittgenstein a cluster concept theorist? To answer that, more must be said about just what a cluster concept theory is. The easiest way to do that is first to describe another account on which the cluster concept view is a variant. I will call that theory '(strict) descriptivism'. It is worth separating the account into a series of tenets, since there could prove to be reason to hold on to some of them while letting go of others. The subject matter of strict descriptivism is the semantics, or the proper understanding of a name on an occasion. If Hugo says 'Wittgenstein was epigrammatic', for example, then the account consists of a set of claims about the semantic properties 'Wittgenstein' had as Hugo used it. (This is to be distinguished from an account of who Hugo had in mind or meant by the name. It is concerned, centrally, at least, with the contribution the name made to fixing what literally and strictly speaking was said in Hugo's words, and whether that is true.)

The first tenet of descriptivism is that the proper understanding of a name (on a speaking), or its semantics, is not exhausted by the fact that the name referred to so-and-so. Its having referred to V is compatible with its bearing any of a variety of proper understandings. So, at least

---

[1] Kripke [1972], p. 31.
[2] Ibid.
[3] Ibid., p. 66.

for many purposes, a name's proper understanding will not count as specified or individuated by mentioning that one semantic property of it: that it referred to V. A name, on this view, has more semantic properties than that, and what they are is not determined by its having that one. Note that to say this is not yet to say what functions these other semantic properties perform, nor what reason there might be for taking there to be such. Nor does it specify what sorts of properties these are.

The second tenet of descriptivism is that at least some of these further semantic properties involve, and are specifiable in terms of, general properties[4]—the sorts of properties (typically) expressible by means of a description, such as being the author of the *Tractatus*, or being the author of the *Investigations*. (As the name suggests, descriptivism is often stated directly in terms of descriptions—linguistic items—without recourse to a notion of general property what a description speaks of or expresses. There are several confusions that this often engenders. I will have occasion to mention some of them later.) There is a variety of candidate sorts of semantic properties involving other general properties. For example, there is the property of being to be understood to be speaking (or to speak) of someone with such-and-such general properties. Or there is the quite different property of making a reference which requires (and/or requires exactly) of a referent that it have such-and-such general properties. And so on. So again, descriptivism has not yet taken a stand on just what function these general properties are supposed to have. Whatever exactly the semantic properties which involve general ones, however, we may add here that the proper understanding of a name is taken to be specifiable at least in part *via* mention of these general properties, and that mention of them is at least sometimes required for specifying an understanding. It will do no harm to append here the stronger thesis that such a proper understanding is always specifiable by appropriate mention of the right general properties, together, perhaps, with the fact (where it is one) that the name referred to V.

The third tenet of descriptivism concerns the function of general properties, beyond that of individuating the proper understanding of the name. That function is to impose a condition on being the referent of the name. For any name (and occasion of its use), there is, on this

---

[4] On the notion of a general property, we will follow Leibniz. Think of an individual property as the property, for some individual V, of being V—the property of being Wittgenstein, for example. Then any other property is a general property. By way of positive characterization, suppose that P is a property such that A's having it is compatible with there being or having been some state of affairs in which B would have (or would have had) P, where A and B are distinct individuals. Then P is a general property.

tenet, some set of general properties such that, under any possible conditions of evaluating the reference of the name, an individual would count as the referent just in case it had those general properties. Given that there is, as *per* the first two tenets, some set of general properties uniquely related to, and individuative of, the proper understanding of the name, this, obviously, is but one among many suggestions as to how those properties might function. Nevertheless, this is what strict descriptivism says.

Strict descriptivism might be seen as one particular filling in of a more general idea. On the more general view, the property of referring to V is an evaluative property, on a par with that, in the case of orders, of having been carried out by the doing of such-and-such, or that, in the case of statements, of having been made true by such-and-such a state of affairs. Just as it is in virtue of a statement's proper understanding that one state of affairs and not another would make it true, so it is in virtue of a name's proper understanding that one candidate and not others qualifies for the post of its referent. To find of a given state of affairs that it makes a statement true, or of an individual that it is the one the name refers to is to evaluate what the proper understanding of those words or that name requires. Which is to say that there is more to the proper understanding of the name than is given by the fact that it had the property of referring to so-and-so. On that view, then, there is a of part, or an aspect, of the proper understanding of a name which serves as a guide to the proper identification of its referent. It is that aspect of an understanding which general properties were meant to identify, according to descriptivism. On one understanding of the term 'sense'— the understanding I adopt here—that aspect of proper understanding which guides us to identifying the referent, no matter what else might be true of it, is properly termed the sense of the name. As in the case of other expressions, we will not go wrong for present purposes if we take the semantics of a name to be its sense (if any) plus its referent (or its having the referent, thus the evaluative properties, that it does).

It is also part of the more general idea, on a natural version of it, that this extra aspect of a name's semantics is something which would guide us equally well towards the referent no matter what the world turns out to be like; that is, in any conceivable situation which, if it obtained, would be compatible with our abilities to discern which situation we are in, and compatible with that understanding having been the proper one for the name. It is part of strict descriptivism that the set of general properties which now contribute to specifying the proper understanding of the name likewise provide a guide to the referent which, equally, is indifferent to which of those conceivable circumstances we actually happen to be in. So strict descriptivism may be seen as the view that a name has a sense as well as a referent, combined with some more specific views as to what such a sense, or having it, is like.

It is worth considering briefly the reasons, such as they are, which seem to speak in favour of descriptivism. The most important of these, I think, center on the first tenet and lend decreasing degrees of plausibility to the other two. To begin with a gross example, consider two Lower Austrian schoolboys in the 1920s. One says to the other, 'That Wittgenstein is strict.' Now compare that reference made by 'Wittgenstein' with the references made by that name in this text. All, we may suppose, refer to Wittgenstein. Yet intuitively there is a difference between the way in which the schoolboy's reference is to be understood, on the one hand, and, on the other, the proper understandings of the references made by the name in this text. A sign of that fact is this. It could conceivably be discovered, next week, say, that in fact Russell and not Wittgenstein wrote the Investigations . (Perhaps this was Russell's secret revenge. That this strikes us as preposterous merely shows how successful the ruse was.) That discovery might be highly relevant to the question whom one or another 'Wittgenstein' in this text referred to. But it would have little to do with the referent of the name on the schoolboy's use of it. Conversely, if it were discovered that Wittgenstein never taught in Lower Austria, that would say much about whom, if anyone, the schoolboy referred to, but would be of little importance to the references in this text. The thought then is: where such a discovery is made, whether it ought to impress us or not, in semantic matters of the present sort, is something which varies from case to case. What the variation depends on, the thought goes, is what reference the speaking of the name in question was to be understood to make (or perhaps what reference it is to be understood to have made).

Statements of whom a name referred to may also, often, be viewed as ways of co-ordinating someone else's use of a name with our own. If we are told that the schoolboy's 'Wittgenstein' referred to Wittgenstein, what we learn is that that use of the name referred to the person we (on some appropriate range of occasions) refer to by that name. (We might also have learned that 'Wittgenstein' so used was a private name for a teacher actually named Klaus Trager, say, so that the right individual is one we would refer to in other references, and not in ours *via* the name 'Wittgenstein'.) That information is a useful aid in evaluating what the schoolboy said. To find out whether it is true, for example, we simply have to ask whether Wittgenstein was strict, using the name to make a reference rather than raising explicit questions as to who its referent is. But there are circumstances under which we would be prepared to give it up; ones in which we would conclude that the

'Wittgenstein' the schoolboy spoke of was not 'our Wittgenstein'. What these circumstances are depends not only on our use of the name 'Wittgenstein', but also on the schoolboy's use. The same facts which would show nothing about some references made by 'Wittgenstein'— for example, that Wittgenstein never taught in Lower Austria, or that he did not write the *Tractatus*—would show others not to co-ordinate with our uses of that name (on an occasion or some range of them), so that, as we should then put it, 'that 'Wittgenstein' did not refer to/ mean Wittgenstein'. So there must be something about any given use of 'Wittgenstein' which fixes what any such facts show about it. *What* we need to know about it, the plausible suggestion goes, is what reference it was to be understood to make (or to be making). If we do need to know that for solving some coordination problems, then the first tenet is right.

The last consideration is a bit more subtle. Suppose that it is discovered that Russell really wrote the *Tractatus*. Hesitant about the views expressed, he decided on a pseudonym, and, with Wittgenstein's consent, borrowed his name for the purpose. So 'Wittgenstein' turns out to be one name for Russell, and Russell one of the many people named 'Wittgenstein'—pseudonymously, of course, *but tant pis*! Now, who were we referring to all along when we said 'Wittgenstein . . .'? The present thought is that there is no one right answer to that question. Rather, there would be different correct answers for different of our speakings of 'Wittgenstein'. If the discovery is (more or less) the only way the world deviates from our present picture of it, then most uses of 'Wittgenstein' in this text probably continue to refer to the man we always thought they did. But suppose the name occurs in the context of some textual exegesis of the *Tractatus* (as in 'Wittgenstein, in 2.123, was actually expressing the view that . . ., a thought which he only develops fully in 4.225 and following'). Then that occurrence of 'Wittgenstein' might well most reasonably be taken to refer to Russell. (Similar problems, and similar divergences of answers for different speakings might occur, for example, if it were discovered that 'Wittgenstein' did pretty much all the philosophical work credited to 'him', but was really not a man at all, but, like Nicolas Bourbaki—the better known one—a committee, or that that work was the first computer-generated philosophy, etc.) So, in these counterfactual circumstances, some of our speakings of 'Wittgenstein' would refer to Wittgenstein, while others would refer to Russell. Speakings of both sorts might occur in one and the same monologue.[5]

---

[5] The example here is in fact a variant of one offered by Keith Donnellan [1972], though Donnellan uses it for drawing substantially different morals.

But which speakings would do which? Again, the answer on offer is that depends on how each speaking is most reasonably understood, which means, on the present view, what its proper understanding is correctly taken to be. If that is right, then so is the first tenet.

The point so far, then, is that there are some reasons to think that there is more to the semantics or proper understanding of a name than the fact that, for some V, it refers to V. What sort of support does this give the second and third tenets? As for the second, suppose that a given speaking of 'Wittgenstein' might, for all we know about it, have any of a variety of proper understandings. Suppose that our task is to explain which of these understandings it did have. It is surely a natural thought that we might reasonably resort to descriptions, hence to general properties, to do so. As for the third tenet, there is at least this thought: if we were to explain the proper use of a name by means of descriptions, we would surely be wrong in choosing descriptions which in fact did not fit the referent. So for D to be the right descriptions—the ones which do state how the name is to be understood—they must identify the referent of the name. Conversely, given that D are the right descriptions, no individual would count as the referent unless he fit them. Neither of these considerations is conclusive in favour of its respective tenet. But, as said already, it just is harder to make these tenets plausible. The important points are these. First, there is at least some reason to accept the first tenet of descriptivism. Second, since those reasons always seem to appeal, in one way or another, to the possibility of an individual turning out to be the referent of one 'Wittgenstein' without being the referent of another (restricting attention to instances of the name which in fact refer to Wittgenstein), there is at least some reason to think that the proper understanding of a name—or some part of it over and above the fact that the name referred to so-and-so—functions as a guide to the referent, hence some reason to think that a proper name, on a speaking, has a sense.

This completes the characterization of strict descriptivism. Kripke appends two non-obligatory theses to it, each of which makes it considerably less plausible, and neither of which will be taken to be part of the doctrine as it is understood here. The first is that if the semantics of a name is fixed by some set of general properties, and hence by some set of descriptions which express them, then those descriptions must be synonymous with the name, and substitutable for it at will (at least outside intensional contexts). That this should be so is one of the misunderstandings avoided by talk of general properties. Let the remark be 'Wittgenstein was epigrammatic' and let D be some set of descriptions which fix the semantics of the name so spoken. Suppose we substitute D for 'Wittgenstein' in that remark, generating the new remark 'D was epigrammatic'. Then the important semantic properties of the initial remark will be preserved only if the condition for being the referent of D is exactly that of having the general properties D expresses. (For convenience, we here take those general properties to be invariant across speakings of D, though, given S-use sensitivity, of course they are not.) But on no thoughtful descriptivist view would this be so. Descriptions, like names, make a variety of distinct references on a variety of speakings. Something must distinguish between one such reference and another. One thing that would, on a descriptivist view, is that different such references impose different conditions on being the referent of them. In general, then, these conditions cannot be simply that of having the general properties which the descriptions (invariantly) express.

Kripke's second addendum is a view as to which other facts about a speaking of 'Wittgenstein' determine which set of descriptions or general properties do fix its semantics on that speaking. The idea is, roughly, that those properties are the ones the speaker would have taken the referent to have. On Wittgenstein's view, there is very little (or less) to be said in favour of that view. Be that as it may, we will have enough work in what follows sorting out issues of what kind of semantics names do have without confusing that question with the question how a name, on an occasion, might come by one semantics or another. First we may address the question what readings the sentence 'Mary had a little lamb' does have, and we may then turn to the question how we tell which instances of it did have one of these readings and which instances another. Here we will pursue a similar line with names.

Having exhausted, for the present, the topic of descriptivism, we now turn to cluster concept theories. A cluster concept account is a minor variant on descriptivism. It differs only in the third tenet. Like descriptivism, it supposes that there is some unique set of general properties which fix the semantics of a name on a speaking. It differs from descriptivism in the function of these properties. On the descriptivist view, the referent would always be that individual, if any, who uniquely has all of these. On a cluster concept view, the referent would always be that individual who has most, or enough of these, but not necessarily all (the exact notion of 'enough' varying from one cluster concept account to another). Note that Kripke's story about the gist of the cluster concept view (in the case of the biblical story and Moses) does require that there be, in point of semantics, some specifiable set of general properties which prepare us for whatever might happen, in this sense: no matter what, the referent will always be the one who has most (or enough) of those. If not, then his conclusion as to there being no Moses if that story is substantially false does not follow.

2. 79 AND ENVIRONS

79 begins as follows:

According to Russell,[6] we can say: the name 'Moses' can be defined by means of various descriptions. For example, as 'the man who led the Israelites through the wilderness', 'the man who lived at that time and place and was then called "Moses"', 'the man who as a child was taken out of the Nile by Pharaoh's daughter', and so on. And according as we assume one definition or another the words [*Satz*], 'Moses existed' get another sense [*Sinn*], and so do all other words [*jeder Satz*] about Moses.—And if we are told, 'N did not exist' we do ask: 'What do you mean? Are you saying that . . ., or that . . ., etc.?'

The Russellian view expressed here is, on all points, strict descriptivism. First, it does suppose that there are a variety of distinct semantics for 'Moses' to bear, on all of which it would refer to Moses (if Moses existed). So the semantics of a name is not exhausted by the fact of whom it referred to. Second, each of these different semantics is specifiable in terms of some set of descriptions. And conversely, different such sets specify different semantics. So there is a unique set of descriptions associated with the name (on any speaking) in point of semantics, and, further, this (together, perhaps, with the fact of the referent) individuates that semantics. Third, though this is not said explicitly, it does appear that these different sets of descriptions correspond to different ranges of circumstances under which the name, with that semantics, would refer to no one, thus making true, with reference to the name used with that semantics, the remark 'Moses did not exist'. So it appears, at least, that the descriptions are to be taken as imposing a necessary and sufficient condition on referenthood—one which would hold for all circumstances in which it was to be assessed to whom the name referred. There is, anyway, so far no indication that we are dealing with a cluster concept view. So the most natural assumption is that the Russellian view expressed here just is strict descriptivism.

Moreover, Wittgenstein does find at least something to be said in favour of this Russellian view. He endorses the view that there is a

---

[6] This is a more natural translation of 'nach' than Anscombe's 'Following Russell'. Moreover, it more unambiguously conveys the proper suggestion that the view being expressed here is one being attributed to Russell, and not Wittgenstein's own.

variety of distinct things to be said in negative existentials, that is, remarks, for a given N, of the form 'N did not exist'. So there is a variety of distinct semantics that such a remark might bear, with the name 'N' and its referent fixed. The Russellian view, of course, offers an easy account of how this could be. If Wittgenstein in fact rejects that view as an account of names, we will eventually want to see what Wittgenstein's account of this variety in negative existentials is.

But the Russellian view here is clearly meant as a trial balloon, to be punctured in the remainder of 79. Just where does this puncturing occur? Wittgenstein begins the second paragraph by lofting his own trial balloon:

But when I make a statement about Moses—am I always ready to substitute some *one* of these descriptions for 'Moses'? I shall perhaps say: by 'Moses' I understand the man who did what the Bible relates of Moses, or at any rate a good deal of it.

The last clause here certainly suggests a cluster concept view. We assign the right descriptions to the name, and then demand that Moses, if there was such a person, satisfy most of them. Such a view is suggested again by one later remark in the paragraph:

Is it not the case that I have, so to speak, a whole series of props in readiness, and am ready to lean on one if another should be taken from under me, and vice versa?

Clusters enter here with the idea that the props are in readiness, thus something which might be specified in specifying the name's semantics.

But is this to be taken as Wittgenstein's response to Russell, or merely as another trial balloon to be punctured? We may approach that question by posing another: whatever the moral of 79 may be, what is its intended scope? The beginnings of an answer are suggested in the parenthetical remark with which 79 closes:

(The fluctuation of scientific definitions: what today counts as an observed concomitant of a phenomenon will tomorrow be used to define it.)

The remark is reminiscent of Leibniz in the *New Essays* and, in more recent times, of Hilary Putnam. For the scientific definitions which fluctuate in this way as science progresses are, notably, definitions of 'natural kinds' and 'physical quantities'—'gold', to take Leibniz's example, and 'water', 'aluminum', or 'length' to take a few of Putnam's. So terms such as these, and the concepts which they express, also fall within the scope of the point of 79.

If Wittgenstein's treatment of names falls in line with his treatment of natural kinds, etc., then so far this brings him into line with philosophers like Putnam and Kripke, among others. But the evidence is that 79 is meant to have an even wider scope. In 80, for example, which to all appearances is a continuation of the discussion of 79, Wittgenstein discusses a case involving the notion of a chair. So the point would seem to apply to concepts of artefacts as well. And in 87, in returning to the name 'Moses', Wittgenstein assures us that the same problems arise for concepts or words such as 'red', 'dark', and 'sweet'. So, in traditional jargon, the point seems meant for 'secondary qualities' as well. The point of 79, then, seems, nearly enough, meant to apply to everything—that is, all our concepts and the words which express them.

One thing we can conclude so far is that the moral of 79 is meant to apply where the idea of family resemblance does—for example, to the concepts with which Wittgenstein first introduces that idea, those of a game, and of a number. This is a good point at which to endorse Kripke's view that 79 just is the idea of family resemblance applied to proper names. The text suggests, moreover, that family resemblance is an idea meant to have application to all our concepts, so that there is at least some important sense in which it is wrong to speak of 'family resemblance concepts', as if those were concepts of some semantically special kind. (Note that Wittgenstein introduces family resemblance in 65, in response to a question about the essence of language. His conclusion about the 'essence of language' is stated in 92. All the sorts of concepts mentioned above are discussed in connection with this problem in the space between those two paragraphs.)

We may now raise a second question: is a cluster concept view consistent with Wittgenstein's view of family resemblance—for example, with what he says about that idea in connection with *game* and *number*? Would he, for example, endorse a cluster concept view of those concepts? On some views of the matter, he would. A cluster concept account of *game*, for example, would posit some set of general properties associated with that concept, such that something qualifies as a game just in case it has most, or enough, of those properties. This would give us, in effect, a disjunction of ways that an item might qualify as a game. Each disjunct would consist of some set of properties the item might have such that these jointly added up to a large enough subset of the set associated with the concept. So item X might qualify as a game in virtue of having properties P_1, P_2 and P_3, item Y might qualify as a game in virtue of having properties P_3, P_4 and P_5, and so on.

To assess this view of the matter, we must look briefly at the discussion between 66 and 76. In 66, Wittgenstein introduces the notion in this way:

Don't say: 'There must be something common, or they would not be called "games"'"—but *look and see* whether there is anything common to all.—For if you look at them, you will not see something that is common to *all*, but similarities, relationships, and a whole series of them at that. To repeat, don't think, but look! . . .

And the result of this examination is: we see a complicated network of similarities, overlapping and crisscrossing: sometimes overall similarities, sometimes similarities of detail.

Again, in 67:

And we extend our concept of number as in spinning a thread we twist fibre on fibre. And the strength of the thread does not reside in the fact that some one fibre runs through its whole length, but in the overlapping of many fibres.

So there is supposed to be no common strand running through, for example, all cases of what would (recognizably) fit our concept of a game; no set of features present in all such cases (or at least none which, by their presence, distinguish such cases from all cases of non-games). The minimal conclusion, in traditional jargon, is that there is no necessary and sufficient condition for being a game.

The trouble with all this, if a cluster concept view fits, is that there is a necessary and sufficient condition for being a game. In fact, we have already stated it: having enough of the properties in the set associated with the concept. Equivalently, we might say that there is a disjunctive condition, where the disjuncts correspond to the large enough subsets of this set. Now in fact Wittgenstein does consider the possibility of such disjunctive necessary and sufficient conditions. His first treatment of the topic is in 67:

But if someone wished to say: 'There is something in common to all these constructions—namely the disjunction of all their common properties.'—I should reply: Now you are only playing with words. One might as well say: 'Something runs though the whole thread—namely the continuous overlapping of the fibres.'

Here Wittgenstein's response to the suggestion of disjunctive necessary and sufficient conditions, or common strands, appears to be: 'That's not what I call a necessary and sufficient condition.' Such a response raises Ramsey's spectre of a canonical form for many philosophical arguments:

Philosopher A: 'I went to Grantchester yesterday.'

Philosopher B: 'No. I didn't.'

For another philosopher might always reply, 'But that is what I call a necessary and sufficient condition'. We had better hope that philosophy is made out of something more substantial than that.

Fortunately, Wittgenstein also has a more robust response. In 68, he considers a form of the disjunctive proposal:

the concept number is defined for you as the logical sum of these individual interrelated concepts: cardinal number, rational number, real number, etc.; and in the same way the concept of a game as the logical sum of a corresponding set of sub-concepts.

He rejects this proposal on the following grounds:

I *can* give the concept 'number' rigid limits in this way, that is, use the word 'number' for a rigidly limited concept, but I can also use it so that the extension of the concept is *not* closed off by a border. And that is how we do use the word 'game'.

The point here is reiterated in 76:

If someone were to draw a sharp boundary, I could not acknowledge it as the one that I too always wanted to draw, or had drawn in my mind. For I did not want to draw one at all.

The point made in this response is stated succinctly, in another context, in 208:

We should distinguish between the 'and so on' which is, and the 'and so on' which is not and abbreviated notation. 'And so on *ad inf.*' is *not* such an abbreviation.

For a concept to be definable disjunctively, on the plan of 68, it must be determinate what the disjuncts of the definition would be. If, for any candidate set of disjuncts which might distinguish cases where the concept fits from those where it does not, there is some (possible) item which falls under the concept, but does not satisfy any of the disjuncts, then the concept does not have a disjunctive necessary and sufficient condition for its application. If a concept fits the cluster concept model, then this condition on the possibility of such a disjunctive definition is satisfied, and in that sense there is a necessary and sufficient condition for falling under it. But it is just this possibility that Wittgenstein denies where, and in so far as the idea of family resemblance fits. So a cluster concept view cannot be the result of applying the idea of family resemblance—whether to proper names or to other items. We must read further in 79 to see how the Russellian balloon gets punctured, and what view of names Wittgenstein does recommend.

3. SECTION 79 REREAD

The main ideas for deflating the Russellian balloon are stated in the second half of the second paragraph:

If I say, 'N is dead', then something like the following may hold for the meaning [*Bedeutung*] of the name 'N': I believe that a human being has lived, whom I (1) have seen in such-and-such places, who (2) looked like this (pictures), (3) has done such and such things, and (4) bore the name 'N' in social life.—*Asked what I understand by 'N', I should enumerate all or some of these points, and different ones on different occasions.* . . . But if some point now proves false?—Shall I be prepared to declare the words, 'N is dead' false— even if it is only something which strikes me as incidental? *If I had given a definition of the name in such a case, I should now be ready to alter it.* [My italics emphasize the key lines.]

Let us first note the elements in the Russellian trial balloon which are not under challenge here. On that view, names have a sense as well as a referent—that is, an element of their semantics which is a guide to the referent and on which questions of referenthood depend. There is nothing in this passage to cancel that idea. Second, it is supposed that the sense of a name is specifiable in terms of general properties, so in giving descriptions which would then be taken as saying to whom the name is to be understood to refer. Properly understood, these descriptions would then state what guide to a referent the sense counts as providing. This idea appears to be endorsed in the first italicized passage, where Wittgenstein states how he would say how the name was to be understood. Third, it is supposed that the sort of guide that sense provides is such that the descriptions which specify the sense provide a condition on being the referent: in Kripke's terms, the referent is whoever satisfies those descriptions. Wittgenstein does not take it, at least in this passage, that he can state the sense of the name in giving a description that does not fit the referent. He does not dispute here the idea that it is a requirement on a description's stating the sense of the name that it does identify the referent. So there is so far no harm to be seen in the view that if descriptions D do state the sense, then, in some sense, the referent of the name is whoever fits D.

Any of the above points might be challenged. In fact, all of them have been. One might deny altogether that names have a sense. This is the line taken by Kripke, or at least commonly attributed to him. Because of its currency, practically anything further that we say on the assumption that names do have a sense will be controversial. But for the present, our concern will be what one ought to say about names if one does say that they have a sense. That assumption will be discussed further in section 5.

One might also agree that names have a sense, but deny that this is something which can be stated by means of descriptions. The usual way to pursue this line would be to invoke homophony[7]—the idea that

---

[7] An interesting and cogent development of a homophonic approach is to be found in McDowell [1977]. Though the present approach diverges from his on important points, I think that there is much more in common to the motivations of each than may be readily apparent.

the way to state the sense of the name 'Wittgenstein.' for example, is by saying, 'Wittgenstein' names (means, etc.) Wittgenstein'. I have said something about homophony in connection with other parts of speech in chapter 1, and will say more about it in connection with names later. But, for the time being, let us set that option to one side. It is, at any rate, not an option Wittgenstein considers in 79.

Finally, one might allow that names have a sense and that this is specifiable by means of descriptions, but deny that these descriptions provide the sort of guide to the referent envisioned above. One very simple way of doing this is a cluster concept account. Another more interesting way has already been mentioned. It is to deny that the sorts of semantic properties of a name which involve general properties (of a sort which might characterize a referent) are such that the condition they impose on referenthood is having those properties, or even most of them. For example, if the name is to be understood to be speaking of someone with those properties, then the condition on referenthood might be being the most reasonable candidate for that post given that, in the circumstances of the speaking, such-and-such would have been properly taken to be so of the referent. It could happen that the most reasonable candidate did not even have most of the properties a referent was to be understood to have. On Wittgenstein's view of the matter, it will emerge, there is something to be said for this position. But it is not the main burden of the cited passage.

What Wittgenstein challenges in the Russellian view is a further tacit assumption. Part of the intuitive idea of a sense was that a sense is something which equips us equally well for determining the referent of the name no matter what circumstances we might conceivably be confronted with. Further, there is something in particular which is what the sense of the name is. The sense of the name is what one would understand about it, for example, on the occasion of its speaking, in understanding it correctly (and fully). This intuitive idea makes natural a further thought which is incorporated in the Russellian view. We state the sense of a name in stating a guide to its referent. That is how descriptions function to say what the sense is. The guide we thus state, if we state the sense correctly, is just that guide which the sense of the name provides. Hence the guide that we state must serve equally well to determine the referent in any circumstances which conceivably could confront us. The sense of the name, or the way it is (was) properly understood, guides us to and determines the referent; if the sense of the name is A—that is, fixed by the semantic properties 'A' mentions—then the name's having those semantic properties must provide exactly the same guide to, and conditions on its referent as is provided by, the name's having the sense or proper understanding that it had (or has).

There is no denying that this last idea is a natural one. In fact, it is so natural that it has formed a major block to seeing what Wittgenstein's view of names actually is. Nevertheless, in the cited passage, Wittgenstein presents at least two ideas which challenge it. The first, contained in the first italicized remark, might be called the *non-uniqueness* thesis. On it, on any occasion on which someone was called upon to state the sense of a name, he might do this equally correctly in any of a variety of distinct ways. He might do this by means of one set of descriptions, and he might do it by means of another. There is no set of descriptions—nor anything else—which is uniquely qualified to perform that function. Since different sets of descriptions state different guides to a referent, this challenges the idea that the guide to a referent which the sense of a name provides is nothing other than that guide which a correct statement of that sense provides or states.

The second thesis, parts of which are in both italicized remarks, might be called *the occasion sensitivity thesis*. On it, what would count as correct statements of the sense of a name on some occasions for stating the sense would not do so on others. That is, correct statements of sense vary across possible occasions for providing them. Part of the reason for this may be that the guide to a referent which a particular statement provides may count as correct on some occasions, and as incorrect on others. On some occasions, while not on others, it may correctly reflect what the sense of the name requires; it may count as one way—though not in general the unique way—of saying what that sense (or the name's having it) requires of a referent of the name. But the passage makes clear that there is also another reason for this variation. On the present scheme of things, we specify the sense of a name in mentioning some of its semantic properties. The semantic properties which we thus say it to have on some occasions, in stating the sense correctly, are ones which the name would not count as having on other occasions. So if the name (on a speaking) is properly understood on some occasion of considering it as requiring that a referent fit such-and-such description, on other such occasions it would not be properly understood as requiring this of a referent. Or if, on some such occasions, it is to be understood to speak (or have spoken) of an individual fitting such-and-such description, then it may be on other occasions that it is not properly so understood. That is, the semantic properties which a name would count as having on some occasion of considering it are not, or need not be, those it would count as having on some other. So, given that names have a sense, the semantics of a name is an occasion sensitive matter. This is consistent with the thought that the name, as spoken, had some sense or other. The point here is that when it comes to saying what the sense of the name was, different things on different occasions will count as correct answers to that question, or more simply, there will be different things on different occasions which that sense counts as being (or having been).

Each of the two italicized remarks makes a different point about the scope of the occasion sensitivity thesis—the range of occasions across which the above variation may take place. The second remark asks us to consider the range of occasions which could confront us consistent with our abilities to tell which occasion we are on; all the circumstances in which we could find, or could have found ourselves consistent with those abilities. Alternatively, all the sets of possible facts which could turn out to be facts, and ones we had not grasped in understanding the name correctly. That is, we are asked to consider all those situations for evaluating the referent of the name across which its sense was meant to provide us with equal guidance to the referent. Each such occasion might provide us with a different set of candidates for the post of referent of the name, or a different set of facts about each candidate. So far, we can suppose that all these occasions but one are counterfactual ones—ones we could have been on, but not ones we might be on. The situation in which Wittgenstein discovers that Mr N did not look like his pictures is not one that might arise if Mr N in fact did look like his pictures. But the first remark points us also to occasions which might arise as things are. There are pairs of occasions Wittgenstein might have for stating the sense of the name 'N' on each of which he would say different things in doing so correctly. The sorts of variations across these two ranges need not be exactly the same. We will consider some possibilities for difference later.

Suppose that 'Wittgenstein', on some occurrence in this text, has a sense which is now correctly specifiable by means of some description, D. One implication this might be thought to have is that under no conceivable circumstances would it have turned out to be the case that that name referred to someone who did not fit D. But it is just that implication which the occasion sensitivity thesis is meant to block. The sense of the name is *now* specifiable by means of D, and, as long as it is so specifiable, it is a requirement that a referent of the name must fit D. But under other conceivable circumstances the sense of the name would not have been so specifiable. So fitting D would not have been a requirement on the referent. So the referent might not have fit D. In other words, no current facts about the sense of the name—that is, nothing which now counts as a fact as to what that sense is—require, for any D, that, no matter what, the referent would have fit D.(Nor, equally, could such facts require that, no matter what, a referent would have to fit most of the descriptions in some fixed set.) For those current facts do not require that they would have been facts no matter what. Wittgenstein is prepared to retract judgements about what the sense of a name is in the light of possible discoveries, which is to say that we are prepared to recognize those judgements as incorrect (for all of which the judgements may be correct, given the facts as they are).

Here Wittgenstein recognizes an important phenomenological point: we do not in fact use names such that nothing ever could have counted as their referent unless it fulfilled such-and-such a descriptive condition. This is recognizable as one of Kripke's main phenomenological theses in his discussion of proper names. So far, then, Wittgenstein and Kripke share an important piece of common ground. They part company over what they make of the phenomenology. Kripke retains the classical Russellian assumption that (if names have senses) what the sense of a name is—or what it counts as being—is an occasion insensitive matter. That assumption, together with the shared phenomenology, requires Kripke to reject the idea that names do have a sense (or, not yet to prejudice things against homophony, one specifiable by means of descriptions). For if the truths as to what the sense is would have remained so no matter what, then there can be no such truth statable in terms of descriptions. Wittgenstein, on the other hand, rejects the idea that what the sense of a name now counts as being is what it would have counted as being no matter what. With that, he is free to retain the idea that names have senses, and even that these are specifiable, on an occasion, in terms of descriptions or the general properties these express.

The remainder of this section will consider some of the significance of the non-uniqueness thesis. The next section will say more about occasion sensitivity. We might begin by noting that in stating the Russellian view, Wittgenstein uses the word 'Sinn'—a word that he does not use frequently in the *Investigations*. It would be wrong to conclude that he intends this word to bear Frege's, or anyone else's proprietary sense for it. But he was certainly well acquainted with such proprietary senses, Frege's in particular. He was also well aware that, like most terms in semantics—like the term 'semantics' itself, for example—the term 'Sinn' is hardly ever used in philosophy without some proprietary sense (since most such terms get their sense, on an occasion, in the context of a theory some philosopher is propounding, hence invariably carry around a lot of baggage). This is simply to underscore the point that when Wittgenstein advances theses about the sense of a name—or, as he later puts it, the meaning (*Bedeutung*) of a name—he does not mean merely to make some point about ordinary usage. It is not as if, for example, his point is merely that there is a diversity of things which we ordinarily call, or count as stating the sense of, a name, or a diversity of things which do state what we ordinarily call or count as 'the sense of a name'. The point is one about the sort of semantics names do have, and the way they have it. This makes Wittgenstein open to a particular form of refutation. Suppose that a philosopher could identify some central semantic function for a sense to perform. Suppose the philosopher could show that, at least typically, something about a name or its proper understanding does perform that function. Suppose he could further show that, at least on any occasion, there was a unique correct way of specifying that aspect of the name's understanding which performed that function, or at least some unique set of identifiable semantic properties of the name which did this. If that feature of a name turned out not to be 'sense' in the ordinary sense, then the philosopher might just dub it, for example, sense*. Wittgenstein would then be wrong about sense*. If he remained right about sense, in the present context, that victory would be pyrrhic.

Wittgenstein's two theses, then, must be taken to hold for any central semantic function in terms of which one might plausibly define sense, or whatever feature of a name fulfills that function. There are, in fact, two candidate functions which have been most prominent in philosophy, and which Wittgenstein actually discusses in the family resemblance discussion. There is also a third important candidate function which has not been prominent in philosophy, but which is suggested by a Wittgensteinian view of sense. The next section will discuss that one. The two traditionally prominent functions are, first, as imposing a condition on the having of evaluative properties— referring to V, in the case of a name, or, in other cases, being true of such-and-such, having been carried out by the doing of such-and-such, etc.—and second, as imposing a condition on understanding. The idea is that the sense of W is either something such that if one knew it he would qualify as an understander of W, or if one did not know it he would not qualify as an understander of W, or both, and that correct answers to the question what the sense of W is are provided by mentioning either items knowledge of which would make an understander of someone, or items ignorance of which would make a non-understander of someone, or items with both these statuses (the disjuncts corresponding to different ideas on the requirements for the sense of W being such-and-such). Non-uniqueness means that in general, in the case of names, there is no uniquely best-qualified candidate for performing any of these functions.

Let us first discuss conditions on referenthood. The idea here is that (where a name is understandable enough for there to be facts as to what it refers to) there is some aspect of the proper understanding of a name which imposes a particular condition on being its referent. Now consider a name, N, and a range of candidate specifications of its semantics. Some of these may count as correct statements of its semantics while others do not. The thought which bears on (non-) uniqueness would be that some of these may be correct, and some incorrect in virtue of their relation to the condition on referenthood which N's proper understanding (or the designated aspect of it) imposes. More specifically, some candidate statements and not others may attribute to the name's semantics the imposing of that condition which that semantics does impose, either by actually stating that condition, or by specifying a proper understanding of the name on which it would impose that condition. For example, a candidate which states the semantics by means of a description might be properly understood as imposing a particular condition on a referent, namely, fitting that description, and that condition may or may not count as the one imposed by the name's proper understanding.

Given that we do assign such a function to the proper understanding of a name, and define sense (or sense*) accordingly, the non-uniqueness thesis is threatened only in so far as it is generally possible to identify a unique condition as the one the proper understanding of a name, N, imposes, and/or a uniquely best-qualified means of stating or specifying 'the condition that N's proper understanding imposes'. Which condition this would be in any given case would have to depend on other facts about the use of the name, or the relevant speaking of it—on facts of the sort Wittgenstein alludes to, in the cited passage, in speaking of what he took to be so of N. In the terminology of chapter 2, it would be what it would be shown to be by correct solutions to disambiguation problems posable for the name (on that speaking). It is as input to disambiguation problems that what Wittgenstein took to be so has a bearing on what the semantics of the name as he used it was. So we might ask after the power of other facts to choose between the various conditions that N's proper understanding might (rightly or wrongly) be thought to impose. Wittgenstein's thesis, applied in this case, is that these other facts generally will not show any condition to be uniquely best qualified for the role envisaged for it here, on any plausible understanding of that role. Otherwise put, granting the right sorts of semantic properties to names, there will generally fail to be unique correct solutions to disambiguation problems posed for those properties.

To see the power of other facts to do the needed choosing here, we must ask what might be required of a condition in order for it to qualify for a role of the envisaged sort—some role meriting the title, 'the condition which the name's semantics/proper understanding imposes on being its referent'. At a lower limit, it might be required that the condition in fact identify the actual referent of the name. Obviously, where there is a referent, many different conditions do this. So if that is the requirement, other facts which might be input to a disambiguation problem cannot show just one condition to satisfy it. The upper limit would be that a condition must correctly identify who the referent would be in all conceivable circumstances; not only as things in fact are, but also however they counter-factually could have turned out to be. By the occasion sensitivity thesis, no condition satisfies this requirement. Nor could it, given Wittgenstein's and Kripke's common ground. Confining attention to the correctness of the results a condition would deliver, the only possible middle ground is this: a condition must be required to be satisfied by the actual referent and by the individual the referent would be in some, but not all, of the counter-factual circumstances in which such questions might arise. Other facts about the use of the name, to pick out a unique correct condition, must then select some range of counter-factual circumstances as the right one to look at for deciding which condition would be the correct one for the envisaged role.

But now Wittgenstein's point is that it is just this that other facts typically do not do. Take a typical philosophical reference *via* the name 'Wittgenstein'. Consider two candidate conditions on being its referent: being the author of the *Tractatus*, and being the author of the *Investigations*. Each condition identifies the referent of that instance of the name. Each would not be (or have been) satisfied by the referent in some conceivable counter-factual circumstances. Typically, the proper understanding of the name gives us no more reason to be interested in the one range of circumstances than in the other. There are speakings for which that is not true. But then the same point could be made in terms of other pairs of descriptions. There is, then, no interesting sense in which the one description, as opposed to the other, may qualify as stating what the semantics of the name requires of the referent, hence none in which the one as opposed to the other might qualify as specifying what that semantics is. On Wittgenstein's view, the point holds for any means for saying such things. To this he adds the view that such things can be said. So, on the right occasion, either of the above descriptions, among other devices, might state the right understanding of what the name, as it was spoken, requires of a referent—of the guide its proper understanding provides to the referent, and hence of what its sense, in the present sense of 'sense', is.

Non-uniqueness is largely a consequence of the phenomena of disambiguation. There is no uniquely correct way of saying what the sense of a name is, *inter alia*, because there is no unique assignment of semantic properties to a name which other facts about it show to be correct. This is not to say that other facts show no such assignment to be correct. Hence nor is it yet to say that we ought not to regard names as having a sense. Disambiguation problems and their solving will prove to lie at the core of Wittgenstein's other theses about names as well. And as we shall see later, they provide a good view—quite plausibly the best one—of what family resemblance in general is all about.

The considerations regarding possible links of sense with understanding are much the same as those just covered. Beginning with the weakest view, suppose we take it that one specifies the sense of W in stating facts (and thereby some semantic properties of W) knowledge of which would make someone an understander of W. Let us take it initially that someone counts as an understander of W when he performs enough like understanders of W—that is, he is prepared (nearly enough) to do the right things with W, and to recognize the right things about its semantics and its proper evaluations and P-uses. The idea is this. Suppose we consider some appropriate largish set of candidate understanders of W. We may well know that at least some of these must be understanders. For it might be unreasonable, hence wrong, to maintain that no one understands W; there may be no serious question of that. It would be wrong to suppose, for example, that no English speaker understands the word 'candidate', or 'consider'. The problem, then, is to separate out understanders from non-understanders within the chosen group. Suppose that on any reasonable way of doing this, with reference to the sorts of performances and preparednesses just mentioned, A would be grouped with the understanders. Then A counts as an understander of W. On this criterion it is obvious that typically there are a variety of distinct things one might know which *might*—given an adequately reasonable treatment of the knowledge—qualify him as an understander of a name. Someone who knew that Wittgenstein wrote the *Tractatus*, for example, would be a good bet for understanding references *via* that name in this text. But so would someone who knew that Wittgenstein wrote the *Investigations* (to mention only two obvious examples). So far, then, considerations of understanding do not select any uniquely correct way of specifying a sense.

One might hope to impose more stringent criteria on 'true' understanding. The general idea for such criteria (if they are to help in present matters) would be to ensure that the understanding an understander has of W exactly match (or match in designated respects) the proper understanding of W. The hope would be that there be some unique way of specifying what the understander must know for this to be so, or at least some unique set of facts (or semantic properties of W) which he must know. But this idea simply returns us to square one. Criteria for stating a sense which are based on considerations of understanding will now pose a threat to the non-uniqueness thesis only if we already see that there is some unique specification of what W's sense is which is best qualified for the title 'the correct/ proper specification'; only if there is some unique set of specifiable facts whose obtaining makes the sense of W what it is. Now we are back to Wittgenstein's original point that in the case of names this is, as a rule, precisely what we cannot see.

To sum up, if there was some unique set of facts one must know to qualify as an understander of W, and if this set were rich enough to plausibly fix a semantics for W (so that its obtaining is not compatible with there being too many distinct semantics that W might have), then present ideas on linking sense with understanding might lead some-where. But given the diversity of ways of qualifying as an under-stander—the diversity of knowledge that might put one in a good position in this respect, in so far as we have the means of choosing between the goodness of one position and that of another—there is no hope, in most cases, at least, that there might be such a set of facts. So far, the thesis is confined to names. But it is clearly one Wittgenstein holds in general. The point, once again, turns on the ability of other facts to dictate solutions to appropriate disambiguation problems (for names) once we have assigned a given function to their semantics.

Our understandings of words or concepts, and the ways we convey these to others, form one of the main topics of the family resemblance discussion. It is at this point, notably, that Wittgenstein raises questions as to how an understanding of a word can determine its evaluative properties in the situations which might confront us (how our understanding might determine what we are to do next) and which are the subject of the 'rule following' discussion a bit later in the *Investigations*. He also anticipates one objection to the view just expressed. In pointing to the diversity of things we might say in conveying our understanding of a word or concept, he is careful to emphasize that, typically, what we *say* is no less than what we know. It is not as if we are holding something back, or as if there is something else which we are unable to express. (So the problem about rule following will be, in the end, a problem about how *that*—what we actually say—might determine what we are to do next, or how words are to be evaluated.) This emphasis on our explicitness, in the present context, has the following point. One might think that any of various bits of knowledge might qualify someone as an understander of a name only because he already has certain background knowledge to which this knowledge is tacitly added, and that it is this background knowledge, or that plus the knowledge on display in the cases alluded to above, which actually constitutes understanding. It is this background knowledge, then, and not facts of the sort mentioned above, that might constitute a threat to the non-uniqueness thesis. Here, on the one hand, Wittgenstein agrees that there are no facts knowledge of which would guarantee understanding (for example, of a name) no matter what else. On the other hand, he emphasizes that this 'logical gap' between knowledge of the sorts of facts we mention in explaining the proper understanding of a name and understanding it is not filled by knowledge of more facts—certainly that there is no set of further facts knowledge of which would close the gap. I will say more about the nature of this gap at the end of the next section.

So far, we have supposed that the sense of a name might be stated by means of descriptions, having temporarily set the possibility of homophony to one side. It is now time to make a few remarks about that possibility. The idea is that we might state the sense of some 'Wittgenstein', for example, in saying, '"Wittgenstein" refers to Wittgenstein.' If this is not to amount to requiring some set of general properties of a referent, then the point is this. We use the name 'Wittgenstein' to identify the individual that other occurrence of 'Wittgenstein' referred to. And it is in stating that fact—the fact that the name, so spoken, referred to that individual—that we specify what the proper understanding of the name is. So it is that fact which identifies this understanding. The first point to be made about this idea is that Wittgenstein has no principled objection to it. The sense of a name might be statable in this way; whether it is or not, on his view, is an occasion sensitive matter. If we accept the idea argued in section 1 that there are a number of distinct semantics the name 'Wittgenstein' might have while referring to Wittgenstein, then the above form of statement will not by itself identify which of these semantics the name so spoken did have. Or if it did, then there must be much more to be said about what was said in saying it, since that, too, may be any of a variety of things. But this is no principled bar to homophonic statements of a name's semantics. No matter how much disambiguation we do for any expression, there will always remain more conceivable disambiguation problems in the offing. 'Complete disambiguation', occasion insensitively, is a fiction. What counts as complete disambiguation on an occasion is what satisfies our purposes on that occasion.

The question we must now raise is whether homophonic statements of a name's semantics promise to perform, in a uniquely best-qualified way, either of the candidate functions for statements of sense discussed above. The first function is correctly identifying the condition which a name imposes on being its referent. Again, there is a sense in which it does this: as things are, no candidate could be the right one for that post unless that candidate is Wittgenstein. But there is also a sense in which it does not. At least for typical references made by 'Wittgenstein'—for example, at least most of those in this text— there are conceivable circumstances in which the name would have turned out not to refer to Wittgenstein, that is, to the individual the homophonic statement identifies. In the case of this text, for example, there are some of the situations in which it turns out that the *Investigations* was really Russell's secret revenge. In this respect, homophonic statements are on a par with others.

Things might seem different when we turn to questions of understanding. Here one might have the following thought. Though any of various bits of other information might qualify one as an understander of the name 'Wittgenstein' (on a speaking), one thing one must always know to count as an understander of the name is whom the name referred to. Thus any of these other items of knowledge will qualify one as also knowing the fact the homophonic statement states. In that respect, homophony is in a privileged position. This thought appears wrong in two respects. First, its premiss is mistaken. Suppose that, although Wittgenstein did write the *Investigations*, tomorrow I am given good reason to believe that he did not. For example, a great 'exposé' might appear in the *New York Review of Books*. I, at least, would have doubts as to whether many of the 'Wittgenstein's in this text did refer to Wittgenstein. For many purposes, I could then truly be said not to know this. For many of these purposes, it could also truly be said that I did understand the name as I have used it here. Second, the homophonically stated fact may, on occasion, not count as sufficient for understanding the name. Someone may know that in a certain book, at a certain place, the name 'Wittgenstein' occurs, and that it refers there to Wittgenstein. If that is all he knows, then he does not know whether the proper understanding of the name is such that, if Russell wrote the *Tractatus*, it would still refer to Wittgenstein. For many purposes, that ignorance would make no difference. For some purposes, though, it might.

Here we can agree with Leibniz[8] that an individual concept is not equivalent to any set of general ones. We can also agree with the thought that a name, if it expresses a concept at all, must express an individual concept—exactly the concept of being such-and-such individual. Homophony serves these intuitions by identifying the

---

[8] See Leibniz [1686], section 8.

individual the right concept is of, and, to all appearances, doing nothing other than this. Which makes homophony attractive. But to this we have appended two observations. First, which individual concept a name expresses depends—at least—on the way the world happens to be, that is, on the circumstances in which we find ourselves having to take it as expressing one such concept or another. Second, given the world as it is, there are many ways, and not just one, of saying what the right individual concept is. For many purposes, there may still be reason to favour homophony. The point is only that it is not capable of doing what other means, such as statements by means of descriptions, in principle could not do.

The morals of 79, after trial balloons are punctured, are these. First, we need not reject the idea that a name (on a speaking) has a sense; nor the idea that the sense of a name, on occasion, is richly specifiable in terms of sets of general properties. But the price of retaining these ideas is recognizing that what the sense of a name (on a speaking) now counts as being is not what would count as its sense in all possible circumstances. Rather, what counts as the sense of a name (and what correctly specifies it) is liable to vary across occasions for assigning the name a sense—whether by way of specifying the sense it in fact had, as thus spoken, or by way of applyng its sense in recognizing its referent. Second, this variation across occasions is not merely across possible ways for the world to be, each with its own array of candidates for the post of referent—thus, across one actual situation and many counter-factual ones. It is also variation across the occasions we may have for taking the name to have some sense, given the way the world in fact is. Further, on an occasion, such a sense may admit multiple specific-ations.

Third, hence the task for a given occasion for viewing the name as spoken on some other is twofold: not just to provide an array of candidates for the post of referent of that speaking of the name, presented in some given perspective; but also to provide facts to fix what the sense of the name (as so spoken) counts, on that occasion, as being, given the different correct answers to that question that different occasions would provide—thus, not only to fix the choices for referent in which a proper understanding of the name must guide us, but also to fix just what the guidance is which the name or its sense then provides. (What that array of candidate referents is like may be prominent among the facts of the occasion which thus show the name's sense, as it then counts as being.) Correspondingly, the point of a prior understanding of the (spoken) name, as it might be brought to novel occasions, is not just to show (where there is something to be shown) how to choose from among the candidates for referent, as they are there presented, but also likewise to show how the other facts of the novel occasion fix what then counts as the name's sense. Only appropriate occasions, sufficiently up to the two fold task, will yield determinate facts as to the name's sense (determinacy here admitting of degrees). The role in fixing its sense of occasions for viewing a name is substantive.

In so far as a sense for a name is a guide or 'path to', or 'mode of presentation of' its referent, the path or mode it provides, and what it is like to follow that path, or for the referent to be so presented, depends on the occasion for using the path, or for viewing in that mode. That the name *did* count as having such-and-such sense on some other occasion may be one factor with a role in fixing what sense the name does count as having on this on, and so what path or mode it then provides. That the other occasion should thus have provided the best guidance it could as to what sense the name now counts as having may be important for fixing what the name's sense counted, on it, as being. But the sense the name *does* count as having need not coincide in all its features with the sense the name *did* count elsewhere as having.

In brief, all the usual phenomena of S-use sensitivity arise for the notion of sense, if that notion is to have application at all. The moral of 79 being general, the point applies not just to the sense of names, but to sense for any expression or concept. That is the core of family resemblance which remains when the more superficial features made seductive by its application to general concepts like game or number are stripped away.

4. OCCASION SENSITIVITY

One moral of the discussion of non-uniqueness is that a statement of a name's semantics by means of a description admits of more than one conceivable understanding. Suppose we are told, '"Wittgenstein" means the author of the *Tractatus*.' One might understand that so as to exclude the correctness of, for example, '"Wittgenstein" means the author of the *Investigations*.' If that is its proper understanding, then the remark would be incorrect at least for most speakings of 'Wittgenstein', and on many occasions for its making. By non-uniqueness, the semantics of the name is statable equally correctly in any of a variety of ways. And the above two ways are reasonable candidates for correct ones for many speakings of 'Wittgenstein', if any such way might count as correct at all. Then again, a remark like the above need not be understood so as to exclude non-uniqueness. That is

one respect in which there may be a variety of things to be said in such
a remark.

Suppose that each of the above remarks is a correct specification of
semantics for some speaking of 'Wittgenstein'. Now let us ask what
those remarks might say about counter-factual circumstances (ones
that we could have been in). Suppose that it emerged that the author of
the *Tractatus* was not the author of the *Investigations*. Wittgenstein
wrote the *Tractatus*, for example, but the *Investigations* were really
written pseudonymously by Russell.[9] If we regard the above descriptions as dictating who the referent of the name would be in those
circumstances, then they yield inconsistent results. So, so regarded,
both could not be correct statements of the name's semantics.
Moreover, if Wittgenstein and Kripke are right as to the phenomenology of names, then neither description could state the sense of
the name correctly. Conversely, if those two statements of semantics
are correct, then they must not be so to be understood.

Suppose that we found ourselves in the counter-factual circumstances just mentioned. Suppose that we encountered a name, N,
which, in them, had a semantics specifiable with equal correctness in
either of the above ways. Then there could be no fact as to whom N
referred to. In particular, for no individual, V, could it be a fact that N
referred to . . For the correctness of the first specification would give us
good reason to take N to refer to Wittgenstein. But the correctness of
the second would give us equally good reason to take N to refer to
Russell. Names being names, we could not take both things to be so.
And that is as far as evaluation of the name could go.

The second minimal conclusion, then, is that if the above-
mentioned 'Wittgenstein' had, in the counter-factual circumstances, a
semantics specifiable in either of the above ways, then there would be
no one whom it referred to. But that does not mean that we, in those
circumstances, would be constrained to find that the name referred to
no one. Perhaps if we were in such circumstances we would not have
assigned the name a semantics correctly specifiable in either of the
above ways. Perhaps we would have assigned it a semantics specifiable
in other ways. And perhaps we would have been correct in all this. For
in the counter-factual circumstances, the facts which might show one
assignment of semantics or another to be correct, or those which might
make us take one thing or another to be reasonable in these regards, are
different from the facts we in fact face given the way things are. So
perhaps correct solutions to the disambiguation problems we would

---

[9] If it proves a distraction to have Wittgenstein around in these circumstances, we
could have let Russell write the *Tractatus*, and let the *Investigations* be computer
philosophy, or written by a committee.

then face would be different as well. For example, suppose that the name occurred in the context of a close textual exegesis of some part of the *Investigations*. Then taking it to mean the author of the *Tractatus* might require regarding the remark in which it occurred as a radically (and boringly) false one, whereas taking it to mean the author of the *Investigations* might yield an understanding of that remark on which it is interesting, insightful, etc. Which, depending on our purposes, might, though it need not, give us good reason to regard the second, but not the first, specification of the name's semantics as correct. So it could turn out, for example, that in these circumstances the name would count as having a semantics specifiable in one of the above two ways, but not in the other. As a consequence, there might have turned out to be a fact, in those circumstances, as to whom the name referred to—to Russell, say.

The semantics a name counts, under one set of circumstances, as having need not be the semantics it would count as having under others. Or better, what its semantics counts as being under one such set need not be what it would count as being under others. For the facts which might make it reasonable to take the semantics to be one thing or another are liable to vary, and vary significantly across such circumstances. This observation about disambiguation solves a problem as to how the sense of a name might be statable at all. The fact of a name's having the semantics it does cannot entail what is not so about the name, in particular—in so far as there are such facts—what is not so as to whom the name would have referred to under one or another set of counter-factual circumstances. The fact that a name has such-and-such semantics, or that its semantics is such-and-such, where this counts as a fact, cannot entail what the name's having the semantics it does does not, hence also cannot entail what is not so as to whom the name would have referred to if . . . . If S is a correct statement of what the name's semantics is, then S cannot entail such things either. The above discussion provides an account of what facts of the second sort need not entail: (some of) what would have been so had they not obtained. It thereby provides an explanation of how there can be statements of a name's semantics—*inter alia* by means of descriptions—which do not entail such things either.

The fact that a name's semantics is (or now counts as being) such-and-such need not, and in fact cannot by itself, entail all the facts as to what the name's semantics would have been or would be under one set of counter-factual circumstances or another—notably not all the facts as to what its evaluative properties would have been. Minimally, such a fact cannot entail the facts as to what the semantics of the name would have been under conditions which would have shown it not to be a fact. Such depends on what those conditions are, and what reaction would be reasonable in them. Here there is a distinction to be preserved. Suppose it is now a fact that N's semantics is A. Having semantics A might, in some counter-factual circumstances, entail B. B would then be so of any item which, in those circumstances, counted as having semantics A. But the fact that N has semantics A need not entail that B would be so of N in those circumstances. For it might be that in them that would not have been a fact. Now the idea is that the way for S to state N's semantics correctly, on an occasion, is for it to state no more and no less than some fact about N of the above sort. Properly understood, it would then require no more for its truth than what counts as so where that fact counts as obtaining. In particular, it will not be properly understood to dictate who N's referent would be where that fact would not obtain.

We can sometimes recognize, within limits, to whom a name, properly understood, would have referred if such-and-such. We might, on occasion, count the name as having some semantics, A, which entails some of these facts, and demand of a correct specification of the name's semantics that it too entail them. Nothing above shows it wrong to require such things. Of course no such specification can entail all of what would have been so were there facts to show it incorrect. Nor can any semantics we might now correctly ascribe to the name entail all of what would have been so where it would not have been correct to do so. If what the semantics of a name is is an occasion sensitive question, then there is no reason why the semantics a name counts as having on an occasion should not be ascribable to it in mentioning one semantic property or another involving some general property as expressed in some description. The object is to fix the semantics N then counts as having; not the semantics it would have had had it not counted as having that.

Occasion sensitivity suggests a third function for a specification of a name's semantics to perform, in addition to those of stating a condition on a referent, and stating something either sufficient or required for understanding. A statement of a semantics, made under given conditions, might be taken as a guide to what the semantics of the name would count as being under different conditions. The way in which a given statement performs this function might provide a criterion which selects certain such statements rather than others as correct. Not that we might expect a statement of N's semantics which is correct given things as we now take them to be to *entail* what the semantics of the name would count as being were things, or had they been, not as we take them to be. But where we confront such a situation, the fact that S would have stated N's semantics correctly under conditions which were taken to obtain may point to the semantics now to be ascribed to N in this way: we may pose the question what semantics is now most reasonably assigned to N given that S would have assigned semantics correctly under those conditions. Some present statements of N's semantics might provide better guides than others to the answers to such questions across given ranges of such occasions which might conceivably confront us. *If* we accept this as a further criterion on the correctness of a specification of a name's semantics, then we may note that it incorporates the mechanisms, if not the outward manifestations of S-use sensitivity. For the sort of goodness involved here depends in at least two ways on what such a statement would lead us as reasonable judges to do and/or recognize. First, there is the question, for given occasions which might confront us, which answers to those questions it would lead us to regard as reasonable if we did confront those occasions. Second, there is the question which such range of occasions we ought to look at in evaluating a statement's correctness; for what range of eventualities ought we to expect a statements of N's semantics to prepare us? Both of these issues are questions of our (or a reasonable judge's) reactions, which, whether they actually do so or not, are liable to vary across relevant occasions for our having them. This third function for a statement of sense, then, provides one means for developing Wittgenstein's idea that, as things are, he would define the name N differently on different occasions for doing so.

Bracketing this last remark, occasion sensitivity as it has been developed so far differs from full S-use sensitivity, as that notion was developed in chapter 1. S-use sensitivity requires pairs of situations such that we might, in fact, find ourselves on either at some time or other, given suitable (but possible) co-operation from circumstance. We might, for that matter, find ourselves in both situations, though not simultaneously. Each member of the pair would differ from the other in what the correct judgements, hence the truth, would be, in that situation, about the relevant S-use sensitive notion. If the truth in question is that about some aspect of W's semantics, then there is something which that semantics would count as being on the one occasion but not the other; some semantic property that W would count in the one situation but not the other as having. All this in support of the thesis that we should sometimes say one thing and sometimes another (correctly) about the relevant notion—in this case, as to what W's semantics was, the variation taking place across circumstances which could be made to confront us, given world, time and ingenuity enough.

By contrast, the main point about occasion sensitivity has involved variation across occasions at most one of which could be actual, hence at most one of which we could be made to confront. Either Wittgenstein wrote the *Tractatus* or he did not. (For present purposes, we will not consider cases in which 'he sort of did and sort of didn't'.) If he did, then we cannot be put in circumstances in which he did not, and asked to judge, in them, whom some instance of 'Wittgenstein' referred to. The variation is across occasions we are on, or conceivably could have been on. The occasions we are or ever will be on can take at most one value from within that range. So far, then, there is no support for the view that it might sometimes be correct for us to say one thing, and sometimes correct for us to say another as to what the semantics of some name is (though that is a view Wittgenstein expresses in 79). In particular, we have not seen that a name might sometimes count as having one set of evaluative properties, and sometimes another—that it might sometimes truly be said to refer to V, and sometimes to some distinct V*, or to nothing; or even that there might be variation across occasions we could confront in what it is true to say about whom the name would have referred to if . . . . Without this sort of variation we have also failed to capture that semantic indeterminacy which, in chapter 1, was a cornerstone of the alternative picture, and which is so much in evidence as a theme in the family resemblance discussion.

The point so far, then, might be put as one about world involving-ness, rather than as one about full-fledged S-use sensitivity. It might be thought of in this way. If a name was spoken intelligibly, then on an occasion—for example, that of its speaking—one might grasp how it was to be understood, or what reference it was to be understood to make. Here we have endorsed the natural idea that what one thus grasps—the proper understanding of the name—is something which prepares us for any eventuality; something which shows how the reference of the name is to be evaluated in any circumstances in which such evaluation conceivably might need to be done. So a grasp of the proper understanding of a name would be, *inter alia*, a grasp of its sense in the present sense of 'sense'. In other terms, the fact that the name was to be understood as it was shows how it is properly evaluated in any circumstances in which such evaluation might need or have needed to be carried out. But that fact, and, in fact, all the facts as to what would properly have been taken to be so of the name on that occasion (and, if we like, all the facts as to what the speaker or his audience did take to be so, or intend, or expect of the name), is compatible with a variety of distinct and mutually incompatible answers to the question what the proper understanding of the name was or is, and the question what correctly specifies that understanding, or says the name to have it. Which such answers are correct depends, at least in part, on the actual state of the world in which the answers are to be given—notably, the actual candidates for the post of referent, and the facts about them. So grasping the correct answers to such questions, in grasping how the name is to be understood, requires grasping the right facts of the world in which those answers are to be given. It might, for example, require knowing who wrote the *Tractatus*.

Maintaining this 'world-involving' feature of the semantics of a name brings Wittgenstein in line with other philosophers, such as Putnam, Kripke or Leibniz, in their views on the semantics of other parts of speech—in Putnam's case, for example, words expressing concepts of 'natural kinds' or 'physical quantities'. We may, for example, now understand the word 'aluminium' correctly, so know or grasp how it is to be understood. But, on Putnam's view, how it is to be understood, or the semantics it now in fact counts as having—for example, what it requires for a thing to be as it says a thing to be— depends on the relevant physical facts of our world, for example, on the correct theory of the elements. So we might correctly specify the semantics of 'aluminium', at least in part, in terms of facts which atomic theory states, provided that those are the facts. If they were not, then the semantics of 'aluminum' would be specifiable otherwise. Wittgenstein's account of names—and, as he indicates, his account of natural kind terms too—makes their semantic properties, and the correct specifications of these, similarly dependent on the way the world is.

We might lament the fact that we have not yet exhibited true semantic S-use sensitivity for names. We might also now go on to try to do so. But, since names occur in 79 as an illustration of a more general point, it is more important to observe just how close world-involvingness of the sort just described—a sort recognized by Putnam and others—brings us to full S-use sensitivity. Wittgenstein begins with a name (or elsewhere with other words) which he may be presumed to understand. So, on the occasion with which he begins, he may be taken to grasp what the proper understanding of the name is. The problem is then to see how what counts on one occasion as the proper understanding of the name might lead us, under other circumstances, to assign one or another set of specific semantic properties to the name, and how it would lead us to do so if we were doing so correctly, respecting what the proper understanding (or sense) of the name requires in those circumstances. The circumstances in question may be ones we could actually be under, or they may be ones we must consider in thought—ones we could have been under compatible with our having had the understanding of the name we did.

The point of principle is that the assignments we would make in thus assigning semantics correctly vary with these circumstances; under different ones, the fact of the name's having been to be understood as it was (and the fact of its having counted, on the initial occasion, as having the proper understanding it did) will count as requiring different things of assignments of semantics, so that different such assignments will count as correct.

To take a Shavian tone, it now only remains to negotiate the price of this variation: what sorts of variation in circumstance could thus yield variation in correct assignments of semantics? Could this, for example, vary with our purposes in taking a word to have one semantics or another—for example, in taking it to be true or false of V? Or with the consequences of doing so? Or could it, perhaps, vary with variations in the candidate evaluative properties which are in question on occasions we might confront (for names, the candidates for referenthood, for a predicate, the candidate items for it to be true of, etc.)? In the first case, the yield would be true S-use sensitivity. In the second, the yield might be just what we would expect family resemblance to be from Wittgenstein's initial descriptions of it in the case of games and numbers. In either case, the question is one of how that sort of variation might affect our reactions, as reasonable judges, to the facts which might serve as input to relevant disambiguation problems; which *might* make it reasonable to take their solutions to be one thing or another.

Perhaps these sorts of variations cannot be found for names, at least across pairs of occasions both of which we might encounter. But if not for names, then there is still hope for other parts of speech. Names contrast with most predicates, for example, in this: while the success of one candidate for the post of referent of a name excludes that of any other, the success of one candidate for the title 'item of which the predicate is true' does not generally exclude the success of others. The first point makes it intuitively plausible, though not necessarily correct, that what a name requires of an item for it to be the referent cannot vary from item to item among the ones we might actually consider: if one item satisfies its requirement, then all others *must* fail theirs. The parallel point is much less plausible in the case of predicates. Its failure there may make family resemblance there come out looking much more as it is usually supposed to. This Shavian attitude towards the principled point of 79 is also, I think, the proper attitude to take, for example, towards the kind of variation which Putnam has allowed in the semantics a word might count as having.

The function of the sense of a name, on Wittgenstein's conception of it, is attenuated *vis-à-vis* some classical views of the function of such a sense. So attenuated, in fact, that one might wonder why it is worth bothering to speak here of the sense of a name at all. There are two reasons. One is to preserve our intuition that we assign a referent to a name, when we do so correctly, in accordance with what a proper understanding of a name requires, and that when we recognize the facts as to whom a name refers to, we recognize something about what its proper understanding requires. That intuition may be developed in harmful ways. It will do harm if it is matched with the wrong conception of what it is for a proper understanding to require something, or of what it is for a name to have the proper understanding that it does. But when such things are spelled out in the right way, there is no harm in the underlying intuition that there is something to be understood about a name which guides us to its referent, and without which the facts about whom it refers to could not be what they are.

The second reason is that it would be tempting to construe a denial that a name has a sense as pointing to a contrast between names and other parts of speech; names lack a sense in a sense in which predicates or common nouns, for example, have one. The suggestion would be that the functions a sense could not perform for a name are functions which are performed by the sense of these other expressions. One might think, for example, that the sense of a predicate does impose a requirement on its truth of an item such that what it requires of an item in matters of truth is invariant across all occasions on which its truth of some item might need assessing. But it is just such suggestions that Wittgenstein wants to resist. The limitations on what a semantics for a word might do, and on its susceptibility to being spelled out, are meant to be illustrated by the case of names, but intrinsic and general features of having a semantics, for any item that might have one. They show what it is to do so.

In chapter 3, we observed a distinction between (the fact of) a word's meaning what it does, and (the fact that) it means/names such-and-such. What the first fact fixes for the word is, in several senses, more than what the second alone does. Here we have drawn a similar distinction, one between (the fact of) the proper understanding (or the sense) of a name being what it is, on the one hand, and the proper understanding of the name being such-and-such, on the other. That the proper understanding of a name is what it is (or simply its proper understanding) determines what semantic properties it is assigned correctly (*inter alia*, those of referring to so-and-so): on any occasion, it is correctly assigned just those semantic properties which its proper understanding then requires, given as input the (other) facts which that occasion provides, and the circumstances it furnishes for assigning semantic properties. That the proper understanding of a name is such-and-such, on an occasion where that counts as fixing the semantics of the name, also determines just which assignments of semantic properties to it are correct: the properties correctly assigned to the name on that occasion are just those which that fact then counts as requiring. The divergence between the two facts comes in this: if it is now so (or counts as so) that the proper understanding of a name is A, then for all that, there may be occasions (and are conceivable ones) on which what the proper understanding of the name requires is not what would be required by the fact, if it were one, that the proper understanding of the name was A. Such an occasion would then be one on which it would not be a fact that the proper understanding of the name was A; one on which that fact would not count as obtaining. It is because there may be such occasions that the obtaining of such facts is an occasion sensitive matter.

We might better see why this should be so if we ask why we might want to have a proper understanding of a name, or what we might want a proper understanding to do. Understanding a name properly, or grasping how it is to be understood, equips us for assigning semantic properties to the name correctly on occasions we might have for doing so, given the other facts with which we are presented on such occasions (that is, facts other than those we grasped in grasping the way the name was to be understood), and the circumstances they provide for assigning the properties. For example, it equips us, on an occasion, for recognizing whom the name referred to (given sufficient input of the facts of that occasion). Conversely, recognizing correct assignments of semantics across a broad enough spectrum of occasions demonstrates a proper understanding of the name. Which is to say that a proper understanding of the name equips us for solving disambiguation problems for it as these might arise on one conceivable occasion or another. It is how to solve these that we grasp in grasping how the name is to be understood, or equivalently, the fact that it is to be understood as it is. On an occasion, we may grasp how the name is to be understood in grasping given facts about this, so in grasping the fact, on that occasion, that its proper understanding is such-and-such. To think that is just to think that it is possible to say what the name's proper understanding is. But now the divergence between these two sorts of facts comes to this: it is conceivable for an occasion to present us with facts which would make correct solutions to disambiguation problems ones which did not assign that semantics to the name which was mentioned in saying its proper understanding to be such-and-such.

Solving a disambiguation problem for W requires a proper appreciation of the other facts about W on which its semantics depends. It requires seeing what was or was properly taken to be so of W and the use being made of it on the occasion of that use, and properly appreciating what is to be made of those facts in the light of further ones where semantic matters are concerned. To have such an appreciation of what gives W its semantics is to be prepared to recognize the right things—to assign W semantic properties correctly, or to see which semantics properties it would have given such-and-such further facts. Saying what the proper understanding of a name is is saying what, for semantic purposes, a proper appreciation of those facts would be. But what such an appreciation would come to, and what would say what it is, may vary with the facts which such an appreciation must lead one to treat in one way or another. So there is occasion sensitivity in (what says) what such an appreciation would be. Hence in what states the semantics of a name. Hence in what counts as a fact as to what that semantics is.

The present points have a close connection with one set of problems about private language. The differences, for example, between a word's meaning what it does and its meaning such-and-such may suggest a certain picture within which the idea of private language thrives. For they may suggest, first of all, that whenever we state (for example) what the meaning of a word is, no matter what we say we always say less than what the meaning of the words is. Or, if that sounds too close to nonsense, that what we state is always less than the fact that the word means what it does. There is then a temptation to think that there is some fact which we grasp in grasping what the word means, but which we did not state, and could not have stated in saying what it means; which 'for some reason' is inexpressible (cf. 71). From here it is not such a long step to the view that the meanings each of us attaches to words, or at least to some words, are private; each person attaches his own meaning, or at least there is no determining that this is not so.

In discussing family resemblance, Wittgenstein is conspicuously concerned to avoid just such suggestions. He insists repeatedly that when we say, as we sometimes do, what the proper understanding of a word is, what we say is no less than what its proper understanding is. There is nothing that we know about it but have left unexpressed. Nor is there anything which is so about its proper understanding but left undetermined by what we said. If we say that the word means such-and-such, and thereby correctly answer a question as to what it means, then the fact we state, as long as it counts as being a fact, determines just what is determined by the word's meaning what it does. There are conceivable occasions on which the fact we stated about the word would not count as being a fact. The fact we stated does not determine the semantics the word would have on such an occasion. Nor does it by itself determine what facts about the word on such an occasion would determine this. But that is not an indication that there is some other fact which obtained (or counted as obtaining) where we stated what we did, and which does determine such things. Rather, such matters are determined by what the facts of those further occasions make it reasonable for us then to take the proper understanding of the word to be. Such further semantic facts will be what there counts as required by the word's having the proper understanding that it does. But that shows only that there are various things that understanding might count as being, and that what counts as (being) that understanding on one occasion—such as the occasion of our statement—might fail to do so on some other.

The fact of W's proper understanding being what it is is not to be thought of as a fact which may count on some occasions but not on others as obtaining. In contrast, the facts as to what W's semantics is may do just that. We cannot now say truly of W what does not now count as a fact about it, though we may now know how to solve disambiguation problems for W where some such thing would count as a fact. It is a mistake to think that such knowledge consists in grasp of a fact which now counts as obtaining, but which we cannot state.

Wittgenstein combats the idea of our understanding more than we can tell in grasping how a word is to be understood by giving full value to the ideas which lie at its source—in this case, to our different ways of speaking of the fact of a word's meaning what it does, or having the proper understanding it does on the one hand, and various spellings out of that fact on the other. Those differences allowed for, the remainder that he rejects is familiar from other contexts. If we think of what a word means, or its proper understanding (or semantics, or sense) as a mechanism which generates correct assignments of evaluative or other semantic properties to it for all the various inputs of facts to which such assignments may be sensitive, then if we can find no such mechanism in what we state in stating the proper understanding of a name, we may think of the mechanism as of a different sort, residing in that aspect of a proper understanding which cannot be stated or expressed. Similarly, if, with Descartes,[10] we think of our uses of words as generated by a mechanism and can find no material one, then we may be tempted to postulate an immaterial one. Such 'immaterial semantic mechanisms' are part of the conceptual apparatus which makes (and appears required to make) private language plausible. In the semantic case, as in Descartes', the way to resist the temptation is to reject the idea of an underlying mechanism. And the way to do that is

[10] See Descartes [1637], section 5.

to reject the idea of an occasion insensitive semantics for a word which, occasion insensitively, determines all the semantic truths about it. Elsewhere, Wittgenstein says (36):

Where our language suggests a body and there is none; there, we should like to say, is a *spirit*.

Family resemblance is, among other things, an account of what might tempt us to look for a semantic 'body' where there is none, and how to conclude that there is none, rather than postulating one which is 'spiritual' or ineffable.

5. DIRECT REFERENCE

Wittgenstein is not a cluster concept theorist. But his view of names does leave intact the thought that the semantics of a name might be specified correctly, on occasion, by means of descriptions, and that this might be so where the descriptions are properly understood as imposing a condition on being the referent of the name. So some elements of descriptivism remain in his view. Saul Kripke has deployed several arguments against descriptivism, whether strict or of a cluster concept sort. It is worth seeing how these arguments fare against the elements of descriptivism left in the Wittgensteinian view. Moreover, Kripke has proposed his own account of the facts on which the referent of a name depends. It is worth comparing that account with the account which emerges from 79. Kripke's arguments and his account are by now deservedly well known. To set out the arguments, I will draw on a taxonomy suggested by Nathan Salmon.[11] Salmon lists three distinct arguments, which he terms *modal*, *epistemic* and *semantic*.

The model argument begins by pointing to some modal data. Wittgenstein might not have written the *Tractatus*. Or the *Investigations*. And so on for any general property in terms of which one might plausibly state the semantics of an occurrence of 'Wittgenstein' (on which it refers to Wittgenstein). Somehow this fact is supposed to conflict with the idea that the name, on a speaking, or on a use, might be definable in terms of descriptions. It is not at all clear why this should be so. But the most plausible story is probably this. Suppose that I have stated a series of modal facts of the above sort, using the name 'Wittgenstein' to state each one. Suppose that the name, as I used it, is 'backed by' some description, D. That is, D is properly taken to

[11] See Salmon [1982].

impose a requirement on being the referent of the name so used. Suppose that one of the facts I happened to state was that Wittgenstein might not have been D. Then what I said must be false. So what I said to be a fact must not be one. But this contradicts the data with which we began. The suggested conclusion is that my use of 'Wittgenstein' could not be thus backed by D.

Perhaps Kripke had no argument like this in mind. In any event, the argument is totally without force. The reason, in brief, is that what is on offer at present is a theory of *reference*. Nothing has been said so far in this text about the proper evaluation of modal statements. Nor about what is required for a modal fact of the above sort to be a fact. To see this, let us consider the argument as directed against strict descriptivism. Consider a statement, 'Wittgenstein might not have been D', and suppose that 'Wittgenstein' to be backed by D. On strict descriptivism, nothing could be its referent without fitting D, and moreover, in no conceivable circumstances could it turn out that that name referred to someone who did not fit D. The first point tells us who the referent in fact is: Wittgenstein. The second is irrelevant for present purposes. We now know whom was spoken of, and what was said about him: that he might not have been D. Now what is required for a statement which says that about that individual to be true? On that subject, the theory of reference is silent. It says no more about this than it says about what is required for the truth of 'Wittgenstein is blue', given that it spoke of Wittgenstein and said him to be blue. On an implausible account of modal statements, the statement could not have been true unless 'Wittgenstein' in it could have referred to Wittgenstein without him fitting D. On a more plausible account, the statement is true if the person it spoke of—Wittgenstein—might have avoided doing what D says him to have done—writing the *Tractatus*, say. But strict descriptivism advances neither account, though it is compatible with either. From both points above we can deduce that if Wittgenstein had not done what was required for fitting D, then the name as used in the statement could not have referred to him. That conclusion is mistaken on Wittgenstein's account of names. But it still stops far short of saying that Wittgenstein could not but have been D.

The second argument is the epistemic one. The idea here is that if, for example, 'Wittgenstein' is definable in terms of a certain description, say 'the author of the *Tractatus*', then one could not understand that name (or wholes of which it was a part) without knowing that its referent was the author of the *Tractatus*, or, on some versions of the argument, without knowing that Wittgenstein wrote the *Tractatus*. Whereas in fact there is no such fact that we must know to count as

understanding the name correctly. So 'Wittgenstein' cannot be definable in terms of any such description. There are a number of things
wrong with this argument if it is meant to apply to Wittgenstein's
account. Here we will stick to two main points. First, by non-
uniqueness, any 'Wittgenstein' might be definable in a variety of
distinct ways. The most that could reasonably be demanded of an
understander is knowledge of one of these specifications of the name's
semantics, and of the facts which it reflects—for example, that the
referent (if any) fits the descriptions contained in that specification. So,
an understander of the above-described 'Wittgenstein' might not know
that its referent (if there is one) wrote the *Tractatus*, because he might
qualify as an understander by knowing other facts instead.

There is a sense in which this first point does not really speak to the
problem Kripke poses here. For Kripke's interest is largely in cases of
understanders with, as it were, highly defective knowledge. For
example, a non-philosopher, reading some portion of this text, may
count (for many purposes) as understanding it, and the references the
names in it make, even though he knows virtually nothing about
Wittgenstein. (He might justly *suppose* that Wittgenstein is some
philosopher or other.) Such a person would not know the information
incorporated in any adequate specification of the name's semantics (at
least by means of descriptions; I have argued that this may well be so
for homophonic specifications as well). The whole story of Wittgenstein's treatment of such cases, being the whole story of his
understanding of understanding, would be quite complex. It suffices
here to note just one point. The epistemic argument supposes, or
supposes that its targets suppose, a principle something like the
following: if X understands N (properly), then there must be some
specification of N's proper understanding such that X knows that—or
at least knows the information it incorporates. Without some such
principle, the conclusion of the epistemic argument would not follow
from the data. But Wittgenstein clearly rejects any such principle.
What the semanticist might say—what in fact fixes the semantics of
the word—and what an understander must know are two different
matters. Here is the bare beginning of a story which might explain the
rejection. Suppose we take it that someone counts as an understander
of N when he is prepared to solve (enough) disambiguation problems
which might be posed for N. That is, he is prepared to recognize what
assignments of semantic properties to the name (such as that of
referring to V) would be correct given further facts with which he
might be confronted. Then, depending on what sorts of further facts we
allow him to be presented with, or what sorts we require him to react
to correctly, various backgrounds might equip him to qualify as an

understander. If we are liberal enough in how much more someone may be told before he is required to react correctly, then someone with 'defective knowledge' of the kind Kripke has in mind might qualify as an understander. The indications are that we sometimes would (correctly) be so liberal. There is nothing in Wittgenstein's account of names to suggest otherwise.

We come now to the third argument: the semantic one. Consider a statement, 'Wittgenstein is D.' Suppose that D happens to be one of the descriptions which 'back' that 'Wittgenstein'. Then it must be so, according to this argument, that that statement is true, provided that the name refers to anyone at all. It could not be an empirical discovery that that statement was false of someone. Moreover, from (our grasp) of a proper understanding of the statement, we can deduce *a priori* that it must be true if the name has a referent. But, for plausible descriptive backings, such as 'the author of the *Tractatus*' , we can never deduce a priori that such a statement is true. Therefore, a name has no such descriptive backings. This argument does show strict descriptivism to be wrong. It can no doubt be extended to show cluster concept theory wrong as well. But it does not touch Wittgenstein's account. By occasion sensitivity, if D does correctly specify that 'Wittgenstein's semantics, that is consistent with there being conceivable occasions on which it would not do so, and on which the name would refer to someone who did not fit D. So if D specifies the semantics correctly, given things as we take them to be, we cannot deduce from that fact alone that the above statement is true. So we cannot deduce this *a priori* from a current grasp of that statement's or that name's semantics. Unless, of course, part of what we grasp in grasping that semantics is the fact that the name's referent, Wittgenstein, is D (for example, the fact that he is the author of the *Tractatus*). For if we grasp that fact then we may also recognize the fact that we never will be confronted with circumstances which would show D not to specify the name's semantics correctly. But there is no harm here in the thought that the truth of that statement may be deduced from the fact that Wittgenstein is D.

Let us turn now to Kripke's positive account of the reference of proper names. On it, a name, N, refers to an individual, V, only if, or perhaps just in case, there is a causal chain (of an appropriate sort) linking V to the relevant speaking or use of N. On one interpretation of this idea, Wittgenstein says nothing to contradict it, and it may well be right. On this interpretation, causal chains impose a sort of global constraint on solutions to disambiguation problems for a name. The constraint is that, whatever semantics we assign to N on an occasion, if this assignment has the result, for some V, that N refers to V, then there must be an interesting causal relation between V and the relevant speaking of N. The intuitive thought would be something like this. Suppose that Russell wrote the *Tractatus*. That fact could not be interesting or important enough to give us *good* reason to take some instance of 'Wittgenstein' to refer to Russell unless there was some intimate causal relation between Russell's writing the *Tractatus* and that instance of the name having been used as it was. Perhaps so.

A 'causal chain' account *might* also be seen as an alternative to the story told above on which a name refers to what it does in virtue of (something about) the way in which it is to be understood. So interpreted, a causal chain account would hold that the referent of a name does not depend on any other semantic properties it may have, but simply on the actual causal facts, known or unknown, and regardless of what anyone would now take to be so of the name as so used. So far, then, there would be no need to take the name to have any further semantic properties. The obvious task for a causal chain theorist would then be to say precisely what sort of chain there must be between V and N if it is to be the case that N refers to V, and to say this in a way that decides cases, so that we can see that it is just that sort of chain which is present in cases where some N does refer to some V, and absent otherwise. Kripke explicitly and wisely refrains from saying anything about what an adequate causal chain must be like. He thus fails to address the problems with which the present account was concerned. Consider all instances of 'Wittgenstein' which refer to Wittgenstein, for example. Why is it that under certain conditions some of these would have referred to Wittgenstein while others would have referred to Russell? In virtue of what features of a name is the one thing or the other so, and what features distinguish a name for which the one thing is so from one for which the other is? A sense for a name was postulated to answer just these questions. So far, the idea of a causal chain says nothing about them.

Perhaps Kripke holds that there are no such problems; that names never require disambiguating in such respects. In that case, we can only repeat the reasons for thinking that there are. Suppose someone uses 'Wittgenstein' repeatedly—in a single monologue, perhaps—and always so as to refer to Wittgenstein. Sometimes the use is in reminiscing about the times he spent with Wittgenstein in Ireland. Sometimes it is in an exegetical remark about some passage in the *Tractatus*. For each use, the causal chain linking it with Wittgenstein is much the same. It depends on facts of the sort Wittgenstein describes in saying what he took to be so of Mr N. Now suppose it were discovered that Russell wrote the *Tractatus* pseudonymously. Then each use would have causal links both to Wittgenstein and to Russell.

At first sight, each link would appear to be much the same for each use. Yet the fact of Russell's authorship would have different consequences for different uses. On the present account, that is due to differences in the ways different uses were properly understood. Now, of course, in each case the causal link to Wittgenstein would differ from the causal link to Russell. If we compare two of these speakings of the name, we *may* also be able to detect differences between the causal links each bears to Russell, and between those each bears to Wittgenstein. The question is why these differences make a difference, or better, precisely what about them makes the difference. For any given 'Wittgenstein', either the one link or the other must dominate. The present account of names says something about why it would: because of what that 'Wittgenstein' was most reasonably taken to be doing. It is difficult to see how there could be any adequate account of the matter which bypassed reference to this factor. No more than that need be involved in the idea that a name has a sense.

6. NEGATIVE EXISTENTIALS

79 begins with the remark that 'Moses did not exist' may mean any of various things. This is not just part of the Russellian account, but a view Wittgenstein actually endorses. So it is part of his view that, for a given name, N, there are various things to be said in saying 'N did/does not exist'. In cases where N does have a referent, these would be various (false) things to be said in using N to refer to that individual. The question then arises: on Wittgenstein's account, what distinguishes one such thing to be said from another?

Where a name, N, is spoken intelligibly[12], we may suppose that any account of the matter must respect the principle that 'N does not exist' counts as true just in case N counts as lacking a referent. Given that, the Russellian view provides a neat account of the variety in such remarks. N, as it occurs in such remarks, may bear any of various senses, or correct definitions. Each imposes a different condition on being the referent of the name. The conditions under which nothing satisfies one such condition differ from those under which nothing satisfies another. The conditions for the truth of the corresponding remarks vary accordingly. Hence there are various things to be said. On a slightly more involved view, we might take it, plausibly, that N, in a remark, 'N did not exist', typically refers to some other use of N in

---

[12] Suppose that, in the middle of this text, I write the sentence, 'Gwendolyn did not exist'. There is no good reason to take it that I thereby said something true, although there is certainly no one to whom my 'Gwendolyn' referred.

some other remark. Hugo says, 'Dagobert loved *choucroute.*' Odile asks, 'Who was Dagobert' and I reply, 'Dagobert did not exist.' My remark is correct just in case Hugo's 'Dagobert' referred to no one. On this view, 'N did not exist.' is true just in case some indicated range of other uses of N, in what purport to be statements about someone, in fact refer to no one. Since in different remarks N might be thus linked to different such other uses of it, the Russellian view continues to provide a nice account of the variety.

The trouble is that Wittgenstein rejects the Russellian view. So what is his account of the variety? Consider a name N, other words W, and two different remarks (and speakings), NW. Call these remarks A and B respectively. Now consider two remarks, 'N did not exist', where the first is to be understood as referring specifically to A, and the second specifically to B. So that if it should turn out that N, in A, referred to no one, whereas N in B referred to V, then it might be correct to say of the first remark that it 'was not speaking of *that* N', and *mutatis mutandis* for the second remark. Suppose that N has a different sense in A than it does in B. No matter what precisely the proper spelling out of a sense is, this could conceivably lead to the result that N, in A, referred to someone, whereas N, in B, referred to no one. That much of the Russellian account is left intact on Wittgenstein's. In that case, the first negative existential above might well be false while the second is true. So that is one way that there may be variation in what is said in a negative existential. Deleting what he rejects in the Russellian account, Wittgenstein is still left with an account of the variety which follows the general Russellian pattern.

But now consider a single remark, NW, and two different comments, 'N did not exist', each referring specifically to that. Could these differ in what they say, or say to be so? Wittgenstein's account of names leaves room for such a difference. Suppose that each comment was made on a quite different occasion. Each such occasion supplies different conditions under which to assign semantics to the original remark NW. Suppose that the semantics to be assigned correctly on the one occasion is one on which N, in that remark, would refer to no one, whereas the semantics to be assigned on the other is one on which N so used refers to V. The first circumstance is plausibly enough to make the first negative existential true, while the second is equally enough to make the second one false. So this is another conceivable way in which one negative existential might differ from another. The idea here might be put as follows: a negative existential involving the name N is to be understood as referring to some given range of uses of N—in the limit case, to its own use—and counts as true just in case on the occasion of its making it counts as so that there is no individual N refers to. In that sense, the negative existential also contains a reference to the occasion of its making. If that outcome for N is something which may count as so on some occasions but not on others, then some such negative existential may be true while others are false, and there may be S-use sensitivity in questions of what exists and what does not. This would be another—and a more general—way in which what is said in one such comment may differ from what is said in another. It is, I suggest, Wittgenstein's general account of the matter.

The general idea in more concrete terms is something like this: when, for example, all the facts come out as to why the biblical story is the way it is, the ways in which it corresponds to fact and fails to, and so on, the conclusion we might be driven to is that it 'sort of' is correct and 'sort of' is not correct that Moses existed; there are two reasonable views of the matter. If there are, then, on the present view of semantics, there are occasions for taking each of them—that is, for each, occasions on which it would be the right view to take. The above view of negative existentials falls in line behind that thought. If the thought is correct, then it yields true S-use sensitivity in the semantics to be assigned to a name. Which puts substance behind Wittgenstein's thesis, in 79, that he would assign semantics to a name differently on different occasions (which he might have) for doing so.

7. FAMILIES

When we turn from names to predicates or common nouns, the most conspicuous feature of family resemblance is what might be called the *'no common thread'* thesis. On it, there is no set of (other) features running through all cases of what a given predicate or concept applies to—all cases of what would fit the concept, or what would be as the predicate says a thing to be. So if the concept is one of being P, then there are no other features in common to everything we are prepared to count as a case of being P. To take Wittgenstein's example, there are no other features in common to everything we would call a game.

The no common thread thesis may be given a stronger or a weaker interpretation. On the strongest version, 'no set of (other) common features, means just that—there is *no* feature in common to everything we would recognize as a case of P. On a weaker interpretation, the point would be that there is no set of common features which not only are present in all cases of (being) (a) P, but further, which distinguish all such cases from cases of what is not P; which is absent in all cases of the latter sort. That is to say, there is no set of other features which exactly coincides with (being) (a) P. The strong version is both daunting (Could there really be a case of a game which was not even an activity, for example?) and tempting (Must a chair be a physical object? Suppose they develop portable force fields.) Wittgenstein does not unmistakably opt for one of these choices. As we will see in a moment, it is not very important, for present purposes, to do so.

There is a problem in seeing how the discussion so far provides an approach to the no common thread thesis. The problem is that the discussion so far has been what might be called concept-oriented, whereas the thesis now of concern is, as it were, object level. We have discussed the guide that a word, or its proper understanding, or a concept words express, provides to what that word or that concept applies to—what it refers to, in the case of a name, or what it is true of or fits in the case of a predicate or a concept. We have also discussed the sort of requirement imposed in virtue of that guide on being something the word or concept applies to, and how that requirement is imposed. One result, by non-uniqueness, has been that there is no unique correct way of saying what this requirement is in any given case—that is, of saying what condition an item must satisfy to be what the concept applies to. This is no help with the no common thread thesis. For it does not challenge the idea that there is a condition to be satisfied, and that, however you say what it is, you will identify some set of features in common to anything which does satisfy it.

The second main result so far, by occasion sensitivity, has been that there are different things, on different occasions, that the requirement (for fitting a given concept) would count as being: sometimes one condition would count as that which was to be satisfied, and sometimes another. This, too, appears to promise little help with the no common thread thesis. For it does not challenge the idea that, on any given occasion, there is something such a requirement counts as being, and that this can be spelled out, on that occasion, in a way which would require some set of common features in anything which counted as satisfying that requirement.

In fact, occasion sensitivity seems much closer to S-use sensitivity than to the no common thread thesis. Suppose we grant, in the case of a predicate or a concept it expresses, that the requirement it counts as imposing on its application may vary substantively across occasions which we might encounter—different occasions we may have for using that predicate or concept to discuss items. To say that is to say that it would be possible for there to be an item which satisfied the requirement imposed on one such occasion, but not that imposed on some other. Such an item would sometimes count, and sometimes not, as fitting that concept. If the concept is of being P, then it would be sometimes true and sometimes untrue to say that that item was P. This is true S-use sensitivity. By itself, it carries no implications as to common threads (on an occasion).

If we have identified a mechanism which yields a no common thread thesis, then it is interesting to note that S-use sensitivity and no common threads are different manifestations of that mechanism. One might put the common point this way. The mechanism provides for some kind of variation in what a concept requires of an item. If that variation is across occasions of our considering or using that concept, and judging candidate items for it to apply to, then the result is S-use sensitivity. If the variation is across items to which the concept might apply, then the result is a no common thread phenomenon.

Given S-use sensitivity, one might have doubts about the idea of no common threads. For that idea might be read to suggest that, for a given concept C, there is some set of items which just are *tout court* the items C applies to, and that that set has a certain structure; that there are no features in common to those items. Whereas in fact what we would want to say is that different items qualify on different occasions as fitting C. In general, nothing about an item qualifies it as fitting C (or failing to) *tout court*. Nor is there anything (specifiable) about any item which *tout court* is that in virtue of which it fits C (or fails to). Rather, different things are required of an item on different occasions for its fitting C. There are consequently different things to be said on different occasions as to why or in virtue of what it does. On the other hand, on many occasions, we can, if asked, successfully identify a large number of things as chairs, and a large number of other things as not. There are limits to what we can do. There may be things we do not know how to classify, but which could be classified successfully in one way or the other on some occasion or other. Still, this sort of activity, though hardly a typical one, is a possible one. The no common thread thesis may then be taken to apply to what we would correctly count as a chair (or whatever) on an occasion. So it would be wrong to reject the problem posed here.

We must note some modalities which are to be read into the no-common-thread thesis. The point is not that there could not be common features to everything that would count as fitting a concept, or that a concept could not be definable in terms of these. Nor, on Wittgenstein's view, is it that there are concepts for which this could not be so. Wittgenstein's advice here is to look, and not to think. We cannot deduce *a priori* whether a concept fits the no common thread thesis. We must see what is in fact so of what it applies to. When we look, we see that some concepts can be defined in terms of a common thread—the concepts of aluminium or of water, for example. Given

the way things are (and bracketing problems about mixtures, addenda
and so on), nothing could ever count as aluminium unless it was a
certain element with a certain atomic number. This is not to say that it
could not conceivably turn out that something was aluminium but did
not satisfy that condition, or even that there was no common thread to
all things which were aluminium. It is not to say that there is
something about the concept of aluminium which prohibits our
recognizing such a thing correctly, given the right input of other facts.
Still, given the facts as they are, there is something which is essential
and sufficient for being aluminium. The thesis, then, is that a concept
might fit (or might have fit) the thesis. Further, we will suppose, there
is no concept that could not do so, and equally no concept that must.
And if a concept does happen to fit the thesis, there is no harm to the
coherency or determinacy of the concept in that.

Suppose that we think of a concept or a predicate as having a sense,
and of that sense as imposing a requirement on the concept's fitting an
item. Then, if the no common thread thesis holds for the concept on an
occasion, we must think of that sense as requiring different things of
different items if the concept or predicate is to apply to them. If the
concept is of being P, and we say V to be P, then what is required for the
truth of that may differ from what is required for truth if we say some
distinct item V* to be P. We may be helped in seeing how this could be
if we note a sense in which a no common thread thesis does apply to
names given what has been said about them so far. Consider all
conceivable occasions on which we might be required to assign a
referent to a name N, each occasion with its own set of candidate
referents, and its own set of facts about each one of these. Now
consider the range of all successful candidates on some such occasion,
and what is so of each on the occasion of his success. By what has been
said so far, there will be no feature in common to these, or at least no
set of features which, on every such occasion, distinguishes the
successful candidate from all the others. So there are no (relevant)
features in common to all cases of what we would recognize correctly
as satisfying the requirement that the sense of the name imposes.
What makes this so, it has been suggested, are facts about the solving
of disambiguation problems—that is, about what the requirement
imposed by the sense of the name would correctly be taken to be, given
various sets of other facts with which we could conceivably be
confronted. What the requirement would be given some such sets
differs from what it would be given others. That idea may be seen as
the key to the no common thread thesis in general.

Being true of V, saying what is true of V, or being a concept of (being)
something that V is are semantic properties, on the present view of

things. If the problem, for given words or concept W, is whether W has those properties (for a given value of V), then there are two approaches one might take. One might try first, through the solving of other disambiguation problems, to fix all of the rest of W's semantics, or some large subset of it—roughly, that semantics associated specifically with sense rather than reference. One might then try to see what assignment of the above properties must be made to be compatible with the semantics assigned already. Or one might try to solve the disambiguation problem posed by the property of being true of V directly, without explicit reference to the rest of W's semantics. Sometimes, for example, we use what we know about what 'bachelor' means—the fact that it has such-and-such other semantic properties— to solve the problem of whether 'bachelor' counts as true of Hugo. But sometimes part of what we do know already is, say, that 'chair' is true of this and that. In that case, the fact that 'chair' is true of V, for example, may be used to demonstrate that it does not have some other semantic property—saying something to be an item with legs, for example. What drives the no common thread thesis emerges when we approach disambiguation problems for evaluative properties like the above directly.

Suppose that, on an occasion, we consider a concept, C, and an item, V, and pose the question whether C has the property of fitting V. We might then try to assemble reasons in favour of saying that it does, that is, facts which would make it reasonable to reach that conclusion. The first thing to remark is that, if it is a question of what it is reasonable to judge about this, then what these reasons are cannot be an occasion insensitive matter. What would make it reasonable to conclude this must depend on what reasons there are, if any, to suppose that C might fit V, or that it might not—that is, on what (real) doubts there are about this. For example, if C is the concept of a chair, and V is the item I am sitting on, then it may just be certain that C fits V, so that no reason could make this more certain than it already is. In that case, it may be that nothing now counts as a reason for taking C to fit V (though it does). But suppose that is not so. So we do assemble reasons for taking C to fit V. At a certain point, these reasons may just make it overwhelmingly reasonable to take C to fit V, and unreasonable to judge otherwise. We may also suppose that this situation is stable: there are no further facts to be adduced about V or about C which would change what was reasonable in these respects. In that case, given what disambiguation is, C counts as having the property of fitting V. The matter is settled. (If C does now count as fitting V, and if reasons are to the point, then there must be reasons in favour of thinking so which would yield a situation like this.)

At this point, the work of chapters 4 and 5 comes into play. Because of it, among other things, where a situation of the above description is produced, it cannot be required that the reasons in favour of taking C to fit V make it inconceivable that C should not do so. If certain facts about V have been cited in those reasons, or certain of V's properties mentioned, it cannot be expected that there could be no conceivable item for which those facts held, or which had those properties, but which C did not fit. If the properties mentioned were P, then perhaps there are conceivable items with P but which C does not fit. The question is whether V might (or could) be one of those items. If there is no reasonable doubt as to C's fitting V, so that it has been demonstrated that C does so, then there is no reason with any force in favour of classifying V among such items. There is no real doubt about it. Whatever conceivable doubts there may be as to C's fitting V, and whatever the other facts about V may be, the above situation establishes that C does count as fitting V. No more is required (on this occasion) than what has already been mentioned in order for this to be so.

Let us now pose the same problem for a new item, V*. Again, we may assemble reasons in favour of taking C to fit V*. Now suppose there is some fact about V, mentioned above, which does not hold for V*. Must this show that the reasons in favour of taking C to fit V* are not conclusive—that they leave over some reasonable doubt about this? If the fact is that V is Q, then we may suppose that there are some (conceivable) items which are not Q which C would not fit. The question is whether there is any reason with force in favour of classifying V* among such items, or thinking that it might be reasonable to do so. The point to be made here is that there is no *a priori* bar to thinking that there is none. Since Q was mentioned as a reason in the case of V, and since it did provide reason for taking C to fit V, we may suppose that without Q there would have been some real doubt as to whether C fit V (a real doubt perhaps to be settled in other ways). It does not follow that the absence of Q yields any real doubts as to the status of V*. In some cases, we need reasons for thinking that the pig in the sty really is one. In others, we neither need nor could have any.

If, despite the absence of Q, the reasons in favour of taking C to fit V* make it more reasonable to do so than not to (and there is no fact to be adduced which would change this situation), then C counts as fitting V*. Q could not then form part of a common thread. If there are enough properties of V to which some item stands as V* stands to Q, then there will be no common thread. Whether this will be so in the strong or the weak sense of the no common thread thesis depends on just how many such properties there are. The point of present considerations is simply that there is no *a priori* way of deciding such matters. The upshot is that if we do think of a concept as imposing a requirement for fit on objects in general, then we must be prepared to relativize what that requirement counts as being to different ranges of objects for which application of that requirement may be considered.

There is a conception of knowledge and proof on which, no matter what might actually be in doubt or to be doubted on an occasion, there is some set of facts about V such that, had any of them not obtained, there would always have been a real doubt as to C's fitting V. What we doubt, or ought to doubt, about the pig varies from occasion to occasion. What varies, on this conception, is merely whether a conceivable doubt about the pig shows it incorrect to ascribe knowledge of the pig to someone. But the conceivable doubts remain fixed. There is a fixed set of facts about the pig such that the failure of any of them to obtain would always demonstrate that there were doubts one ought to have about the thing being a pig. If something like this held for V and C's fitting it, then there would be something in the idea that there must be a common thread running through all cases of what C fit. But it is just that conception of epistemology that has been under challenge in chapter 5. It is in this way that Wittgenstein's idea of hinges and his conception of proof form a preliminary to the idea of family resemblance in its general form.

Family resemblance, on Wittgenstein's description of it, exhibits two crucial features. The first of these might be called anti-Socratic, and the second anti-Fregean. The anti-Socratic idea runs against the thought that a concept, if it is coherent, ought to be definable in other terms; that there should be a specifiable and non-trivial necessary and sufficient condition for fitting it. Family resemblance denies that thought in two main ways. First, it denies the idea that any such thing could be so occasion-insensitively. For any such definition, there are always counter-examples in the sense that there are always conceivable circumstances under which something would fit the concept and not satisfy the definition, and vice versa. On the Wittgensteinian view, this point shows something about the possible functions of counter-examples as criteria of correctness for such 'Socratic' definitions. For some such conceivable circumstances are also ones in which the concept would not have been definable as it now in fact is. Hence some such 'counter-examples' would not show some 'Socratic' definitions to be wrong. In opposing the idea of necessary and sufficient conditions, it is important not to deny what we certainly can do, as in our scientific definitions of aluminium or water, just as it is important not to think that such definitions accomplish more than they do. Second, family resemblance denies the thought that a 'Socratic' definition must be possible given things as they are. How a concept may be defined is, if you like, a partly empirical matter. Here Wittgenstein points to one more area not ripe for philosophical theses.

The anti-Fregean feature runs counter to the thought that the semantics a concept or expression now counts as having fixes all the semantic facts, and all the semantic truths there could be to tell about it. The general idea is that the semantics an item now counts as having, though it forms one input into disambiguation problems for the item to be performed on other occasions, does not by itself determine what the outcomes for such problems will be. S-use sensitivity is one way of making the point. The object level no-common-thread thesis provides another powerful one. Consider all the items C now counts as fitting, in so far as these count as being facts of such matters, and what C requires of each of these for it to qualify for that role. All those facts are compatible both with there being a novel item which satisfied any or all of those requirements and which C fit, and with there being a novel item which did that but which C did not fit. Novel items pose novel disambiguation problems whose solutions are not dictated by solutions to similar problems for items already encountered. It takes the item to show what C requires of it, as well as particular circumstances for considering that question. That this anti-Fregean feature is at the core of the family resemblance discussion shows family resemblance to be one main expression of Wittgenstein's commitment to the picture of semantics, and of having semantics, described in chapter 1.

7

The Autonomy of Fact-Stating

The account of chapter 2 proceeded on the supposition that there are semantic facts—for example, facts as to what was said in various speakings of English (such as these). The model discussed what, on that supposition, those facts would most reasonably be taken to be; hence, on the model, what they would count as being (when). But what of the supposition itself? That is the topic of this chapter. More generally, the chapter will discuss what it is for discourse to be fact-stating, hence for there to be facts of a sort that a given sort of discourse states, or at least purports or appears to state.

On that topic, Wittgenstein has a striking thesis. That thesis might be viewed as containing an anti-anti-realist moral—for some conceptions of anti-realism. Since the private language discussion, to be treated in the next chapter, may fairly be viewed as containing some sort of anti-realist moral (one already hinted at in chapter 2), the present thesis may be important for putting that anti-realist moral in proper perspective.

Wittgenstein's thesis concerns a range of problems. The following will serve as illustration. Compare:

1. Odile is wearing a brown suit.

2. Oysters are delicious.

An intuitive view would spot a contrast. Words 1 state a fact, or purport to; there is something which they say to be a fact (or so). And their correctness depends on that thing's being a fact. Whereas none of this is true of 2. It is not a fact that oysters are delicious; nor is it a fact that they are not. Some people like them and some do not. Beyond that, there is no fact of the matter. So there is nothing (which might be a fact) which 2 says to be a fact. But then nor would 2 (on a typical speaking) purport to state a fact. Someone who liked oysters might speak 2 and thereby speak correctly; the correctness of what he said would in no way depend on its being a fact that oysters are delicious. To sum all this up, we might say that 1 is fact-stating, whereas 2 is not. Much the same contrast might be made in terms of truth. Words 1, on a typical speaking, are at least eligible for being either true or false, and, *ceteris paribus*, will be one or the other. Whereas words 2, on a typical speaking, are not so eligible. There are no circumstances in which they would be either the one or the other. So, as terminology will be deployed here, we might say that 1 (typically spoken) is a truth-bearer whereas 2 is not.[1]

Such is an intuitive enough view. But what is required for it to be a correct one? If 1 is a truth-bearer, what features decide that it is—mark it as one, or show it to be one? Similarly, if 2 is not, what features mark it as without that status? In general, how is a classification of items into truth-bearers and non-truthbearers to be done? Under what conditions is such a classification of any given item correct? This is the problem to which Wittgenstein's present thesis is addressed.

1. TRUTHBEARERS

The contrast just illustrated by 1 and 2 could almost have been made in the following terms: 1 says to be so what either is a fact or is not one; whereas 2 does not do this. (In fact, 2 does not say anything to be so— on the intuitive view; but it is not so of what it says that it either is a fact (or so) or is not.) Or, equivalently, 1 but not 2 says what is either true or false. That would almost have been to draw the same distinction, but not quite. For even in the best of cases—a case of a truth-bearer with the best possible initial pedigree—things may go wrong, so that that item is neither true nor false, and what it states neither so nor not so. Or at least such is a possibility on the present view of semantics. Not all would agree that such things may happen to well-behaved central cases of truth-bearers. As will emerge soon, what is to be said here about truth-bearers ought not to be vitiated by that possible difference of opinion. Still, for present purposes, these are lines along which we will want to sharpen the notion of a truth-bearer.

Consider a favourable case. Hugo says, perhaps in admiration of Odile's maintenance of form,

3. Odile weighs 50 kilos.

---

[1]   Someone might want to drive a wedge between being fact-stating and being a truth-bearer. I can find no cases where it would be correct to say that it was true that W without its also being correct to say that it was a fact that W. So, for present purposes, I will use these notions more or less interchangeably. For convenience, I will most often speak of truth-bearers, and what is required for being one. But it is to be supposed throughout that where W is a truth-bearer, there are facts of a sort which W states (or purports to), so that the requirements for being a truth-bearer are also, in substance, those for there being facts of some corresponding sort.

If that is not fact-stating discourse, it is difficult to see what would be. Still, things might go wrong. Suppose we take enough interest in his remark to make a serious attempt at confirming or disconfirming it. Then we might discover that there is something quite remarkable about Odile. For example, though she always looks about the same, she produces wildly varying results when put on scales, and for no apparent reason. The upshot is—suppose—that *when all the facts are in*, there is exactly as good reason to count Hugo's words as true as there is to count them as false; nothing is hidden, but nothing dictates that the one judgement rather than the other is the one to be made. So it is not a fact that Odile weighs 50 kilos, and it is not a fact that she does not weigh 50 kilos; Hugo's words are neither true nor false. If that were to happen, still, in the sense of the present discussion, his words would be fact-stating, and remain a truth-bearer. The world turned out to be unexpectedly unfavourable for evaluating them. But it is not what happens when things are that unfavourable that is meant to show whether an item is a truth-bearer.

The kind of situation envisioned here is most forcefully illustrated, perhaps, by such things as contingent liar paradoxes. Complaining about student evaluations, I say, 'What my students say about me is always false.' This is unlikely to be true. But its credentials as a truth-bearer are good enough. Still, suppose that one of my students, loitering in my doorway, overhears my remark, and, misunderstanding it, pops his head in the office and says, 'What Travis just said is true.' The result is that my original words are unevaluable as to truth. We have strong reasons for thinking that it could not be correct to maintain that they were true; but nor that they were false. Still, things might have been otherwise. Were my students perverse enough (but not this perverse), then my words might even have been true. The point is that the kind of situation illustrated here could, in principle, arise for absolutely any potentially truth-bearing words whatever.

Words 1 or 3, or any item, for that matter, are liable to lack a truth value given enough lack of co-operation from the world. The rest of their semantics, no matter what it might be, is not enough to guarantee otherwise. Or such is the present view. In any case, the important point is this. Words 1 or 3 have an appropriate sort of (other) semantics for having a truth value. Given the rest of their semantics, it is proper to evaluate them as to truth; that is a sort of evaluation to which they are to be, or may be, subject. Moreover, world willing, such an evaluation would have as a result either that they were true, or that they were false. There is no difficulty in conceiving of circumstances under which they would have the one or the other property, while having the other semantics that they now have. (Similarly, it is correct, for each, to say that there is something it said to be so, or a fact, and, world willing, that thing will either count as being so—or a fact—or as not being so.) Any words might come to have, for example, the property of being true, through changing the rest of their semantics enough. But the point about words 1 or 3 is that their present semantics is compatible with their having such a property. Not only is it compatible with that; their present (other) semantics makes it reasonable to expect them to have either that property or the property of being false. If they do not, then something has gone wrong; there is something defective about them. Whereas, on the intuitive view, 2 may fail to have either of those properties without anything having gone wrong. Such need not reveal some sort of lack of expected co-operation from the world. We might also say this: 1 and 3, given their current semantics, do have some truth-involving properties, even if not the simple properties of being true or false. For each, there are some situations or items, V, such that it has the property of being true, or what would be true of, V. Again, none of this is so of 2 if the intuitive view is right. There is no need to aim for more precision here than circumstances warrant or require. But we may say that these features of 1 and 3 are what characterize them as truth-bearers, and that it is these features which generally characterize what that notion applies to.

It might be useful to distinguish at least the following four ways that words might lack a truth value (though there will not always be sharp distinctions between the one sort of case and the other.) Consider the following two cases (adapted from Wittgenstein):

4. She milked me sugar. (498)
5. After he had said that, he left her as he did the day before. (525)

Words 4 are not either true or false, for they do not even make sense.[2] It is not as if, like 2, they might be something else instead of true—say, an accurate expression of the speaker's likes, or simply, sincere. Words 5 are a good English sentence, and, to that extent, do make sense. But they require appropriate circumstances for expressing a definite thought. And we are supposing here that such circumstances are missing. (Imagine those words to occur in the middle of this paragraph, but not as an example.) In appropriate circumstances, they might well have said something either true or false; they are the right sorts of words for that. Again, 5 contrasts with 2. For 5, as it were, part of the

---

[2] As Paul Ziff pointed out long ago, it is difficult to find an example of English words which are truly and completely senseless *tout court*. Having written down this example, I, at least, can already begin to think of sensible interpretations for it. But then, of course, surroundings are missing. So it would merge with 5.

semantics it would need to have in order to express a thought is missing. The situation is this. There is a variety of semantics that 5 might have, with some of which it would say something true, and with others of which it would say something false. We must rely on circumstances to choose between these semantics. But, in the above case, circumstances do not do that choosing. So there are not enough other facts about the semantics of 5 for it to be either true or false. The variety of semantics to be chosen from are all semantics compatible with all the semantics 5 does in fact count as having; so that semantics is compatible both with 5 being true and with it being false. In the case of 2, there is, or appears to be, no further semantics for it to have, compatible with the semantics it does in fact have, on which it would be either true or false. It is not as if choosing needed to be done between a variety of possible further semantics, on some of which 2 would be true, and on others of which it would be false. For it is not compatible with 2's present semantics that it should have any semantics on which it was either true or false.

In the same way, 5 contrasts with 3, at least taken as illustrating the phenomenon it was meant to. Here again, there are no choices between further semantics for 3 to have, on some of which it would be true, while on others it would be false. The facts as they are settle all that we could want to know about 3's semantics; it just turns out that an item with that semantics is neither true nor false. As it turned out, the reasons in favour of 3's truth and those against it neatly balance. There are possible semantics, of course, on which some of the reasons on one side would weigh more heavily than any of those on the other. On some possible semantics, certain weighings and not others count, for example. But those are not possible further semantics compatible with the semantics 3 in fact has. For it is part of that semantics that none of those reasons do count more heavily than any of the others with respect to that which, on that semantics, 3 is to be understood to have said.

Words 2, 3, 4 and 5, then, illustrate four different ways of lacking a truth value. Wittgenstein's thesis concerns the ways illustrated by 2 and 3. Words 2 have all the semantics we could wish for them; but that semantics is incompatible with their being either true or false (given the intuitive view). So they are not a truth-bearer. Words 3 also have all the semantics we could wish, among which some truth-involving properties (since there are some situations of which they would be true, and others of which they would be false.) And the semantics they have makes them properly evaluable as to truth. So they are a truth-bearer. As it happens, though, evaluation leads nowhere; they are not correctly judged true, or false. The point is that Wittgenstein's thesis applies equally well to both these cases. That is why someone who does not follow the present view in allowing for truth-bearers without truth values may still, in good conscience, read on.

It may help further to sharpen the notion of a truth-bearer if we consider one more case. I said above that 2, on a typical speaking, would not, intuitively, say anything possibly either true or false. But there are always atypical speakings. Consider Pia, the gastronomic realist. According to her, what is delicious and what not is not all a matter of taste; there really are facts of the matter—a view which she is in the process of making abundantly clear. In the course of doing this, she illustrates her point by saying 2. Clearly she does not mean merely to say what her taste is in the matter; nor, I think, is that the full account of what she did say. If you share what I have called the intuitive view, then you will agree with me that what Pia said in her speaking of 2 is wrong. It would not be stretching a point too much, I think, to say that what she said was false. Such would not be a clearly mistaken description of it. If we do speak that way, then in virtue of what are the words false? One thing required for the words to be correct is that there be some 'fact' which they count as having said to be a fact— that is, something which at least might count as so (or not so); something which could at least be judged or taken to be so in judging or taking something to be so, and which counts as what those words said to be so. Such would also be one requirement for the words being true, if they could be. And it was to be understood of them (and part of their proper understanding) that they were properly taken to be saying what was either true or false. That is a semantic feature they were to be understood to purport to have. Which explains why there is this requirement on their correctness. But that requirement is not met. That, if anything, makes it correct to count the words as false.

Let us now ask what was said in Pia's words. One view would be that this was (roughly) that oysters are delicious, and that that is a fact (and not just her taste). On that view of what was said, the second conjunct, at least, is straightforwardly fact-stating discourse; false fact stating discourse, at that. On those grounds, we might count the whole as fact-stating, and a truth-bearer, though one containing non-fact-stating elements. This may be a tendentious view of saying; but on it, the case poses no special problems for the notion of being a truth-bearer. But one might also take the view that what was said in Pia's words was simply that oysters are delicious. True, the words were to be taken to be fact-stating, and in such a way that their actually being so is part of what is required for their correctness. But it was not strictly speaking said in them that they were fact-stating. They spoke of oysters, and not of themselves, or of what they said. For the sake of the exposition, let us adopt this view of what was said.

Non-controversially, Pia's words were to be understood to be fact-stating. But on this last view of what they said, they were not in fact fact-stating. There is nothing which might have been so or been not so which qualifies as what was said to be so in saying what was said in Pia's words. No state of affairs which might obtain or might not counts as what was said to obtain in those words. Pia's words, we decided, were false, or at least might, properly be said to be. We could decide to use the term 'truth-bearer' in such a way that that alone is enough to make them a truth-bearer. But I have promised to make that term follow along with 'fact-stating'. And, on this view of what was said in them, Pia's words were not fact-stating, even if they purported to be, and were to be understood to have the feature of being properly taken to be. I will stipulate, then, that on this view of what was said in them, Pia's words were not a truth-bearer, even though it was part of their proper understanding that they were to be taken to be one, and that the term 'truthbearer' is so to be used that the considerations just mentioned are always enough to show an item not to be a truth-bearer.

On this restricted use of the term, Pia's case points to the following moral. By making it plain enough what one means to say, one can always get one's (declarative) words to purport to be fact-stating (and to be a truth-bearer.) They would then have the semantic property of being to be understood as to be taken to be a truth-bearer (or the property that it was to be understood of them that they were so to be taken); part of what there was to be understood about them was that they gave themselves as so to be taken. But being so to be understood is not enough actually to get words to be fact-stating or a truth-bearer. So, too, one cannot get one's words to be fact-stating merely by making it plain enough that that is what one means them to be. For them to be fact-stating, we must be able to identify something they say such that there is something which is said to be so in saying that; something which we could take to be what was so, or what was not. That Wittgenstein's thesis applies intact to truth-bearers, on this understanding of what being one involves, will help show, when the thesis is stated, just how radical a thesis it is.

2. THE THESIS

Wittgenstein states his thesis on truth-bearers in 136. The main part of the thesis reads as follows:

Now it looks as if the explanation—a *Satz* is that which can be true or false—determined which things were *Sätze* by saying: what fits the concept true, or, what the concept true fits is a *Satz*. So it is as if we had a concept of true and false with whose help we could then determine what was a *Satz* and what was not. What *meshes* with the concept of truth (like a cog-wheel) is a *Satz*.

But that is a bad picture. It is as if one were to say, 'The king in chess is *the* piece that one can check.' But that can only mean that in our game of chess we only check the king. In the same way, the statement that only a *Satz* can be true can only mean that we only predicate 'true' and 'false' of what we call a *Satz*. And which things are *Sätze* is determined in *one* sense by the rules of sentence construction (of German, for example), and in another sense by the use of the sign in the language game.[3] And the use of the words 'true' and 'false' may be an ingredient in this game; and then for us it is *a feature of* the *Satz*, but it does not *'fit' it. As we might also say that check is attached* to our concept of the king in chess (as it were, as an ingredient of it).[4]

We may distinguish three main ideas in this passage. *First*: the concept of being true (and that of being false), or, as we might also say, the concept of stating a fact (what is so, or what is not so) do not impose any determinate requirement on being a truth-bearer, such that an item qualifies as being one, in virtue of its other features, by satisfying that requirement. There is no requirement specifiable in terms of other features of semantic items which effects the classification of these items into truth-bearers and items of other sorts. Conversely, no other properties of a semantic item—semantic or otherwise—in themselves require that it be a truth-bearer, or that it not be one. (Plausibility here requires some sharpening of the notion of 'other properties'; that will be discussed in the next section.)

Note that Wittgenstein characterizes the opposite of this—the picture on which there is such a requirement, and a fact as to which items, in virtue of their other properties, satisfy it—a 'bad' picture, and not a false one. This suggests that there is an important sense in which it is mistaken to think in these terms; but there may also be some sense in which it is harmless to do so. The differences here between badness and falsity will be explored in the next two sections.

Second: Being a truthbearer is a *semantic* property of an item. That is, it is an element in an item's semantics that it is to be regarded as a truth-bearer (or that it is not). Putting the point in terms of language

---

[3] Recall that Wittgenstein has said he would sometimes use the expression 'the language game' to refer to 'the whole, consisting of language and the actions into which it is woven' (7). That use fits here. But it would also do to read 'the language game' as whatever game a candidate *Satz* counts as a part of.

[4] I have changed Anscombe's translation in ways which I hope allow the ideas to come through more clearly. Of course, if you think that my reading of this passage is totally off target, then you might view these changes as obscuring the point rather than as an improved rendering.

I have let the word *Satz* stand untranslated to remind us of its special use in the *Investigations*. For 'is a feature of' one might substitute 'is attached to'. That might be regarded, reasonably, as more literal.

games, that an item is a truth-bearer is (partly) constitutive of its role in the game; it is part of what there is for the rules of a game to specify in one way or the other. It is part of what there is to be specified—what is open for specifying—as a fundamental or identifying fact about the rules of the game; that is (recalling that language games are abstract items which we construct), part of what is open to stipulation in setting up what the standards of correctness in the game are to be. Given the status of this feature in the game as such, and given the way in which the idea of a language game is to be applied in describing various doings or sayings as the playing of one language game or another, the property of being a truth-bearer qualifies as part of the semantics of items which have it.

Note the difference between what we say in saying that being a truth-bearer is a semantic property and what we said in describing Pia's case, in the last section. If an item is a truthbearer, on the present account, then that is what it *is* on its proper understanding. Since its being so is a semantic matter, we may say that it is properly understood (or regarded) as a truth-bearer, and properly understood to be one. That it is a truth-bearer is part of its proper understanding; part of what there is to be understood about it. Such is what Pia wanted to be so of the semantics of her words. But, on the above view of them, it is what she failed to achieve for them. What she did achieve is something rather different. It was part of the proper understanding of her words that they were to be taken to be a truth-bearer; but not part of that understanding that that is what they were. That is what they were supposed to be; and that they were supposed to be that is part of what there was to be understood about them. But it is an important general rule in semantics that an item can be supposed to have some given status without actually achieving it. The importance of the distinction here should not be obscured by the fact that it is a subtle one; nor by the fact that in practice one side of it may sometimes tend to slide over into the other. In sum, for something to be a truth-bearer is for it to have a certain semantic property. But that is not some other property in virtue of which it qualifies itself as a truthbearer; it simply is the property of being one.

Third: The (semantic) property of being a truth-bearer is autonomous. That is to say, no other semantic properties that an item may have strictly speaking require that it also have that one; nor, strictly speaking, do they forbid its doing so. It is an independent property, which an item either is to be understood to have, or is not, full stop. We might think of it this way. Suppose we took some range of semantics for items to have, some of which contain the property of being a truth-bearer, and some of which do not. We strip away the property of being a truth-bearer from all the sets which contained it. Then there would be no way of reading off from the result which items did, or must have, that property, and which items did or could not. Not merely that we could not tell; no remaining facts about the way those semantics are require that one answer or another to this question be correct. This, of course, merely restates part of the first point. Again, it will be subject to some minor qualification in the next section. But its unqualified form conveys the right idea.

Leaving the term *'Satz'* untranslated in Wittgenstein's statement of the thesis serves to remind us that, given his general view of semantic phenomena, he is not, and would not be, making a point which is 'merely about words'. We might recognize other items—perhaps (some of) what is said, or thoughts—as truth-bearers. A thought, for example, may be of something's being so, or (of) what might be. If we do think in any such way, then Wittgenstein's thesis applies equally to sorting among items of these sorts, picking out those candidates which qualify as truth-bearers and those which do not. Reminding ourselves of this point allows us to see the difference between the point Wittgenstein is making and a somewhat similar, but more innocuous, one that might be made in terms of a Fregean distinction between sense and force.

The Fregean point is fundamentally about words. The idea would be, in that arena, that anyway we *can* count thoughts in a way which makes it correct to say that in expressing one thought we might also express any of a variety of attitudes towards it. If the thought, for example, is of its now snowing, then that thought may be expressed in saying or claiming that it is, in asking whether it is, in wishing that it were (or were not), or in demanding that you see to it that it is, etc. (There may be a parallel point to be made here about propositional attitudes: about the various attitudes we may take towards some one given thought while 'entertaining' it.) But for Frege, words are true, anyway, only in a derivative sense: words are true when they express a true thought. Thoughts are the fundamental truth-bearers. And the thought that it's snowing remains a truthbearer (and, for that matter, true or false as the case may be) regardless of the attitude expressed towards it in expressing it. In fact, for Frege, thoughts certainly have this much of their semantics intrinsically and essentially. Whether a *thought* is true cannot depend on which of various forces it bears. If the notion of force were to have any application here at all (which it does not), then there could not be more than one force that any given thought could have.

Speaking in this Fregean vein, we would have to say that Wittgenstein's thesis is precisely concerned with the right way of sorting between thoughts, distinguishing those thoughts which might be either true or false, or represent what might be so (as being so), from those thoughts without this status. Or, if, for Frege, thoughts are truth-bearers by definition, then distinguishing genuine thoughts from other candidates which might masquerade as ones. The main thrust of the thesis is not in the arena of distinguishing, say, statements from orders or promises. It rather concerns distinguishing that which genuinely says (rightly or wrongly) how things are, so that there is at least some way for things to be which is the way it represents them, from that which, though it may at first appear to do so, really specifies no way for things to be, so that it could not be a factual issue whether things were that way.

Wittgenstein's thesis, viewed in this light, has obvious philosophical significance. For it is a natural enough idea that certain items just do say the right sort of thing for being either true or false, whereas other items do not, so that there are sorts of things to be said which are just the right sort to 'mesh' with the notion of truth, while there are other sorts which are not. It is also a natural step from that idea to the idea that there are requirements on being a thing of the right sort, where these at least sometimes effectively pick out what is the right sort of (expressible) thing for truth-bearing, and what is not. Given that idea, one might even think to be able to specify some such requirements. So, for example, philosophers have tried to link being a truth-bearer with requirements on ways in which an item, if a truth-bearer, would have to be open to confirmation, or verification, and to disconfirmation—for example, some requirement that such an item would have to have truth conditions specifiable in 'experiential' terms (whatever that might be taken to mean). With the idea of some such requirement in mind, some philosophers have then thought they discerned, for example, that statements as to what caused what, or statements about what could, must or might have been, or about ways in which an item could not have been different, or conditional statements (where not truth-functional), or, pertinently for present purposes, statements as to the semantics words have or had on a speaking, could not be genuine truth-bearers; they could not be saying to be so what, as a matter of fact, either was so or was not.

Wittgenstein's thesis is opposed to all such lines of thought. It is a natural idea that some things to be said are just the right sort to be either true or false while others are not. Natural, but incorrect. Or at least, on Wittgenstein's thesis, there is something seriously wrong with it. The idea that there might be a requirement, much less a specifiable requirement, for being a 'thing of the right sort' fares, on this thesis, even worse. With the incorrectness of that idea goes a whole methodology. One cannot, on Wittgenstein's view, hope to *demonstrate* that such-and-such is not fact-stating by demonstrating that there is (or simply producing) such-and-such a requirement on an item's having truth-bearing status (or on that status attaching to what we might say) and that the relevant items fail this requirement. There can be, on his view, no such demonstration. For, first, to understand an item as, or to be a truth-bearer is, on the view, to do just that, and not to understand it in some other way where being to be understood in that way entails being a truth-bearer—there are no such ways. And second, if we do so understand and treat an item, then—subject to one qualification to come two sections hence—that is the end of the matter. So, for example, if it comes naturally to us to take causal, conditional or modal statements as fact-stating, if that is the semantics we naturally assign them, then, no matter what other semantics they may count as having, and subject to the qualification to come, that is what they are. There can be no further issue to settle on this score. Unless, of course, the same sorts of homely considerations that might show that we had misunderstood some speaking of 'Mary had a little lamb' would show that, precisely in this respect and no other, we had misunderstood what was being said, assigning it a possible semantics, but, by chance, not the one it happened to have.

It is now clear that the thesis has an anti-anti-realist import, for at least some species of anti-realism. For some anti-realists do hope to be able to discern some definite and at least sometimes effective requirements which somehow limit the range of facts, or possible facts that we could state, and do so in a way so as to rule out of the domain of fact-stating discourse at least some items which some other philosopher might have thought to belong within it. Wittgenstein certainly endorsed the idea that it is possible for syntax to outrun semantics, so that there might be words which looked as though they stated a fact, or expressed a thought that might be so, but did not do so. But we will have to look for the import of that idea elsewhere. For him, the project of identifying requirements that fact-stating discourse might have to meet, where these might succeed in disqualifying, perhaps to our surprise, what we had always taken to be such, is definitely not on.

In one sense, it is clear that Wittgenstein must take the position he does in 136, given the model of semantic fact set out in chapter 2, and given that he reckons being a truth-bearer as among semantic properties. For, so reckoned, the model applies to it. One feature of that model was that, on it, no non-semantic properties of an item can entail that it has any given semantic property—so, *inter alia*, that of being a truth-bearer—apart, that is, from our natural reactions to them. In the present case, there is nothing unintuitive about that idea. It is not, for example, the sound of 'Mary had a little lamb' that makes us classify it as among truth-bearers. But it is also a feature of the model that, in exactly the same sense in which non-semantic properties of an item

cannot *entail* that it has any given semantic one, so too no given
semantic properties can, strictly speaking, entail the presence of any
further one—again, independent of our reactions to them. In that
sense, other semantic properties which an item might have—say, the
property of saying something of such-and-such sort—could not entail
either that it has or that it lacks the property of being a truth-bearer. In
that sense, being a truth-bearer is autonomous. Seeing Wittgenstein's
thesis here as a special application of the model helps, I think, to place
it in proper perspective.

On the other hand, part of what was built into the model was that
there are semantic facts. What the model described was how to
determine what the semantic facts are, given that there are some. But
it is just that supposition that is in question when it comes to
discussing the present thesis at all. For we are now interested, *inter
alia*, in what it is for semantic discourse to be fact-stating, hence, too,
in what it is for there to be semantic facts. Whether there are such facts
or not may well depend on what the right account of this matter is. So
it may seem question-begging to invoke the model to answer the
present question. On that point, two comments. First, it might be fair
to say, at least sometimes, that the model proceeds on the supposition
that there are semantic facts. But we might also ask: 'Is there any
doubt that there are? Is it proper to doubt this? If so, what sorts of
doubts are there? And when (and how) would these be settled?' What
would answer these questions? I can think of nothing better to
recommend here than applying the model itself, thus asking: would a
reasonable judge take there to be any such doubts? when would he take
them as settled? as things are, would such a judge take there to be
semantic facts or not? (For these questions to make sense, of course,
specific doubts first need to be raised.) Given what I take to be the
reasonable view of reasonable judges, there is nothing question-
begging in 'supposing', in the way the model does, that there are
semantic facts. There just is no question about it. Second, whatever
the credentials of the model in this case, it is clear that Wittgenstein
accepts the results that the model, if applied, would deliver. There is
no harm in regarding those results as an independent thesis, to be
argued for on its own. The argument will not sound very different from
what has been said so far in defence of the model (and, importantly, in
defence of its epistemology). But, for what it is worth, we can just let
the present thesis stand on its own legs.

3. AUTONOMY

Wittgenstein's thesis has a more spectacular side, and a homelier but
more practical one. The spectacular side matters less, but I begin with

it anyway. As with most spectacular theses, some qualification may be called for. If, for example, we claim that no other features simply make an item 'the right (or wrong) sort of thing to be a truth-bearer', so that any other semantics it may have is compatible both with its being a truth-bearer and with its not being one, that does not mean that it is within our powers to regard just anything either as a truth-bearer or as not, or that for just any other semantics an item might have, we could regard both views of an item with that semantics as even remotely reasonable, much less equally so, nor even that for both views of the item there are at least some circumstances in which we would find them reasonable—any more than it is generally within our powers to believe whatever we like, or than we could find it reasonable to believe just anything we decided to. Perhaps we just react to the other semantics of some items by taking them to be truth-bearers (or not), and, given that other semantics, we just cannot help ourselves in this respect. (Such reactions are, after all, part of what *makes* the semantic facts what they are.) So there is a sense, at least, in which we may not find just any other semantics an item might have as compatible both with its being a truth-bearer and with its not being. What the spectacular thesis is meant to point to is that such facts, in so far as they are facts, depend essentially on facts about us and what comes naturally to us; on our ethologies, as the point has been put previously, and not *just* on the other semantics to which we are reacting. That dependence is the homelier point to be explored in the next section. With this qualification in, we now aim for the spectacular.

Let us briefly examine Wittgenstein's chess analogy. The analogous question would be: what identifies a given piece as the king in a game of chess, or in virtue of what might some piece qualify for that role? A quick answer would be: the fact that it is stipulated that that piece is the king. If we think of the piece as a concrete object which we move around on the board as the game proceeds, then it is no part of the rules of chess that *that* piece is the king. But if we think of ourselves as having made certain stipulations (probably implicitly) about the playing of this particular game, then we might think of such a stipulation as one of the rules governing our playing of this game of chess. So viewed, it is an essential and ineliminable part of the rules. As we might put it, it is partly constitutive of this game of chess that such and such piece, K, is the king. To say this is to say that it does not follow from any other features of K that K is the king, or at least none that hold independent of K being the king. It would have been possible to stipulate that some other piece, J, and not K was to be the king. We would still have had a game of chess, and the fact would have been that J and not K was the king in it.

If we think about how we do recognize the king in actual games of chess, then other sorts of answers may suggest themselves. Typically, we recognize the king by its shape. We do not have to wait to observe the way the players treat a piece, or their attitudes towards it, nor do we need to discover what stipulations, if any, were made. But we also recognize immediately that the shape of a piece does not *require* that it be the king; there could have been a stipulation that a piece of some other shape was to be the king, and then it would have been. (Though we might find it difficult to make ourselves treat pieces of certain shapes as kings, if we are used to certain standard sorts of chess games.) We might take this as one model of the way in which other facts about an item do not require that it be a truth-bearer. It is a model that is revealing in some ways, misleading in others.

We might also observe that the king in *chess* can be defined, in one sense of 'define', in terms of its initial position and the moves permitted it during the course of the game. It is then a further feature of chess that *the* piece subject to those rules is the piece one can check. So, within chess, it follows from the fact that a piece has the property of being subject to those rules, or movable in those ways, that it is checkable (and conversely). But of course we can invent games in which the piece subject to those rules is not checkable, and/or an other piece, or other pieces, defined in parallel ways, is/are checkable. Would such a game be chess? Well, chess may sometimes count as surviving at least some changes to its rules. But that does not matter for present purposes. What does matter is that being checkable follows from being movable in such-and-such ways not because being movable in those ways as such requires being checkable, as if things simply could not be otherwise, but rather because it is an extra and fundamental feature of this game (chess) that that is part of what is stipulated to follow, or to count within the game as following; those inferential relations are set up by the fact that, within that game, they are to be understood to hold. (Wittgenstein makes the same point in terms of the relation between being checkable, or being movable in such-and-such ways and being the king.)

The parallel here is between being checkable and being properly evaluable as to truth, that is, being a truth-bearer. It is true that we regard items with certain sorts of other semantics as truth-bearers (or not)—as illustrated by 1 and 2. And we are correct in doing so. But what makes us correct is not that things just could not be otherwise in these respects. Rather, what makes us correct is simply that (roughly) that is the way we regard them; that it is part of our game, or way of treating those sorts of items, or those sorts of semantics, that within it such is to be taken to follow; that for the items or semantics we deal with, as dealt with by us, such inferential relations are to be understood to hold. So again, items with such-and-such semantics are properly taken to be truth-bearers because that is what they are to be understood to be; because, for those items, being a truth-bearer is to be understood to follow from that semantics, and not because that semantics, of itself, leaves no other options (any more than those movement rules which in fact apply to the king in chess leave no other options, for example, with respect to being checkable).

Note that in certain contexts—for example, while playing chess—we may be incapable of regarding an item movable in certain ways as other than checkable or the king; in those contexts, we might take it, correctly, that the facts as to the other rules governing the piece do not leave open more than one possibility in these regards. Similarly, in certain contexts we may not be able to regard words, say, with certain semantics as even possibly other than a truth-bearer (or non-truth-bearer); we are unable to see two ways for things to be in this respect. But again, it is not these semantics themselves which require this; it is the way in which we fit such semantics into the overall determination of the semantics of the items in question. So again, such facts reflect, in part, facts about us. Such possible inabilities on our parts, and their source in us, and not just in the properties we are regarding, points to Wittgenstein's reason for speaking of a 'bad' picture, rather than a false one. The 'bad' picture, applied where the role of our reactions is taken as read, need not be mistaken.

The spectacular thesis, then, is that the property of being a truth-bearer is autonomous. That is to say, for any other semantics that an item might have, it would be possible for an item to have that semantics and have the property of being a truth-bearer, and it would be possible for an item to have that semantics and lack that property. That is to say, in principle there are two kinds of case. Immediately some qualification is called for. First, as mentioned at the outset, something is a truth-bearer if and only if it has at least some truth-involving properties (and is grammatically of the right sort—for example, not a predicate). Since being a truth-bearer cannot be independent of having truth-involving properties, such properties are to be excluded from the other semantics in question. Second, it may be that some more specific verbs which we sometimes use to replace 'say'—for example, 'assert' or 'claim'—may fit only where some truth-bearer has been produced.[5] (Though, on the other hand, it is not clearly wrong to say, 'She claimed that oysters are delicious.') If so, then the

---

[5] There may well be verbs of propositional attitude like this as well. Chinese appears to contain one nice example: *'yiem'*, which means roughly *to despise (deplore?) the fact that.*

other semantics in question is to be specified without the help of such verbs. Third, conversely, some specific verbs of saying may exclude application to truth-bearers—for example, 'asked'. These too are to be left out of account.

In fact, it would avoid extraneous issues here, and help to get a grip on the thought we are after, if we permitted ourselves enough of the Fregean picture to think of the autonomy thesis as operating at the level of thoughts, or at least candidate thoughts, before issues of force have entered the picture, rather than at the level of language. A truth-bearer would then be something which was at least eligible for being expressed in saying something either true or false.

Alternatively, we might think of the issue as concerning what was said in words. The point would then be that we can allow ourselves any specification we want of what it was that was said, excluding other verbs of saying. We can specify, however we like, which items were spoken of, which properties or candidate properties (such as being delicious) were mentioned and/or attributed, and so on. Then the property of being a truth-bearer is autonomous, in the specified sense, *vis-à-vis* all that.

Part of the autonomy of being a truth-bearer can be expressed in terms of language games, keeping in mind the relation to semantics that has here been assigned them. The thought would be this. Take any declarative form of words, W; so, with that restriction, any candidate truth-bearer or vehicle for expressing one. Now define a game, G, in which W is a move. With one restriction, you may do this however you like. So the parts of W may turn out to name or speak of whatever you like, in G, in Wittgenstein's broad sense of 'name'. (If you would not speak of 'is delicious' as naming being delicious, we can at least say that it speaks of being delicious, and says things to be, or characterizes them as delicious.) And G may impose whatever standards of correctness on W that you like. For example, if W is 1, then it may be part of what is required for correctness that W is to be spoken only in situations in which Odile is wearing a brown suit. Here is the restriction. It is not to be already part of the rules of G that W is to be assessed as to truth or falsity, so nor that there are such-and-such standards for such an assessment being carried out correctly. For good measure, let us add that it is not part of the rules of G that W is not to be so assessed. The easiest way of achieving this is simply to exclude (explicit) assessments as to truth or falsity from being moves in G at all. So thinking of G as, as it were, containing no truth predicate. As a rule, players simply make moves; assessing them is not part of the game. (We might allow players to accept or reject moves; a player might protest that some making of a move was an infraction of such-

and-such rule, or that it really had to be done in such and such way or situation, and not that one. But if we do allow protests, we will restrict them to this vocabulary and form.) Then the thesis is that G may be embedded in two further games, G_1 and G_2—that is, games with rules permitting all the moves of G and more as well—such that in G_1 W clearly is a truth-bearer, whereas in G_2 W clearly is not.[6]

The simplest, though not the only way to conceive of this is to suppose that G_1 and G_2, unlike G, do contain explicit means for assessing things as to truth—as it were, a truth and a falsity predicate. That is, for each of these games, there is some range of its moves (and perhaps other items as well) such that finding one of these moves true, or finding it false, is itself a move in the game. For each game, there will also be some range of moves in the game such that finding them true or false is not a move in the game; if someone were to try to say such a thing, he would be making a clear mistake—expressing something incorrect, and perhaps even false in that game; and we might even allow *that* fact to be expressible as a move in the game. We might also suppose that these games contain some other terms of assessment, a range of moves (and other items) to which these terms may be applied as a move in that game, and rules to the effect that these terms of assessment may be applied only where the truth predicate may not be (in playing the game). G_1 and G_2 would then differ in that W belonged to the relevant range in G_1 but not in G_2. It would be part of the rules of G_1 that W could be assessed as to truth, and those rules would provide standards of correctness for such an assessment. Whereas it would be part of the rules of G_2 that W was not so assessable, and that anyone who tried to express such an 'assessment' would simply be committing a mistake—a conceptual error, as it were. It could not possibly be true, in G_2, that W was true, or that it was false, whereas in G_1 at least one of these thoughts could turn out to be true. Yet the situations in which W itself would be correct in G_1 would be exactly those in which it would be correct in G_2.

Part of the autonomy thesis is that for any initial G, as described, there is always some pair of games, as G_1 and G_2 were described above, which are coherent games. That is to say, it is coherent and consistent both to regard W as governed by the rules of G and a truth-bearer and to regard it as governed by the rules of G and a non-truth-bearer. It should be recalled here that any other (non-truth-involving) semantics that W

---

[6] Reflecting on what it would be, on the account of chapter 3, for W to count, on some occasion of our regarding it, both as a move in G and as a truth-bearer (e.g. as true or as false) should help to keep the spectacular thesis from seeming more spectacular than it deserves to. Anyway, it will presently be subjected to some small amount of deflation on that account.

might have is capturable in the rules of some game G, on the notion of language game as developed in chapter 3. But the autonomy thesis also says more than this. Recall that it is up to us, according to 136, to *make* it part of our game that W is a truth-bearer, or part of our game that W is not. (We need not do so through stipulation; we may do so *via* what comes naturally to us.) This means that there must be at least conceivable circumstances under which both G and G_1 (but not G_2) would count as among the games being played in some speakings of W, and similarly for G and G_2. One might also add: there are conceivable speakings of W which we would recognize and correctly count as playings of G and G_1, and others which we would recognize as playings of G and G_2—though that thesis is both less central to the present point (particularly to its anti-realist moral) and less certain.

4. AN EXAMPLE

An example may help fix the force of the thesis. Consider:

6. Hugo needs a cleaning service.

I am supposing that as we in fact would use and express 6, it is neither a clear case of a truth-bearer, nor a clear case of a non-truth-bearer. Reasonable people might disagree as to whether it did or did not state a (purported) fact; and neither one side nor the other would be demonstrably wrong. On the one hand, if it came to deciding who did and who did not need such a service, we might take it that often we could clearly perceive what the result should be. Hugo, for example, is an unusually hard-working and reasonably well-off bachelor, with an apartment which is clearly a mess by generally accepted community standards. That would strongly incline (some of) us to say that 6, or what it said, was so. So far, 6 looks fact-stating. But suppose we find ourselves among serious revisionary moralists. Tidiness, we are told, is a much overvalued bourgeois value. Your revulsion at certain messes merely reflects your bourgeois upbringing. Mental labour, à la Chairman Mao, should really be combined with physical labour, so that cleaning his apartment would do Hugo a world of good. Then there is also the puritan view: if Hugo were to rise earlier and work still harder, he could care for the apartment himself. We might be inclined to think that (some) such views did not get the facts wrong; they expressed values which it was not perfectly wild to have. When we were so impressed, reflecting on how they tend to impugn 6, we might feel that 6 could not really be a case of fact-stating after all. I am supposing that neither of these feelings is clearly and demonstrably the correct one. If you do not share this intuition, then you should change the example accordingly (unless you think there are no such examples at all).

Now let us consider two hypothetical communities, which I will call the Fastidians and the Pluralians.[7] The Fastidians are extremely concerned with getting (judging) it right in matters of neatness, and with assigning praise and blame for such things correctly. They assign very great importance to the consequences which ride on such judgements, and may assign them very important consequences too.[8] (For good measure, we may suppose that Fastidian society is prepared to spend almost unlimited time and resources to finding out how matters really lie within this domain; they are deeply interested in it.) The Fastidians take it that there are as a rule facts as to who needs a cleaning service and who does not (these facts existing within a wider domain of facts about tidiness). In fact, no normal and otherwise reasonable Fastidian would ever question this. It is something which stands fast for them; which they do not doubt. (Once in a while, a radical moral revisionist may appear among them.) So any Fastidian would understand a normal speaking of 6 as saying what, if correct, was a fact, and to be understood as saying what either was so or was not. (As always, the concept of fact-stating tolerates the occasional exceptional case where, through non-co-operation by the world, what 5 said turns out to be not quite a fact and not quite not so either—for example, Hugo's apartment is a borderline case of messy. It is not guaranteed to be a fact either that 6 is true or that it is false. Nor are the Fastidians irrational enough to think otherwise.)

The Pluralians, on the other hand, could not care less about the distribution either of messiness or of cleaning services, or of needs for these in the world. Unlike the Fastidians, they are prepared to spend 0 per cent of their GNP investigating such matters. (You cannot get a grant at a Pluralian university this way.) Just as much as the Fastidians take their above attitudes without question, so (almost) no Pluralian would think to question that views on needing a cleaning service are all just a question of attitude; there is no question of there being facts of the matter here. For Pluralians, in matters of tidiness, *non disputandum est*. So any Pluralian would understand a normal speaking of 6, without hesitation or reflection, as merely expressing an attitude, thus as a non-truth-bearer. Any doubt about that would be regarded by them as hyperbolic. Nor would a Pluralian think that it even made sense to investigate further whether these words 'agreed

[7] The Pluralians may fit some conceptions of Californians.
[8] Perhaps, for example, unextenuated messiness is a capital offence.

with the facts'. Concepts such as agreeing with the facts, representing the world as it is, etc., as a Pluralian might put it, simply get no grip in this case.

The thesis at its most spectacular is now this. Not only would the Fastidians and Pluralians regard 6 in the ways just described, but they would, at least on occasion, count as correct in doing so: typical Fastidian speakings of 6 would (at least sometimes) count as expressing a truth-bearer; whereas typical Pluralian speakings of 6 would (at least sometimes) count as expressing what was not one. I have tried to make clear that neither Pluralians nor Fastidians are us. So what was just said is not a discovery about the status of 6 as we speak it, or what we express in doing so. It is not as if the Fastidians, for example, discover that what we have been doing all along is stating definite facts (or falsehoods) in saying such things as 6, whereas we thought that 6 simply lacked a clear status in this respect. But it does mean this. Fastidian speakings of 6 would count as expressing a truth-bearer on (some) occasions for our considering them, so, as considered by us; that would (at least sometimes) be the correct (true) thing for us to judge about them. *Mutatis mutandis* for Pluralian speakings. This spectacular thesis is part of the most natural interpretation of the idea that seems to be expressed in 136, that it is partly constitutive of the role of an item in *our* language game that the concepts of truth and falsity are to be applied to it; that this is something for the rules of our game to specify in one way or another (just as it is up to the rules of chess to specify one way or another whether the king may be checked). But, though it is the most spectacular side of that idea, we will see presently that it is not the most important part of it.

We might usefully think of the difference between Fastidians and Pluralians in this way. The Fastidians suppose without question that there are facts as to who needs a cleaning service and who does not, or equally, when, or under what circumstances someone would or would not. (That supposition exists within a wider network of related ones, of course; but that point can be left to one side here.) That there are such facts is part of what there is to be understood about what they are saying in their speakings of 6. (But, of course, that such is to be understood to be so is not enough by itself to make it so.) The problem for the Fastidians is then this: given that there are such facts, what is the most reasonable distribution of cases into cases of someone needing a cleaning service and cases of someone not needing one (modulo, perhaps, a tolerable number of exceptional cases where there is no choosing between several equally reasonable distributions, thus cases which do not determinately count one way or the other)? That is, given that there are facts of this sort, what are those facts most reasonably taken to be? It is to research on that problem (and ones like it) that the Fastidians devote a considerable portion of their GNP. If this problem has a sufficiently good solution, then, on our thesis, a Fastidian is stating a fact in speaking 6 just in case what he states would be a fact on that solution. It is because what the Fastidian thus says is related in this way, in virtue of its proper understanding, to this problem that it counts as fact-stating discourse. The Pluralian, on the other hand, explicitly rejects the supposition of there being such facts as these. So for him, the problem of the most reasonable distribution of cases with respect to such facts does not arise. It is a problem to be rejected out of hand. And that it is is part of the proper understanding of what he says in a typical speaking of 6. (That is one sort of explanation, perhaps, of why Pluralians devote 0 per cent of their GNP to researching such questions.) So, for the Pluralian, such a problem could have no solution—or better put, any solution to such a problem, no matter what its credentials, would be powerless to show anything about 'when he was stating a fact' in speaking 6.

We ourselves now enter the picture like this. Reflecting on the Fastidian's problem, we may be able to see that there are at least some facts as to what its solution, if any, would be. We may be able to see, for example, that if we were to suppose the problem to have a solution, then Hugo would surely get classified on the side of cases of people who needed a cleaning service; no reasonable classification scheme could put him on the other side, given that there are disjoint and reasonably large classes of cases on each side; that there genuinely are the two kinds of case. Otherwise put, if a substantial number of people need cleaning services, then there is every reason to think that Hugo would be among them. Or, if we cannot see this of Hugo, then perhaps of other cases (the invalid with the horror of dust, for example).[9] Recognition of such facts would enable us to see how speakings of 6 could be determinately fact-stating discourse. We would see how that could be; but the fact that the problem at hand has as neat a solution as

---

[9] This is an appropriate time to remind ourselves that if we were to suppose the Fastidian's problem to have a solution, we might well also expect such a solution to be an S-use sensitive matter. So it might well be part of such a solution that whether the invalid counts as needing a cleaning service depends on the circumstances under which, and the purposes for which, we are classifying things one way or the other. If the government is passing out cleaning-service grants, then perhaps yes; if we are contemplating anti-dust-aversion therapy, then perhaps no. That taking there to be a solution to such a problem may (and typically will) require accepting a certain amount of S-use sensitivity is a not an inconsiderable factor in showing how it could be that discourse with given other semantics may be treated correctly either as fact-stating or as not. We may be free, to at least some extent, to choose just how much S-use sensitivity we are prepared to live with before concluding that some problem of the form just described really has no solution at all.

it does does not force us to recognize any speaking of 6 (to say Hugo to need a cleaning service) to be fact-stating discourse. (Nor need there be only one possible view of just how neat that solution is; or how important the cases, and their number, which do not get classified on it.) The Pluralians serve to remind us of that. Though we could allow problems of this sort to arise, and though if we did they might have solutions, we (or the Pluralians) are not forced to allow such problems and their solutions as relevant to what we or the Pluralians say in our speakings of 6—even if we continue to take such speakings as saying Hugo to need a cleaning service.

We might note that if there are enough facts about what the solution to the Fastidian's problem would be, then their supposition might, in the end, confer more semantics on their speakings of 6 than simply the property of being a truth-bearer. Notably, such words would typically have some further range of truth-involving properties: if, on the most reasonable solution, C would be a case of someone needing a cleaning service, then such words would typically have the property of saying what would be true of C. Further truth-involving properties might bring with them further properties of other sorts as well. But the fact that additional semantics is likely not to come bit by bit ought not to obscure the point of the example: 6 with the other semantics we now assign it could function in the two different ways just described if there were two societies as different from us as the Fastidians and the Pluralians.

To illustrate the spectacular thesis, I chose a case of what for us counts neither as determinately a truth-bearer nor as determinately not. But the thesis was meant to have more generality than that. It ought, for example, to have application to 1 and 3 as well. Here is a way of thinking of how it might. We might think of ourselves in relation to the Fastidians and the Pluralians as at the base of a two-tined fork, with each of those other hypothetical societies at the tip of one tine. At the base, there is a semantic item, a candidate truth-bearer, whose status in that respect is indeterminate. At the tips of the tines, the status is determinate: on one tine it is a truth-bearer; on the other it is not. If we think of 1, for example, which determinately is a truth-bearer for us, then we might think of our position on the fork as having shifted: now we are at the end of one tine, and we can try to imagine two other societies, one of which would be at the base, while the other would be at the tip of the other tine. Similarly, *mutatis mutandis*, for 2, if we agree that that is as clear a case as anything could be, for us, of non-fact-stating discourse. In such cases, the people at the other positions on the fork would, no doubt, be quite different from us. They might have radically different purposes and values; and they might embed the semantic items in question in, for us, very strange activities. Nevertheless, the thesis is that there are such positions to be occupied, and that there might be people to occupy them without lapsing into total irrationality.

In its full generality, this thesis might be broken down into components. The first part of it, for 1, is that in treating 1 as a truth-bearer, we situate ourselves on one tine of a fork, on the model of the fork for 6, on which there are the other two corresponding positions to be occupied by some hypothetical community or other. On the other tine would be a community which took it, unquestioningly, that what was said in saying a suit to be brown did not divide up situations, or ways for the world to be, into ones which made *that* so, and ones which did not, so that there was no conditional problem to be solved. Differences of opinion over whether some suit was brown would be, like ones over the delectableness of oysters (for us), intrinsically just that and no more. At the base of the fork would be a community which, like us with regard to 6, did not treat 1 clearly in the one way or the other.

The second part of the thesis is that we can conceive of circumstances in which these communities would be correct in treating their productions or considerings of 1 as they do, just as much as we are in fact correct in treating our encountered instances of 1 as we do. As produced by us, 1 is a truth-bearer; as produced by our counterparts on the other tine, it would not be. On the present view of semantics, we can conceive of this simply by conceiving of there being further judges whom we could recognize as reasonable who would find that these people were correct in thus taking those items as they did; that in doing so they were understanding the relevant words as they were to be understood.

A third part of the thesis—the most spectacular part—is that we can conceive of people to occupy the other positions on the fork whose activities, purposes, etc. were such that we would be correct in regarding them as in fact occupying those positions, which is to say that they would in fact count as doing so (on our occasions for judging the matter one way or the other). There could be people, for example, who would count as saying Odile's suit to be brown in producing 1, but not as producing a truth-bearer in so doing; not just that we can conceive of their having turned out to be right in regarding their productions of 1 as they do, but that they do in fact count as right in this. That is the most spectacular suggestion of 136, on the present reading of it. But it is also the least essential for present purposes. One might think that we just could not imagine circumstances for producing 1—meaning brown by 'brown', etc.—in which one would not count as having said thereby what either was a fact or what, as a matter of fact, was not so; so what was either true or false (exceptional cases of non-co-operation by the world excluded). The point would then be that our semantic reactions do not allow us so to regard 1. For, even if there are those conceivable language games to be played, it is not an arbitrary matter for us which language games we play, or even which ones we can see others as playing. My own view is that we can conceive of such circumstances, though just barely. But the central thrust of the thesis of 136 does not require making good on this. Still, I will end this discussion of the spectacular side of the thesis with a few brief comments on this issue.

There may be an asymmetry between the case where we take what we regard as clearly a truth-bearer and try to imagine a community treating it—or something with its relevant semantics—such that, produced by them, it is not one, and the reverse case, where we begin with something we regard as clearly not a truth-bearer; thus, for example, between what we should say of 1 and what we should say of 2. Let us begin with the first case. Here it would be a start in the right direction if the other community regarded activities such as confirmation or disconfirmation, and disputes of the sort we have over facts, to be inapplicable to 1; not only that they took no interest in such things, but that they would regard someone who tried to test what was said in 1, or dispute it in the way we dispute matters of fact, to have missed the point of the remark. Nor would they be prepared to accept anything as demonstrating that what was said in such a remark was not so. It is as if one of them said 1 (properly) when that was how it struck him; demonstrating that he was wrong, if that were possible, could only mean something like demonstrating that that was not how it struck him; and that makes as much or as little sense as our trying to demonstrate to someone that he was wrong in saying 'Oysters are delicious'.

The above would show one way in which the other community did not share our values and purposes. To this we might add that there is room for further relevant divergence. It strikes us that the conditional problem for 1—the problem of which cases would be cases of something being brown on the supposition that there are facts of such matters—has a straightforward and obvious solution; as good a solution as we ever have a right to expect in such cases. But we may note how our values play a role in that view of the matter. Consider a contrasting case, such as 'Oysters are delicious'. Here we might take it that the corresponding conditional problem has no adequate solution. If there is any reason for taking 2 not to be fact-stating beyond 'That's just what we do', then surely such reason must lie there. Now, there are two reasons why we might take this view of the conditional problem. One would be that no one has any view on the subject at all; or, more generally, that we could not imagine anything being even a *prima facie* reason in favour of one solution to that problem over another. (Note that a reason for or against some solution to the conditional problem is not directly a reason for or against its being a fact that oysters are delicious. There could be such reasons, perhaps, only if 2 is already reckoned within the realm of fact-stating.) More plausibly, however, we take the conditional problem to have no correct solution because, though we can recognize some reasons in favour of some candidates, there is at least too wide a spectrum of conflicting candidates such that the reasons in favour of one do not outweigh those in favour of another. That Odile finds oysters delicious is at least some reason in favor of thinking that they are; but that Hugo finds them revolting provides equally good reason for thinking that they are not, for example.

That kind of balance between competing solutions to the conditional problem is supposed not to arise in the case of being brown. But there are often enough at least some reasons both for and against taking something to be brown—a building built of brown bricks, perhaps, or muddy water, or a chestnut-coated horse with normal mammalian innards. Our taking the conditional problem for brown to have a straightforward solution commits us to taking one of several attitudes towards cases which present such conflicting reasons. First, we might just regard the reasons on one side as much more impressive than those on the other, so that the correct solution is what the more impressive reasons indicate. Second, we might view the case as exceptional or unlikely to arise, or etc. Then we can say that the solution is correct modulo that case (perhaps among others). *That* case, perhaps, is a case of *isostheneia* in nature;[10] but such *isostheneia* is exception rather than rule. When and how often we can take that attitude depends on how much non-uniqueness in a solution we are prepared to tolerate. Third, we might take the attitude that while there is *isostheneia* for the question whether the item is brown *tout court*, what that shows is that it is an S-use sensitive matter whether the

---

[10] The Greeks, or anyway Sextus, had in mind by '*isostheneia*' an equal balancing of the reasons available (or which might be available) to us for and against judging some given thing, F. By '*isostheneia* in nature', I mean an equal balancing of all the reasons there are for and against counting a situation as one of F's obtaining; nature has hidden nothing from us, or so we may suppose, but the world does not come down determinately on the side of F's obtaining or its failing to. Sextus, no doubt, would have regarded the position being described here as a negative dogmatism, as opposed to the sort of scepticism he favoured. I am endebted to my colleague Jim Hankinson for making the ancient notion of *isostheneia* as clear to me as it now is.

item counts as brown; on some occasions we assign more weight to some of the reasons, and on other occasions to others. Again, the extent to which we can do this depends on to what extent we are prepared to live with S-use sensitivity rather than throwing up our hands and saying that the apparent need for it really shows that the conditional problem has no adequate solution at all. (Note that it is the latter rather than the former course that we would find reasonable in the case of 'Oysters are delicious'.)

Again, our reactions in these respects, in taking one such attitude rather than others in particular cases, reveal something about what our values are. And we may expect these values not to be shared by communities in the other positions on the fork. The community that took 1 not to be fact-stating, for example, might just throw up its hands at the first sign of conflicting reasons, and refuse to allow after that that the relevant conditional problem could have an adequate solution. If, for example, they were unprepared to live with as much S-use sensitivity as we are, they would not be clearly beyond the pale of rationality, nor would they clearly fail to be speaking of brown, and taking the problem to have no solution in that case. (Recall the diversity in rules which might govern what names brown.)

One final remark. Suppose we encountered people who found any attempt to dispute a claim made in 1 by one of them, or to check it, not merely *gauche*, but reflecting a positive misunderstanding of what was said. Then we might be tempted to describe their speakings of 1 in the following way. The thought they express in 1 is, like the thought we would express in so speaking, straightforwardly a truth-bearer. Their expressions of that thought, however, carry a peculiar illocutionary force. Given that, it is inappropriate to assess their *words* as true or false. Those words should be understood merely as saying, roughly, how things seemed to the speaker, and not as expressing a judgement as to how things are. On the level of thoughts, however, we have not yet seen how something could have the rest of the semantics of 1 and not be a truth-bearer. I think that nothing prohibits describing such a case in this way. But nothing requires it either. In the right circumstances, we might also describe them as having said the suit to be brown, but having done so such that what was thus said is not eligible for being either true or false. Again, people who said things like that would not be carrying out activities much like ours in doing so.

Now for the reverse case: people committed to treating typical speakings of 2 as stating facts (or falsehoods). Could we possibly regard them as doing so correctly? First, all the above comments apply in reverse. For example, such people might be much more tolerant of S-use sensitivity here, and deploy it in a much different way than we

would. For example, they might think that there are some speakings of
2 for which Odile's reaction to oysters counts much more heavily than
Hugo's—perhaps even decisively, and then, if so, for the truth of what
was thereby said. (It is far from clear that we do not in fact sometimes
treat some speakings of 2 in this way. In the right group, you may
speak 2, and, anyway, be counted as having spoken the truth.) For other
speakings, Odile's reactions might count not at all, and some other
reason might be decisive. Or perhaps quite often, though not always,
no reason is decisive: you need very appropriate circumstances for
expressing a definite thought in 2.

Second, we may note that some conceivable states of the world
would present a much better chance for there to be an adequate
solution to the relevant conditional problem than we take to be
presented by what we take the actual state of the world to be. Suppose,
for example, that people's reactions to oysters were much as they are,
but that the only other kinds of comestibles found on earth were
universally regarded as revolting. Then, on the supposition that there
were facts as to what was delicious and what was not, 2 would be a
good candidate for stating a fact if anything did, whereas for any other
comestible, C, 'C is not delicious' would also be an excellent candidate
for stating a fact. There would then be a good case for regarding 2 as
within the realm of fact-stating discourse, even by our lights. We do
not hold out much hope (or fear), perhaps, that the world will turn out
to fit anything remotely like that model. Thus, we are not gastronomic
realists. But the other society, on the other tine of the fork, might have
an inextinguishable hope that something like this will be the case (but
without everything but oysters being revolting). The result might be,
not that speakings of 2 actually did state a fact (given that we, and not
they, are right about the world), but that such speakings are at least
properly regarded as falling within fact-stating discourse. If they fail to
be in fact either true or false, that will be because of the hazards to
which all fact-stating discourse is liable.

5. ERROR

Now leaving fantasy behind, let us consider what the thesis means for
the semantic items we in fact produce and treat. This will be the
homely but practical side of the thesis. Many of the semantic items we
produce do count as truth-bearers; some do not. We have no difficulty
recognizing most of these items as truth-bearers, or as not. In fact, in
most cases, we could hardly do otherwise. Such is part of what our
natural semantic reactions require. One might then ask what identifies

these semantic items as truth-bearers (or as not). Or what identifies them for us; what is it about them to which we are required to react in that way? Part of Wittgenstein's answer to this question, as one would expect, is that being a truth-bearer, or a *Satz*, is a family resemblance concept, so that there is no common identifying thread running through all cases of what we identify as a truth-bearer. As he puts it,

But haven't we got a concept of what a *Satz* is, of what we understand by '*Satz*'? —Yes; just as we also have a concept of what we understand by 'game'. Asked what a *Satz* is—whether it is another person or ourselves we have to answer— we shall give examples and these will include what one may call an inductive series of *Sätze*. In *this* way we have a concept of a *Satz*. (Compare the concept of a *Satz* with the concept of a number.) (135) [cf. 68 on the concept of a number.

In 136, Wittgenstein also offers an answer of another kind. Part of what makes an item count as a truth-bearer, in a typical case, is that we treat it as a truth-bearer—for example, we take it to be subject to evaluation as to truth, and we take certain sorts of disputes over it to be in order, or at least to make sense. So we might ask what identifies items that we would treat in that way. But we might also, as it were, reverse the question. It is possible for someone to understand, and take an item to be a truth-bearer when it is not. So, presumably, it is at least conceivable that we should all take some item, or perhaps even some area of discourse to be fact-stating when, in point of fact, it is not. Under what circumstances would it be so that we were regarding some item, or range of items, as truth-bearers (or as non-truth-bearers) and were mistaken in so doing—that is, were thereby taking to be so what was not? (A related question: suppose that we correctly understand an item to be a truth-bearer. Then we will suppose, ceteris paribus, that it either says what is a fact or it says what, in fact, is not so; so that it is either true or false. Under exceptional circumstances, that supposition might turn out to be false. When would that be so?) Wittgenstein answers this question in the last sentence of 136. Having compared the way in which being evaluable as to truth is an ingredient of a *Satz* to the way in which being subject to check is an ingredient of being the king in chess, he then says:

To say that check did not *fit* our concept of a pawn would be to say that a game in which pawns were checked, in which, perhaps, players who lost their pawns lost, would be uninteresting or stupid or too complicated or something of the kind.

Let us abbreviate the epithets to 'too stupid'. Then the comparison is this. An item, W, which we produce and/or deal with, is not a truth-bearer just when treating it as a truth-bearer is too stupid for us, or too stupid by our lights. A start on being too stupid might be that we were never inclined to regard W as a truth-bearer to begin with (though that *need* not be decisive). But, in a case where we did regard W as a truth-bearer, we could only be wrong, on this line of thought, through having failed to notice or properly appreciate some aspects of so treating W which, when properly attended to, would make doing so too stupid by our lights. (As per the model of chapter 2, 'too stupid for us' should be taken to mean: counts, on our occasions for considering it, as too stupid for or by the lights of a reasonable judge. The point being that it is not enough simply for us to react by *saying* 'Too stupid!', or 'Not!'; we must count as reacting reasonably in so doing. This wrinkle will turn out to be significant in the long run.)

Suppose that we have (or may be described as having) a practice of treating a certain item or items as truth-bearers, and that it is part of that practice that, under certain circumstances, or on certain occasions, we regard one or another of these items as having stated a fact, under other circumstances as having stated what is not so, under still others, we take it that it is not settled, or still open to dispute whether what the item states is a fact, and so on. I will say that the practice is coherent if it is clear enough, often enough, when, given the practice, one of these items would be treated in one of these ways or another that is, when it would be part of that practice so to treat it. We (the users of these items) will regard the practice as coherent when we take it that it is thus often enough clear enough how the practice is to be followed, or what following it would be; what, that is, would be part of this practice. What is often *enough*, and clear *enough* is a question of what we find too stupid (in the present sense); that is, of when the clarity and its frequency are enough for us to find it not too stupid to suppose that there is such a thing as what engaging in the practice would be, and facts as to what following it would require. We may also be said to take it that there is some point to the practice if it *is* our practice, and if we have not renounced it. Suppose that no facts we are unaware of would, if we were exposed to them, change our reactions in these respects. Suppose further that a reasonable judge would not find that we had committed some positive error in so reacting; that we were being plain and simply irrational in so doing. Then there is no further issue as to whether the items in question are fact-stating. To be treated in this way just *is* to be fact-stating. And if items are fact-stating, then there are facts of the sort they state (unless, as a matter of fact, the world just happens never to provide circumstances under which, as part of that practice, one or another of these items would count as having stated a fact). There is no further issue as to whether there are or are not facts of that sort. That is the practical import of Wittgenstein's thesis of 136.

The point may be put in terms of the conditional problems discussed in the last section. Suppose that we regard some range of (one or more) items as fact-stating. Then we may consider the problem what the facts would be on the supposition that there were facts of that sort. When would one of these items count as having stated, or as stating a fact (or as true)—*if* there were/are such facts to state? Part of the point of 136 is that that range of items is fact-stating if there is an adequate (that is, sufficiently reasonable) solution to this conditional problem. Given the solution, there is simply no question of demonstrating that 'really' there are no facts of that sort; if we took the relevant discourse to be fact-stating, then there is *no* room for a demonstration that we were mistaken in doing so. To render the point in a motto, no more is required for there to be facts of a given sort than sufficient coherence in the supposition that there are (and our preparedness to make it), so no more than an adequate solution to the conditional problem the supposition of such facts would pose. We may regard this as Wittgenstein's ontological criterion.

A further part of the point of 136 concerns what an adequate solution would be. An adequate solution is, on that view, a solution which we find to be adequate—one that is good enough for us to continue to engage in the relevant practice; unless a reasonable judge would find us to be plainly mistaken and irrational in so finding it, or as simply failing to see what is required by our standards of stupidity. A given candidate 'adequate solution' may tolerate, or make for more, or fewer cases where the reasons for and against taking some given relevant item to state a fact do not add up to any clear result as to whether it does so, so that, in that case, we must say that it neither is nor is not a fact that F; there fails to be a fact of the matter (otherwise put, it may tolerate more or fewer truth-value gaps, or cases of *isostheneia* in nature.) It may make for more or less determinacy in the way the facts of that sort are. Or it may make for more or fewer cases where the reasons for and against taking it to be a fact that F yield a result one way or the other only S-use sensitively. Or it may yield more or fewer cases where we must say that, while there may be a fact as to whether F, we do not, and perhaps cannot know it. We do tolerate cases fitting each of these descriptions, at least as exceptional ones. But how much of such phenomena can we tolerate before we must say that the solution in question is inadequate, or worse, that the practice which poses such a conditional problem is too stupid, or is an incoherent one? The answer, on Wittgenstein's view, depends on us. It is a question of when we find practices too stupid to engage in, or find it too stupid to take there to be such a thing as 'what engaging in the practice requires', or 'what is, and what not, in accord with the practice'. Beyond our reactions in such respects, there is nothing to decide the issue.

The thesis has local, as well as global, import. Given discourse—say, discourse about the colour of clothing—may or may not be fact-stating. But, given that it is, a given bit of that discourse—say, some remark that Odile's suit is brown—while properly regarded as a truth-bearer, may happen to state a fact, or what is not so, or may happen to count as stating what is neither quite a fact, or quite not so. We must always allow for the exceptional case where Odile is wearing a very peculiar suit: there is no uniformity in the judgements of 'normal observers' as to its colour, nor are we helped in deciding the matter by available scientific criteria or tests. But when, in fact, will we have encountered such an exceptional case? That depends, first, on how we weigh the reasons we do have, and second, on when we judge that there are no further reasons we do not have, or none that would change the picture; when we give up on researching the question further. As for this second question, it might be said that what makes it correct for us to judge this is its being too stupid to judge otherwise; that is, the practice involved in supposing otherwise is one that would be too stupid by our lights.

It should be clear by now that 136 is directed, at least in part, against revisionary metaphysics, as represented by selective ontic scepticism. On the present conception of fact-stating, arguments along such lines are simply off-target. A pointed example is the domain of semantic fact itself. It is part of our practice to take it that there are semantic facts— for example, that sometimes someone says or said someone to have eaten *lamb* in saying 'Mary had a little lamb'—and to talk about them. Quine, notoriously, has argued that such facts are not constructible (uniquely) out of the sort of facts that Quine happens to like—as he puts it, facts about 'surface irritations', on the one hand, and noise-makings or other 'observable behavior' on the other.[11] (Donald Davidson, in a more liberal spirit, has required that the other facts which determine semantic facts 'be of a sort that would be available to someone who does not already know how to interpret utterances the theory is designed to cover: it must be evidence that can be stated without essential use of such linguistic concepts as meaning, inter-pretation, synonymy, and the like.'[12] This is to demand that semantic facts, in so far as there are any, be determined by, so constructible out of, non-semantic facts. Quine, I think, would take his argument to survive Davidson's more liberal characterization of the other facts in question.)

Assuming that we accept Quine's result as a result, what should we conclude from it? If I understand Quine, what he suggests that we

---

[11] See Quine [1960], ch. 2.
[12] Davidson [1973], p. 128.

conclude is that, in so far as semantic fact is not recoverable uniquely from other fact, we should conclude that there really are no semantic facts. So Quine suggests that we content ourselves with a sort of *ersatz* semantic fact (for example, facts about so-called 'stimulus meaning'). On Wittgenstein's view, such a conclusion could not follow from Quine's 'result'. Conceivably, we could have regarded what Quine shows about the relation between semantic fact on the one hand and 'facts about stimuli and behavior' on the other as an intense surprise. And we could, conceivably, have reacted to this surprise by suddenly taking our practice of stating semantic facts—such as those about speakings of 'Mary had a little lamb'—to be incoherent. But suppose we do not react in this way (as, in fact, we have not). We continue to regard our practice as coherent—which is to say that we take ourselves to know well enough when, on the practice, one is to assign one or another semantics to an item: for example, when to say that one thing or another was said in 'Mary had a little lamb'. Then the supposition that there are semantic facts, and of just the sorts we always took there to be, remains unimpeached, and so far unimpeachable. The only conclusion one might legitimately draw from Quine's result is that being reducible to facts of Quine's favoured sort is not part of what is required for there to be semantic facts; nor are there particular requirements for the obtaining of particular semantic facts which might be stable in such terms. What must go is Quine's ontological criterion, not the facts of the sort that Quine questions.

Saul Kripke has recently represented Wittgenstein himself as a sceptic about semantic fact. As Kripke expresses it,

The sceptical argument, then, remains unanswered. There can be no such thing as meaning anything by any word. Each new application we make is a leap in the dark; any present intention could be interpreted so as to accord with anything we may choose to do.[13]

Further,

Now, if we suppose that facts, or truth conditions, are of the essence of meaningful assertion, it will follow from the sceptical conclusion that assertions that anyone ever means anything are meaningless.[14]

Again,

Wittgenstein's sceptical solution concedes to the sceptic that no 'truth conditions' or 'corresponding facts' in the world exist that make a statement like 'Jones, like many of us, means addition by "+".' true.[15]

[13] Kripke [1982], p. 55.
[14] Ibid., p. 77.
[15] Ibid., p. 86.

So, for example, on Kripke's rendering of Wittgenstein's view, it is not a fact that 'plus' in English refers to a function which maps 68 and 57 into 125. Nor is it a fact that 'is brown' says something that is true of Odile's suit, given the way that suit is, rather than something false of it (nor vice versa). The reason for this is that semantic facts fail to satisfy a certain requirement that Kripke takes Wittgenstein to have imposed on them, namely, that for each semantic fact there should be some other facts incompatible with that fact being otherwise.

But it has now been shown why this could not be a correct reading of Wittgenstein. Wittgenstein could not draw sceptical conclusions in Kripke's sense from results of the kind described as to the relation of semantic facts to others. Such conclusions could only follow if the 'revelation' of such results caused us to regard our practice of ascribing semantics to items as being too stupid, and to renounce that practice. But, as Kripke acknowledges, Wittgenstein does not suggest either that we would or should do anything of the sort. At most, results about the relation of semantic facts to others can only show something about what is required for there to be semantic facts, or for particular ones to hold. In this case, what is shown is that it is not required that there be other facts which, independent of our reactions to them, are incompatible with the semantic facts being otherwise—a result described in the model of chapter 2, in describing how the relations of semantic facts to others (including other semantic facts) depends essentially on our reactions to them.

Kripke's Wittgenstein does allow that our discourse about semantic 'fact' is 'in order as it is'—even though the sceptic has really shown that there are no such facts. He allows, further, that that discourse certainly *looks* fact-stating—for example, we do apply the concepts of truth and falsity to it. Kripke attempts to account for this with his own reading of 136:

> Wittgenstein's way with this is also short. We call something a proposition, and hence true or false, when in our language we apply the calculus of truth functions to it. That is, it is just a primitive part of our language game, not susceptible of deeper explanation, that truth functions are applied to certain sentences.

On Kripke's reading, what Wittgenstein does in 136 amounts to offering us a *façon de parler*. Really, the sceptic has shown that there are no semantic facts; but we can continue to talk *as if* there were. That is our practice, and there is no impeaching practice. This is simply what we do. But that is to reverse the point of 136. Wittgenstein is telling us there what it is for discourse to be fact-stating; not what it is for it to be *soi-disant* fact-stating. Given that our discourse about semantics is in order as it is, it sometimes states facts; those are what the semantic facts are. There is no further room for a sort of fact which a sceptic might tell us there is not. Nor is there room for the sceptic's considerations to even tend to show that what we state in our (true) semantic discourse is anything less than one aspect of the way the world is—facts in the fullest sense, in case anyone might suspect that there were some other. Wittgenstein's epistemology, to begin with, makes it impossible for him to be a sceptic; that is simply never the business he is in. His view of what fact-stating is (which is not a suggestion on what might substitute for it) makes it impossible for him even to make sense out of semantic scepticism, much less to have advanced such a view himself.

The moral of 136 for revisionist ontic scepticism is a moral for revisionist anti-realism as well. If there is anti-realism in Wittgenstein, it cannot be of a sort that would claim of something that we naturally regarded as a truth-bearer that it *could* not be. The only way of showing that would be to produce some sort of consideration that would make us react by taking it to be too stupid to treat that item as a truth-bearer; that is, something that would make us find the practice of so treating it incoherent. Nor could it be an anti-realism which proposed conditions that a practice must meet in order to count as sufficiently coherent—for example, that for an item within such a practice, 'the condition which must, in general, obtain for it to be true' be 'one which we are capable of recognizing whenever it obtains, or of getting ourselves in a position to do so.'[16] If we did take an item to be a truth-bearer, and were unimpressed by its failure to satisfy that requirement, then it is the requirement that would have to go.

One prominent idea in the *Investigations* is that syntax may outstrip semantics, taking us, as it were, beyond the bounds of sense. A combination of words may be in order according to the rules of sentence formation. It may *look* on the surface as if it stated some fact. But it may fail to express a definite thought. It is tempting to respond to that insight by looking for some extra requirement, beyond appropriate syntax, that an item must meet in order to express a definite thought—in order, that is, to enter the domain of fact-stating discourse. And, if one convinces oneself that there must be such a requirement, it is easy to think of what it must be in anti-realist terms, for example, in terms of our ability to grasp or recognize the conditions under which what it stated would be so (and to put a particular interpretation on what 'grasping' here must be). The moral of the present story is that the idea of such a requirement is a mistake.

In fact, as pointed out in previous chapters, the thought of syntax outstripping semantics, in at least many of its manifestations in the

---

[16] Dummett [1973], p. 224.

Investigations, points not at anti-realism, but rather at S-use sensitivity. What is missing, where we have a well-formed combination of meaningful words, is typically *appropriate circumstances*. For example,

> You say to me: 'You understand this expression, don't you? Well then—I am using it in the sense you are familiar with.'—As if the sense were an atmosphere accompanying the word, which it carried with it into every kind of application.
>   If, for example, someone says that the sentence, 'This is here' (saying which he points to an object in front of him) makes sense to him, then he should ask himself in what special circumstances this sentence is actually used. There it does make sense. (117)

The problem here is not, for example, one of words stating something 'verification transcendent', but of them not stating anything identifiable at all, outside of special circumstances. The function of such circumstances has been discussed already. This is not to deny that the *Investigations* has anti-realist content. That content may even be hinted at in the above passage. But Wittgenstein's anti-realism cannot be of a revisionist sort. To find what it does amount to, we will have to look elsewhere.

6. PARALLELS

The idea of autonomy has interesting and plausible applications outside of the area of fact-stating. Proper names offer one striking example of such an application. A brief look at it may help us to focus better on the force of the thesis as applied to truth-bearers. It may also help tie together some of the remarks about names that have been made in various preceding chapters.

  Restricting attention to expressions which are grammatically speaking devices for referring to individuals—at least on the surface—an autonomy thesis for names can be stated as follows. That a name is a (proper) name is a semantic property of it; an item has that property, that is, just and exactly when that is part of its proper understanding. Moreover, having or lacking that property is independent of any other semantic properties an item may have. So being a name is autonomous with respect to the rest of an item's semantics. An item is a name, one might say, because (and only because) that is what it is to be understood to be. As one might also say, an item is a name when we treat it as a name and when a reasonable judge would not find us to be misunderstanding it in so doing; when it is part of *our* game, to use that image, to treat it as a name, so, as it were, to apply 'the calculus of name-bearers to it'—that is, the sort of discourse that is appropriate to, and only to names; the sorts of assessments that fit names. And, one might add, when our so treating the item is not too stupid (for us). If and only if that requirement is satisfied, it is a fact that the item is a name. And beyond that, there is no further factual issue as to whether it is a name or not.

The thesis is a plausible one; enough so for me, at least, to believe it. But the present purpose is not to argue for it. Rather it is to see how the thesis may help with a problem about names, specifically, in the first instance, one raised by Russell.[17] Russell thought that names have a special sort of semantics, and insisted that that sort of semantics always be distinguished from any other possible sort of semantics for a referring expression—that is, for an item in the broad category mentioned above. He further insisted that any name, to be a genuine name, be distinguished from any item having one of these other sorts of semantics. Russell saw that this requirement posed a problem. For it made difficulties for the view that there could possibly be names which named such things as people, their pets, bits of geography, or 'material objects'. The problem Russell saw was that the needs created by referring to items such as these appear (from a certain perspective) inconsistent with the requirement that a name should have the semantics of a name, and not the semantics of any other sort of referring device.

There is a tension, then, between the requirement on being a name and the requirements of referring to individuals as we ordinarily conceive them. The present claim is that autonomy relieves that tension. But before saying how, let us briefly examine the two sides which are supposed to be in tension. First for the requirement on names. It is certainly an intuitive idea that names have a distinctive sort of semantics. But in my view—autonomy aside—it is very difficult to say just what is so distinctive about it. One test proposed by Russell is this: if N is a name, then it should be impossible to count as understanding N without knowing who or what N names. I think there must be something right in this idea (though not if combined with Russell's views on what *knowing who* requires). There are, though, at least two problems. First, the criterion is psychological and not semantic. It tells us what we must do to grasp the semantics (though knowing-who ought not to be assumed to be some one sort of identifiable accomplishment); but it does not tell us anything about what that semantics is. This need not be a fault. Still, we so far have no

---

[17] The Russell referred to here is throughout Russell [1918].

answer to the question we originally wanted to pose. Second, there seem to be many counter-examples to the criterion as it stands. To take the simplest case, we might all have been competent users of 'Lewis Carroll' without knowing that Lewis Carroll was Charles Dodgson; thus, in some sense (or better, for some purposes), without knowing who Lewis Carroll was.

Another more semantic approach would be this. If N is a name, then, in happy circumstances, where N names something, there is an individual, V, such that N names V, is to be understood to name (or as naming) V, and for any individual, V*, N names V*, if at all, because V* is V, and not (merely) because V* satisfies some other criterion. To this, some would add that, for any general description, if there are possible circumstances in which V would not fit that description, then there are possible circumstances in which N would name an individual who did not fit it, and/or would not name an individual who did. Some would also add: if N names V, then it could not (could not have?) but name V; there are no possible circumstances in which, through variation in the distribution of general properties in the world, N would name something or someone else other than V, or no one (nothing). Again, there is no doubt something deeply right about at least the first of these ideas. Again, there are problems with the idea as stated. One is that, as pointed out previously, there are at least conceivable circumstances under which, for example, some instances of 'Wittgenstein', as now used, would name Russell and not Wittgenstein—though, as things in fact are, they name Wittgenstein. Another is that though, no doubt, for any genuine general or descriptive property V has, either V could have lacked it, or some individual other than V could have had it without being V (Leibniz's insight), it is not so clear that just any such alterations could come about while the name N would, in those circumstances, continue to name V. One of the general properties V could have lacked may be, after all, being named by N. And there is no obvious reason why that general property could not be linked with others which served as a condition for having it. Aristotle could have gone into shoe repairs, perhaps. It is a different thought, though perhaps also true, that the name 'Aristotle', as we use it, could turn out to name a cobbler. Thoughts about what Aristotle could have done or been do not rule out there being descriptive conditions on our *name* 'Aristotle' referring to someone, or indeed, being regardable coherently as a name at all. The deep truths in the above ideas, if any, must be reconciled with these facts.

Actually, though, a proper account of what is distinctive about a *name's* semantics is not crucial for present purposes. For what really concerns Russell is that, whatever the semantics of a name may be like, we certainly want to contrast it with one other sort of semantics that it would be at least possible for some referring device to have. We can imagine some referring device, R, being associated with some set of descriptive or general conditions or properties, D, such that it is part of the semantics of R that, under all possible circumstances, R refers to that unique item, if any, which has D, whatever item that may happen to be, and if there is no such item, then R refers to nothing. However names contrast with other actual referring devices, it is clear that R would not be a name. (And note, for example, that, in contrast with names, there is absolutely no difficulty at all in supposing that someone understands all there is to understand about R without having the faintest idea who R refers to—a fact that particularly impressed Russell.)

It is this contrast between names and referring devices like R which Russell thought it would be difficult to maintain for names of such things as people, pets and bits of geography. The reason, in brief, is this. First, Russell thought that the exigencies of referring to items such as the above would require any item which did so to have 'descriptive content'. That is, it would have to be part of the semantics of any such item that it was to be understood to be referring to whoever or whatever (uniquely) satisfied some certain descriptive condition, or had some given set of general properties, D. Second, Russell thought that an item could not admit such descriptive content into its semantics without sliding over into being the sort of referring device R is. Russell was deeply impressed by Leibniz's insight that, for any individual, V, and any descriptive condition, D, being V, and satisfying that condition must be, logically speaking, two distinct and independent things. As Leibniz might have put it, the concept of being V and the concept of satisfying D are logically distinct. Nor could the concept of being V be individuated (for all purposes, at least) by D. Russell takes this to mean that if D is part of N's semantics, and is to be understood to be a requirement on being the one N names, then N cannot be a name at all.

Russell's reasons for thinking that a 'name' of, for example a person, pet or city, must have descriptive content are, in my view, not the best possible ones. I have said what I think those are in chapter 6. Still, some of Russell's reasons are certainly worth stating. One is what we might call the re-identification problem. Items like people or pets may occur at a variety of times, under a variety of conditions and in a variety of states. Suppose we stipulate of a given individual, V, as V is found at some time in some condition that N names V. The re-identification problem is then: in what other circumstances will we have encountered (or will there be) an individual such that N names it?

That is a question which, on Russell's view, a general criterion for being the one the name names would have to settle. Russell thinks that—for possibly recurrent individuals—there would have to be such a criterion. And he thinks that it would have to be specifiable in general terms; hence, that N would have to have descriptive content. Something about what N means—or how it is properly understood— must guide us in distinguishing circumstances which present us with a case of what N names—or which are a case of the presence of that item—from circumstances which are not. That element of N's semantics, to be of any help to us, or to draw the required distinction effectively, would have to be descriptive. But if there is such an element in N's semantics, then, on Russell's view, N could not be a name.

A second of Russell's reasons concerns what to say in or of the unhappy possibility that N should lack a referent altogether. Ask yourself, Russell says, what we should say if told that N referred to no one or nothing. First, would we admit that this possibility was compatible with N's current semantics at all? Second, would we say that, in that unhappy event, N was, in any case, meaningful—would we then be able to assign it such-and-such definite semantics? If the answers to these two questions are 'Yes', then N is not a name, on Russell's view. For there would then have to be some component of N's semantics which would be present equally whether N referred to anything or not. That component would have to be descriptive content. Conversely, any property of naming V could not be part of N's semantics under the hypothetical circumstances. Hence, on Russell's view, it could not be part of that semantics as things stand. For both these reasons, N would not be a name. One reason Russell seems to think this is that the semantics N would turn out to have in the case where it turned out not to refer would have to be a semantics that it would have both in that case and in the case where it did refer to something (for example, the actual state of affairs). In that case, that semantics could not be other than descriptive. On the present view of semantics, that is a bad reason. The semantics N would have in some counter-factual circumstance need not be a semantics it now counts as having. But another reason behind Russell's view is, I think, just another version of the re-identification problem. If it is both possible for N to turn out to refer to something and for N to turn out not to, then there must be some criterion which distinguishes the one sort of case, and when we are in it, from the other. But again, that criterion, to be any use to us, would have to be at least partly descriptive, and would have to be (now) built into the semantics of the name.

Russell takes it as obvious that ordinary 'names' of people, pets, cities, etc. would still be meaningful if it turned out that they had no referent, and so that it is possible for such things to turn out to be so. I think that Russell is right in this, though a comment is in order on his reasons for thinking so. Russell tries to persuade us that this is so by presenting us with examples like 'Romulus' and 'Homer'. Most of us believe that Romulus did not exist. Yet, in some sense at least, we would allow that 'Romulus' was a name. Since we use 'Romulus' as we do in the belief that there is (was) no one it refers to, it must be that the semantics it now counts as having is one that it would count as having if it did not refer. (In fact, given my belief about Romulus, that is not even quite grammatical.) So far, so good.

But now consider the name 'Russell'—since that is also within the intended scope of Russell's thesis. Could that name turn out to lack a referent, and if it did, what should we say about it then? Well, in a sense, at least, I think this is possible. But we must distinguish two quite different sorts of case. First, there is the case where we all sit around speaking freely of 'Russell', but it then emerges that we have all taken LSD. Coming out of our trance, we are all amazed to learn that while under the influence we all actually thought that *that* was someone's name. What a silly idea! In that case, I think we would be inclined to say that 'Russell' was just nonsense. It masqueraded, perhaps, as a name, but it is not and never was one. It never had any definite semantics, or, in-so-far as it did, not that of a name. But second, there is the case where we pick up the latest issue of the *New York Review of Books*, read the large headline 'Gigantic "Russell" Hoax Exposed', groan 'Oh, no', and read on to have our worst fears confirmed. In that case, we should admit, I think, that 'Russell', in our mouths, was and is perfectly meaningful, but that it names no one. I would then be willing to suppose that descriptive content was at least part, and perhaps all, of its semantics. What we should not so cheerfully just assume is that the descriptive content it would then count as having is a semantics it would have counted as having, had that respected journal proved mistaken in this case.

Despite all this, however, Russell's underlying intuitions seem most plausible here. Anything we ordinarily regard as a name could, under bizarre enough circumstances, turn out to be meaningful, but without a referent. We need some criterion to distinguish (possible) cases where we have actually arrived in such a situation from ones in which we have not. It is reasonable to suppose that some version of such a criterion is part of the present semantic content of the 'name'. And it is at least plausible that that requires that that present semantics include at least some descriptive content.

So Russell has raised a problem as to how what we ordinarily regard as names could possibly be names. Russell's problem does not quite have the status of a paradox. It is not as if we could not imagine any way out of it at all. Still, at least it is a problem, and as such, deserves to be faced somehow or other. One approach to it would be to deny that our ordinary names do have descriptive content as part of their semantics. Without that assumption, Russell, at least, would have provided no reason to suppose that these names slide out of the category of name into the other semantic category about which he worried. But, of course, it will not do to stop there. Russell has, after all, provided some reason to think that ordinary names must have descriptive content. For ordinary names, he has provided at least two classification schemes for situations we might be in: situations of confronting the referent of the name and others; and situations of the name's having a referent and others. The pressure towards descriptive content comes from the idea that, in each case, there must be such a thing as the way in which the classifying of situations within the scheme is to be done, and that some understanding of what the right way would be is (normally) part of the proper understanding of a name—or at least an ordinary one. It is difficult to see how one such understanding might be distinguished from another except in descriptive terms. Someone who denies that ordinary names have descriptive content owes us an account of how this pressure is to be resisted. Many of the latter-day 'Russellians' who have taken this way with Russell's problem have realized that there is this further job to be done. That, I think, is the motivation for 'causal (or historical) chain' theories of the fixing of the referent of a name. For reasons pointed out in the last chapter, I think it is doubtful at best that such theories actually do offer solutions to the problems Russell poses.

The other approach would be to admit that ordinary names have descriptive content and to deny that that entails any slide on their part into some other semantic category, such as the one with which Russell contrasts genuine names. The autonomy thesis for names suggests how that approach might be carried out. Consider some ordinary name, N. ('Russell' will do.) Suppose it to be settled in advance that a certain descriptive content, D, is part of N's semantics. On the autonomy thesis, that fact about N, by itself, leaves it an open question whether N has the semantic property of being a name: both its having and its lacking that property is compatible with its having that much other semantics. Suppose that N does have that property (hereafter E). Then there are two components to N's semantics, E and D.

What these two components are supposed to do for N, specifically, is to allow it to have descriptive content while keeping it out of the semantic category of the hypothetical referring device R. That means that with the two components there should be some possible situations of which it is now true to say that, should they obtain, or had they obtained, the item in that situation which N would refer to and name is not what N would refer to on the rule that it referred, in that situation, to whatever uniquely fits D.[18] That would be true of a situation, S, if in S treating N as a name was incompatible with taking N's referent to be whatever satisfied that requirement, and further, treating it as a name was the right thing to do.

Take the last point first. By hypothesis, we are now correct in treating N as a name, since it is one. What is required is that the counter-factual situation, S, not be one in which we would have to admit that we were mistaken in taking N to be a name. The supposition is that S is a situation in which the guidance we would get by taking fitting D to be the requirement on being a referent conflicts with any advice we would get by taking N to be a name. The problem then is: what would be the most reasonable advice to follow? S is a situation of the required kind if the latter advice would be the most reasonable to attend to. Our way with Russell's problem supposes that there are some situations like that.

Now for the first point. S would be a situation in which taking N to be a name was incompatible with following the advice provided by the requirement of fitting D—on the view that being a name is an autonomous property—if following that advice made it too stupid for us to treat N as a name, or to apply 'the calculus (discourse) of name-bearing' to it. On the autonomy thesis, one might argue, this 'if' should be made an 'iff', though that is stronger than what is needed for the present point. It may be part of applying the calculus of names to 'Wittgenstein', for example, that it is to be supposed that there is some man such that that name is to be understood to be him. Supposing that may be stupider than anything we could ever regard as correct if we must also suppose that being (uniquely) the author of the *Investigations* and the *Tractatus* is to be understood to be the (or even a) condition on being the referent of that name, and if it emerges that both these works were long-term joint projects of the Cambridge Moral Sciences Club (depending on just what the facts of that discovery were). The most reasonable course may then be to suppose that 'Wittgenstein' is not, and never was, a name. But it may also be to attend to what treating it as a name would most reasonably indicate (if there must be some man it was always to be understood to mean, then it would most reasonably be taken to be that one) and to go on treating

---

[18] It is perhaps worth a reminder that the issue of keeping N out of the category of R is distinct from any questions about how to evaluate modal statements in which N might occur. The latter issue poses no problems in any case (see ch. 6).

'Wittgenstein' as a name, rather than to attend to the requirement suggested above. In such a case, the mere fact of 'Wittgenstein' being a name, and always properly so understood, would make its behaviour differ from what that behavior would be if it were guided by descriptive content alone, so keeps the name from falling into the category of R.

That there is more to the semantics of a name than just its descriptive content, and more which is independent of what that descriptive content is, is enough to make the name's behaviour in counter-factual or other possible circumstances differ from what that behaviour would be if it were determined, in the way R's is, by descriptive content alone. In a case like the above, we might correctly drop the idea that the above-mentioned properties of Wittgenstein were part of that name's descriptive content. But that we would then do so does not show that that is not now in fact part of that name's descriptive content. For, as just shown, its being so need not be taken to determine what we would have to say if we were in such counter-factual situations as just described. That it cannot by itself do so is shown by the fact that the property of being a name is also and autonomously a part of 'Wittgenstein' 's current semantics.

A final note on Putnam's problem of chapter 3. What 'makes it the case' that 'Wittgenstein' names Wittgenstein rather than someone else, when all the other facts about it—particularly, in Putnam's case, facts about its behaviour in wholes of which it is a part—are compatible, in some sense of that term, with other hypotheses? First, it is part of its proper understanding that it is a name. That is the most reasonable solution to disambiguation problems for it. Aside from that, nothing else requires that it be so treated. Second, as part of the calculus of names, or name-bearing, it is to be supposed that there is a fact as to who the name names. Third, what that fact is most reasonably taken to be, on that supposition, is that 'Wittgenstein' names Wittgenstein. That is what strikes us as the most reasonable way of applying that calculus, or discourse in this case. Nor ought one to want or expect any more of an account than that.

8

The Problems with Private Semantics

'Is this [everyday] language somehow too coarse and material for what we want to say? *Then how is another one to be constructed?*' (120) Suppose, specifically, that we want language which excludes S-use sensitivity: its predicates, for example, have a determinate extension, and have that extension independent of occasions for assigning them (parts of) one. How are we to construct such language? Or, how might we assign such language a semantics which rules out its applying to things in S-use sensitive ways? Private language is a case against which to test an answer. The answer it suggests—or so it will be argued here—is the answer Wittgenstein means to suggest in 120: it is not possible to construct such a language—or more generally, there could not be semantic items which thus excluded S-use sensitivity in their applications. (As noted in chapter 1, if that is true for *any* sort of semantic item, then any language is intrinsically liable to have its semantics S-use sensitively; so there will be at least the possibility of S-use sensitivity at the semantic level as well.)

The bearing of private language on other, non-Wittgensteinian, models of language or semantics does not, to be sure, exhaust its interest. No doubt private language has epistemological significance as well—at least in so far as it has traditionally been tied up with the idea of an incorrigible statement; and, as we shall see, the demise of private language does spell the demise of incorrigibility in *statements* (or thoughts) as well. Moreover, the impossibility of private language is connected to an anti-realist moral; one which has its bite especially in the area of our psychological properties—our having sensations or after-images, etc., but also our propositional attitudes. It is no accident that Wittgenstein introduces the idea of private language, in 243, in connection with examples involving sensations. Nor that he later connects the moral of private language with his application of chapter 2's model of semantic fact to the semantics of our propositional attitudes. The anti-realist moral, and its connection to our psychologies, will be discussed briefly at the end. But my main concern here is simply to connect the private language discussion to the semantic issues which have occupied the bulk of this book, and to show how private language and those issues are crucial to each other.

The idea of private language does not obviously speak one way or the other on the issue of S-use sensitivity. If there could be private language at all, there is no apparent reason why some of it, at least, should not be S-use sensitive. The crucial fact about private language, for present purposes, is rather this. If there could be private language, then it would appear—and, as will be argued, correctly—that the model of chapter 2 could not apply to its semantics. Reasonable judges could not play the substantive role that they do on that model in fixing what the semantic facts (of the private language) are; for reasonable judges could not have appropriate informed reactions to all the other relevant facts at all. Or at least not, as the model demands, an indefinite number of novel judges. So private language is a test case where the model does not apply. Conversely, it will be argued, the failure of the model to apply makes for the impossibility of private language. So, what private language is meant to show is that where the model does not apply there could be no semantic fact. If there are items to which the model does not apply, then it could not be a fact that those items have any semantics at all, and there could be no facts as to that semantics being or requiring any one thing rather than any other. Put positively, wherever there are facts as to what the semantics of an item is—so wherever it is sensibly taken to have a semantics at all— the model does apply to the item, so that its semantics is subject to the public access principle, and the facts as to that items semantics are, as per the model, what the reactions of reasonable judges show them to be.

About making language more exact, Wittgenstein says,

No *single* ideal of exactness has been laid down; we do not know what we should be supposed to imagine under this head . . . (88)

The connection of private language with S-use sensitivity may now be seen by developing a parallel point. Suppose we encounter some particular bit of S-use sensitivity in English. There is no reason in principle why we should not be able to revise language—or at least the language we use for some particular purpose—so as to get rid of it. We note, for example, that the predicate 'is red' may, on occasion, say what is true of some ripe apples, and, on occasion, say what is false of them. So we introduce some new predicates—say, 'is apple-red' and 'is solid-red', pointing to the above distinction to define what we mean. 'Is apple-red' does not sometimes say what is false of those apples; it always says what is true of them (at least as far as we can see so far). So we are rid of that particular bit of S-use sensitivity for the predicate 'is apple-red'. None of this is yet philosophically interesting. On the other hand, no one (who accepted S-use sensitivity in the first place) would expect 'is apple-red', as so introduced, not to exhibit S-use sensitivities. It would just exhibit them at different places. For example, it has not yet been settled in any unique way what to say about apples that look different in different sorts of light. As for the picture of semantics developed in chapter 1, if we were inclined to think that it fit 'is red', then we should be just as inclined to think that it fits 'is apple-red'.

Now consider a philosopher who, when he thinks of eliminating S-use sensitivity, is not thinking of piecemeal operations such as this. His aim is to construct language whose semantics prohibits it from being S-use sensitive at all, or ensures that it cannot be. So he aims for language which is radically different in kind from the language with which we are familiar, and not just different in the way that 'is apple-red' is different from 'is red'. A language with semantics of the sort he seeks would be, for example, in virtue of that fact alone, one for which one could state a homophonous 'truth-theory' which would be, taken literally and seriously, both sensible (coherent) and correct (true). That such a theory could be stated would be a feature of the kind of semantics involved itself, and would distinguish this philosopher's 'more precise' language, free as it is from S-use sensitivity, from any language we now know.

For a philosopher with this sort of aim, the model of semantic fact proposed in chapter 2 poses a substantial problem. For suppose that P is some predicate of his constructed language. Then P must have some semantics such that, for any V to which P might apply, and for any occasion of considering the question, there is just one thing that that semantics requires with respect to P's truth of V: it requires that P have either the property of being true of V, or that of being false of V, or that V be an irremediably borderline case. That that semantics requires what it does must be an intrinsic part of its being the semantics it is; what it requires must be independent of any further facts, and particularly of facts which are liable to vary across occasions for judging P's semantics. So, in particular, it must be independent of further facts about the reactions of otherwise reasonable judges.

But this requirement on the ideal constructed language is at loggerheads with the model of chapter 2. On that model, applied to P, P's having or lacking the property in question is a matter of the reactions of reasonable judges to other facts about it. Conversely, what any given semantics requires with respect to P's truth of V is a matter of the reactions of reasonable judges to P's having that semantics. Given that the role of such judges is substantive, there is always more than one reaction that it would be conceivable for them to have; the other facts themselves cannot require any one given reaction independent of what reasonable judges are, in fact, like. But then it is always conceivable that occasions should turn up which would make reasonable judges treat P S-use sensitively in the relevant respect. The possibility for this to happen cannot be eliminated by the nature of the semantics involved (as the rest of P's semantics). It cannot be that that semantics is intrinsically the wrong kind for allowing P to be S-use sensitive. P may in fact be such that reasonable judges never will react to other facts so as to treat it in S-use sensitive ways. But the possibility of their doing so cannot be eliminated. So nor, in principle, can the possibility of P exhibiting S-use sensitivity, as long as the model applies. What is needed, then, for constructing an ideal language of the sort envisioned by the above philosopher is that the model of chapter 2 should not apply. The aim of the private language argument, or at least that facet of it to be considered here, is to show that the applicability of that model is ineliminable if there is to be coherent talk of semantic fact at all.

1. TWO ARGUMENTS

As we are now speaking, some language—say, some predicate—or some concept or thought is private when the public access principle does not apply to it. If W is the private item, this means that at least part of W's semantics is such that a reasonable judge could not be in a position to appreciate properly what other facts require with respect to having or lacking that semantics. Such a judge could not stand in the right sort of relation to the other facts, and to the semantics in question—a relation such that his reaction to the other facts, when so related to them, settled the question whether W had or lacked that semantics. More precisely, if some judges, reasonable or not, could do this, it would not be indefinitely open to novel reasonable judges to do so.

We might think of any of a number of reasons for such a state of affairs. Perhaps the semantics in question is not graspable by an indefinite number of judges: there are semantic properties involved such that no more than some fixed group of judges could, in principle, know or understand what those properties are. For example, Pol detects, or claims to, a certain ineffable quality of some of his sensations, and reserves some word or concept W for ascribing just that quality to novel sensations. The property of saying a sensation to have just that quality would be one we could not grasp. If Pol's word does say that, we could not, in principle, understand what was being said in it. Or it might be that some of the other facts on which W's having that semantics depends were ones to which no more than a fixed group of judges could stand in the right relation (the right one, that is, for having reactions that count). This might, but need not be, because, for example, no one but Pol can know the relevant other facts to obtain. For instance, no one but he can 'observe' his present sensation—the one he is characterizing as 'W'. But it might be that we could stand in the right relation to the other facts without knowing, or being able to know, them to obtain. If we could be told what they were, for example, we might be able to say what those facts would show about W's semantics if they did obtain. And it might be that the reactions we thus evinced were the ones which settled what W's semantics was in the relevant respects. Since W is private, we must suppose that either we could not even be told what the relevant other facts were, or that the reactions we evinced on thus being told were not such as to settle the relevant issues of W's semantics—for example, that you had to be able to see the facts to obtain, in the full surroundings in which they do, to have the appropriate reaction to them. One might also imagine a third possibility: we can all see all the other facts on which W's semantics depends, and grasp what semantics is in question; but, in principle, no one's reaction to those facts except for Pol's could possibly have a role in showing what W's semantics was. I do not think that this is a genuine third possibility. But the point does not matter much for present purposes. Nor does it matter much in which of these ways you conceive of privacy. The argument to come will apply equally in any of these cases, provided that the public access principle is violated.

It will help if we make some simplifying assumptions. It is not built into the notion of private language that such items must be spoken, or thought by only one person. But it will change nothing if we consider a private language which is spoken by only one person. Let us imagine a solitary private linguist, then, who we will call Pia. It does not matter for the argument whether the private semantic items are words or, for example, concepts or thoughts. But for simplicity let us consider a private word, 'gronch', which we will suppose to be, grammatically, a predicate. Finally, we have said that an item is private if it has even part of its semantics privately; that is, if there is part of its semantics which is not just what it would be shown to be by the reactions of a reasonable judge to other facts which were appropriately available to an indefinite number of further judges. For all that, part of the item's semantics might be public. But it will facilitate the argument if we suppose all of the semantics of 'gronch' to be private except whatever semantics is entailed simply by the fact of 'gronch' being a predicate. In allowing that much semantics to be public, or at least beyond dispute, we depart, perhaps, from Wittgenstein (see 261). But that will not destroy the argument. Supposing all of the rest of the semantics to be private saves us the trouble of adding qualifiers, as in 'there are no semantic facts about W in so far as its semantics is private'. These preliminaries done, let us consider two arguments.

The Epistemic Argument (EA)

Suppose that Pia takes some semantic fact to hold of gronch. For example, for some item, V, she takes 'gronch' to be true of V. (It does not matter whether V is a public or private item.) She would probably express this attitude simply by saying, 'V is gronch' or 'This is gronch', referring to V. (The mere fact that we cannot understand her need not stop her from speaking out loud.) We, however, cannot say that she takes it that V is gronch. For in saying that we purport to say what it is that she has taken to be so. And, by hypothesis, that is something we either cannot grasp or at least cannot know: we do not know what it is for 'V to be gronch'. But we can describe the semantic property she is ascribing to 'gronch' in the above terms—one use of semantic ascent.

   The epistemic argument now begins by supposing, first, that there is some posable question as to how Pia knows that 'gronch' has the semantic property in question—being true of V. (This may be a question that only Pia could pose to herself.) Second, it is supposed that Pia does know the fact in question only if there is some satisfactory answer to that question. So if there is none, then it is fair (and true) to conclude that she does not know. Third, the argument urges on us a certain conception of what it would be for there to be an adequate answer to questions of this sort. Suppose there is a pair of cases in which Pia might take 'gronch' to have the relevant property, in one of which it did have it, while in the other it did not. Then Pia must now have at her disposal some (further) information which shows her to be in the first sort of case and not the second. For suppose that the second situation is deceptive—that is, it is such that if Pia were in it, she would have all the further reason she now has for taking herself to be in a situation in which 'gronch' is true of V. Then, it is urged, there is no satisfactory answer to the 'How does she know?' question, and, in fact, she cannot know the semantic fact in question. So the requirement is to hold for any such pair of cases. It will be recognized that to insist on it is simply to invoke the indiscernibility principle (IP) discussed in chapter 4.

   Fourth, the argument will expend some ingenuity on demonstrating that there always is such a pair of cases, one of which is deceptive—so that IP can never be satisfied. For example, we might appeal to the fact that, if Pia has conferred some meaning on 'gronch' in the past, or if it has somehow come by one, and that meaning is supposed to determine whether it is now true of V, then Pia may have misremembered what that meaning is. (Compare 265.) One might try to resist this stage of the argument, urging that the nature of private semantics leaves no room in logical space for a deceptive case in this matter—which is to say, no room for a gap (at least in the right sort of case) between Pia taking 'gronch' to have a semantic property of this sort, and it actually having that property. We will consider this move in due course. But, for the time being, let us take this fourth stage of the argument to be successful. The conclusion would then be that Pia could never know any fact about the (private) semantics of 'gronch'.

This argument, if successful, would, I think, spell the demise of the idea of incorrigible statements. Obviously, some additional argument would be needed before it had been shown that private language was impossible. But it is not our present concern to provide such argument. Our concern is merely to consider whether EA, as far as it goes, is a correct argument.

The Ontological Argument (OA)

The (sample) claim now is that 'gronch' has the property of being true of V. The second argument begins with a demand to be shown some other facts which make that purported fact so, or in virtue of which it is so. It then urges two principles on us. The first is that if, for given other facts, F, it is conceivable that F should hold while it was not the case that 'gronch' was true of V, then those facts do not meet the demand. The second is that if there are no other facts which meet this demand, then it is not a fact that 'gronch' is true of V. In the last stage of the argument, ingenuity is expended on showing that there are, and could be, no other facts which meet the demand, as bolstered by the principles, so that the purported fact is not a fact. Further (more ingenuity) the point would hold no matter what purported semantic fact about 'gronch' was in question. So 'gronch' cannot count as having a semantics at all. Again, the last stage of this argument might be resisted. One might try to show that there are, or could be, other facts which leave no room in logical space for the purported fact about 'gronch' not to hold. For example (with reference back to EA), the other fact might simply be that Pia takes 'gronch' to be true of V. Again, we will have more to say about this sort of move at a later stage. But for the moment let us take this last stage of the argument as not in question. So given the principles appealed to, the argument would be correct. At any rate, if it is correct, then it does follow directly that private language is not possible (i.e., that it is not possible for there to be 'private language' with a semantics).

There are two striking facts about the arguments just cited. The first is that, in the public case, the stage at which ingenuity was expended is a stage which we accept as correct. The rule, at least, when it comes to our knowledge of publicly available facts, is that there is no withstanding IP. Nor, for the sorts of facts we normally recognize to obtain or not, is there any withstanding the requirement imposed by OA on other facts: that their obtaining leaves it inconceivable that the fact in question should fail to obtain. Public knowledge and public facts are what they are despite these requirements, not because of them. That is why we are not yet directing attention to the stage of the argument at which ingenuity is expended in the private case. If that stage of EA or of OA were mistaken, that would make the private case radically unlike public ones. We would then want an explanation of how there could be private facts which were genuinely facts, and which behaved that differently from the ones we normally recognize and sometimes know to obtain. But it is not yet time for such considerations.

The second striking feature of the arguments is that they are ones which Wittgenstein rejects as invalid, at least in general, in the public case. For each depends on principles which he rejects. The rejection of EA was considered in chapter 4. OA was rejected, in progressively greater detail, in chapters 5, 6 and 7. So, it would seem, Wittgenstein must reject these two private language arguments. For to accept them would be to impose substantially higher requirements on Pia—for example, for her to know something about her private language—than we are willing to have imposed on ourselves. And that, as many have hastened to point out, would not be fair.

Unless

Suppose it could be argued that there is some crucial and relevant difference between the private and the public case. So that, while IP and the principles invoked by OA were not valid in the public case, or, in general, they were valid in the case of facts about private semantics. With that supplementation, EA and OA might be seen to be good arguments. It would follow immediately that private language was impossible. In line with this thought, we might note the following. Resisting the principles in the public case involved invoking certain resources; the principles failed because, it was claimed, such-and-such else was correct. Suppose it could be shown that those resources were not available in the private case, and that there could be there no suitable substitute for them. Then the principles could not be resisted in that case, and EA and OA, as applied to Pia, would be correct. The private language argument to be given here will be a development of that thought.

2. WITTGENSTEIN'S CHALLENGE

In the public case, we know that EA and OA are wrong. But why? Consider EA first. Wittgenstein rejects this form of argument. But not because when it comes to knowledge anything goes. On the contrary. The sceptic is mistaken, on Wittgenstein's account of the matter, because, notably in advancing IP, the sceptic relies on a conception of knowledge which conflicts with that conception which Wittgenstein argues to be correct. Otherwise put, Wittgenstein is not content merely to point out that the sceptic's argument must be mistaken, or to complain that it imposes higher standards on us than we could reasonably accept, or something of the sort. He specifically identifies what the sceptic's mistake is. To review the most central point: the sceptic supposes that any doubt (or conceivable deceptive state of affairs) which might ever show A not to count as knowing F, or which A must at least be in a position to settle if he is to count as knowing F, is a doubt which always has this status, and the power to show such things. Whereas Wittgenstein argues that a doubt which sometimes has this status and power may often lack it, the variation being across occasions for judging whether A knows that F, and equally across the various things to be said, on various such occasions, in saying A to know F. So a correct statement of truth conditions for knowledge claims requires recognition of a distinction between two classes of doubts, or potential deceptive states of affairs—in present terminology, real doubts and mere doubts, where the former but not the latter have the power in question. The category of mere doubts will always be a non-vacuous one, containing some substantial array of doubts that would be capable of showing, or tending to show, on some occasions (though not on ones where they were mere) that A did not then count as knowing that F.

Now let us ask: how is the real/mere doubt distinction to be drawn on an occasion for a given A and his knowledge of given F? What makes it the case that a given conceivable doubt counts as on one side or the other of this distinction (when it does)? Part of the answer, on Wittgenstein's account, depends on the way the world impinges on us (or on whoever is judging A's knowledge of F), and, given that, on what it is worth to us, or in lives like ours, to treat that doubt in one way or the other; what the consequences are for our activities and our roles in them. But, given that the world impinges on our activities as it does, part of the answer also depends on the reactions of a reasonable judge (so of reasonable judges) to that. In short, a doubt counts as a real one just in case a reasonable judge, in this position for ascribing knowledge of F to A, would react to the facts about A and A's position (and about F) by taking that doubt to be real; by expecting A to be able to settle it if indeed A does know that. So, on the Wittgensteinian view, our right to dismiss, in the ways we do, sceptical worries in matters of someone knowing that F—when and in so far as we do have such right—rests on the reactions of reasonable judges, or at least of a reasonable judge. Our practice is unimpeachable—when it is—because there is no impeaching a practice that a reasonable judge would find a correct one to engage in. It is for that reason that, in the face of the sceptic's arguments, we are entitled serenely to retain our conviction that we have a concept of knowledge, and that it is one about whose extension we were not so far off in practice as all that.

Let us now turn to OA. Again, this is a form of argument which Wittgenstein rejects. Again, he rejects it because he thinks the ontic sceptic mistaken in his conception of what it is (or would be) for such-and-such to be a fact, or for there to be a fact of such-and-such matter. And again, Wittgenstein does not stop there. He has specific views on just how and where the sceptic's conception is wrong. There are various ways of describing the mistake, any of which would do equally well for present purposes. The most convenient is in terms of the view of chapter 7. First, if we treat given discourse as fact-stating, and if it is not too stupid (for us) to do so, then it is fact-stating. There is *no* further issue as to whether it is, and hence no 'deeper sense' in which it still might not be. Second, if, or in so far as, there is a most reasonable view of what the facts would be, in the matters spoken of in that discourse, on the supposition that there were such facts at all, then those are the facts of the matter. In particular—to approach present issues—semantic facts, such as the facts as to whether some predicate, W, says what is true of some item, V, are what they would most reasonably be taken to be, on the supposition that there are semantic facts at all. So there are facts of the matter just where there are most reasonable views of what such facts would be.

Once again, there is the obvious point to make. Whether it is reasonable, for example, to take W to have the property of saying something which is true of V depends on the (other) facts as to the way the world is. But it also depends on the most reasonable reactions to those other facts. The most reasonable reactions are the ones a reasonable judge, appropriately related to those other facts, would have. On the Wittgensteinian account, it is the reactions of reasonable judges which show what those of a reasonable judge would be, and, moreover, which play a substantive role in making such reactions what they are. So again, our right to reject or resist sceptical pressure to give up the idea that there is some fact as to whether F—where and in so far as we have it—rests on the reactions of reasonable judges, and so on there being such. It is worth noting that, even in the public case, what our rights are in such respects depends on what the reactions are. We are not always guaranteed, for any candidate value of F, that there is a fact of the matter as to whether F—even where F does belong to fact-stating discourse. We do know of two kinds of case: some issues are just such that nothing about the way the world is settles them one way or the other. The reactions of reasonable judges, and of a reasonable judge, play an essential and ineliminable role for us in separating out the one sort of case from the other. Or so it has been the burden of this book to argue.

The problem for the private linguist is now evident. *Prima facie*, Pia is not entitled to the reactions of a reasonable judge; still less to those of reasonable judges. For *prima facie*, wherever public access is violated, there can be no such reactions, and no facts as to what they would be. So far, the point is no more than *prima facie*. Strictly speaking, all that is entailed by violation of private access is that there could not be an indefinite number of other judges in a position in which they stood in the right relations to the other facts in which to evince appropriate reactions; reactions which would at least be of the right sort to be telling in questions of what the private semantics in question was. One might still suppose there to be such a thing as how a reasonable judge would react to all the other facts of the case if only such a judge could have access to them, so facts about what such a reaction would be. Such facts would have to be established, if they could be established at all, by appeal to something other than the reactions which (novel) reasonable judges *do* have. But it still must be shown that this could not be done.

If there are ever to be facts as to private semantics (for some item), and if anyone (the private linguist included) is ever going to be capable of knowing any of these facts, then one of three things must be the case. Either, despite first appearances, there really could be facts as to the semantics a reasonable judge would take a private item to have by way of reacting to the other facts about the item. Or there are some alternative resources in the private case given which there may be facts, in particular cases, as to how the real/mere doubt distinction is to be drawn. Similarly, there must be resources which allow a sufficiently large range of discourse about the semantics of the private item to count as fact-stating, and within that range of fact-stating discourse, permit there to be facts as to the correct drawing of a distinction between bits of that discourse which actually succeed in stating what is or is not a fact, and bits which do not. More generally, the resources must allow there to be facts as to what the facts would be within this putative domain of discourse given the supposition that there are, as a rule, facts of the relevant matters. Or, finally, the private linguist must have means for resisting EA and OA which do not depend on drawing any of the crucial distinctions for which Wittgenstein appeals to the reactions of a reasonable judge.

Wittgenstein's challenge to the private linguist, then—that is, the philosopher who holds private language possible—is to show how any of these three conditions could possibly be met. His own conviction is that they cannot. The aim of what follows is to support that conviction with argument. Wittgenstein *appears* to be unfair to the private linguist, imposing higher standards on Pia, or on facts about private language, than he would accept (for us) in the public case. For example, he says, commenting on private ostensive definition,

But what is this ceremony for? For that is all it seems to be! A definition surely serves to establish the meaning of a sign.—Well, that is done precisely by the concentration of my attention: for in this way I impress on myself the connection between the sign and the sensation.—But 'I impress it on myself' can only mean: this process brings it about that I remember the connection *right* in the future. But in the present case I have no criterion of correctness. (258)

Remarks such as this stand in blatant contrast with his view in the public case, as expressed in remarks such as,

If I have exhausted the justifications, I have reached bedrock and my spade is turned. Then I am inclined to say: 'This is simply what I do.' (217)

To use a word without a justification does not mean to use it without right. (289)

Imagine someone suggesting to us that perhaps we are misremembering the way in which 'brown' is to be used, or which things are to be called 'brown'. We can, perhaps, give no justification for our use of the word, or proof that we are using it correctly. Yet our failure to have anything to say here does not jeopardize our counting as knowing what we are saying, or what the word means, or how it is to be used. Yet the possibility of there being facts about private semantics—such as facts as to what the future correct use of a private word requires, or what would be cases of such use—and the possibility of the private linguist knowing such facts is supposed to be called into question by the possibility of Pia misremembering her definition of her private word. Why cannot Pia respond to such sceptical doubts, with us, that while she has here reached bedrock and her spade is turned, for her thus to use her word without justification is not for her to use it without right? Is Wittgenstein not just maintaining a double standard?

The answer to this charge of unfairness is this. It is clear what entitles us to proceed without justification. Wittgenstein has gone into great detail in establishing that right for us, and examining just when and where we have it. It remains to be shown that anything could ever entitle a private linguist to proceed without justification. The resources that do the job for us are *not* obviously available to Pia. And it is no double standard to ask the philosophical private linguist to provide a metajustification for Pia's right sometimes to proceed without justification, of the sort, or at least of the efficacy of the metajustification that Wittgenstein has provided for the public case.

3. A PRIVATE VIEWING

It is all too easy to think of private language as easy to do. It may seem no less commonplace than, for example, what the following fantasy suggests (or anyway it is easy to fall into thinking of it on the model of this fantasy). Pol falls through a crack in the earth, and enters the wondrous world of Outreterre. He is equipped with a radio transmitter, so that we can communicate with him; but we are for ever barred from seeing the wonders he sees. At a certain moment, we become interested in the question how many Outreterrian widgets are mauve. We ask Pol to study a sample for us. But, it emerges, he does not know what mauve is. So we explain it to him the best we can. After several attempts, Pol says, 'I've got it', and goes off to do the study. His report is, '17 per cent are mauve.' Later he tells us that while he was studying the widgets he noticed another kind of object which he cannot quite describe, but which he has decided to call 'dralps'. As he speaks, he says, 'There goes one now', and from then on includes reports like this from time to time in his communications.

Consider first Pol's widget study. It is always possible that Pol has not understood what mauve is, or that he is unreliable and uses that word in no consistent way at all. For we have no very good way of checking on how he has taken our instruction. Possible, but, if you know Pol, not likely. He is, after all, generally reliable in his use of English, and in general reasoning abilities. Moreover, we may suppose, he is generally sensitive to colours and good at colour identification. So, though there are various possible views of Pol's reports in this matter, none of which is positively and once and for all refutable,

surely the most reasonable view is that what Pol is reporting to us is
how many Outreterrian widgets are mauve, and that, for his sample, at
least, he has got this roughly right.

Now for 'dralps'. Again, various views are possible. Perhaps Pol
simply uses the term at random. Or perhaps he frequently forgets what
he has decided to mean by it, so that he calls all different sorts of things
dralps on different occasions. But again, considering Pol's general
reliability, such things are not likely. The most reasonable view is that
there is a certain kind of strange object in Outreterre, that Pol has
named this sort of object a 'dralp', and that, by and large, he goes about
saying that there are dralps about (when he does) because there are
dralps about.

Does Pia differ relevantly from Pol? From time to time she says,
'(It's) gronch.' (We might as well suppose that she does this out loud.)
With Wittgenstein, we may suppose, for convenience, that she does
this, or purports to do it, by way of characterizing 'private objects'—
her sensations, or the like. But of course that is not all that she does.
We may also suppose her to be a competent English speaker. So she can
communicate with us. If it helps, we may also suppose her to
demonstrate, in such public behaviour, that she is an eminently
reasonable (sagacious and judicious) person—as a rule. Again, there is
no end to possible accounts of what she is doing in her 'gronch'
utterances, none of which are definitely refutable (at least from our
point of view). Among these, she might, as it were, just be mouthing
off randomly. But surely, it will be urged, that is not the most
reasonable view of what she is doing. The most reasonable view, it
might be claimed, is that there is an explanation for it, namely: some
of her sensations, etc. have a certain (observable) quality which she
refers to as 'gronch'—or perhaps, as 'being a gronch'. When she says
'It's a gronch', she is saying the private item in question to have that
quality. And as a rule, though not always, the explanation for her
saying that is that the item does have that quality. As it were, her use
of the word is under the control of that property (the one she uses the
word to name)—whatever precisely this means, but in any case in
much the way that our use of the word 'brown', if we are competent
with it, is under the control of the property of being brown, or simply
the colour brown. If the above line of thought does not fit Pia's case,
and if, indeed, she is not to be thought of on the model suggested by
Pol, then it is important to say something about what the differences
are. This section will at least take some preliminary steps in that
direction.

The suggestion of Pol's case for Pia's is that, while it could never be
established conclusively (by us, or perhaps by her) that she was

speaking meaningful, coherent and hence private language, rather than, say, being under some strange illusion that that was what she was doing, it at least could be the most reasonable explanation (for us) that that was what she was doing. And it is always, or nearly so, reasonable to accept the most reasonable explanation. So it could be that we ought to judge that Pia was speaking private language. But, as has been observed before, we can compare explanations to see which is the most reasonable only after those explanations have, as it were, entered into explanation space. The explanation must itself be coherent and describe a possible state of affairs. (One might also insist, churlishly perhaps, that it *explain* something.) What is at issue now is precisely whether the idea of speaking a private language is a coherent one, and whether there is any possible state of affairs that would count as someone doing that. Those questions are not to be settled by appealing to the idea of reasonable explanation. So that comparison with Pol's case is at least premature at this point. At the end of this section, we will return to considering whether the idea of Pia speaking a private language genuinely does explain anything. Meanwhile, the aim is to break down the idea that what Pia does in speaking private language is something familiar—even something as familiar as what Pol does in speaking to us from Outreterre.

For convenience we have been supposing that Pia speaks her private word 'gronch' in characterizing or identifying private objects. But if 'private objects' are simply sensations or things like them, then speaking of such things is neither a necessary nor a sufficient condition for speaking private language. Chapter 2 canvassed the idea that a private 'gronch' could be used for characterizing public objects such as ashtrays, ascribing to them a putative ineffable quality which only Pia could be in a position to grasp or recognize. So that only Pia could stand in the right relation to other facts about an object for judging whether those facts made it a case of what counts as having that quality. Only she, if anyone, could have the reactions that might establish that an item did or did not so count, or might make for there being cases of its doing so.

On the converse side, Pia might say such things as, 'I am having a greenish after-image.' That would be English, so presumably public language, though apparently about Pia's 'sensations or something of the sort'.[1] (In the past, some have held that talk about after-images, while English, also is private language. It is difficult to see how this could be, the problems with viewing English in that way being

---

[1] It is notoriously difficult to say just what an after-image is, other than an after-image. It is not quite a sensation. A visual phenomenon, perhaps, but does that help? In any case, it seems a reasonable candidate for a private object, in so far as there are any.

notorious. Wittgenstein, in any event, insists that such bits of English are public language. It should at least be clear by now that the issue is not settled against him without some further account of just what sort of semantics that part of English is supposed to have.) If ordinary after-image talk is public language, then it follows that all the other facts on which the correct employment of such talk, and its semantics, might depend are facts to which an indefinite number of novel judges could stand in the right relation for having reactions which established (and determined) what those facts about the use and semantics of such talk were—that is, which established what the reactions of a reasonable judge in such matters would be. So, for example, the facts on which the truth of such remarks as Pia's depended would be available in principle, in whatever the appropriate form of availability might be, to an indefinite number of novel judges. And the facts about truth here would be decided by the reactions of such judges to these other facts along the lines described in chapter 2. The implications of that thought will be examined further in the last section of this chapter. For the present, the point is merely that talk about such 'private objects' as after-images might, for all that, be public language.

Pia's remark about her after-image is, at least on my intuitions, public language. But what is presently crucial is that if that is not so, it is not shown not to be so merely in virtue of the fact that it is, after all, a remark about an after-image. Now suppose that Pia announces to us that she has a word in her vocabulary, 'gronch', which characterizes or identifies some of her sensations, etc. She cannot, she tells us, explain to us what it means, or when it would be used correctly. Or rather, she gets so far as telling us that it stands for a certain quality, but then claims inability to explain to us what quality this is. What decides whether this is private language? (Rather than being no coherent language at all, or none with the semantics Pia has told us it has; or being public language.) Confine attention to the choice between its being public and its being private language. (There might also fail to be a fact of the matter. There may be genuine room left by the facts for choice on our parts as to how we will regard this language of Pia's.)

Pia might, for a start, tell us that 'gronch' was private language. But we would be under no automatic compulsion to believe her. Some English speaker might, bizarrely, believe that his use of the word 'hand' is private language, and even intend it to be such. (Russell believed that his use of the name 'Piccadilly' was private language. I believe that Russell was wrong about this.) The person with the bizarre attitudes towards 'hand' might, despite them, be using that word to mean what it does mean in English, hence as an instance of public language. (He might also, given his attitudes, be using it to say many false things.) What would make this so would be facts about the semantics most reasonably assigned to his words in the circumstances of their use—facts about the way we all (reasonable judges, that is) would react to them. (That it is a publicly decidable issue whether private language is being spoken is a theme to be expanded in the next section.)

It is a possible view of Pia that, despite her protestations, she is really speaking public language. (It is consistent with taking that view that we should also view ourselves as not yet having caught on to which property she uses 'gronch' to name. We might persist in that view for quite a long time—until doing so proved too stupid by our lights.) If her language is public, then its semantics is whatever it is shown to be by the other facts about it available to us, or at least to an indefinite number of novel judges. Given that, we might on occasion be in an authoritative position to establish that Pia was wrong in various of the semantic facts she took to hold of such utterances, including facts as to their truth. It might be possible to demonstrate publicly and conclusively that such things were so. On the other hand, there might be (for all we know so far) a possible view of what Pia is doing on which her utterances are private language. In that case, perhaps, we might still have *evidence* as to her going right or wrong in her semantic judgements about it. But the true facts of the matter would depend on the proper reactions to facts in principle forever beyond our ken (or proper appreciation). So, it would seem, conclusive demonstration, from our perspective on the matter, is excluded. At least such demonstration could not consist in actually producing the facts on which those semantic facts depend.

If one of the above views of Pia, rather than the other, is the right one, then there must be some facts which show it to be. Presumably, those facts will be publicly accessible. On the other hand, there may be no such facts: it is possible to take the one view, and it is possible to take the other, and that is the end of the matter. We would then be free to view Pia either as speaking public or as speaking private language. What (and how much) we will say about the semantics of her words will, of course, vary accordingly. Whatever the right view on that score, the point is this. To view Pia as speaking private language is to impose a certain conception of meaning (or semantics) on the semantics of her words. That conception should not be allowed to inherit familiarity from the familiarity of the rest of her doings, or of doings such as Pol's, in so far as such doings are available to us—and in so far as they do seem familiar. For those familiar doings, where we can find them, do not of themselves require that conception. On that conception, to repeat, there are facts controlling the semantics of the words (or concepts) which are in principle opaque to all judges of relevant matters (if any) other than Pia herself. The semantics of the words is what it is, only given that there are such hidden facts to be reacted to (by Pia, though not by us) and that those facts do require that their semantics be taken to be that. (It is important, though perhaps not yet immediately obvious,[2] that on this conception, to get into a position to see what Pia was saying of her sensations in saying 'gronch' of them, one would have to get to *be* Pia. That is certainly not our ordinary conception of sensation or after-image talk.) That Pia uses 'gronch' to speak of the sensations, after-images, etc., which she has does not force this conception on us—any more than it is forced on us in Pol's case by the fact that he is speaking of Outreterrian objects. We may think of her speaking of such items and doing so in ways such that semantic questions are settled in principle by facts appropriately available to further judges, and not just to her. That, in fact, is how we do think of such talk when it is done in English. That may be the wrong way of thinking of Pia's words. But if so, this cannot be because they are words of a familiar sort, or because their semantics is of a familiar sort.

If there really are two views to take of language, as having a private semantics or as having a public one, then presumably both those views are available for remarks in English such as Pia's 'I am having a greenish after-image'. In the case of English, it is reasonable to suppose that the facts decide in favour of the public view. Similarly, either view should be available, at least as a possible view, for Pol's talk of dralps. That fact in itself shows that the familiarity and plausibility of Pol's case in no way suggests that private language is an easy thing to bring about. We might view Pol as speaking private language. Perhaps even no other facts show this view to be incorrect. We might even imagine further facts showing it to be correct. But to take that view is to do more than merely view Pol as fitting the description provided at the outset of this discussion. Perhaps we can see what it would be like to view Pol as speaking private language if we consider what it would be

---

[2] One might think: perhaps we could grasp *what* Pia was saying, but just not be able to be in a position to see or judge of what cases it would be true. The problem is that if we are systematically and in principle barred from seeing this, then it is difficult to see how we could be in a position to distinguish between various things to be said which differed precisely in of which of these cases they were true. What the thought supposes is a conception of what is being said which is independent of a grasp of the cases of which it would be true, but which requires a certain distribution of truth values across such cases. Such runs afoul of the general problem of how any semantics can require any further semantics—a problem dealt with for the public case in ch. 2. Anyway, it is not part of our ordinary conception, e.g., of after-image talk that we cannot grasp, or even be familiar with, the cases of its correct application. It is easy enough, for a start, to give oneself after-images.

like to take the contrasting public view of what he is doing. So let us ask what it would be like to take that view of him.

The circumstances are that Pol has slipped through the crack into Outreterre, and *we* cannot follow him. So if Pol encounters some object, and calls it 'dralp', we cannot be there to see whether he has got it right. (As things stand, we do not even know what we should look for if we were there). There are three points to make. First, we cannot be there to be shown a dralp. That does not mean that there could not be an indefinite number of otherwise reasonable judges in such a position, and, more generally, in a position to react to all the other facts relevant to the semantics of 'dralp'. Moreover, if there were such further otherwise reasonable judges to check on Pol's semantic judgements, there is no reason why we should be barred from knowing and appreciating that fact, and reacting to it appropriately in our judgements as to the semantics 'dralp' in fact had. We have not said whether there is anyone else in Outreterre. Perhaps there is not. Perhaps even there could not be (for some peripheral reason, such as cracks closing up.) But no fact about the sort of word 'dralp' is, or the sort of semantics it has, requires that there not be such an indefinitely expandable array of judges. It is not part of the concept of a dralp, or part of the semantics of the word, that being a dralp is not the sort of thing ordinary folk such as you and me could be in a position to judge about. So far, in fact, the *concept* allows anyone to have a view (since so far, a dralp is just an ordinary, though difficult-to-describe sort of object), though the world might not provide the occasion for just anyone to do so. We could, perhaps, build it into the concept of a dralp that this was not so. But to do so would be to add to the story told so far. And not in the direction of making it seem more familiar or easier to bring about.

Second, for the same reasons as those just mentioned, we need not take such a modest view of our own abilities in such matters. We cannot observe dralps since we cannot slip through the crack. But that may be viewed as a peripheral matter. It is not as if the sorts of facts about dralps and non-dralps which would be relevant are facts beyond our capability to appreciate or to perceive. So far, there is a clear sense in which we *could* react to all the facts relevant to the semantics of 'dralp'. We could, for example, if the crack were widened. There is no similar way of getting us, for instance, to have Pia's after-images. So if it is built into the concept of (a) gronch that that is what we would have to do in order to be in the right position for reacting to all relevant facts, then we could not be in such a position. Moreover, when we conceive of 'gronch' as private language, that *is* how we are conceiving of the position we would have to be in—if we do not actually have to have Pia's after-images, we do have to be made privy to facts we are equally barred in principle from coming in proper contact with. That is just how 'gronch' differs from what might be familiar or common-sensical.

Third, we can be privy to many relevant other facts about 'dralp' and its proper use. We can be told such facts. As we can be told what sorts of facts would be relevant to determining where 'dralp' applied. (Pol cannot quite tell us what sort of thing a dralp is, or not in a satisfactory way. But that sets no definite limits on how much he *can* tell us about this). The role of what we thus can be told has not yet been settled. (It was not settled by the initial story.) We may certainly react to these facts as a reasonable judge in taking 'dralp' to have one or another semantics (though, of course, reason will set limits to the amount of semantics we would thus assign it.) Since, on the public view, the actual semantics of 'dralp' is made what it is by the facts we or a reasonable judge might react to, and could not be made to vary by facts the force of which no indefinite number of such judges could have access to judging, it may be part of the semantic judgements we thus reasonably would make that we know 'dralp' to have such-and-such semantics—that in these respects what the facts we do appreciate show to be so could not be changed by further facts which by chance have remained beyond our ken. For given what we know about the force further facts might have, it would not be reasonable to suppose that there is any doubt as to whether such a thing might happen. This is to assimilate 'dralp' to our own public language: it is conceivable for there to be more facts that we do not know which would be relevant to some truth-involving properties of 'brown', say. But we are often in a position to say, despite that, that we know which of those properties 'brown' has. In this way, we might sometimes be in a position to demonstrate, authoritatively, that Pol is wrong in some of his judgements about 'dralp'. Whereas it is at least much less clear that we would be able to judge, reasonably, that there is no (real) doubt as to whether the semantics of words is what the facts in our possession would show it to be where the existence of such doubts must depend on the force of further facts whose force in these semantic matters we could not be in a position to appreciate—as would be the case with Pia's 'gronch' on the private view of it.

The above considerations show why Robinson Crusoe was not a private linguist, and conversely why private language is nothing so simple as what we might easily imagine Crusoe doing. To get some idea of the problems unfamiliarity breeds here, we might consider how private language could accommodate the phenomenon of S-use sensitivity. First a preliminary remark. Private language being un-familiar as it is, we cannot just assume that it would be S-use sensitive at all. This much we can say: public language is often S-use sensitive. Further, public language as we know it is intrinsically liable to showing S-use sensitivity at any point. As far as we know, nothing about the semantics of public expressions prohibits them from being S-use sensitive when it comes to their applications, or ensures that they cannot turn out to be as new occasions for applying them to items or situations arise. In fact, we have no idea how we might confer such a thoroughly non-S-use sensitive semantics on an item. As emphasized in the opening of this chapter, our inability to do so is, in a sense, built into the public nature of our (normal) language. So if a private word like 'gronch' has a semantics in virtue of which it cannot exhibit S-use sensitivity, and the problem of dealing with that phenomenon no longer need be considered, then that is a sense in which it is a deeply unfamiliar sort of language. Far from being able to appeal to parallels between it and cases, like Pol's, with which we feel comfortable, we are in urgent need of an account of how such a strange sort of semantics could be conferred on an item at all. The idea of such an account will carry us into succeeding sections. Meanwhile, let us suppose that S-use sensitivity is a phenomenon which private language must be prepared to deal with.

In another connection, Wittgenstein says,

The great difficulty here is not to represent the matter as if there were something one could not do. As if there really were an object from which I derive its description, but I were unable to show it to anyone.—And the best that I can propose is that we should yield to the temptation to use this picture, but then investigate how the *application* of this picture goes. (374)

Here, too, the best method will be to yield temporarily to the temptation to picture private language as an easy accomplishment, and then to work through some of the problems of applying that picture. So let us suppose that Pia has conferred a meaning on 'gronch', as follows: she picked out some property (perhaps by concentrating her attention on it), and decreed or resolved that 'gronch' should name that property. Call that property 'P'. The result, we will suppose, is that 'gronch', as Pia uses it, names P, and that she uses it to name (mean) P—that is, that is what she means by it. 'Gronch' is private language, we will suppose, in virtue of the fact that, given the nature of P, we cannot be privy to all the facts needed for judging just which property P is, or for distinguishing between P and other candidates. But in what follows, it will nowhere be questioned that 'gronch' indeed does name P.

We now encounter a problem to which Wittgenstein gives great prominence in the private language discussion. He points to it, ironically, as follows:

Once you know *what* the word stands for, you understand it, you know its whole use. (264)

Suppose that Pia now encounters some private object, V, and says of it, 'It's gronch.' Is what she said true? And what other facts about the semantics of her words determine this? In the general case, as we know (if private language is at all like the public variety), there is a variety of language games to be played in producing the words Pia did, in all of which 'gronch' names P, where, by the rules of some of these games, those words would be true (of V) while by the rules of others they would be false. Perhaps the semantics already conferred on 'gronch' chooses between these games, or does enough choosing to decide whether the words Pia spoke are true or false. But again, if this is regularly true, then Pia's private language is radically unlike public language. The general rule for public language is that the semantics words have (where they name such-and-such) is compatible with their figuring as moves in a wide variety of language games, including ones whose rules differ over cases in the way just described. Moreover, that special semantics will not have been conferred on Pia's language merely by getting 'gronch' to name P. The naming relation is intrinsically labile. So, given the story with which we succumbed to the picture, we are still owed an account of how 'gronch' came by this extra semantics—a semantics capable of choosing between games to be played in the way described. So to view the semantics of 'gronch' as regularly settling such questions is to view it as radically unfamiliar, contrary to our current hypothesis.

The naming relation is, as said, labile. But what public words mean is often fixed by what they name. Which corresponds to the fact, just mentioned, that what public words mean typically does not choose, in and of itself, between some variety of language games which differ over truth values for particular cases in the way just described. On the assumption of the familiarity of Pia's private language, neither does the semantics of 'gronch'. That is not part of what Pia's naming ceremony, however successful we allow it to have been, conferred on that word. In the public case, it is just this failure of meanings to choose between games that opens up the possibility for S-use sensitivity to manifest itself. For there must be an appeal to further facts of the case, and this appeal is liable to work out differently for different occasions of making it. This same possibility of S-use sensitivity is presumably open in Pia's private case as well.

What is obscure is how Pia, in the private case, could have the means for dealing with it. For recall that, in the public case, the games being played in a given speaking, and thus the truth value of the words as thus spoken, is a question of the games it would be most reasonable to be playing under those circumstances. What further facts about the circumstances must do is fill in which of the variety of games consistent with the given facts about naming it would be reasonable to play; circumstances must make some such games more reasonable than others, and they must do enough of this in the right ways. In effect, given that a public word, W, names Q, we ask ourselves the question: of the various ways of counting things as being Q or not (or of dividing up the world into the Q and the non-Q), any of which would be reasonable sometimes, what is the most reasonable way of doing that under these circumstances (the ones of that speaking)? What appears to require publicity is the way such questions get answered. For, it has been argued, what the most reasonable games or ways of counting in fact are (under those circumstances) are just those games and ways of counting which reasonable judges, hence which a reasonable judge, would find so. (That reasonable judges *could* react differently under different circumstances—that such is, *ex hypothesi*, not forbidden by the semantics of the words as such—is what opens up the possibility of S-use sensitivity.) Which *appears* to require that those are questions that a sufficient number of reasonable judges could, in principle, judge.

But, *prima facie*, Pia is deprived of facts, in her private case, as to what reasonable judges would find most reasonable, and hence of facts as to which games a reasonable judge would take to be the ones being played. Without such facts, it remains deeply obscure how any other facts could yield facts as to which game was being played, hence as to the truth value of Pia's words. So it is obscure how anything Pia might say in private language, even given the success of her ceremony, could have any truth value at all. Whatever facts or factors, if any, might bring it about that they did so would have to be radically unlike those which make for such facts in the public case. In which case, private language ought to seem thoroughly unfamiliar and puzzling. Our ability to communicate with Pol and to credit him with coherent language, even where he speaks of dralps, is far from showing how private language is possible, or even that it is.

Let us now return briefly to the issue of private language as a reasonable explanation of what Pia is doing in saying, from time to time, 'It's gronch.' The thought was that the explanation was to consist of the points, first, that there was some property, P, that Pia was, as a rule, reacting to (or at least took to be present) in so doing, and second, that 'gronch' named it. The question was whether that 'explanation' was a genuine denizen of explanation space. We must first observe that, since 'gronch' is *private* language, P must be a private property. If we could be told which property P was, or could be in a position to judge authoritatively as to which of some variety of candidates it was, then 'gronch' would not be genuine private language. Second, as shown by the above discussion of S-use sensitivity, the explanation is far from complete, and it is so far obscure how it might be completed. For the fact of 'gronch' naming P would not be enough to explain Pia's calling things 'gronch' unless there were also an explanation of why she takes those uses, rather than some rival, also consistent with the facts about naming, to represent the correct way of then describing things a 'gronch' *given* that 'gronch' names P. If it is part of the explanation that her utterances are to be taken to *say* something of the items of which she speaks, it must also be possible to say why and how she takes 'gronch' on occasion to say one thing rather than another. The 'explanation' on offer sounds very much like a paradigm non-explanation: something or other (call it P) is making Pia do what she does, but we have no idea, and in principle can have no idea, what it is. Which seems to be saying: there is no explaining her behaviour. To this non-explanation we have added the thought: furthermore, that whatever-it-is is such that 'gronch' names it. But if it is this addition which lends the appearance of explanation here, then we must note that it is an appearance generated by supposing semantic description to fit (and be true of) Pia's private words. It is just that which we are not entitled to do without argument, and just that which will be challenged in what follows.

4. INTERNAL AND EXTERNAL

The semantics of Pia's 'gronch' could have been other than it is. Nothing about the word 'gronch' requires that Pia use it so as to have just that semantics. (Similarly, even if no concept could have had a semantics other than it does, where Pia has or applies the concept *gronch* she might have had or been applying some other.) This is just to say that the semantics of 'gronch' depends somehow on how the other facts are. So it is fair to ask how it might do so, and on what other facts it might depend. How might other facts make for a case of 'gronch' having such-and-such semantics—or of any other word having that semantics—and what other facts might do that? That question might be posed (or might arise, even if we cannot pose it) for any particular semantic feature which 'gronch' in fact has. If such a question were posed for any semantic feature of a public word, we would expect that a correct answer, and which other facts it would cite, would depend on the circumstances of the asking, and just which questions we were then raising as to the word's having that semantics. Occasion insensitively, we would not expect there to be such a thing as *'the* facts which make that semantics what it is'. That sort of occasion sensitivity in answers to such specific questions might also be tolerated in the private case.

One might also pose a more general question; one at, as it were, a meta-level. The question would be, not what accounts for some given word having this or that semantic feature, but rather how *any* other facts could possibly make for a case of a word, or of this word, having any semantic features at all, or any of some given sort—rather than say, the word's having some other rival set of semantic features, or none at all. How could there be facts with such powers, and what sorts of facts would these be? Wittgenstein has answered that question at some length in the public case. We are now concerned to see how it might be answered in the private case—for example, in the case of Pia's 'gronch'. (Note that seeing there to be an answer to this question—or seeing there to be none—need not require us, *per impossibile*, to see the putative hidden private facts on which the semantics of Pia's word is meant to depend.)

The meta-question we want to pose might, again, be posed in either of two arenas. First, and most obviously, it might be posed for the semantics of 'gronch' itself. We would then want to be shown how there could be other facts which would make 'gronch' have that semantics rather than, say, some other private one. Call this the internal problem. But we may also note that what we want to come out true, if private language is possible, is some statement to the effect that 'gronch' is private language—one made in just those words, for example—where we are supposing that to be private language is first, to be private, in the sense of violating public access, and second, to be language in the sense of having a definite and coherent semantics— and, as we are supposing for present purposes, a semantics on which it is a truth-bearer (or figures in them), and at least sometimes is true or false of items. So we might consider the predicate, 'is private language'. This is a specimen of English, and public language. It had better be if we now know what we are talking about. On speakings, it is a predicate with truth (or satisfaction) conditions. We want these conditions to be (at least sometimes) such that the predicate, so spoken, may be true of something. To say that it is, or would be, true of various items or bits of language, W, is to ascribe further semantic properties to it. Since it is public language, its having or lacking any given semantics of the sorts just mentioned must depend on our reactions, or those of reasonable judges, to the facts to which we might, in principle, have the appropriate sort of access. And it is on just those facts and no others that these semantic questions may depend. We may then pose the meta-question how there could possibly ever be publicly accessible facts which would make the predicate 'is private language' count, for some W, as having the property of being true of W. Call this the external problem. It is with that problem that we will be concerned in this section.

If W is private language, then we cannot be shown (all) the facts on which W's having one private semantics rather than another depends. What we may expect to be shown, though, since 'private language' is public language, are publicly accessible facts which make it true to say that there are such further private facts. The image is that enough of W's semantics may be fixed by public facts to ensure that it does have a semantics, and one on which it is truth-bearing at that, but that these public facts might stop short of determining just which semantics that is. The present aim, of course, is to erode that idea—the thought that there is room for the publicly accessible facts to do just so much and no more. One qualification: It may be, in public cases, that the semantics of some language is fixed, in part, by facts which we cannot be *shown*, for boring peripheral reasons, even though those facts are publicly accessible. Such might be true of a statement about the properties of some very distant region of space—that there is a woman there, say, with a mole directly over her eighth vertebra. It is presumably true of Pol's remarks on mauve widgets. It is conceivable, then, that the applicability of 'private language' to Pia's 'gronch' is determined by facts which we are peripherally barred from viewing. Unlike the case of distant women, however, it is not particularly plausible that this is so. Our access to Pia is not restricted relative to something else it might be, or at least this is not built into the case. So if there are publicly accessible facts which fix that her language is private, there is no reason why we should not have access to them. Assuming peripheral blocks, though, will anyway not change the case.

In the public case, for simple fact-stating discourse, there is a simple model available. Here it is in Austinian terms.[3] The thought that A is (or all, some or most A's are) B, or saying that, presupposes some way or scheme for classifying cases, or some way in which this is to be done. The scheme would be for a classification of cases of ways the world could be into ones which would count as (some) A's being B, and ones which would not. Given the scheme, one might go wrong in one's thought about A because of what A is like: A just does not have what the scheme requires for being classified as a case of something (being) B. A second way of going wrong in such a thought is, given the way A

---

[3] Austin's fullest discussion of this model is in Austin [1952/3].

is, mistaking what the scheme is, or what it requires for classifying on one side or the other of the division being made. As Austin puts it, there is the difference between mistaking the colour of this blouse, and mistaking what colour mauve is, for example. Wherever the scheme fits, it is always conceivable, where someone thinks or says that A is B, that he should have made a mistake of either of these two sorts.

Not all public language fits this model. Here are two contrasting cases. First, there is Hugo, who considers himself super-sensitive in interpersonal matters. He claims to detect a property that some people have, which he calls 'glumfing'. Some people glumf and some do not, according to him; and he values the ones who do more highly. We, however, cannot detect what Hugo is talking about. Eventually we conclude that there is no such thing as glumfing. If we are right, then 'glumf' is public language in so far as it is language at all; but in crucial respects it lacks any semantics at all. There is nothing which it says things to be; it has no truth-involving properties, etc. Second, consider Odile. From time to time, she says, 'Aya!' There is not even a pretence that there is something she is thereby saying to be so. There may be various sorts of occasions when she is more inclined to say it than at other times—when she is pleased, perhaps, and/or when she is shocked and/or when she is hurt, or something untoward happens. There may also be situations in which it would be more or less inappropriate to say it. But the basic semantic rule governing 'Aya!' is: when you feel like saying it, say it (which does not make it a report of one's desire to say it). Again, everything about the semantics of 'Aya!' is public. We know exactly what semantic properties it has; there is nothing about its proper use that we cannot grasp; nor does its having the semantics it does depend on any further facts which are even in fact, let alone in principle, beyond our ken.

Both of these cases contrast with the Austinian model when it comes to error. Hugo certainly is wrong if he takes himself to be saying something of someone in saying him to 'glumf'; but he cannot go wrong in saying (or thinking) a person to glumf when he doesn't. There is no such mistake to make. For Odile, though 'Aya!' is meaningful language, there is no possibility of her making a mistake (or at least of saying something mistaken) in using it at all. Fact-stating words, 'A is B', as pointed out by the model, always leave more possibilities for going wrong, or at least more ways of going wrong than that. One might, perhaps, grant that given discourse fits the model, and then try to imagine someone with cognitive powers which were so great that, at least when directed at some given area covered by that discourse, they left the person in fact incapable of making a mistake. Certainly for many an ordinary statement, such as 'There's tea in the tea-basket (if you want some)', it may sometimes be true to say of the person who made it that he could not be (or have been) mistaken. We may also be able sometimes to say truly, for example, of someone who is very careful about examining and keeping track of tea-baskets, that he is so good at it that he cannot be wrong about such things. But suppose we wanted to strengthen such remarks to the point of maintaining that it was just not conceivable that the person should be making a mistake; that there was no conceivable way for him to do so, or no conceivable mistake for him to make. That would be to drop the thought or remark in question out of the Austinian model. And it is difficult, to say the least, to see how to do that without moving it into one of the patterns exemplified by Hugo and Odile above.

For 'private language' to be true of W, W must steer a course between the three models just described. For it to do so, there must be, in addition to those models, a fourth position in the relevant conceptual space. W cannot be some sort of subspecies of the model exemplified by Odile. For there is nothing private about the semantics of an item that fits that model. If any item does fit that model, then we can be told that it does. And, in the absence of special reasons to disbelieve what we are thus told, having been told that may be good enough reason to take it to be so. Nor can W be a subspecies of the model exemplified by Hugo. For, to do that would be to have, in relevant respects, no semantics at all, and in no respect a private one. So W must fit the Austinian model at the points where that model leaves possibility for error. The difference would be that, whereas in the case of a public remark 'A is B', we can grasp what that error would consist in in the specific case at hand, and need not stop at the general description of this error provided by the model, in the private case we could not do that. In the public case, we can grasp the difference between mistakenly taking A to be B, and—if 'B*' and 'A*' are also public language—taking A to be B*, or taking A* to be B, and, more generally, we can count as grasping what the person in error was mistakenly taking A to be (and, conversely, what he was mistakenly taking to be B). In the private case, we are barred from grasping at least half of this, and, in particular, from grasping what was mistakenly taken to be so in that taking of A to be B. Despite which, since W is meant to be private *language*, there must in fact *be* answers to these questions as to what the mistake involved was or would be, even if these are not answers with which we could be provided.

It is at this point that our external meta-question arises. The question is what publicly accessible facts could possibly carve out this putative place for W in conceptual space. The question is not one about necessary and sufficient conditions for being at that place. All we want to be shown is even one case where other facts would most reasonably be taken to make W classify in that way. The other facts must show that answers both to the question whether Pia had made either of the two mistakes the Austinian model allows for in saying 'W' of an item, and, where she had, to the quesion what the gap was between what she thus took to be so and what in fact was so, depend on facts we could not appropriately confront. But nevertheless that those were genuine questions with genuine answers. It was not as if Pia were simply mistakenly taking herself to be saying something, in the way Hugo did, or saying something whose public semantics precluded her being wrong at all, as with Odile. But it is obscure how publicly accessible facts could even tend to move us (or the reactions of reasonable judges) in such a direction. To the extent that there are graspable regularities in Pia's use of 'gronch', we have, *ipso facto*, good reason to take 'gronch' as she uses it to stand for a publicly graspable property—the property which those regularities point to. Which is to say that such would be a reasonable reaction to the other facts. Whereas to the extent that there are no such regularities, we have *ipso facto* exactly the same reason to classify Pia as fitting Hugo's model as we had in the case of Hugo himself.

It is not possible for other facts to move us away from one of our three models without moving us in the direction of the other (at least for discourse with the surface appearance of Pia's). Nor ought we reasonably to be moved by Pia's protestations, if any, against what these public facts indicate. She, after all, is but the user of 'gronch' and the candidate private linguist; she is not an infallible semanticist, nor an infallible user of such bits of English as 'private language'. On such matters, she is - at best—no more an expert than we are. Such is the burden of one of the principal arguments against private language. It does not depend on trying to see things from Pia's point of view. For all of which, it ought to be enough. But, in case it fails to be fully convincing, we will turn next to the internal perspective.

5. THE INSIDE STORY

We will now pose the internal meta-question: how could other (private) facts possibly have the effect of making for a case of 'gronch' having some given semantic property—being true of some item, V, say, or saying such-and-such, where that is something that is or would be true of V? This section will be concerned with but one aspect of that question: could there be facts as to how a reasonable judge would react (in relevant respects) to such other facts, so that the reactions of reasonable judges might confer on the other facts the semantic effects that they have? The point will be to argue that there could be no facts within the private realm as to what a reasonable judge would do. It should be emphasized that the aim is only to block substantive appeals to such facts. If there is some other way of making for private semantic facts, and if, given that, it is anyway a fact that 'gronch' has some semantic property, P, then no doubt a reasonable judge in Pia's position—or as well related to the other facts as Pia might be—would react to the other facts by taking 'gronch' to have P. At least there is no reason to dispute that idea. What is in dispute is whether it could be the case that 'gronch' had some private semantic property P (or had P privately) *because* a reasonable judge would react to the other facts by taking it to do so, where without the right independently establishable facts about reasonable judges, or a reasonable judge, the other facts would not have had that semantic effect.

If there are such substantive facts as to the reactions of a reasonable judge, then there are two cases to consider. Either other otherwise reasonable judges are the measures of what those facts are, so that there are facts about them (us, for example) which show how a reasonable judge would react to the other facts in the private case at hand; or Pia is similarly the measure of what those facts about a reasonable judge are. A third alternative is that (some) other facts just do show what a reasonable judge would do here, independent of any facts about what any actual (or possible) judges would do. But that is to dispense with substantive reliance on reasonable judges altogether. It is just to maintain that the other facts have the private semantic effects they do 'in the nature of the case'; that is what they require, full stop. That is not the alternative I now mean to consider.

To begin, then, how might facts about judges other than Pia help establish what the reactions of a reasonable judge would be to the other facts for semantic questions arising in the case of Pia's private language? The obvious problem is that other judges could not be in a position to have (relevant) reactions to these other facts. So the facts about other judges which might play the role just described could not, in principle, include facts as to the reactions they did have to these facts. One might, though, have roughly the following thought. Suppose we confine attention to public language. Typically, when we assign semantics to an item, or take it to have some, we do not have to wait to observe the reactions of other judges. Typically, in fact, we do not observe such reactions. Rather, we know, or can tell, how reasonable judges would react. (Significantly, we are occasionally wrong about this, and there are always ways we could turn out to be. But that point does not matter yet.) Our abilities to perceive the reactions that reasonable judges would have, in the absence of (other) reasonable judges actually having them, suggests the following. There is such a thing as the sort of reaction (or sorts of reactions) that reasonable judges produce (as a sort or on the whole)—that is, the sort of reaction that reasonable judges would show the reaction of a reasonable judge to be. There are facts as to what sort (or sorts) of reaction this would be.[4] These facts enable us to identify particular reactions, in particular cases, as being of this sort, or not of this sort. For example, someone says,'I bought red apples this time'; we go to the refrigerator and look; we see that reasonable judges would react to the facts by judging the remark true. That is the reaction that would be of the sort that reasonable judges would have (on the whole) in this case.

Now the thought is that such facts about the sort of reaction reasonable judges (and thereby a reasonable judge) would have may help in the private case. For consider the possible (semantic) reactions to some set of other facts about Pia's 'gronch', and, say, some object, V, of which it might or might not be true. It may just be that some of these reactions are of the same sort as those reasonable judges (so a reasonable judge) produce, or would produce in cases where they are able to do so, while other such are not. The ones which are thus of the right sort will qualify as the reactions of a reasonable judge in the private case; while the others will be disqualified for that role. Given that there are thus facts about how a reasonable judge would react, the semantics of Pia's private language may be taken to be what such reactions would show it to be.

There is an obvious objection to this thought. Let the semantic property in question be being true of V, for some V such that having or lacking this property is not just a matter of reactions to publicly accessible facts. Now we can identify two possible reactions to the other facts of the case, no matter how benighted at least one of these may be: one (Pia) might react by taking 'gronch' to have this property; or one might react by taking it to lack the property. Correspondingly, we can conceive of two sorts of reaction, both of which would agree with the reactions of reasonable judges over any desired range of cases of public semantics, but one of which—call it R—would involve having the first of the above reactions in this private case, while the other—call it R*—would involve having the second. We can even imagine two sorts of possible organism, to one of which it would come naturally to have R—in the same sense in which it comes naturally to us to have the semantic reactions we do in public cases—while to the

---

[4] If you like, you may think of these as produced by facts as to the sorts of organisms or judges that reasonable judges are.

other of which it would come naturally to have R*. What makes R rather than R* (or viceversa) the sort of reaction that reasonable judges have, let alone the reaction that a reasonable judge would have in this case? How, in fact, could there be any fact of the matter here at all?

Suppose that Odile makes a painting and destroys it before anyone has seen it. Consider the question of the applicability to it of the concept of being red, or simply the question of the painting's being red. Again, there are two conceivable reactions: one might have reacted to the painting by taking that concept to apply to it; or one might have reacted by taking the concept not to apply. Ignoring the possibility that she has produced a difficult case to classify, we may safely suppose that there are facts as to which of these reactions is of the sort that reasonable judges would, on the whole, have in this case—or would have had had they been privileged to look. We may even suppose this, and do so for objects that no judge has ever or now ever could encounter—for example, some apples in wild orchards which ripen and perish without ever being seen. But we are helped along the way to facts of the matter in cases such as these by specific facts as to what the sort of reaction in question *is most reasonably taken to be* in relevant respects, where these require no more than the reactions of reasonable judges to facts which they well might be in a position appropriately to react to.

For the sake of argument, let us tell a vastly oversimplified, and so somewhat falsified story. (The falsifications here can only work to the benefit of the defender of private language—at least one who is interested in following the present route to private semantic facts.) Suppose that what reasonable judges react to in identifying items as red (on the whole, and modulo peripheral blocks to reacting according to sort) is some easily identifiable property of the light the item reflects (in cases where it is reflected light that matters), such as the wavelength. If that is so (or better, if it were so), then we could also reasonably take it that it is central to the concept of being red that that property is in general absolutely central for identifying something as falling under that concept or not—at least given the world as it is. (Here too the story is vastly oversimplified. We are ignoring, for example, any possible family resemblance features of the concept. Again, this works entirely to the advantage of the defender of private language.) We can now say which facts about the painting, or the apples, make the one sort of reaction or the other the sort of reaction that reasonable judges have, and, in this case, would have. In fact, let us stipulate that the painting reflected the right wavelength of light (it was a uniform red-on-red painting.) We have just stated a publicly accessible fact; one to which reasonable judges may relate so as to react appropriately in sorting out which reaction is of the right sort in this case. They cannot see the painting, of course. But they can certainly say—and would, given our falsified story—that if that is the way the painting was, then the reaction a reasonable judge would have to it would be to classify it as falling under the concept red.

The point so far is just this. The question of sorting out, in relevant respects, which of various sorts of reactions is the sort of reaction that reasonable judges produce is itself a question that may be settled by the reactions of reasonable judges: the facts about sorts of reactions are what those reactions would indicate them to be. Moreover, in the public case, we are entitled to the reactions of reasonable judges in these last higher-order respects, since they involve nothing more than reactions to facts which are publicly accessible (in so far as, and in all the ways such that, anyone's reactions to them matter). There are, of course, concepts which match our concept of red in all cases anyone (else) ever has observed, but differ from it in the case of Odile's paintings, or the wild apples. There are concepts such that, like our concept of red (on the falsified story), it is wavelengths of light that matter in many cases; but, unlike that concept, such phenomena of light cease to matter in certain selected cases, such as that of Odile's painting. It is also conceivable that, had we actually confronted Odile's painting, or those apples, we would in fact have reacted as one in taking those items not to be red, thus revealing that one of those alternate concepts was really the one we did have (in matters of redness) all along. All these things are conceivable; but none is among what it is reasonable to suppose. That such hypotheses are unreasonable, that no reasonable judge would ever suppose such a thing (or nearly), is the background against which we may judge correctly and truly that the facts as to the sorts of reactions we are evincing in reacting to red (and non-red) things as we do are as just represented above.[5]

This appeal to facts about how reasonable judges would group reactions into sorts is, in the present context, just what is not available for the possible reactions to other facts in the case of Pia's 'gronch' and any one of its candidate semantic properties. For the problem with which we began was to explain how there could be facts as to how a reasonable judge would react to the other facts in a private case—and,

---

[5] Is it not up to science to tell us what we are reacting to in identifying things as red or not? Of course. That is in fact how I know that the above story is falsified. But first, the deliveries of science on such scores only make sense given a background of facts about which concepts we are concerned with here. And second, science only tells us, and arguably only could tell us, how we do or would react to publicly accessible properties or other facts.

on the present strand of the argument, to explain that by appealing to facts as to how otherwise reasonable judges other than Pia would react, wherever such facts might be available. It is no solution to that problem that facts about other reasonable judges would do the job given facts about how a reasonable judge would react to non-publicly accessible facts. But it is just that that we are being told when we are told that it is up to a reasonable judge to react to the alternative possible semantic reactions to the other facts of Pia's case and to classify these as belonging, or not belonging, to one or another sort of reaction which is the (a) sort that reasonable judges produce. The relevant facts to react to, for an application of 'gronch', are, by hypothesis, ones other judges *could* not appropriately react to; *a fortiori* not by classifying one or another reaction to them as of the sort a reasonable judge would produce. If such were possible, 'gronch' would cease to be private. So far, then, other reasonable judges cannot establish what the reactions of a reasonable judge would be in the private case unless there are already assumed to be facts as to the reactions of a reasonable judge in the private case. But to say that is to say that the present line of thought makes no progress at all with the problem at hand.

One might try to suppose, instead, that other facts of the private case simply require that possible reactions in that case be classified in one way rather than another, independent of any further facts about how a reasonable judge would react to them. It is difficult to see how such could be. Certainly it could not be the deliverance of any scientific theory we would ever have reason to accept. In fact, it is not even a fit subject for scientific investigation. But in any case, to take this line is to opt for an alternative that does not yet concern us. It is to suppose private semantic facts to be made what they are in ways that are essentially independent of any substantive appeal to the reactions of reasonable judges, or even a reasonable judge. That option is a topic for the next section.

There is one relevant alternative left. Perhaps there are facts as to how a reasonable judge would react to the other facts in Pia's private case, but these are what they are, not in virtue of the reactions of other judges, but rather in virtue of facts about Pia herself, and her own reactions. Here again, there is an obvious problem. We have already concluded that Pia must be a fallible reactor to other facts if her word 'gronch' is not to fall into fitting the model of Odile's 'Aya!'. But it is difficult to see how there could be a gap between the fact of her reacting in such-and-such way (assuming the possibility of private semantic reactions at all) and that being the way in which a reasonable judge would react, when the latter fact is to depend on nothing but facts about Pia's reactions. The obvious thought would be that we should think of Pia as reacting sometimes in and sometimes out of character, so to speak—her mistakes corresponding to the occasions of her acting out of character. The thought would be that she has somehow or other internalized some proper way of reacting to other facts in matters concerning 'gronch'—for example, by resolving to use the word in such-and-such way, or by being the sort of organism that would use the word in such-and-such sort of way, given such-and-such antecedent facts about it. She may then occasionally, for some peripheral reason, use 'gronch' in some way that is different from the internalized way, or what it requires.

The problems with this last thought simply re-rehearse the problems with the appeal to judges other than Pia. Consider any occasion for Pia to react to other facts—for example, in taking 'gronch' to be true of some V or not. Again, there are the two possible reactions. Again there is the problem of how these reactions classify into sorts. Which if either belongs to the sort which Pia has internalized? That question might be answered by appealing to the reactions of a reasonable judge in that matter. But to do that would be again to admit that we had so far made no progress. Or it might just be taken to be, as it were, a brute fact of nature that Pia's relevant internal state is *thus* and not *so*. (In which case, a fact not made so by facts of her internal state which are publicly available or open for (scientific) investigation.) That is just to take the line to be considered in the next section. It is, in effect, to dispense with appeal to the reactions of a reasonable judge for the making of private semantic fact altogether.

We are to think of Pia, on the present thought, as having got herself into some relevant internal state—perhaps simply the state of having undertaken to use 'gronch' in such-and-such way. But how are we to think of this?

It might be said: if you have given yourself a private definition of a word, then you must inwardly *undertake* to use the word in such and such way. And how do you undertake that? Is it to be assumed that you invent the technique of using the word; or that you found it ready-made? (262)

For each occasion of use, certain assignments of semantic properties, such as being true of some V, are to classify as 'in sort', or faithful to the undertaking, as what the internal state requires; while others are to classify as 'out of sort'. But in virtue of what do they do so? Are we to imagine that each such fact is simply intrinsic to the internal state in question—part of the way in which it is ready-made? Or are we to suppose that Pia conferred each such fact individually, as it were, on the state? And in either case, in virtue of what would this be so? Not, in any event, in virtue of the fact that that is how a reasonable judge would regard things.

Wittgenstein points to the problem here, well in advance of the private language discussion, in pointing to what reasonable judges are called on to do where their reactions are available. We are to think here in terms of what carrying out Pia's undertaking correctly, or remaining in sorts with her relevant internal state, would require. But, borrowing Wittgenstein's words from the public case,

To carry it out correctly! How is it decided what is the right step to take at any particular stage?—'The right step is the one that accords with the order [read: undertaking—as it was *meant*.' . . . But that is just what is in question: what, at any stage, does follow from that *Satz*. Or again, what, at any stage, we are to call 'being in accord' with that *Satz* (and with the intention—the *meaning-it-so*—then put into the *Satz* [read here: the undertaking]—whatever that may have consisted in). (186)

To think of Pia as having internalized some state, where that internal state is then the arbiter of what is reasonable, is to think of her on the model of a machine with a given internal state which determines what it will do (when not malfunctioning). Wittgenstein suggests just this analogy, and uses the comparison to point out:

The machine as symbolizing its action: the action of a machine—I might say at first—seems to be there in it from the start. What does that mean?—If we know the machine, everything else, that is its movement, seems to be already completely determined. . . .
  'The machine's action seems to be in it from the start' means: we are inclined to compare the future movements of the machine in their definiteness to objects which are already lying in a drawer and which we then take out. . . . We *do* talk like that . . . when we are wondering at the way we can use a machine to symbolize a given way of moving—since it can also move in quite *different* ways. (193)

Similarly, we may think of Pia's internal state as representing, or symbolizing, a given sort of reaction—the sort required by her undertaking—though she can, and sometimes will, react in different ways. But which reactions belong to this sort? And what is to determine that? Where we use a machine to symbolize a certain sort of action, our reactions (so those of reasonable judges) can determine what belongs to the sort. But no such appeal is available in the private case. Without it, facts about Pia cannot be used to fix what a reasonable judge would do.

6. EA AND OA AGAIN

The remaining idea is that, for any specific feature of the (private) semantics of 'gronch', that feature should depend on the other, not entirely publicly accessible facts, but that its doing so, and the way in which it does so, should be independent of any appeal to the reactions of reasonable judges to those facts. The thought is that the way the other facts are just does require the presence (or absence) of that feature; that is an intrinsic part of what it is for the other facts to be that way—quite independently of considerations of how that would affect us (when being reasonable), or other otherwise reasonable judges. When we are careful to filter out tacit appeals to our reactions as reasonable judges, this idea can be seen, I think, to be a non-starter. Consideration of EA and OA provides some reasons why. Again we will begin with the simpler EA, although it yields no direct proof of the impossibility of private language.

Suppose that, on an occasion, Pia takes 'gronch' to have some given semantic property. For example, she confronts some object, V (whether public or private), and takes 'gronch' to have the property of being true of V. We might then pose the question whether that is really consistent with the rest of the semantics which 'gronch' must have anyway—for example, the semantics it must have given Pia's undertakings on previous occasions. Could it not be, for example, that Pia has misremembered what the rest of that semantics was, what 'gronch' does say of things? Or that she has misperceived what consistency with that other semantics demands in this case? As Wittgenstein points out, such ways of questioning Pia's judgement can be prolifer-ated *ad lib*, and in ways which cut off the possibility that Pia might have further information which settled all such questions conclus-ively. For example, if a gronch is a kind of sensation,

'Well, I *believe* that this is the sensation S again.'—Perhaps you *believe* that you believe it! (260)

'But surely I can appeal from one memory to another. For example, I don't know if I have remembered the time of departure of a train right and to check it I call to mind how a page of the time-table looked. Isn't it the same here?'— No; for this process has got to produce a memory which is actually *correct*. If the mental image of the time table could not itself be *tested* for correctness, how could it confirm the correctness of the first memory? (As if someone were to buy several copies of the morning paper to assure himself that what it said was true.) (265)

So if Pia were to suggest that her memory of the rest of 'gronch''s semantics was correct because, on reflection, she distinctly remembers having conferred such-and-such semantics on it, the question would then be: how does she know that she remembers what she then did correctly?

If every such question represents a real doubt, then, no matter what situation Pia might be in, it is demonstrable that she does not know that (or whether) 'gronch' has the semantic property in question. So if she might ever count as knowing anything about 'gronch''s semantics, or at least not always count as ignorant on every point about it, then there must be a real/mere doubt distinction of some substance here. It must be a distinction which applies to her as considered on that occasion, mentioned above, of her taking 'gronch' to have that semantic property. There must be facts of the matter as to which doubts are real and which not with respect to her then knowing the point in question. For some substantial range of possible doubts, the facts must be that these are but mere doubts for the purposes of assessing her knowledge on that point. Moreover, those facts cannot depend on any appeal to 'facts' to the effect that we, or more pertinently, a reasonable judge, would react to the situation Pia is in by taking such and such doubts to be real and such-and-such others to be mere.

The relevant real/mere doubt distinctions here, then, are to be thought of as simply built into the nature of the case; as just what the other facts, by their nature, require them to be. The first point is that it is difficult to see how this could be. How could there be facts in *rerum natura* as to which doubts are real and which doubts mere, independent of facts about the interests we take in, and the importance we attach to, the matters in question, and to going right or wrong in judging about them—the interest and importance we assign to things, that is, when acting *reasonably*, which is just the sort of fact we are now barred from appealing to? One might, perhaps, think along lines like these: perhaps there is survival value attached to treating certain doubts as real, where this value does not attach to so treating other doubts. One might think, as it were, in terms of a sort of 'natural' epistemology: there is a certain optimal policy, from the point of view of 'survival' (whatever precisely that may mean) on when to treat certain things as so, or treat oneself or others as justified in taking them to be so; the right way of drawing the real/mere doubt distinction is the way one *would* draw it according to that optimal policy.

But, in addition to its numerous general demerits, this idea encounters special obstacles in the private case. First, 'optimal policies' will presumably involve generalizations of certain sorts. The point cannot merely be that Pia's having or not having some given doubt in this specific case would have survival value, but rather that her doing so would instance some general policy, where that policy is optimal for survival. But then there is the problem of determining which policy her having or not having that doubt would instance; which generalization fits her actual performance in this case. The problems with the fixing of such facts in the private case have been discussed in the last section. Second, it is difficult to see how there could be facts about the survival value of various ways of drawing the real/mere doubt distinction in the private case, or, in fact, of taking 'gronch' to have or lack any (private) semantic property at all without those facts transforming 'gronch' into public language. Here is Wittgenstein's way of worrying about that problem:

Let us now imagine a use for the entry of the sign 'S' in my diary. I discover that whenever I have a particular sensation a manometer shows that my blood pressure rises. So I shall be able to say that my blood pressure is rising without using any apparatus. This is a useful result. (270)

Insofar as it is a useful result, there may also be value—'survival value', if you like, in having various doubts as to whether this is a case where it is correct to say 'S'. But, by the same token, the facts of utility here threaten the privacy of the semantics:

And now it seems quite indifferent whether I have recognized the sensation *right* or not. Let us suppose I regularly identify it wrong, it does not matter in the least. And that alone shows that the hypothesis that I make a mistake is mere show. (We as it were turned a knob which looked as if it could be used to turn on some part of the machine; but it was a mere ornament, not connected with the mechanism at all.) (270)

There are now public criteria for whether the private word, 'S', is being used right or not; and with them, the idea that there is some further private matter which the private linguist is getting right or wrong simply drops out.

The scheme for blocking EA, for Pia, now looks like this. On a given occasion, Pia takes 'gronch' to have some property P. (For the sake of argument, 'gronch' does have P.) In so doing, Pia, perhaps, treats certain doubts about this as real, and, if so, settles those. All others she treats as mere. It is a bare fact of nature—just the way things are—that on that occasion certain such doubts are real and others mere. (Since the real/mere distinction cannot be drawn at all except occasion sensitively, that is how nature must be supposed to draw it too.) Pia's drawing of the distinction agrees with nature's. Thus is she supposed to qualify as knowing the fact about 'gronch''s semantics.

But this mere coincidence between what Pia does and what nature requires cannot be enough by itself to confer knowledge. Pia must also stand in the right relation to these natural facts as to what ought to be doubted.[6] For the concept of knowledge permits us to conceive of someone doubting (and not) as it were capriciously; with neither right

---

[6] This is closely related to the point John McDowell makes against 'criterial' theories of knowledge, as discussed in ch. 4, section 2.5.

to nor reason for that policy. Such a person might, by chance, on some occasion, doubt just what ought to be doubted. This person would, of course, take himself to be doing that; but could, for all he knew, and all the reason he had for that, be in a deceptive situation in which, while he doubted in just that way, there were doubts he absolutely ought to have but did not—on the present suggestion, a deceptive case where the natural facts about doubting were different. Something must qualify Pia as not falling within any such category. Something must make her *entitled* to her policy of doubting as she does. But it is now clear that there is nothing in her situation (*vis-à-vis* 'gronch') that could do that. It is useless to postulate further facts of nature—for example, to the effect that she need not doubt whether she falls in such a category. That would only proliferate the problem, since she would then have to relate appropriately to those. Nor could her entitlement be assumed to be itself a brute fact of nature. That would be to 'defeat' EA simply by denying it. But in this case there is nothing but 'facts of nature' to appeal to. Such cannot be enough in themselves to make Pia relate in the right way to them.

In the public case, Pia's entitlement may come from the fact that she is generally among the reasonable judges, and that there is no special story to be told on this occasion to show that she ought to doubt whether she is performing with these fact-supporting devices. She is, *prima facie*, within the range of judges whose reactions *make* the facts about doubts what they are. But in the private case, even if she were to assume that she was performing, in the above respects, as a reasonable judge would—and even if that were, *per impossibile*, correct—that would be beside the point. For, as things now stand, in relating to private facts, the aim of the game is *not* to perform as a reasonable judge (on the substantive conception of that at work in this book), but, as opposed to that, simply to be in fact 'in tune with nature'. Where performing as a reasonable judge would is not the goal, reasonableness is not a route to entitlement—*inter alia*, to that which is here required. But where it is not, nor could anything else be.

There is a further problem with the idea that, where Pia takes 'gronch' to have some semantic property P, she might count as knowing this. Recall that it is a general feature of knowledge that the right way of drawing the real/mere doubt distinction is fixed not just by what Pia is taking to be so, or the facts of the world in which that is so or not, nor just by that plus the facts of Pia's perspective on those facts, but by all of that plus the facts of our perspective on Pia in taking her to know or not to know the relevant fact. Given that it is Pia we are concerned with, and that it is some particular item, F, which she takes to be so, there are various things to be said—as a rule, if any true things, then both true things and false ones—in saying Pia to know that F. Correspondingly, on some occasions for our considering the matter, she may count as knowing that F; but if so, then, as a rule, there will be others on which she does not. Correspondingly, the proper way of drawing the real/mere doubt distinction in this matter will vary across our occasions for considering it. Where F is a fact of private language, though, we could have no appropriate occasions for considering the question of Pia's knowing (or not) that F—no range of occasions across which the right way for *us* to draw the real/mere distinction might vary. Our perspective on Pia's relation to the putative fact F could not vary like that. Which casts further doubt on the idea that the concept of knowledge is applicable in Pia's private case at all.

Consider the problem to which OA is addressed. Take some candidate fact about the semantics of 'gronch'—say, that it is true of V. Call that candidate F*. We have already agreed that whether F* is a fact—if there is any possibility of its being such—depends on how the other facts of the case are. The problem then is: what would make it so that these other facts were such as to make F* a fact? OA places two demands on an answer. First, on it, if the other facts are indeed such as to make F* a fact, then there must be specifiable such other facts which demonstrate that F* is a fact. Second, for given such facts, G, to demonstrate this, there must be no conceivable case in which G would obtain but F* would not. In the public case, we saw that there is really no question of meeting the demands OA imposes. Rather, we provided the means for rejecting those demands. The private case being as strange as it is, we will not insist to begin with on the same approach to OA here. Still, OA gives us a scheme for classifying ways in which other facts might make F* a fact. First, there might be some specifiable other facts, G, which satisfy the demands OA imposes. Second and third, it might be possible, in the private case, to reject one or the other of the demands; to show how it might be a fact that F* even though that demand could not be satisfied.

In the case of public words, W, we can often appeal to other facts of the case to demonstrate this or that semantic fact about them. This is one of our main devices, at least, for resisting OA in the area of semantic fact. To begin with, we should remind ourselves that the public notion of demonstration is an S-use sensitive one. *Which* other facts would show W to have such-and-such a semantics depends, *inter alia*, on what questions are being raised as to W's semantics, and on what the alternatives are. So other facts which, on some occasion, might demonstrate W to have some semantics S might well fail to demonstrate this on some other occasion we could construct. Still, fix the occasion, and often demonstration can be provided. Odile says, 'Mary had a little lamb.' Hugo is told that she said this, but does not know under what circumstances she did so. So he might need to be shown that her words were, in fact, a remark about meat eating. He might even be initially inclined to disbelieve this, associating Odile more naturally with nursery rhymes. Still, if we tell him enough other facts of the case, we can convince him, if he is reasonable. For there are other facts which, for this purpose, at least, show it. Those facts might not show it on an occasion on which there were other doubts as to the words having that semantics. But if we think of demonstrations as phenomena of occasions, then we may say that demonstrations of semantic facts are sometimes possible.

Where it is possible to demonstrate some semantic fact about the public words W, it is, of course, the second of OA's demands which must be resistible. Whatever we may tell Hugo about Odile's words, we certainly do not believe that there could be no conceivable case in which those facts would hold of words which lacked the semantics we ascribed to Odile's—unless, as might also happen, we simply assure Hugo that what she said was that Mary had eaten some meat. That such other sorts of cases are imaginable typically will not and need not bother us. For, if the reasons we give are good ones by normal lights, then we may rely on the following: though there are such conceivable cases, a reasonable judge (and reasonable judges) would not, if suitably informed, react to Odile's speaking by taking it that it even might be one of these. Such cases do not belong within the range of what Odile's speaking might be (at least on the occasion in question for considering it). Hence, on that occasion, they are not relevant to the issue of demonstration. A demonstration may be supported in this status, then, by the reactions of reasonable judges. And the same reactions may support the judgement that it is so supported. For a reasonable judge, in taking it that G shows that F, would take it that that is how a reasonable judge would react, and vice versa.

This sort of support for facts as to G demonstrating F is, of course, unavailable in the private case. Restricting attention to the present option for responding to OA, that lack makes for a real problem. Consider an occasion for Pia considering the private fact, F*. To exercise the present option, we must maintain the following. First, on that occasion, there are some other facts, G—available, perhaps, only to Pia—which then count as demonstrating that F*. Second, there are some conceivable cases in which G (or in which what thus holds of 'gronch' would hold of some semantic item), but not F*. Third, however, on this occasion, the second fact does not show G not to demonstrate that F*; it is irrelevant to the question of demonstration on that occasion. This third fact, again, is simply to be a further fact of nature; a part of the structure of the world which holds quite independently of what we or any other judge do or would think about it. The world just happens to be set up in such a way that, on this occasion, those conceivable cases of G but not F* just do not find themselves among the possible ways for things now to be.

But now, applying OA to that presumed fact of nature, we may ask in virtue of what it counts as a fact: what makes it thus a basic part of the way the universe is? If we remain within the present form of response to OA, then the answer must be that there are some further facts, G*, which demonstrate this, where again there are conceivable cases where G* would hold but the third fact would not. There would then be need for a yet further fact that those conceivable cases do not now locate themselves among the possible ways for things to be. Obviously, remaining within this option, this proliferation of further facts must be continued indefinitely. (It might be that if, *per impossibile*, we could properly confront all these further facts, we would react by taking it to be reasonable to take them for facts, rather than accepting the conclusion, in each such case, which OA urges on us. But such reactions are intrinsically and necessarily irrelevant to the question whether these supposed further facts are facts; they are not the sorts of facts that depend on our reactions in such ways.) The upshot so far is that we can see how OA would be mistaken (as applied to private semantic facts) if we assume that there are such-and-such further facts which would not be facts if OA were correct; that is, if we take it in the first place that OA is mistaken. What we do not thereby see is how OA might be mistaken *tout court*. And that OA would be mistaken on any given application if we helped ourselves to enough auxiliary facts is something that any ontic sceptic always would have granted. The option that works in the public case, then, does not—at least by itself—provide a means for resisting ontic scepticism when it comes to private semantics.

Let us, then, look at the other alternatives. First, there is the alternative of accepting and meeting the challenge OA poses. For that to work, there must be some other facts, G, which demonstrate F*, and such that there are no conceivable circumstances in which G would hold and F* not. One obvious problem with this option is that if such were the case, then G would be 'facts' which would themselves be outstanding candidates for the application of OA. What, we might ask, makes those 'facts' facts? More important, though, we may note that this is really just a degenerate case of the option just considered. On that option, all the conceivable cases in which G but not F* do not count. On this one, all such cases do not count for the special reason that there are none. But what, we may ask, makes that so? In the normal case, there is no conceivable case in which H, say, but not F, when we do not allow there to be any such; when we do not recognize such a possibility within the range of what we are prepared to call conceivable. That is, there are no such cases exactly where a reasonable judge would react to all the facts as to what H and F are by taking there to be no such cases. In the present case, however, the absence of such conceivabilities is supposed, once again, to be a further fact of nature; part of the basic way in which the world is constituted. That fact, though, is a good candidate for a further application of OA. This variation on the theme just discussed will not yield a different result.

Finally, there is the idea of resisting OA in its entirety. We might maintain that F* is a fact, and further, that, though if other facts were different enough it would not be one, there is no specifiable aspect of the way the other facts are which qualifies as that in virtue of which F* is a fact, or that which makes it a fact; F* is, as it were, a *sui generis* constituent of the totality of facts. So there is no demonstration that F* is a fact, either one which tolerates conceivable cases for which it would give wrong results, or one for which there are none such. The idea of *sui generis* or non-demonstrable facts certainly gains plausibility from the public case. For, on any given occasion, there is much of what we take to be facts about which we would have to say, if pressed, that nothing *demonstrates* them to be facts, though they surely are. That is, nothing then qualifies for the title, 'demonstration of F', if F is such a fact. Part of the explanation of this phenomenon is simply that demonstration is an occasion sensitive notion. Like any such notion, it requires appropriate circumstances in order for it to have intelligible applications. Where the facts of an occasion are not up to choosing between various competing and conflicting proof conditions, nothing can count as a proof. This is just to repeat the main point of chapter 5. Another factor which allows for *sui generis* facts in the public case is that there may also be no (reasonable or real) doubt that F is a fact— where that, of course, is a matter of the reactions of reasonable judges, on that occasion, to F.

All the same, for candidate *sui generis* facts,F, there are two sorts of case: cases where they indeed are *sui generis*, neither admitting nor requiring demonstration, and cases where they are not. There are the unsuccessful as well as the successful candidates. In public cases, reasonable judges serve as devices for doing the classifying. In the private case, the problem is in virtue of what further facts a given candidate classifies in one way or the other. To solve that problem in any given case, we must take some route through the options just canvassed. If F is a *sui generis* fact, then what about the fact that F is *sui generis*? If OA is applied to that putative fact, in virtue of what else are we going to be able to resist OA's conclusion in that case? Since none of the available options promises any progress with the problem at all, we must conclude that, within the private sphere, it has no solution. The upshot is that in the area of private semantics, there is no way of blocking OA or resisting the conclusion it urges on us. Which is to say this. Where the public access principle is violated, there can be no facts as to the semantics of the item in question; the reactions of reasonable judges are required where items may sensibly be supposed to have any semantics at all.

When we confront an application of OA to some F, we may sometimes react by taking it to be more reasonable to reject OA, and its conclusion in this case, than to take it that F is not a fact. If we took G to demonstrate that F, we might find it more reasonable to dismiss some conceivable cases in which one would have G but not F, rather than dismiss the idea that that was a demonstration. Or if we took F to require no demonstration, we might continue to find that the most reasonable reaction to what confronts us. There may be no reason for us to doubt that those are the reactions a reasonable judge would have. We may, in fact, be able to see that they are. (For such are among the cognitive capacities we may reasonably take ourselves to have.) And we are, of course, correct in concluding what it is reasonable for us to conclude. Those are simply not the issues that confront us, however, when we consider the correctness of OA as applied in the private case. There, the issues cannot involve what reactions a reasonable judge would have, since there can be no facts as to this. Rather, the issues, if any, concern the way the facts are arranged in nature, independent of any access we, or any judge, could possibly have to them. When that is the most fundamental and correct way of posing the problem OA presents, there can be no resources for blocking it. Where there are none, there can be no way 'the facts really are' at all.

7. BELIEF

The issues so far are not confined to private *language*. Rather, the central concern has been with private *semantics*. The problems discussed are equally problems for any item which may have a semantics, and the arguments given against private language apply intact for any such item. In particular, if private language is impossible, then so is private belief. Suppose that, for some G and P, Odile believes that G is P. Then what property P is, or what being P comes to, which item G is, whether what Odile thus believes is true, and, more generally, when or where it would be, are all features which characterize what it is that she believes, and hence the semantics of her belief (that is, the one she thus has). Beliefs may have, and perhaps be identified by, their semantic properties. In so far as that is so, any question as to which semantic properties they have must respect the public access principle, if the argument given so far is correct.

This consequence of the private language discussion is worth remembering. For recent philosophy has felt some pressures towards making the semantics of belief a private matter—in some innocuous sense of 'private', perhaps; still, we may learn something about what belief is, or what our concept of belief requires it to be, by checking that no more than innocuous privacy is entailed by such currently prevalent thoughts. The sort of pressure I have in mind here is exhibited, for example, by Michael Dummett in the following passages:

If Alice has been told that her uncle lives in Lima, she can pass on this information even though she herself knows no more about Lima than that it is the capital of Bolivia, Peru or Ecuador, and cannot remember which. In this way, she can use the name, 'Lima'; but can she be said to believe that her uncle lives in Lima? . . . when we are concerned with the precise content of a belief expressed by means of an utterance, we must take that as depending, not upon the public meanings of the words composing it, but on the speaker's private understanding of them.[7]

If we are concerned with exactly what belief a speaker expressed by means of a sentence, it is his private understanding of the words that determines this. We shall usually not go far astray if we take the sentence, regarded as having the meaning that it does in the common language, as determining the belief that he expressed by means of it; but we may sometimes have to take account of the fact that we have thereby characterized his belief only imprecisely.[8]

The correct conclusion is that, when we follow our usual procedure of characterizing someone's belief by means of a sentence considered as having the meaning that it does in the language to which it belongs, we are very often giving only an approximate statement of the content of that belief.[9]

I do not think that Dummett means 'private understanding', in his sense, to be something that requires the possibility of private language. His idea appears to be only that what determines the content or semantics of a belief is the sense or semantics the believer attaches to certain relevant words, where such senses are fixed by the believer's conception of what they are; the semantic properties he would take

[7] Dummett [1981], p. 109.
[8] Ibid., p. 112.
[9] Ibid., p. 116.

them to involve. The thought is not that we should be in principle unable to grasp the private understandings of another, or barred access to the facts which determine what these understandings are. Dummett is not thinking in terms of Russellian privacy, involving literally inscrutable (for us) semantics, or objects of thought in principle beyond our ken. Nor, perhaps, does he think it in principle beyond our powers, on his conception of the matter, to discover or to know precisely what someone's private understandings are, hence *precisely* what it is that he believes. Still, I think that Dummett's conception of belief does in fact conflict with the present view of private language, and that it is important to see how the view does have that sort of import. For what is thus brought into question is something still more general: a conception of belief on which what someone believes is fixed by facts about, as it were, his internal configurations, together, perhaps, with their causal histories, linking them to 'external impingements', but independent of our perspectives on them—a conception with profound consequences for how we view, and might think to be able to investigate, ourselves.

To report what someone believes, we have nothing but public language. Using what we thus have, we might reverse Dummett's conception of belief. Suppose that Hugo says, 'Montreal is on an island.' That is public language, and the semantics of Hugo's words, and what he thus said, is, in the present sense, a public matter. (So far, Dummett would not disagree.) Now let us ask: does Odile believe *that*? (That is, the item Hugo thus produced; what he said.) The following answer suggests itself: she does if she stands in the right relation to it. For example, perhaps, if she would agree to it. Some immediate qualifications are in order. First, what the right relation is is a matter of the precise semantics of belief ascriptions—what we would be saying in saying Odile to believe that. It is not obvious what that semantics is; that remains to be worked out. Second, in all probability, belief ascriptions are S-use sensitive. Which means that the right relation to stand in is an S-use sensitive matter. The relation(s) Odile does bear to what Hugo said may make her count, on some occasions, but not on others, as believing that. But, bracketing issues of S-use sensitivity, there is no reason to expect other than this much. First, whether Odile does stand in the right relation to Hugo's words depends only on further publicly accessible facts. Second, it does not depend on any further semantic facts—say, facts as to the semantics of some further item. For example, if Hugo said what he did in the course of an argument, and Odile would take his side in that argument, then that may be enough. So Odile's having the belief in question—the one ascribed to her above—is a matter of her relation to given public semantics. So far, it is that semantics, and only that, that comes into the picture.

The above model makes no mention of private understandings. On it, what Odile believes is fixed by the public semantics of bits of public language. What is wrong with this model? Why not think that all the facts as to what Odile believes fit it, without the introduction of private understandings of anything? On Dummett's view, when we approach questions of what Odile believes in this way, we arrive—as a rule, at least—only at *approximations* as to what she believes; we never say precisely what her beliefs are. But why should we think this? Why think that the model even inclines us to fall short of precision? Why isn't what Hugo said, with its public semantics, *exactly* what Odile believes? Dummett, I think, has two main reasons for thinking this.

One of Dummett's reasons—the less important one—concerns a puzzle propounded by Saul Kripke.[10] Kripke shows that, given our ordinary criteria for attributing belief, we could, for example, in unusual circumstances, have overwhelmingly good reason both for judging that Odile did believe that Montreal was on an island, and that she did not. (Consider the difference in pronunciation between 'Montreal' and 'Montréal', and the different ways in which Odile might relate to thoughts about the city when expressed in each of those two ways). At first sight, that is a paradox. Dummett, like many others, has reacted to that apparent paradox by concluding that neither of the apparently conflicting belief ascriptions is an exact statement of what Odile believes (or does not). Rather, each is an approximation to some fact which, when specified exactly, would be seen not to be in conflict with the other (when specified exactly). The suggestion is that ordinary standards for belief ascription are lax.

Not only is this suggestion non-compulsory, but as it stands it is incomplete. For we still need to be told what the more exact or exacting standards are to be. (We are not told this simply by mention of the words, 'private understandings'; for the problem then is: what are the criteria for having one or another of those?) Unless some such further suggestion is demonstrably correct, the correct conclusion, if Kripke's 'paradox' really is a paradox, may be that belief is an incoherent notion, and there are no facts as to what anyone 'believes'. More importantly, however, there is no reason to accept that there is any sort of paradox here at all. The phenomena Kripke exhibits are just what one would expect if belief ascription were an S-use sensitive matter—that is, if the relation demanded between the believer and the

---

[10] Kripke [1979].

belief varied with occasions for judging what someone believed. If that is so, they can have even the air of paradox only if the S-use sensitivity which is present in the notion is being ignored—as it is by Kripke, for example. By now it should not be surprising if we did discover such S-use sensitivity in the notion of belief.[11] If that is the conclusion to which we are moved by Kripke's data, then we have so far no reason at all to depart from the public model of belief just presented as a counter to Dummett's.

Dummett's more important reason arises, I think, from a strange play of nominalizations. In referring to what Hugo said, above, we have already specified an item which, we have supposed, Odile might well believe. But now suppose we ask: is this (really) (exactly) (literally) what she believes? Consider the expression, 'what she believes'. We may mark two distinct uses of it. First, suppose that Pol tells a series of stories, or states a series of candidate subjects for belief. After each one—in an appropriate context, at least—he might ask, 'Is *this* what Odile believes?' Or, after the whole series, he might ask, 'Which of these is what Odile believes?' Importantly, context may be needed to show how one ought to go about giving an answer. But whatever answer we did give, we would not suppose that it was the unique qualified candidate for the role of 'what Odile believes', or that it was the only true literal and exact statement of something she believes—except, perhaps, as opposed to some stated range of specific rivals. There is no limit, we ordinarily suppose, to what it might be literally true to say about what Odile believes.

There is also another use of 'what she believes'. We might take it, roughly, as referring to the entire body of Odile's belief. So understood, we might well think of it as being fixed in some unique way. But then we do not think of there being some one object of belief which is the unique correct answer to the question what she believes. We may say that what she believes is consistent with this or that, or that it forbids her doing this or that. But we do not suppose that we could begin to *say* what 'what she believes' is, much less do so by specifying some particular potential object of belief. For one thing, on the public model, there is an indefinite range of things she no doubt does believe—not only that Montreal is on an island, but also, say, that her mother has a gold tooth. Is all of this to be included in a proper correct and exact answer?

Trouble comes when we mix this second conception of 'what she believes' with the first: we ask after 'what she (really) believes', but think of ourselves as asking (really) after what she really believes on

---

[11] For further discussion of these issues, see Travis [1983/4].

such-and-such topic - at first approximation, for example, the topic of Montreal and islands. Of course, we tell ourselves, we are not really interested in *everything* she believes—in her belief about her mother's gold tooth, for example. Drawing on our second conception, we expect the answer to be something unique—when we speak strictly and demand exactness and precision, or completeness. Drawing on the first conception, we expect the answer to consist of citing some particular object of belief—either the candidate object we specified in citing what Hugo said, or some particular rival to it; something much like that, but perhaps with a somewhat different semantics. Given both these expectations, the question is which, if any, publicly specifiable item— which thing Hugo might have said—this uniquely qualified candidate for the role might be. It should not be surprising if *that* has no precise and correct answer.

On the second conception of 'what someone believes', it is quite plausible that what someone believes is a function of the entire course of his experience; *any* difference would make a difference here. So it is also plausible that no two people quite match in 'what they believe'; perhaps even that no two people *could* so match. That is to say: one person's *beliefs* will not quite be the same as another's: on the public model, the entire body of truths there are to be told as to what A believes can never quite match the entire body of truths about what B believes. Compare Odile and Pia, for example. Pia knows that the city she lives in is on an island; that city is Montreal; but Pia does not know it by that name. Odile lives in Tervuren, but has read about Montreal and knows that it is on an island. Of course they differ in their beliefs; we have just described the difference. As the example indicates, the general points about fine differences in belief might even survive some restriction of the topic. Thus, what Pia believes in the matter of, or concerning, Montreal being an island is not quite what Odile believes on this topic, though the differences are hardly indescribable.

Now turning to the first conception, let us suppose that there is some unique object of belief which is that item which Odile *really* believes on the issue in question—if we choose to insist on perfect exactness in the matter. Suppose that this is some public item—for example, something Hugo might have said, with the public semantics it would have had as he said it. Which item might this be? Suppose, for example, that it is the item actually cited above in saying, 'Montreal is an island'. But now, can we not imagine two people—Pia and Odile, say—who both have equally good claim to believe that, even though— referring back again to the second conception—what Pia believes is not quite what Odile believes? Of course we can. What this shows is that that public item cannot be (exactly) the supposed unique item which is 'what Odile believes'. For to identify that as the item would be to fail to distinguish her belief from Pia's, whereas, by hypothesis, what Odile believes is not quite what Pia does. The public item will not do, then, for the just-defined role of 'what Odile believes'. It is at just this point that the pressure mounts to turn to private understandings for an exact and correct specification of what Odile believes.

This turn to private understandings may seem to be innocuous. But we may now notice that the above argument would apply no matter which public item we happened to choose, above, as a candidate for what Odile believes. Which is to say this. Let S be the (full) semantics of that item which is precisely 'what Odile believes' (in relevant matters.) Then S cannot be the semantics of any publicly expressible item. We could not say anything with semantics S. Which is to say that S is a semantics that we could not be in a position to grasp. Nor could we be in a position to judge that S was the semantics of Odile's belief. That is not what we could judge the other publicly accessible facts to show. Dummett's conception of belief which demands that beliefs be specified in terms of private understandings, then, conflicts with the idea that private language is impossible, as that idea was argued for above. Whatever the *prima facie* attractions of Dummett's conception —and I have tried to indicate that there is less there than meets the eye—the conception cannot be correct, or at least not if, as has been argued above, Wittgenstein is right about private language.

This conclusion is important. For Dummett's conception is shared by many. It informs dominant conceptions both of our psychologies and of what a science of psychology might be. Against which we might now say: we identify what people believe—ourselves as well as others—not by looking inside their heads, but rather by looking at those items which might be believed than we can produce for public inspection, and then at the publicly observable ways in which the individual in question relates to them. What Odile might believe is just what we might say; it is fixed just by that, and not by further facts about her internal configurations, at least where these are conceived as being what they are independent of the views of her afforded by the items we might express and the ways we might relate her to those. Which is, in effect, just to apply the main moral of chapter 3 to those semantic items with a role in our psychologies.

8. TRANSCENDENCE

How *could* Wittgenstein give a private language argument? For the conclusion of such an argument would surely be that there could not be a private language. Yet Wittgenstein is the philosopher who continually reminds us that it is the business of philosophy to describe how things *are*, not how they must be; in fact, that a philosopher who thinks that he can see how things must be is apt to be 'held captive by a picture', and thus only under some sort of illusion. He says, for example,

Philosophy may in no way interfere with the actual use of language; it can in the end only describe it.
   For it cannot give it any foundation either.
   It leaves everything as it is. (124)

Philosophy simply puts everything before us, and neither explains nor deduces anything.—Since everything lies open to view there is nothing to explain. For what is hidden, for example, is of no interest to us. (126)

The work of the philosopher consists in assembling reminders for a particular purpose. (127)

If one tried to advance theses in philosophy, it would never be possible to debate them, because everyone would agree to them. (128)

What we are supplying are really remarks on the natural history of human beings; we are not contributing curiosities, however, but observations which no one has doubted, but which have escaped remark only because they are always before our eyes. (415)

Again, Wittgenstein is the philosopher who has enjoined us not to think, but to look:

'But *this* is not how it is!—we say. 'Yet *this* is how it must be!' (112)

The aim of philosophy, in general, is to free us from ideas as to how things must be, and let us simply see how they are. So, one would think, phenomenology, perhaps,—whether linguistic or not; but no transcendental arguments—that is, no appeal to supposed *a priori* considerations for showing how things must be. Yet it seems undeniable that Wittgenstein argues that there could not be a private language; not merely (what is surely so) that we do not ordinarily talk as if there were. He must produce a transcendental argument to do so. How could he be entitled to argue in any such way?

   The answer, I think, is that the private language argument is, or appeals to, an anomaly. Here it is useful to compare Wittgenstein to Descartes—not to Descartes as he saw himself (which, as suggested in chapter 4, is a distorted view), but to what Descartes in fact accomplished. Descartes, as we know, accepted the sceptic's conception of knowledge, and in particular, IP. In fact, he authored both of the usual moves used ever since to resist scepticism by philosophers who do accept IP: first, he posited double sense of 'know', including a weak ordinary sense to which the sceptic's arguments do not apply (he called knowledge in this sense 'moral certainty'); and second, he posited a special realm of facts to which we have, or anyway can have, infallible access *via* special cognitive powers ('natural light' in the first instance, and later 'clear and distinct ideas'). But he also noted an anomaly in IP. Using IP to show that A does not know that F, in any given case, involves finding a pair of conceivable situations, in both of which A takes F to be so (or does what is indistinguishable to him from that), and in at least one of which, A is thereby fooled. The anomaly is that this must be a pair of situations including A. Hence if what A takes to be so is that he exists, then there can be no pair of situations which allow IP to apply. So it is not to be shown *via* IP that A does not know this. This point we can allow as unobjectionable. But it is also clearly an anomaly. It does not, as Descartes in fact thought, exhibit a representative of some wider domain of sceptic-resistant knowledge.

The private language argument similarly represents an anomaly in the Wittgensteinian principles which require that philosophy be, in general, phenomenological rather than transcendental. It is an anomaly in the principles operative in chapter 7, and in those at work in chapters 4 and 5 as well. We might best see how a private language argument is possible (on Wittgenstein's terms) if we view the matter in terms of chapter 7. To recap roughly the principles at work there, we may say that given discourse—W, say—is fact-stating provided, first, that a reasonable judge would take it as so to be understood (so that that feature would be included in correct solutions to relevant disambiguation problems), and second, that a reasonable judge would find it not too stupid for us so to treat it. Given that these conditions are met, W is further unimpeachable. It is not subject to any further possible argument, appealing to whatever *a priori* principles, showing that W does not really state what is a fact or not. What W states is in fact a fact, iff that is part of the most reasonable distribution of facts of the sort W states, given that there are indeed such facts.

But there is an obvious condition on the meeting of such conditions. It must be open to a reasonable judge—and hence, it has been argued, to a potentially indefinite number of reasonable judges—to take W to satisfy the conditions or not. And such judges, or an indefinite number of them, must have access (in principle) to all the other facts on which an informed reaction in the relevant respects is to depend. Hence the anomaly. Discourse for which that condition is not met—hence any putative private language—cannot qualify (in this way, at least) as fact-stating; nor as such that there are facts of the sort it states. So it is subject to impeachment by philosophical argument. And once so subject, it has now been argued, it must inevitably succumb. It is important that the case of private language is an anomalous exception to the general unimpeachability of what purports to be fact-stating discourse—except, of course, by (from the standpoint of philosophy) mundane phenomenological means. For that shows exactly how much room is left for transcendental argument within the Wittgensteinian scheme of things: exactly as much room as the private language argument fills.

As noted already, the private language argument contains an anti-realist moral. The semantics of any item must depend entirely on facts that are in principle available to us or to an indefinite number of other reasonable judges—that is, facts to which we or they could stand in the right relations for forming the semantic judgements which count. The point holds for any semantic property of any item. So, in particular, for truth-involving ones, and specifically, where relevant, for the properties of being true or being false. So further, for any fact we might state (or think), whether it is a fact can depend only on how the publicly accessible facts are. Anything which is not publicly accessible is not relevant to whether it is a fact or not.

The anomalous nature of the private language argument defines the limits of this anti-realism. First, within the domain of what is publicly accessible, it is not open to this sort of anti-realism—or to any anti-realism available to Wittgenstein—to show that, for example, when we say, 'W', we are really not stating what is a matter of fact, or there is no fact corresponding to what we say. So, for example, this sort of anti-realism does not show us whether there could be facts as to moles on the backs of distant women. We may take it, for example, that distant judges might have access to the facts needed for evaluating the semantics of remarks on such topics, and that those judges might count as reasonable by our lights. We may further take it that that makes it *not* too stupid by our lights to suppose there to be facts of those far-off matters—in which case (if we are performing as reasonable judges), such is not too stupid by our lights. If that is how we react, then our discourse on such matters as far off moles is fact-stating. More generally, it cannot be shown by *a priori* argument, nor by the strictures of present anti-realism, that such discourse is not fact-stating when we do not regard it as too stupid to treat it as such. Similarly for remarks about events far off in time, so, for example, for facts of history. Such discourse does not demonstrably fall without the sphere of what fits the present model of public semantics; we are under no compulsion to construe it as so falling.

Second, within the public domain, it is not open to this species of anti-realism to show how some facts we state *must* depend on, or be related to, others. It is not a consequence of it, for example, that the meaning or content of statements about, say, distant women must be

either specifiable or exhausted by 'verification procedures', or principles fixing when one is warranted or justified in making such
statements. Nor are we bound to conclude that such a statement may
state a fact only where we could bear the right epistemic relation to it.
If our conception of things allows for facts which violate such
strictures, and if our so conceiving of the world runs smoothly by our
lights, then we are not wrong, and so not to be shown wrong, in
supposing there to be facts of the sorts our conception of things thus
allows for. *That* is just part of what our concept of a fact allows for. So,
for example, if it is part of our framework of judgement—as it is—to
take the world to have a history, and that history to be replete with fact
in certain ways, then our so supposing is beyond criticism. It does not
depend on those historical facts being related to others more accessible
to us in given ways. All that is required for us rightly to suppose of a
statement that, world willing, it states what either is so or is not is that
we find it not too stupid to suppose that the full semantics of that
statement (including its truth-involving properties) is, in principle,
sufficiently open to adequate judgement by some indefinitely large
range of reasonable judges, from positions such judges may assume.
There can be no *a priori* deduction of where, or under what condition,
we may so find. How the truth of any given statement (where we do so
find) depends on other facts is fixed by nothing other than how
reasonable judges, appropriately related to the other facts, would react
to them. Here, too, there is no room for *a priori* deduction of what such
reasonable judges must do. (In fact, the model of chapter 2 does not
allow for such deductions; that would be to get the making of semantic
fact running in the wrong direction.) In so far as there is anything
general to be established as to the policies a reasonable judge would
follow in any particular case, this can depend on nothing other than
the policies we (or they) happen to regard as too stupid or not. We are
not *bound* by present anti-realism (within the public domain) to find
certain policies stupid or not.

Third, present anti-realism presents no definite or specifiable limits
to what we can regard as within the public domain and what not. *If* it is
private language, then it is really no language at all; but that does not
yet say what we must regard as private language. The point has already
been illustrated in the case of Pia. We have *her* word for it that the
semantics of 'gronch' depends on private facts, to which we are barred
access in principle. And we have whatever evidence we have that we
cannot get the hang of how 'gronch' is to be used, or cannot manage to
establish the relevant semantic facts. But we are not bound to accept
Pia's word—certainly not by anti-realism. Nor are we bound to accept
what the evidence, such as it is, suggests about our shortcomings; *so*

far we have not caught on to the proper use of 'gronch', but perhaps we still will. That Pia is to be taken at her word, and that the semantics of 'gronch' or the facts on which it depends are forever closed to our view, are views we will accept when but only when it is too stupid to suppose otherwise. The strictures on when we must conclude that have already been discussed under point two. *If* we conclude that Pia's 'language' is not public—or if and in so far as we treat it in this way— we must then also conclude that it is really no language at all, and without semantics altogether. But anti-realism does not tell us when we must conclude that.

The real bite of present anti-realism, it seems to me, comes precisely in the realm of psychological fact—facts about our mental states and attitudes, sensations, emotions, and so on. The point in this domain is that the obtaining or not of any such fact must depend exclusively on the arrangements of those facts which are publicly accessible—if, for some peripheral reason, not to *us*, then to an indefinite number of novel judges. Conversely, in so far as some putative fact or phenomenon is accessible in appropriate ways only to the bearer of the psychological property in question, to that extent it does not figure in determining whether that psychological concept applies in that case or not. A person's psychology does not depend on what only he can observe (in so far as observation is relevant at all). It is a corollary of this that sometimes the psychological states or attitudes of other people fall within the range of what it is open to us to observe— observe, that is, and not merely infer or guess at. For if observation is to be given a role in psychologies—as it undoubtedly is—then that cannot be a role from which we or, more generally, other judges are always and in principle cut off. So the private language argument might be viewed as providing a solution to the so-called 'problem of other minds'—or better, as an account of why there was really never any such problem at all. (To think that there was would be to misapply the techniques of the ontic sceptic within the domain of the mental.) But of course that aspect of Wittgenstein's intent was always the most striking feature of the private language discussion. The aim of this book has been to place it properly within the wider framework in which it belongs.

Bibliography

Austin, J. L. [1946], 'Other Minds', in his *Philosophical Papers*, Oxford University Press, Oxford, 1961.

—— [1950], 'Truth', in his *Philosophical Papers*.

—— [1952/3], 'How to Talk:—Some Simple Ways', in his *Philosophical Papers*.

—— [1962], *How to do things with Words*, Oxford University Press, Oxford, 1962.

Blackburn, S. [1984], 'The Individual Strikes Back', *Synthese*, vol. 58/3, March 1984, pp. 281–301.

Chihara, C., and Fodor, J., [1965], 'Operationalism and Ordinary Language', *The American Philosophical Quarterly*, vol. 2/4, 1965, pp. 281–95.

Cook Wilson, J. [1926], *Statement and Inference*, Oxford University Press, Oxford, 1926.

Davidson, D. [1973], 'Radical Interpretation', in his *Truth and Interpretation*, Oxford University Press, 1984.

Descartes [1637], Discourse on the Method in *The Philosophical Works of Descartes*, trans. E. S. Haldane and G. R. T. Ross, Cambridge University Press, London and New York, 1967.

Donnellan, K. [1972], 'Proper Names and Identifying Descriptions', in D. Davidson and G. Harman, eds., Semantics of Natural Language, D. Reidel, Dordrecht, 1972, pp. 356–79.

Dummett, M. [1973], 'The Philosophical Basis of Intuitionistic Logic', in his *Truth and Other Enigmas, Duckworth, London, 1978*.

—— [1981], *The Interpretation of Frege's Philosophy*, Duckworth, London, 1981.

Frege, G. [1918], 'The Thought', in his *Logical Investigations*, ad P. Geach, Basil Blackwell, Oxford, 1977.

Gilbert, M. [1983], 'On The Question Whether Language Has a Social Nature: Some Aspects of Winch and Others on Wittgenstein', *Synthese*, vol. 56, 1983, pp. 301–18.

Kaplan, D. [1988], 'Demonstratives', in Themes From Kaplan, ed. J. Almog, J. Perry and H. Wettstein, Oxford University Press, Oxford, 1988.

Kripke, S. [1972], *Naming And Necessity*, Basil Blackwell, Oxford, 1980. (First appeared in *Semantics of Natural Language*, 1972.)

—— [1979], 'A Puzzle About Belief', in A. Margalit, ed., *Meaning and Use*, D. Reidel, Dordrecht, 1979, pp. 239–83.

—— [1982], *Wittgenstein on Rules and Private Language*, Basil Blackwell, Oxford, 1982.

Leibniz, G.W. [1686], Discours de Métaphysique, ed. G. Le Roy, Librairie Philosophique J. Vrin, Paris, 1970.

—— [1703], Nouveaux Essais Sur L'Entendement Humain, ed. J. Brunschwig, Garnier-Flammarion, Paris, 1966.

McDowell, J. [1977], 'On the Sense And Reference Of A Proper Name', *Mind*, vol. 86, 1977, pp. 159–85.

—— [1981], 'Anti-Realism and the Epistemology of Understanding', in H. Parret and J. Bouveresse, eds., *Meaning and Understanding*, De Gruyter, Berlin, 1981, pp. 225–48.

—— [1982], 'Criteria, Defeasibility and Knowledge', *The Proceedings of the British Academy*, vol. 68, 1982, pp. 455–79.

—— [1986], 'Singular Thought and the Extent of Inner Space', in P. Pettit and J. McDowell, eds., *Subject Thought And Context*, Oxford University Press, Oxford, 1986, pp. 137–68.

Malcolm, N. [1952/63], 'Knowledge and Belief', *Mind*, vol. NS 242, April, 1952, reprinted in significantly revised form in his *Knowledge and Certainty*, Prentice-Hall, Englewood Cliffs, 1963.

Moore, G. E. [1925], 'A Defence of Common Sense', in J. H. Muirhead, ed., Contemporary British Philosophy, second series, George Allen and Unwin, London, 1925.

—— [1939], 'Proof of an External World', *The Proceedings of the British Academy*, vol. 25, 1939, pp. 273–300.

Peacocke, C. [1986], *Thought: an Essay on Content*, Aristotelian Society Series, vol. 4, Basil Blackwell, Oxford, 1986.

Prichard, H. A. [1950], *Knowledge and Perception*, Oxford University Press, Oxford, 1950.

Putnam, H. [1962a], 'What Theories Are Not', in his *Mathematics, Matter and Method*, Philosophical Papers, vol. 1, Cambridge University Press, Cambridge, 1975.

—— [1962b], 'The Analytic and the Synthetic', in his *Mind, Language and Reality*, Philosophical Papers, vol. 2, Cambridge University Press, Cambridge, 1975.

—— [1962c], 'Dreaming and Depth Grammar', in Philosophical Papers, vol. 2.

—— [1970], 'On Properties', in Philosophical Papers, vol. 1.

—— [1975], 'The Refutation of Conventionalism', in Philosophical Papers, vol. 2.

—— [1981], *Reason Truth And History*, Cambridge University Press, Cambridge, 1981.

Quine, W. v. O. [1960], *Word and Object*, The MIT Press, Cambridge, Massachusetts, 1960.

Russell, B. [1918], 'The Philosophy of Logical Atomism', in his *Logic and Knowledge*, ed., R. C. Marsh, George Allen and Unwin, London, 1956.

Salmon, N. [1982], *Reference and Essence*, Basil Blackwell, Oxford, 1982.

Stroud, B. [1984], *The Significance of Philosophical Scepticism*, Oxford University Press, Oxford, 1984.

Travis, C. [1975], *Saying and Understanding*, Basil Blackwell, Oxford, 1975.

—— [1981], *The True and the False*, J. Benjamins, Amsterdam, 1981.

—— [1983/4], 'Are Belief Ascriptions Opaque?', *Proceedings of the Aristotelian Society*, New Series, vol. 84, 1983/4, pp. 73–99.

—— [1985], 'On What is Strictly Speaking True', *The Canadian Journal of Philosophy*, vol. 15 2, June 1985, pp. 187–229.

Wittgenstein, L. [1958], Philosopical Investigations, second edition, trans. G. E. M. Anscombe, Basil Blackwell, Oxford, 1958.

—— [1969], Über Gewissheit/On Certainty, trans. D. Paul and G. E. M. Anscombe, Basil Blackwell, Oxford, 1969.

Vendler, Z. [1977], Res Cogitans, Cornell University Press, Ithaca, 1977.

Wright, C. [1985], 'Facts and Certainty', Henriette Hertz Lecture for the British Academy, delivered 11 December, 1985.

——[1986a], 'Rule Following, Meaning and Constructivism', *in Meaning And Interpretation*, ed., C. Travis, Basil Blackwell, Oxford, 1986, pp. 271–57.

—— [1986b], 'Does *Philosophical Investigations* I. 258–260 Suggest a Cogent Argument against Private Language?', in Pettit and McDowell, eds., Subject Thought And Context, pp. 209–66.

Index

Index